The Resourceful Writer

FOURTH EDITION

The Resourceful Writer
A Basic Writing Course

William H. Barnwell

Robert Dees
Orange Coast College

Houghton Mifflin Company   Boston   New York

Senior Sponsoring Editor: Mary Jo Southern
Senior Associate Editor: Ellen Darion
Assistant Editor: Jennifer Roderick
Project Editor: Elizabeth Gale Napolitano
Production/Design Coordinator: Jennifer Meyer Dare
Manufacturing Manager: Florence Cadran
Senior Marketing Manager: Nancy Lyman

Cover Image: © Sophie Marsham/Photonica
Cover Design: Linda Manly Wade/Wade Design

Contents

22   Preventing Sentence Errors   471

Anthology   493

APPENDIX: Answers to Practice Exercises in Part IV   535

Rhetorical Contents

Classification Analysis

Process Analysis

Cause and Effect Analysis

Argument and Persuasion

Thematic Contents

Education

Contemporary Issues

Identities

Language and Convention

Media

Men and Women

Science and Medicine

To the Instructor

In the fourth edition of *The Resourceful Writer: A Basic Writing Course,* we continue to offer a method that helps students write meaningful paragraphs and essays as they move from personal, expressive writing to more formal, academic discourse. *The Resourceful Writer* also includes an anthology of reading selections chosen to increase students' interest in writing and discussing ideas. In addition, the research paper chapter has been enlarged to include new MLA-style documentation guidelines and additional resource material for suggested research paper topics.

For the fourth edition, we have kept the best features of the original edition. Thus, students still write from the very beginning of the semester. They write first about what they know best: their own experiences and their perceptions of the world around them. They learn early on how to put together a paragraph—how to structure it, how to use convincing details, and how to maintain their own voices in writing the paragraph.

Throughout the book, students use a six-step writing method—*gather, analyze, identify, plan, write, revise and edit*—to guide them through the prewriting, writing, and revising processes. As students master this writing method, they also learn how to draw from and respond to outside resources, such as the reading selections in *The Resourceful Writer* itself, as well as sources they might use to complete a research paper. Additionally, students can practice mastering sentence structure and the mechanics of English by completing the many exercises in Part IV, the "Writer's Workbook" section of the text.

Features of the Fourth Edition

The Anthology includes fifteen new reading selections followed by apparatus to stimulate discussion and writing. These include selections from such writers as Brent Staples, Garrison Keillor, Lance Morrow, Barbara Ehrenreich, and Elizabeth Wong.

- One-third of the professional and student selections are new to this edition. Reading is integrated with many of the writing assignments that accompany each chapter. Thus, Chapter 1 refers students to Garrison Keillor's essay "How to Write a Personal Letter" to provide guidance and encouragement for their first writing assignment. Other writing assignments ask students to respond to essays included directly within the chapter.

- Chapter 14, "Writing the Research Paper," has been expanded and updated in keeping with the guidelines of the Modern Language Association (MLA), especially as they apply to electronic and online resources. In addition to a new sample research paper and extended treatment of documentation techniques,

Chapter 14 includes readings specially intended to provide ideas for research topics, as well as a list of potential sources for such topics. A "Suggested Research Topics" section also describes other topics that would be of interest to most students.

- Chapter 12, "Using the Library's Resources," has been completely revised to include the latest information on using and citing electronic sources.

Organization

The Resourceful Writer, Fourth Edition, is organized into four parts with a total of twenty-two chapters and an anthology of additional readings.

Part I: Part I, "Writing from Direct Experience" (Chapters 1 through 6), guides students step by step through paragraph writing to short essay writing. Chapter 1, "A Place to Begin," asks students to plunge in and write: their first assignment is a letter about themselves, addressed to their classmates or to their professor. Chapter 2, "Locating Your Resources," introduces the six-step Writing Process that will guide students through most of the writing assignments in the book. In this chapter, students progress through various writing assignments, including the classroom interview, the outside interview, and keeping a journal. In Chapter 3, "Gathering and Analyzing Your Material," students learn how to use and analyze brainstorming, free writing, clustering, class discussions, and conversations with others to enrich their writing. Chapter 4, "Identifying Your Main Point," concentrates on helping students write structured, thoughtful paragraphs and teaches students how to develop a main idea and a thesis statement. Chapter 5, "Planning and Writing Your Essay," teaches students how to create an outline in order to formulate their ideas for writing. Students are then guided through writing an essay with an introduction, conclusion, and title. Chapter 6, "Re-Visioning Your Essay," offers a substantial section on revision, reinforcing the importance of students' evaluating and revising their own writing. It gives an example of a student paper taken through the revision process.

Part II: Part II, "Structuring Your Writing," teaches students to use various rhetorical modes and organizational strategies. Chapter 7, "Describing and Narrating," introduces objective and subjective description to students and also provides several excerpts from professional narrations. Chapter 8, "Writing with Examples, Comparison and Contrast, and Classification," guides students through the steps involved in using these modes of development. In Chapter 9, "Writing About Process ('How To') and Cause and Effect," students are taught how to write "how to" and cause-and-effect paragraphs and essays. The final chapter in Part II, "Notes on Writing Essay Exams and In-Class Essays," instructs students on preparing and writing clear and thoughtful in-class assignments.

Part III: Part III, "Writing with Outside Resources," helps students move from writing about their own personal experiences to writing with outside resources. In

Chapter 11, "Reading and Summarizing," students learn how to summarize material they read. Chapter 12, "Using the Library's Resources," describes the various resources available to most students and then has them write short essays about reading material they have obtained from the library (thus employing summarizing skills as well). Also included in this chapter is a section entitled "Reading on Your Own," which includes a list of books that college students generally like to read, thus further encouraging beginning college writers to read as much as they can. In Chapter 13, "Writing Persuasively," students learn how to form an argument and write a persuasive paper supporting their argument by using outside resources. Preliminary exercises at the beginning of the chapter help students formulate arguments and present them clearly. Chapter 14, "Writing the Research Paper," provides instruction for constructing a research paper and shows a sample research paper.

Part IV.   Part IV, "A Writer's Workbook," is designed to be used throughout the course in conjunction with Parts I and II. While students write paragraphs and essays in Parts I through III, they can work on their mastery of grammar and mechanics in Part IV. Chapter 15, "Parts of Speech," offers a review of the parts of speech. Chapters 16 and 17 concentrate on verb use, including subject-verb agreement and correct use of tense. Chapter 18 guides students in proper use of pronouns, and Chapters 19 and 20 offer practice and instruction in spelling, capitalization, punctuation, and numbers. Chapters 21 and 22 help students write correct, whole sentences. All of the chapters in Part IV contain brief instruction and lots of practice exercises for students. Answers to the practice exercises in Part IV appear at the back of the book, answers to review exercises (which appear at the end of each chapter in Part IV) are provided in the *Instructor's Resource Manual.* Many of the exercises concentrate on students' own writing by asking them to write their own sentences.

Acknowledgments

The following reviewers contributed many good ideas to *The Resourceful Writer,* Fourth Edition:

Marcia Bronstein, Montgomery College (MD)
Phyllis B. Burke, Hartnell Community College (CA)
Bobbie R. Coleman, Antelope Valley College (CA)
Ana Hale, Fort Lewis College (CO)
Margaret Harbers, Nashville State Technical Institute
Susan Jackson, Spartanburg Technical College (SC)
David Lang, Golden Gate University (CA)
Arah Pinson, South Carolina State University
Mary F. Sisney, California State Polytechnic—Pomona

R.D.

PART I

Writing from Direct Experience

Dear Students,

The primary goal of this course is to help you say in writing what you want to say, with clarity and style, and to say it correctly. The assumption is that you have much to say that is worth communicating. During the semester your instructor will lead you through various activities and exercises that are designed to help you relax in your writing and to bring forth your strengths.

An important objective of Chapter 1 is to help you present yourself, in your writing, to an audience—your classmates first, and then your instructor. Your classmates, along with your instructor, will be your audience for most of the writing assignments in this book. In Chapter 2 you will learn about the activities of the writing process and how to locate the materials for your writing within yourself—in your thoughts, feelings, and observations—as well as in the people around you. Then, in Chapter 3, you will practice techniques for developing writing ideas as part of the first two activities of the writing process, gathering and analyzing ideas and information. By the time you finish that chapter, you should never have to worry about having something to say when you're asked to write an essay.

Chapter 4 focuses on the third activity of the writing process, identifying your main point. You will also study paragraphs and how they can help shape your writing. In Chapter 5 you will learn how to plan and write a full essay using all the activities of the writing process, and Chapter 6 shows you an easy method for revising and polishing your work. The next three chapters describe different types of essays and show you how to write them using the activities of the writing process. Chapter 10 offers suggestions for applying what you've learned in Parts I and II to essay tests and in-class essay writing in your other college courses.

Throughout Parts I and II you will be the chief resource for your writing—what you see, what you hear, what you can remember. Then, in Part III, you will learn how to draw on outside resources for writing—reading material and the library. You will discover that the same method you used for the personal writing in Parts I and II will work well for the more objective writing in Part III.

Part IV is a writer's workbook that provides instruction and practice in the mechanics of writing: how to write in complete and interesting sentences, how to use tricky verbs and pronouns correctly, how to punctuate, and how to overcome spelling problems.

Your instructor may ask you to work through Part IV from beginning to end while you are completing selected writing assignments in Parts I through III. Or your instructor may ask you to do particular assignments in Part IV that will help you learn certain skills. Either way, Part IV can serve as a reference handbook for you. When you need to know how to write particular constructions, you will be able to find the appropriate rules (with examples and practice exercises) in Part IV.

We hope you enjoy this course and learn to say exactly what you want to say as you learn the craft of writing.

Sincerely yours,

William H. Barnwell

William H. Barnwell

Robert Dees

Robert Dees

The Writing Process

GATHER your ideas and information
ANALYZE your ideas and information
IDENTIFY your theme or main point
PLAN your writing
WRITE
REVISE AND EDIT your writing

1

A Place to Begin

■ Describing Yourself

WHOEVER CALLED WRITING a "one-sided conversation" was right. Experienced writers simply assume an audience to whom they "talk" on paper. Think of the last letter or short note you wrote. You were actually just "talking" on paper, telling whomever you were writing to what was on your mind. You knew the person you were writing to and what you wanted to say. Instead of talking face to face or over the telephone, you communicated your ideas in the form best suited for the occasion, in this case a letter or brief note.

You already have, in other words, the most important skill a writer must possess—the ability to communicate your thoughts and feelings to other people. And you already have a distinctive way of expressing yourself—a *voice*—that is special to you and to no one else. A character in a play by the French dramatist Molière expressed astonishment on being told he had been speaking prose all his life. You, too, may be pleasantly surprised to discover that you have been instinctively practicing the underlying principles of good writing every day in your interactions with others.

Conversations, of course, do differ from writing in being more spontaneous and less organized. When you chat with a friend, any topic, in any order, is possible. Interruptions and wandering off the topic are almost expected. If you are not making your point clearly, your friend can ask you what you mean. And when you talk, you do not have to be concerned about matters of punctuation and spelling.

These differences between talking and writing—purpose and content, organization, clarity, and correctness—are where the majority of writers have to pay most of their attention when they communicate on paper. Many of these differences, however, are differences of degree only. Once you master them through instruction and practice in writing, you will gain real satisfaction from the process of putting your ideas on paper for others to read and react to.

You also will find that writing can be the joyful experience of discovering yourself. Writing is fundamentally self-expression, and it can be much more than that as well. Writing your thoughts will help you understand what you may be thinking. James Reston, a noted newspaper columnist for the *New York Times,* once said, "How can I know what I think until I read what I write?" Learning to write effectively can help give you insight into what you think and feel. You will find your ideas and reactions to the world gaining clarity and authority as you focus on expressing them fully during the writing process. You will also discover how an increased awareness of your audience—the specific group of people with whom you are communicating—influences the final shape of your writing.

You and Your Audience

All forms of writing have specific readers for whom they are intended. One person writes a letter not to the whole world, but to another person, someone whose presence as *audience* determines to a great degree what information the letter contains and how it is expressed. Other writers, such as magazine or newspaper columnists, write to a much larger audience. They do not know all, or even most, of their readers personally, yet the special identity of this mass audience governs what they say and how they say it in exactly the same manner.

When given the opportunity to write for others, always conduct an "audience analysis" to determine both what you will write and how you should say it. Such an analysis usually includes the following kinds of questions:

Who is my audience?
What does my audience need to know?
Are there any special concerns or issues that I need to think about as I write?
What does my audience expect from my writing?
How can I best convey my ideas to my audience?

Answering these questions before you begin to write, as well as during the writing and editing processes later, can save time and increase your writing effectiveness. For instance, if you were writing about the Internet for an audience of beginning computer users, you would need to explain basic concepts and processes. If you were writing for an audience familiar with the Internet, however, you would be free to use technical terms and address complex issues.

Determining your audience will also influence your choice of style and language during the writing stages. Whether you write formally or informally about your subject, for example, will influence your tone, which is regarded as the writer's attitude toward the reader and the subject. Consider the following ways of saying the same thing, for example:

The research was well done and carefully recorded at every step.
They did a good job on the research, I guess.
If you just have to know, the research was OK, too.
I mean, they RESEARCHED!

Your tone will suggest to the audience whether you are excited about your topic, amused or bored by it or irreverent or admiring of it. Likewise, your tone will tell your audience how you regard them—respectfully, formally, casually, indifferently, or with a combination of qualities. For these reasons, good writers are always careful to write with a tone appropriate to their subject and their audience.

Knowing something about your audience before you begin to write is crucial if your communication is to be successful. The writing assignments in this book assume that your audience will be your instructor and other students in the class. Similarly, you will be part of the audience for other students' writing. For both your classmates and your instructor, you will need to write clearly, with well-developed ideas and examples to demonstrate your thinking and writing skills. Think of your audience as people who enjoy getting to know you better, who want to know your ideas, and who appreciate your effort to write well on their behalf.

Writing a Letter of Introduction

Sometimes personal letters are the best way to tell others who we are and what we are thinking. They are also excellent means to practice writing and establish an appropriate tone for the audience you are addressing. If you are not used to writing letters, you may wish to read "How to Write a Personal Letter" by Garrison Keillor on pages 000-000 before you do the following assignment.

Writing Assignment 1-1: Describing Yourself to Others

Write a 200- to 300-word letter about yourself to the other students in your class. Write in your own voice—that is, in the words and style that are closest to "natural" for you while still being good English—and say whatever you want your classmates to know about you. To get some ideas of what you might say about yourself and how you might want to present that information, start by reading the following two student samples. If any ideas for your own letter occur to you as you read, write them down.

Sample A

Dear Classmates,

Hi! My name is Tamara. I am probably unique because I attended two high schools and, as of this year, two colleges as well. First there was Grace King High School, then Slidell High, and then I quit and enrolled in John Jay Beauty College. I attended John Jay for a year. I loved beauty college because I could relate so well to everyone there. A few of us became good friends and would go everywhere together. There was a college atmosphere at John Jay. In other words, you could do as you pleased. The teachers took a special interest in each student. If you weren't sure of a cut or the solution for coloring hair, they came running to your aid. While I liked John Jay Beauty College, I thought I should get a couple of years of regular college while I still had the chance.

I dropped out of John Jay and came to this college because I've always heard it was a hard but good school. My family warned me that people here would be unsociable, and they are. People will look you right in the eye and not speak, as if you weren't even there. Yesterday, when I said hello to a girl who is in one of my other classes, she didn't even look at me. I hope people in this class will be different, and we will get to know each other.

I want to be a teacher when I finish school because I love children.

Sincerely yours,

Tamara

Tamara Orne

Sample B

Dear Fellow Students,

It all started February 19, 1980, and is still going on today. I know you are won
dering what started, so I will satisfy your curiosity and tell you that on that day I was
born. I grew up in a typical Vietnamese-American home, with two brothers and a
sister. My parents and brothers came here from Vietnam the year I was born, so it
was a big year in more ways than one for my family.

So far this has been a good year for me. I share an apartment with another
student named Tom, and we get along very well. He is majoring in psychology, and
I'm majoring in math. He doesn't seem to mind the fact that I play music all the
time, something that drove my parents crazy when I lived at home. Tom wants to
learn Vietnamese, so I am teaching him simple things like greetings and so forth.
He can't believe that my Vietnamese is not all that good, though. That's because
none of us children grew up speaking it, and my family uses mostly English, even
at home.

My father is a dentist, and that's what I want to be when I get through college.
You're probably thinking that being a dentist is not too exciting, but it can be. Besides
the usual things a dentist does, I also want to get involved in reconstructive dentistry,
working on people whose jaws and teeth have been seriously damaged from birth
or accidents. That way I can do something more than fill cavities or give advice about
making somebody's teeth whiter. But until that time, I'm just going to study hard and
enjoy school. That's why I'm here!

Yours truly,

Steve

Steve Pham

How should you go about planning and organizing your letters to the class?
You might begin thinking of the interconnected activities of the Writing Process
as follows:

Gather your ideas and information

Analyze your ideas and information

Identify your main point

Plan your writing

Write

Revise and edit your writing

These activities are neatly ordered here. In reality, the first three *prewriting* activities—*gather, analyze,* and *identify*—may not occur in exactly that order. You may

have your main message or point in mind before you have collected a scrap of information about it. Similarly, you may be performing the *postwriting* activity listed last—*revise and edit your writing*—while you are in the act of writing, or even before you begin to write, when new information you have gathered causes you to revise your theme or point.

However, the order given here approximates the general flow of the Writing Process. Try approaching Writing Assignment 1–1, your letter to the class, using this framework as a guide.

Gather Your Ideas and Information: Begin by collecting the information and self-description you want to present in a letter about yourself to your classmates. Use the spaces provided to jot down statements about your interests, your background, your plans for the future—anything that comes to mind and tells people something about who you are. If you jotted down ideas that occurred to you while reading the study samples, list them in the spaces as well. The following are some topic areas that you might find useful:

Main life interests and/or hobbies
College major
Places lived
Jobs held
Life goals
Likes and dislikes
Special talents or skills
Major accomplishments

1. *Adiss Abeba,* ___ I born on Jan. 5, 1980, in the capital city of Ethiopia. I grew up with my grandmother in Gonder, northern part of Adiss Abeba ___

2. ___ I came in the USA on July 4, 1998. I am excited to be here. My first job was in a Seafood resturantl as a cook. Working in a ___

3. ___ I given in Bristow, VA. With my family. I like hiking, fishing, play Boll ___

4. _____

   _____

5. _____

   _____

Analyze Your Ideas and Information: Now that you have written down some of the material you might present, analyze what you have listed to see which statements and descriptions might be grouped together. Which topics seem to have generated the most ideas for you? Are there any that you could have said more about? Analyze the sample student letters to see how their authors' experiences may be similar to or different from your own, and compare them with your list.

- Which letter interested you the most, and why? Does it suggest ideas for your own letter?
- What would you discuss about yourself that these writers did not?
- Would you want to present a general picture of yourself and your life, or would you rather focus on one or two striking aspects?

Identify Your Main Point: Obviously, in a brief letter you cannot include everything you want your classmates to know about you. You will need to decide on the purpose, or main point, of your letter. That is, you will need to focus on those things about yourself that you most want to tell this audience.

This is something the writers of the sample letters had to do, too. Notice that their letters were focused on the following main points:

TAMARA'S LETTER: "I am probably unique because I attended two high schools and, as of this year, two colleges as well." (Her letter goes on to mention the high schools and to talk about the two colleges she has attended.)

STEVE'S LETTER: "It all started on February 19, 1980, and is still going on today." (Steve's letter talks generally about his life in terms of his past, present, and future.)

Obviously, you have a wide range of possibilities to choose from when you formulate your main point. Notice how each of the following statements of main ideas focuses on different aspects of its author's life and personality:

I was a fisherman before I could walk, and I guess that's been a big influence in my life ever since.

I come from a very rural part of the state, so living in a big city or in a dorm on campus is a new experience for me.

Good-humored, "intellectual," and crazy about cars—that's how I'd describe myself.

Right now my life consists of taking twelve units of study and keeping up with two part-time jobs.

What single statement or main idea about yourself might best introduce you to the other students in your class? After reviewing your list of facts about yourself and drawing on the examples just given, formulate a main point that would summarize what you want to tell your classmates about yourself. Write that main point as a single, complete sentence.

_____

_____

_____

Plan Your Letter: To help you plan what you are going to write, fill out the following worksheet to use as a guide for your letter. Or, if the worksheet does not help you say what you want to say, make up your own outline for the letter.

Worksheet A

Dear Students,
   (Introduction and main point:) _____

_____

_____

   (Describe yourself or a particular part of your life that illustrates the main idea:)

_____

_____

   (Describe other experiences or facts about yourself that illustrate your main point:) _____

_____

_____

   (Tell how you feel about some of the things you have described:) _____

_____

_____

   (Add anything else you want your audience to know about you:) _____

_____

_____

Sincerely yours,

Worksheet B

Dear Students,
    Main point: Some people know a lot about me, but there is more to me than anyone really understands.

_____

_____

_____

Describe things that most people know about you.

_____

_____

_____

Describe some things that very few people know about you.

_____

_____

_____

Describe some things you would like people to remember most about you, and why.

_____

_____

_____

Add anything else you want your audience to know about you.

_____

_____

_____

Sincerely yours,

Write Your Letter: Using the worksheet or outline you have prepared, write your letter on a separate piece of paper. Think of yourself as talking aloud to someone you feel comfortable with. Offer examples to illustrate the general statements you make about yourself.

Revise and Edit Your Letter: Plan on writing at least two "rough drafts," or versions, of your letter, reviewing each one and making additions or corrections as you go. If you have questions about the form for a letter, review the sample student letters.

After you have completed your last, most polished draft, read your letter aloud to a group of four to seven of your classmates. Reading your writing aloud can be helpful in developing a sense of audience and connecting your written statements to your natural speaking voice. You will find yourself gaining confidence in your work as others react to what you have communicated.

When each person has read his or her letter, take turns answering the following questions:

1. What about the person interested you the most?
2. What, if anything, could you identify with?
3. What would you like to know more about?
4. What would make the letter more effective?
5. What are the letters' best features?

Once you have heard the discussions of your own and others' letters, you may want to revise and edit your letter once again to make sure that you have said everything as fully and clearly as you intended.

Revise and Edit Your Letter Again: To revise your letter after you have tested it on your audience, you may want to move certain sections around or add more details to others. Have you told everything in the best order? Would more detailed examples help? Should anything be reduced or taken out entirely? Is the ending appropriate? Does it sound like an ending?

On your final draft, check to see that your sentences are all complete and that the ideas seem to connect smoothly. Does the writing sound natural? Have you written complete sentences throughout? Are you sure that you have spelled each word correctly? An important editing task is correcting problems in grammar, punctuation, and spelling. To help you with this, Part IV provides a complete workbook review of the basic rules of grammar and punctuation. As you read through the chapters that follow, specific points will be referenced to the matching section in Part IV. Use a dictionary to check the spelling of any words about which you are uncertain.

Writing Assignment 1-2:
Writing to Your Instructor

For this assignment, write a letter describing your educational history to your instructor. In addition to covering the major events of your previous education, try to include details that show what kind of student you are and which subjects interest you most. The following letter describes one student's education from kindergarten up to when she started college. You may want to organize your letter differently. After reading this student's educational history, use the steps described for Writing Assignment 1-1 to prepare your letter.

August 18, 1997

Dear Professor Hernandez:

My educational history is probably not very different from other students' in this class. I was born and raised in Gratton, Michigan, and went to school first at Hamilton Elementary and then at Barton Junior High. I was always a pretty good student, and at Barton I was class vice president for both years I was there. My best subjects were art and science. That is, I liked them the best and got good grades—A's and B's—pretty easily. I was never very good at math, so that was always a struggle. I remember trying to learn algebra and thinking it was really hard and something only a chemist or rocket scientist could ever understand!

Once I got to high school, I at first had a hard time getting used to things. My courses seemed more difficult, and the other students on campus seemed much, much older than all of us freshmen. I think that scared me a little—that along with the gangbangers. I gradually got used to them and figured out they were about as confused as I was by everything I got mostly C's and B's during my freshman and sophomore years and didn't do much more than just go to class every day.

But things picked up when I got to be a junior. I joined the swim team, and I got mostly A's in all my courses both that year and the next. You will be glad to know that I did pretty well in English. That was mainly because of my teacher, Mrs. Carr, who made us write in class almost every day. I hated it at first, but after a while it got to be easier and we all made great progress. I was also very good in chemistry and plan to make that my major, providing that I can conquer the math requirements, of course.

I am looking forward to being in this class and at this college. I started a new job this week demonstrating computer software at Sears, so I know I'll have to pay more attention to school than I usually do. Please let me know if I'm not doing all I should do to succeed in this course.

Sincerely,

Candice Washington

Candice Washington

In this chapter you learned to use a six-step group of interconnected writing activities to create a personal letter introducing yourself to your classmates. You will use this method, which we call the *Writing Process* for short, throughout the writing assignments in this text, and you will gradually recognize how it applies to the writing you will undertake in other courses and on the job.

The chapters that follow will explain the Writing Process in detail and will give you extensive practice in applying it to your own writing. You will study each of the prewriting, writing, and postwriting activities in turn and learn to incorporate them in your approach as you gain experience and confidence in sharpening your writing skills.

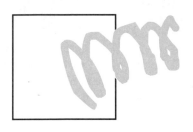

GATHER your ideas and information
ANALYZE your ideas and information
IDENTIFY your theme or main point
PLAN your writing
WRITE
REVISE AND EDIT your writing

2

Locating Your Resources

■ **The Writing Process**

THE LETTER YOU wrote to your classmates in Chapter 1 gave you practice in using the Writing Process with a definite audience in mind. You also learned about discovering ideas to write about and ways of organizing those ideas. You will need to write more than letters in college, of course, but in many ways creating a thoughtful essay is not so different from writing a letter. You will find that expressing ideas on paper can be as stimulating and natural as a good conversation and that your writing style can be just as uniquely your own as your speaking voice.

The writing method presented in this book is a flexible framework that allows you to perform easily and effectively in many types of writing tasks. Using the Writing Process to gather, organize, and record your impressions will help you transfer your "voice" from the spoken to the written word. You will learn to know your audience, know what you want to say, and know how you want to say it—in writing.

Writing Is a Process

What do we mean by *process?* A process is a series of actions that brings about a result. The process of writing as we describe it here consists of a series of activities that end in a finished piece of writing.

You have already gained some experience in using the Writing Process in Writing Assignment 1-1, your letter to the class. This writing method consists of six interconnected activities that can be applied to almost every writing situation:

Gather your ideas and information

Analyze your ideas and information

Identify your main point

Plan your writing

Write

Revise and edit your writing

Although it is helpful to think of them in this sequence, the activities that make up the Writing Process do not always occur in a 1-2-3 order. Sometimes you may begin with a main point and then gather information and ideas to support it. Other times you may find yourself reidentifying your main point in the course of planning or writing your essay. The main thing to keep in mind is that the complete experience of writing includes preparation (prewriting) and review (postwriting), as well as simply putting words on paper.

The writing method we call the *Writing Process* is easy to learn and apply. Let's look now at each of the activities in turn.

Gather Your Ideas and Information: Collecting ideas and information is the first step you will learn to take whenever you approach any writing task, no matter how large or small. As you discovered in Chapter 1, your most important starting resource is you—your attitudes, feelings, and beliefs. Determining what you already know or feel about a topic is essential in writing. Finding out what else you need to know before you can write is important as well, and you will also need to draw on resources outside yourself for your material.

Analyze Your Ideas and Information: Once you have gathered material, you must sit back and think about it before you begin to write. In the chapters to come you will learn to analyze your ideas and information to determine what they really amount to, which ones are important and which are not, how to organize your thoughts, and how best to give them expression.

Identify Your Main Point: All writing serves a purpose. Whenever you write anything, you will have a main point to make, the result of analyzing your ideas and coming to a general conclusion about them. You will learn how to state that main point effectively and use it to shape your writing.

Plan Your Writing: Even after you have determined your main point, you will still need to make a plan before you begin writing. You will learn to organize your writing to present important ideas in the best order and to convey your main point effectively to your readers. Knowing what you are going to say before you start to write—details and examples as well as general points—is an added bonus of planning. Careful preparation will give you confidence and make the experience of writing enjoyable. Remember also that a plan is a flexible tool that sometimes does and should change. You should expect to find that your plan will change in the course of writing if you see that you can best accomplish your purpose some other way.

Write: Look at your main point—perhaps you will want to state it first—look at your plan, and begin to write. New ideas will come to you as you write, some of which you will certainly want to use. Notice that the act of writing itself comes *after* you have completed the important first four activities, and for good reason. Writing can be as easy as talking—after you have determined what you want to say and have thoroughly organized how you want to say it. The kind of preparation involved in the prewriting activities of *gather, analyze,* and *identify* (as well as the postwriting activities of *revise and edit*) is the major difference between writing and speaking.

Revise and Edit Your Writing: No writer, no matter how experienced, ever passes up the chance to perfect his or her work. When you finish your writing, evaluate it. Were you able to carry out your purpose? Did you give enough examples and details to support the points you made? Did you bring your writing to a clear ending?

Part of the revising activity is to proofread and edit your writing to correct as many mechanical errors as possible. Some students prefer to edit during revision, some afterward. Because it is difficult to look for all possible errors in just one or two readings, plan to proofread your writing at least three times: twice to catch errors you are particularly apt to make and once to catch any other errors.

Many students complain that they cannot identify errors in their writing because it is too familiar, especially if they have read a passage over several times. If you have this problem, try the following for your last reading: Proofread and edit your paper a sentence at a time, starting with the last sentence and moving backward to the first sentence. Working this way will force you to look at each sentence separately.

You may revise and edit your writing while you compose as well as when you have finished your final draft. At whatever stage you perform it, this activity is crucial to the success of any writing. The act of revision often prompts you to rethink the ideas behind your writing, and you may find yourself either gathering new information or reanalyzing what you already have. As already noted, you will often find yourself doubling back and repeating certain activities as you move through the prewriting, writing, and postwriting activities of the process.

"This is all very well," you may be thinking as you read about the variety of activities that make up writing. "But *what* am I going to write about? What can I possibly say in 300, 400, or even 500 words?" Self-doubts of this kind are common among students in college English courses. This chapter will introduce you to two readily accessible and inexhaustible resources for your writing: yourself and the people around you.

Writing Resource 1: Yourself

Your feelings, ideas, memories, and perceptions of the world, taken together, form your personal experiences. One definition of the word *experience* is "the act of living through an event." You have experienced anything you have heard, seen, touched, smelled, or tasted. Such experiences are excellent sources for your writing.

Writing from experience requires that you develop an awareness of what you are experiencing. *Awareness* means "knowing or being conscious of what is happening." Awareness is a skill that can be developed. You can choose to become aware—by observing closely, by noticing fine details, and by remembering vivid images and experiences exactly as they happened. Becoming more conscious of your experiences, ideas, and feelings helps lay the groundwork for any writing project. One of the best ways to develop your awareness, as well as to provide yourself with an ongoing source of new ideas for writing, is to keep a journal.

Keeping a Journal

Skill comes from practice, not inborn genius. This is as true for you as a writer as it is for an artist, a musician, or an athlete. One of the best ways to learn to write effectively is to practice writing—a lot. This is where your journal comes in handy.

Take twenty minutes at the beginning or end of each day to write about something that caught your attention during the previous twenty-four hours. The topics you write about may be personal to you, or they may relate to broader social, cultural, or political issues or events. Besides giving you practice in writing, keeping a journal also will give you an abundant supply of personal material to shape your thinking.

We often tend to think of journals and diaries as sanctuaries in which we may safely pour out our most heartfelt and personal feelings. They are this, but they are more as well. The journal has an equally long and honorable tradition as a mental tool, a record of serious thought and opinion, as well as of passion. Take this journal excerpt from the famous lifelong diary of the writer Anaïs Nin, for example:

> What causes the choice of memory? What causes certain events to fade, others to gain in luminousness and spice? . . . Some portions of my life were lived as if under ether, and many others under a complete eclipse. Some of them cleared up later, that is, the fog lifted, the events became clear, nearer, more intense, and remained as unearthed for good. Why did some of them come to life, and others not? Why did some remain flavorless, and others recover a new flavor or meaning?

From now on, think of your journal as a handy medium for generating, exploring, and "rehearsing" ideas before you communicate them to an audience of other people. A journal is a place where you can practice *thinking* as well as writing, where you can develop a real sense of accomplishment by thinking your ideas through.

The key to keeping a journal is learning how to ask yourself the kinds of questions that start you talking about yourself and your experiences. If you feel self-conscious about writing when your only audience is you, try asking yourself these questions (you may begin to think of many more):

1. What was the strangest experience I had today? How did I feel about what happened?

2. What or who has been most on my mind today? Why?

3. What new understanding about my life did I gain today? What happened to give me that insight?

4. What conflicts did I experience today? Were those conflicts within myself or with others? What happened?

5. What is the most striking thing I have seen, heard, touched, smelled, or tasted today?

Many journal writers prefer to make entries strictly by topic rather than by self-questioning. For example, you may decide to write about a single person, event, or subject that interests you, regardless of whether you encountered it on the day of your journal entry. Or you may want to use your journal to practice a specific kind of writing, such as a book or movie review. As you will discover, the possibilities of journal writing are limited only by the bounds of your imagination.

Read the sample journal entries that follow and note how the writers used questions like those given earlier to examine the day's experiences.

Sample A: What Made Today Different from Other Days?

I've decided that next semester I am going to enroll in the Emergency Aid course in the P.E. department. Here's why. Today when Joanne Selkirk and I were sitting in the Three Sparrows Restaurant, a man across the aisle from us started choking on his food. We heard some grunting and choking sounds, and it suddenly was clear he wasn't getting enough oxygen. Pretty soon the whole restaurant was watching, but nobody seemed to know what to do.

Then, without saying a word or anything, Joanne—all 106 pounds of her—dashed across the aisle and seized the guy, spinning him around and grabbing him from behind, both arms locked below his chest. She gave him a sort of quick, hard jerk—and that was it! He spit up a tiny piece of food that had lodged in his throat, and it was all over. Everybody in the restaurant applauded, and the man thanked Joanne and hugged her. She turned red with embarrassment, but she was smiling, too. Joanne told me later she had used something called a "Heimlich maneuver," a rescue technique she had to learn this year in her Emergency Aid class. I want that class!

Sample B: What Has Been on My Mind Today?

On my way to class this morning I suddenly became conscious of what the new construction along the freeway meant: They were going to add three new lanes to handle all the traffic better. At first I was glad about this because heavy traffic has made what used to be a twenty-minute drive to campus into forty-five minutes of stop and go every morning now. More lanes would surely help the situation.

But then a thought occurred to me: For how long? How long before all the new housing brings in more people and more cars until the freeway becomes just as jammed again as it is now? When Bob and I first moved to our house in Park Acres, there were no more than three or four housing developments. The hills were all rolling and covered with nothing but thick brush and low trees. Now nearly every hill is shaved off and covered with new homes. And how are all those people going to get to work or school every day? They'll be on the freeway, blocking up those three new lanes. In a hundred years the planet will be literally overflowing. This thought has bothered me all day.

Sample C: What New Understanding Did I Gain Today?

My five-year-old son Kenny was with me today when I drove past a long line of cars following a hearse for a funeral. He asked me why all the cars were lined up and moving so slowly. "Because they are all going to the cemetery to bury someone they loved," I said. "Then what will the people do?" he asked. "Then they'll say some prayers and all go home again," I answered. "If they love someone, why do they go away and leave him in a cemetery?" he asked. I really didn't know what to say, because I didn't want to make death and funerals sound gruesome or anything. Before I could say anything, though, he came up with his own answer. "I guess they all have to go back to work or school and he doesn't," he said. "That's right," I answered.

How did he figure that out by himself? I'm amazed at times how children understand some things so easily and so, <u>so</u> clearly.

Sample D: What Conflict Did I Find Myself in Today?

After the lecture today in my biology class, I'm not sure how I feel about using animals for medical experiments or even keeping them as pets. It's clear that some of them suffer—rats with electrodes implanted in their brains, for instance, or monkeys who are injected with experimental vaccines that ultimately prove ineffective. On the other hand, without those experiments, an awful lot of people would suffer and die, too. I read just last week that a possible vaccine for Lyme disease was developed through experiments with lizards.

Then there is the question of keeping animals as pets. If they are intelligent, don't they want to be free and on their own? Should I let my parakeets out of their cage? Probably, but how will they survive in a city environment with all the pollution and lack of open spaces? And what about my cat, Kenya? She probably wouldn't be any better off than those cats I see scurrying around in alleys eating out of trash cans. Or am I just arguing to keep my pet cat? I don't know right now. This is something I want to think about some more.

 ## Writing Assignment 2–1: Keeping a Journal

Begin keeping your own journal, following the suggestions outlined in this section. Write in your journal for at least twenty minutes every day, using that opportunity to explore events and topics that interest you. Write as much in these entries as you care to, going back to them later if you find you have more to say. Because your journal is a private rehearsal space and resource for generating essay topics, you do not need to follow the formal Writing Process too closely in making your entries, but you will probably find yourself performing most of the activities automatically as you think, write, and review your writing.

What should you write in your journal? The range of subjects is limited only by your imagination. Whatever you write in your journal, consider it a rich source of information about yourself and your thinking. Besides asking yourself the kinds of questions listed earlier, here are some other questions you may want to address as you write in your journal:

1. If you were writing to Dear Abby or Ann Landers (columnists to whom many people write for personal advice), what would you ask? Explain the prob-

lem in detail. Now play the part of Abby or Ann, and write an answer to yourself. (For example, you may want to ask what you should do about a boyfriend or girlfriend who drinks too much or drives too fast. Or you may ask for advice on how you should respond to a parent whom you can never please, no matter what you do. Or you may want to ask how in the world you can get a child to eat vegetables—and so on.)

2. What headline would you most like to see in tomorrow's newspaper? Write the article that would appear underneath the headline. (You may choose a headline that might appear in the sports or entertainment section as well as in the front section of the newspaper.)

3. What advice would you give a daughter or son about family relationships, education, friendships, or another subject you feel has been important in your life? Write that advice in your journal as though you were speaking directly to your daughter or son.

Reread your journal at the end of every week. Do further thoughts on any of the topics occur to you after time has elapsed? Make a note of them. Thinking is never a static process, and your writing is a valuable tool for recording how your thoughts on a given subject change and develop over time.

Also notice, for each point you cover, if you would have presented it differently had you been writing for your classmates as an audience instead of yourself. How does the presence of an outside audience affect the way we express our opinions? Would your expression be different still if you were writing for only your family? For students from another culture?

With these questions in mind, let's look now at the other major resource—and audience—you have as a writer.

Writing Resource 2: The People Around You

To become a good writer, you need to learn to receive and organize ideas and information from a variety of sources, including other people. A good writer must have a keen ear for what people say. The better a listener you are, the better you will know what questions to ask to get good material for writing. Learn to listen actively. Much of the skill of active listening is simply deciding to concentrate on what other people are saying.

The following exercise provides you with an opportunity to practice active listening by taking turns with another student to interview each other for twenty or thirty minutes during or outside of class. Your goal will be to find out enough to write a short introduction of each other and to describe a "famous deed," an event in each of your lives that other people remember and like to remind you about.

Writing Assignment 2–2: Introducing Another Student's "Famous Deed"

If you are a fan of late-night television talk shows, you have undoubtedly watched David Letterman or Jay Leno interview celebrity guests, each of whom has done something unusual, something for which he or she is well known or famous (or possibly even notorious). Believe it or not, all of us are "famous" for something unforgettable that we did sometime, somewhere. We may not be as famous for what we did as the people who appear on David Letterman's or Jay Leno's show, but we have all done something for which others remember us and enjoy talking about.

How many times have you seen old friends or just been relaxing with your family when someone has suddenly said something like "Hey, remember the time we were lost and you got us home by . . . "—and the story goes on from there? Or maybe one of your aunts or uncles likes reminding you and the rest of the family about the time you used their airline tickets as a bookmark—and then returned the overdue book to the library! Or how about the time in high school when you . . .

People like you and your classmates do remarkable, memorable things all the time, things for which you remain "famous" to friends and families long afterward. Some of those famous deeds are more widely known than others, and they can include unforgettable accomplishments that range from saving a drowning child to coming off the bench in the last minute to sink the winning shot in a championship playoff game. Are you famous for filling the chemistry lab with smoke the time you mixed the wrong chemicals and made everyone run outside for fresh air? Did you surprise everyone by getting selected to be your city's mayor on Student Government Day? Famous people like you are everywhere. Take a few minutes to look around at your classmates. What do you suppose each of them is famous for?

Interview a Famous Classmate

Here's a chance to see what kind of talk-show host you would make. Sit down with one of your classmates and take turns acting as *interviewer* and *subject*. Your goal is to find out about each other so that you can describe the other's "famous deed," something each of you has done for which others like to remember you. After you finish interviewing, each of you will write a few paragraphs introducing the other and giving an account of that person's "famous deed."

As the subject of the interview, your role will be to volunteer information about yourself and your famous deed. Try not to be shy. Tell about your famous deed as though you were a celebrity on a talk show and wanted to entertain as well as fully inform your audience.

As the interviewer, you will need to ask questions, listen closely, and (later) jot down some notes. Encourage your famous classmate to relate the full story of what he or she did that people still talk about. Spend a few minutes preparing your questions and planning your interview before you begin. You may want to ask some of the questions listed here, in any order you think appropriate, or you may want to devise your own questions for the interview. In either case, be prepared to modify your questions in response to your subject's answers or preferences.

Questions to ask about the subject:

1. What is your college major, and how did you happen to choose it?

2. What hobbies do you have? Which is your favorite? Why?

3. What feature of your personality are you most proud of?

4. What takes up most of your time outside school?

Questions to ask about the "famous deed":

1. What have you done that other people remember and remind you of?

2. Can you explain what you did in detail for me? Please do so.

3. How did you feel while you were doing this?

4. Why do you think people remember your famous deed?

5. How do you feel today about being "famous" for such a deed?

6. If you had the chance to do your famous deed over again, would you do anything differently?

7. What kinds of famous deeds do you hope your children will accomplish?

Here are some further suggestions to follow when you assume the role of *interviewer* during the interview:

- Do not take extensive notes while interviewing. Listen attentively and jot down your impressions and what you recall after the interview.

- Invite the subject to answer each question in detail, but do not push for answers that are not easily given. The object of this exercise is to get to know the person and to enjoy sharing the account of a famous deed.

- From time to time, summarize aloud what you have heard the subject say. Your summary or clarifying questions will show that you have been actively listening and will give the speaker a chance to correct anything that you misunderstood.

Before you begin your interview, read the following essay to get an idea about the kind of introduction and description of a famous deed that you may want to write.

Genius at Work

When it comes to doing remarkable things by the age of five, Mike Graham is right up there with Mozart and Macaulay Culkin. Now nineteen years old and in his second year of college, Mike is currently taking Spanish, calculus, English composition, and advanced swimming. Mike is an engineering major, an interest that relates both to his love of swimming and to the reason why, at the age of five, he became ever-lastingly famous as "that crazy kid who made his grandmother's cellar into a swim-ming pool."

Mike's fame as a creator of recreational spas began the summer day his older sister and three cousins went off to the local public swimming pool without him. Mike could not swim yet, so he was left to play by himself in his grandmother's back-yard, first riding his tricycle up and down the driveway, then looking around the yard to see what else he could do.

It was when Mike raised the door to his grandmother's cellar that the idea of making his own swimming pool first occurred to him. Mike's grandmother used the cellar to store jars of homemade jams and jellies, plus a few boxes of old clothes and an old table that she never used anymore. Looking down the steps into the small underground room, Mike immediately recognized the as yet unrealized potential of his grandmother's cellar. Here, right in front of him, was a wonderful, deep, square hole in the ground, with cement sides and cement steps leading down—exactly like a swimming pool without water! No problem, thought Mike.

Mike quickly went to work. He started by putting two of his grandparents' gar-den hoses into the cellar and turning on the water. Next, he added more hoses from the neighbors' yards. Then he patiently waited while the water from all the hoses flowed and flowed into the cellar. After about an hour, Mike saw the boxes of clothing his grandmother stored in the cellar begin to float, bobbing slowly up and down in about three feet of water. By this time, the water had covered the first three steps up from the cellar floor. It wasn't long until his grandmother's table began floating awkwardly on its side, bobbing along with the boxes and other de-bris carried about by the water. Mike watched this scene for another ten or fifteen minutes, and then he decided it was time to go into the house and change into his swimming trunks.

Once changed, Mike went through the kitchen and past his grandmother, who just happened to ask what he was doing in his swim trunks. "Going swimming," he an-swered and went out to enjoy his new pool. Luckily, however, Mike's grandmother fol-lowed him outside. When she saw her cellar half full of water and her boxes and table floating about, his grandmother yelled, "Michael, what have you done? You could have drowned! Just look at my cellar!" She rushed Mike into the house and immediately called his mother to tell her what he'd done. By the time Mike's mother arrived on the scene, the other kids had returned from the public pool and were busy using buckets to bail the water out of the cellar. His sister and cousins were joined by oth-ers from the neighborhood, and soon a line of children and adults were passing buck-ets and making jokes about what Mike had done. Mike's mother gave him a spanking and promised him another one—which he got—later that night from his father.

Today, fourteen years later, Mike says the floor and walls of his grandmother's cellar are still damp and moldy. He's not sure his grandmother has ever really for-given him, even though she laughs when her neighbors tease him about the time he made his own private swimming pool. His cousins have grown up and moved out of state, but whenever Mike sees them, they all laugh and say things like "Hey, Mike! Drowned any cellars lately?"

After you and your classmate have interviewed each other, use the Writing Process outlined earlier and described in the steps that follow to write a short paper about each other.

Gather Your Ideas and Information

Following the interview, jot down as much as you can remember from your conversation with your classmate. These notes will serve as the raw material for the introduction of your classmate and an account of the famous deed. Check to see that you have gathered enough details and that they are accurate. Have you spelled your classmate's name correctly? Do you have enough information to compose a good introduction? Can you describe the famous deed with enough detail to allow readers to share it? Do you need to ask your classmate for any other information that would strengthen your account?

Analyze Your Ideas and Information

Study the material you have gathered about your classmate to decide which details you may not need to include or which ones might best be put together. What has the interview told you about your classmate as a college student? What overall picture of this person do you have? What is your view of the famous deed? Was it humorous or tragic? Worthy of admiration? Make notes about your answers to these and any other conclusions that come to mind.

Identify Your Main Point

Try to decide on a main point or dominant impression to present about the classmate you interviewed. Notice that the writer of the sample essay about another student's famous deed was able to relate her subject's college major and interest in swimming to express a main idea about him:

> Mike is an engineering major, an interest that relates both to his love of swimming and to the reason why, at the age of five, he became everlastingly famous as "that crazy kid who made his grandmother's cellar into a swimming pool."

Plan Your Writing

Your goal will be to create a brief piece of writing that will introduce your classmate as well as his or her famous deed to other members of your class. You will need to decide such things as where and when to state your main point or dominant impression about your subject, what order to put your ideas in, and where and how many concrete details to include. Will you stick only to the facts your classmate told you, or will you also mention your own impressions of the person and the famous deed? As you make your plan, be sure that it allows you to focus the content of your writing around the main point or dominant impression that you identified earlier. You may want to jot down the order of the ideas you want to present, along with relevant supporting examples.

Write Your Passage

Now you are properly prepared to begin writing. Write as much as you feel necessary to introduce your subject and the famous deed to your classmates. Do not try to tell everything you learned in the interview. Keep your overall purpose and plan in mind in order to emphasize those features that are most interesting and that illustrate the main point about the person or famous deed.

Here are some suggestions to follow in your writing:

1. Begin your piece of writing with one sentence that names the person you have interviewed and states or suggests something about the main point or dominant impression you will be making. Try to make the sentence say something interesting enough about the person to capture your readers' interest.
2. Throughout your discussion, state examples or details that illustrate and amplify the ideas you expressed in the first sentence. For example, if you stated in your first sentence that "*X* is a person of unusually varied interests," you would want to support your main point by mentioning at least several of those interests in your paper. If you described the famous deed as something "exciting," you will need to include details that support and illustrate that description.
3. As you move from point to point in your writing, make sure that you use smooth transitions. In writing, *transitions* are words or sentences that build bridges between different thoughts. Transitions are discussed more fully in Chapter 4, pages 63–65 For now, note how the student author of the sample essay used transitions to lead the reader smoothly from one event in time to another:

   > He started by putting two of his grandparents' garden hoses into the cellar and turning on the water. *Next,* he added more hoses from the neighbors' yards. *Then* he patiently waited while the water from all the hoses flowed and flowed into the cellar. *After about an hour,* Mike saw the boxes of clothing his grandmother stored in the cellar begin to float, bobbing slowly up and down in about three feet of water. *By this time,* the water . . .

4. Do not leave your audience dangling. Instead of simply stopping, close your discussion by leading your audience away from the material on which you have been focusing and into a broader view of it. End with a single sentence that signals a conclusion or sums up what you have been saying so far. Notice how the writer of the sample paper handles such a conclusion:

   > Today, fourteen years later, Mike says the floor and walls of his grandmother's cellar are still damp and moldy. He's not sure his grandmother has ever really forgiven him, even though she laughs when her neighbors tease him about the time he

made his own private swimming pool. His cousins have grown up and moved out of state, but whenever Mike sees them, they all laugh and say things like "Hey, Mike! Drowned any cellars lately?"

Revise and Edit Your Passage

Once you have written your passage, reread it and study it carefully to make any necessary changes in the content, order, or style. Be sure that you have written in complete sentences and that your voice remains the same throughout. You may find that you need to rearrange some parts of the passage or add material to illustrate or emphasize certain points more effectively. If necessary, ask your subject for more details and examples.

Next, check the whole passage for oversights in grammar or punctuation. Refer to Part IV of this text if you need to review any rules of grammar or punctuation. Use a dictionary to check the spelling of any word you are unsure about.

When you have finished planning, writing, and revising, read your passage to your group or to the class. After you have read your passage aloud, first ask yourself if it sounded like you, that is, does it have your voice? When you composed it, did you write with your audience of classmates in mind? Were you able to predict your audience's reactions accurately? After others have read their introductions, ask yourself the following questions:

1. Did you get a clear picture of the person being introduced?

2. Was there a main point? Did the writer support his or her points with examples?

3. Was the writing straightforward, or did it sound awkward? Could you spot sentences that could be improved?

4. What more would you want to know about the person in the passage?

Once you have answered these questions about your own passage as well as those of your classmates, you may want to repeat the *revise and edit* activity to make sure your passage says everything as you intended. Consult the person you are writing about if you need more information.

Writing Assignment 2-3: Introducing Another Person

Now turn your attention from the immediate arena of your classroom to the world outside for more writing resources. Write a passage of about 150 words on one of these subjects:

1. A foreign student on your campus
2. One of the athletic coaches at your school

3. Your oldest relative or the oldest person in your neighborhood
4. Someone you work with at a job outside school
5. A professor or dean in the discipline of your major
6. A person you went through grammar school and high school with
7. Your doctor or dentist
8. A person who holds a job you would like to have
9. A student of the opposite sex (from outside your class) who appears intelligent, interesting, and willing to cooperate with this assignment
10. Someone no one else would think to interview

Interview your subject using the questions and hints provided in Writing Assignment 2–2, jot down your notes after the interview, and use the Writing Process activities to compose, edit, and revise a final draft. As you write, remember that you are writing *to* your classmates.

Read your introduction to a group of your classmates and listen to their feedback. Then revise your draft again.

Listening to Others

In gathering ideas and information for your writing, it helps to listen closely to others as they speak and to record what they say. When you let people speak for themselves, you make your writing exact, specific, and interesting—always important goals in writing.

In your college writing, you may never have to record a whole conversation. However, the following writing assignment asks you to do just that so that you will gain skill in recording what people say. From time to time you will want to quote the people you write about. Also, by completing one or more of these assignments, you will learn to apply the tricky mechanical rules for recording dialogue.

 Writing Assignment 2–4:
Recording a Conversation

Position yourself near two or more people who appear to be having an interesting conversation—in the campus coffee shop, in the halls, outside the library, on the bus going home, or somewhere in your neighborhood. Write down as much of the conversation as you can. Be sure to use the speakers' words and not your own. If you object to listening to such a conversation, record a recent conversation in which you participated, or record a conversation from a radio or television talk show.

First, study the following rules for recording dialogue:

1. Use quotation marks at the beginning and end of each speaker's statements, but not after each sentence.

2. Always place periods inside the quotation marks.

3. If you quote an entire sentence that asks a question, place the question mark inside the quotation marks—for example, "How are you doing?"

4. If you drop a letter to make a word sound the way it was pronounced, use an apostrophe to show the omission—for example, "How are you doin'?"

5. If there are only two people talking and it is clear which one is speaking, drop the names before each speech after you have introduced each speaker.

6. Indent the line (that is, begin a new *paragraph,* to be discussed in detail in Chapter 4) each time the speaker shifts.

Next read the following student sample and notice how the dialogue is set up according to the rules just discussed.

Sample

There were cops coming from every direction, shouting for us to put our hands against the wall. There was screaming, pushing, and shoving. About twenty of us were taken to Central Lockup.

When we arrived, we were allowed one phone call. Bernice and Sylvia made their calls first, and their parents agreed to come get them right away. I then called home. Of all the people in the house, my mother had to answer the phone. The conversation went something like this:

"Hello, Mom," I said.

"Bernetta, what happened?" she asked.

"I'm in Central Lockup."

"Oh, my God! My child is in jail!"

"Come and get me out before it's too late and I have to spend the night."

"Bernetta, how did you get arrested?"

"The Blue Light got raided."

"You told me you were going to a party."

"I lied."

"Well, since you lied to me, I'm going to lie to you and say I'm coming to get you out."

"But Mom!"

The phone clicked off, and I thought the world was coming to an end.

The next morning my father picked me up and took me home. There was no conversation all the way home. When I opened the door, my mother was standing there, waiting.

"You are the first one to bring the family name down," she said.

My brothers and sisters were also waiting for me.

"What kind of birds don't fly?" my brothers asked.

"Jailbirds," my sisters answered.

Now write about 200 or 300 words reporting your conversation. Begin with a brief introduction explaining the occasion for the conversation. Study the rules for recording dialogue again, and also see Chapter 20 Section 7 for more rules on how to use quotation marks.

When you have finished writing your story, read it aloud in a small group. After each person has read his or her paper, answer the following questions:

1. Did the dialogue really sound like people talking? Explain.

2. What more would you like to know about the people talking or the conversation itself?

Exchange papers with another student to check for proper dialogue style, punctuation, and capitalization. Then revise your story, making use of the feedback you received from your classmates. As noted in Chapter 1, you will find that class reaction to your writing is a valuable tool in enhancing your work. Your audience's response is as important a factor as your intended message and how you composed it. As you listen to your classmates read their work, you will also come to appreciate the ways in which other writers compose. And as you gain experience in sharing your writing in class, you will discover that writing is not just an exercise, but a dynamic way of communicating ideas that are important to you.

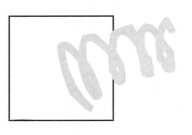

The Writing Process

GATHER your ideas and information
ANALYZE your ideas and information
IDENTIFY your theme or main point
PLAN your writing
WRITE
REVISE AND EDIT your writing

3

Gathering and Analyzing Your Material

- **Free Writing**
- **Focused Free Writing**
- **Visualization**
- **Brainstorming**
- **Clustering**

YOUR JOURNAL WRITING and class introductions have given you some initial practice in using the Writing Process for communicating ideas and information drawn
from your own experience and from the world around you. Your journal especially
can be a rich resource for developing essay ideas and gaining confidence in expressing yourself on a wide range of topics.

In most writing situations, however, you are expected to write on a specific
topic assigned by a teacher. This means that you will have to come up with ideas
on the topic and assemble them in some kind of systematic way. When you sit
down to perform this task, however, you may find, as many students do, that your
mind is a complete blank. What do you do now?

Experienced writers use a number of techniques to "prime the pump"—that
is, to initiate a flow of ideas that will ultimately result in a finished essay. Other
tricks of the trade help them to sift and evaluate the raw material they have generated. This chapter will explore specific tactics for generating ideas and information from yourself and the world around you.

Getting Started: Free Writing

Free writing is an excellent warm-up exercise you can use anytime you are having
trouble thinking of what to write. When you free write, you let ideas come out any
way they want to. The principle of free writing is quite simple: You just plunge in
and *write*. Write whatever comes into your head without stopping to worry about
phrasing, grammar, or spelling. Try to free write in complete sentences when you
can, but do not let concern for appearances keep you from being completely spontaneous.

Free writing usually works best when you set a time limit—say, five or ten minutes—within which to write. If you are writing at home, you may even want to set
the alarm clock. Simply keep writing at a pace that is comfortable for you until the
time is up.

If your mind goes blank, write "My mind has gone blank" a few times until something else occurs to you. Do not be surprised if you stray from your original idea
before you finish or if you write down words that are nonsensical to someone else,
or maybe even to you. The mere act of putting words on paper is relaxing and puts
you in a better frame of mind for moving on later to more focused writing.

Your journal is an excellent place to practice free writing. An entry that may
begin as haphazard often becomes the basis for serious thinking and writing.
Whenever you cannot think of a topic to write about in your journal, use free writing to get started. You may be surprised at the ideas you create.

A touching and unforgettable example of free writing in its ultimate form
comes from the pen of the Soviet dissident writer Andrei Sinyavsky, sentenced to
twelve years in a work camp and allowed by law one pencil:

> I began scribbling some nonsense, whatever came to mind . . . mostly about the
> book I intended to write someday. I couldn't think of any other way to be of

help to myself. It's not that my mind was teeming with ideas. And I was not moved by the passion to write or by a literary impulse, but by the instinct for self-preservation, prompting me to hold on for dear life to my pathetic profession just as it was being taken from me for all the world to see. . . . The book would be about its own writing. A book about a book. . . . I had neither heroes nor images apart from that dream of a book whose purpose and beginning were unclear, and, were it begun, I would still have no idea how I was going to write it. . . . I have not written that book, and there's little chance I ever will. But to make mental contact with it always buoys me up in my darkest hours.

Writing Assignment 3-1: Free Writing

On a blank sheet of paper, practice free writing for a full five minutes. Do not worry about what you are writing or about spelling, punctuation, and grammar. Instead, write without stopping, trying to fill the page.

To get an idea of what free writing looks and sounds like, read the following example.

> Well here goes—I'm free writing. Doing my best to write as much as I can without stopping so that nothing gets in the way of letting things go. It's sort of like holding your breath and trying to run at the same time and seeing how far you can get before the whistle blows—or like when the track coach tells us to run a whole quarter mile at full speed and knowing that you probably won't be able to keep it up all the way around the track, but you try anyway just to see how far you get—how'm I doing? Is it time yet I am writing and trying not to think but I do think about some things of course of course of course like why did I ever sign up for physics when I know I'm no good at that stuff math and all—barely understood algebra in high school. There ought to be some class for nonmath people to learn physics, like the Theory of Physics or something—that would be a great course, just ideas and no math so people like me could appreciate physics, like the class in music appreciation that I took where I didn't have to write music to appreciate it wow! TIME!

Now try your hand at free writing. Sit with paper and pen ready, let your mind relax—and start writing! When you finish, look over what you have written. Answer the following questions about your free-writing experience:

1. Did you find it easy to free write? If not, what things made it difficult?

2. Did anything you wrote surprise you in some way? What things? Why?

3. Are there any words or sentences that seem particularly effective or well chosen? Which ones?

4. Did any patterns of ideas evolve out of your free writing? What were they? Could you write more on those ideas?

Share your free writing with others in your class, and compare your experience of the exercise with theirs.

Focused Free Writing

Now that you have gained some experience with free writing, you are ready to apply it to the task of generating ideas on a specific topic. This technique is called *focused free writing*. Whereas free writing involves putting down whatever comes into your head, in focused free writing you try to write spontaneously about ideas that relate specifically to your assigned topic.

Writing Assignment 3–2:
Focused Free Writing

Write for five minutes about an event in your life that seemed to be a negative experience at the time but later appeared more positive (or taught you a valuable lesson).

Before you begin, read the following focused free-writing sample on this topic.

> Summer with my aunt and uncle and cousin in Oregon and not being able to talk to my cousin Sharon because she is deaf. What kind of fun if we couldn't talk to each other? Aunt Patty could talk—sign language, all those hands and fingers moving all the time all the time and I remember helping weed the berry patches every day and at first didn't even try to communicate with Sharon smiling and those berries! What work, bending over all day hands raw, legs sore, getting about 25 cents a basket 25 cents! And it took about a half an hour for me to find those things and fill a basket and I wanted to go home. It wasn't fun. No stores to go to. It was work all the time and no other kids around. Phoning Mom—"I don't like it here!"—and then I started to catch on to the sign language and pretty soon I could sign Do-you-like-television? Want-to-go-swimming-tomorrow? Telling jokes in sign! I got really good at it. Now I can talk to any deaf person and make friends all the time. Maybe a good college major or career for me.

Now you are ready to try the technique of focused free writing. First select an experience that fits the assignment, and then tell your story from beginning to end. Use a blank sheet of paper and write without stopping for at least five minutes. Try to write in complete sentences, but do not be too concerned with spelling, punctuation, or grammar. Do not worry if you get sidetracked, for you may be uncovering important parts of your story.

When you have finished writing, you will find that you have performed the activity *gathering your ideas and information*. You now have raw material to analyze and shape into a finished piece of writing. Put this writing sample aside for now and try a few more exercises in free writing.

Writing Assignment 3-3:
Finishing Passages

As a writer, you can gain skill in using effective language and arranging details by practicing free writing to complete an imaginative story or an essay begun by someone else. This exercise is designed to give you that kind of practice.

Examine the following passages. Choose one of them and continue the story by free writing on a blank page of paper. First, copy the passage. Then let your imagination take you wherever it leads. Write for at least ten minutes, or longer if you can. These passages have no "right" ending; feel free to finish them any way you please.

1. I found myself at the age of twenty on the outskirts of Chicago, with no money in my pockets and no relatives or friends to turn to. It was getting dark, and it was chilly in the early fall air. I was hungry and I did not know what to do, but I knew I had to do something, so . . .

2. I have always believed that somewhere in the world there lives the perfect mate for me. I was at a small party the other night, and when I happened to look up toward the door, I saw him (or her) standing there alone. I knew, as I have never known anything so definitely before, that this was the right person for me. I gathered my courage and I . . .

3. Words and what people say have always been especially important to me. I grew up hearing statements like "Just Say No to Drugs," "Love is where you find it," "God helps those who help themselves," and a good dozen or more declarations that you have probably heard as well. I remember my dad always saying, "Don't break anything that isn't yours"—which is not only good advice for children, but for adults, too. Certain words or sayings, in fact, have had a pretty profound influence on my life. For example, there is the expression . . .

4. I don't always think of myself as the courageous type, but I have done my share of asserting myself when I thought it was important for my own sake or the well-being of another person. Once, for example, I found myself calling on all the courage I could muster to stand up against a friend of mine on someone else's behalf. I was having lunch with . . .

5. Our society has an obsession with guns. We hear every day about someone shooting another person as the result of a crime or the outcome of an argument. There has even lately been an outbreak of guns being brought to school by children in the third or fourth grades! This crazy addiction to guns has to stop. I think it's time that . . .

After you have finished your free-writing practice, revise it by adding to it, deleting from it, or changing it in any way needed to make it a completed piece. Then make a final draft, checking to see that you have written everything in complete sentences.

Brainstorming

We all have more ideas and know more information than we are willing or able to express. Before writing anything at all, you may worry about what others will think of your thoughts and fear that you will sound stupid to the instructor, to other students, or even to yourself. This fear may make you decide to play it safe and write only those things you are sure will not be criticized or laughed at. But what you do *not* say—or are afraid to say—is sometimes far more interesting than what you think you *ought* to say.

The poet W. H. Auden called the internal force that keeps us from expressing ourselves freely the "Watcher at the Gate." The Watcher always wants us to say things perfectly, always wants to make sure we do not say the wrong things, and is thus always ready to slam the gate shut on what we are capable of saying. Your Watcher performs a valuable service when it comes time to proofread and revise an essay, but if the Watcher is allowed to close the gate too soon on what you *could* say, you may find you have very little to write about. A second-semester freshman wrote the following to explain how the Watcher at the Gate prevents him from writing what he wants to write.

The Watcher at the Gate

My Watcher at the Gate is a built-in critic who is tougher on the writer than Rex Reed is on movie producers. I often imagine my Watcher as a duplicate of my eleventh-grade English teacher, a slightly balding man in his early thirties, always wearing a doorman's uniform. He sits in a straight-back chair in front of the gate and lets nothing escape his discriminating eye.

I believe that deep inside me is a writer, as well as a Watcher, who is waiting to surface. This writer is very small compared to my Watcher. The writer strives to be original and let the thoughts flow from my mind to the paper without stopping at the gate. Only at certain times, however, can my Watcher be caught off guard. One of these times is at three o'clock in the morning. While my Watcher is dreaming away, I am left alone, free to express myself. The Watcher can also be caught off guard in the closing moments of a deadline. At this point, the Watcher is frantic about making the deadline, so he becomes less critical and allows thoughts to flow freely.

My Watcher hates to take chances. He would rather block my thoughts and copy the style of another than risk failure. Because of this, most of my writing sounds as if it were taken from the pages of an English text instead of from my own mind. When all is taken into account, however, the Watcher at the gate is necessary in the writing of proper English. He does make me look up words in the dictionary and insists that each of my "sentences" is a sentence. Who knows? He may even have helped me write this description of him.

Brainstorming is a technique that helps you open the gate, allowing all the thoughts—perfect, imperfect, silly, beautiful, or ugly—to flow freely from your brain to the paper without stopping at the gate. This technique asks simply that you make a decision to open the gate and jot down as many thoughts as possible. Later, once you have written down all the thoughts, you can pick and choose which ones to use. Here is how one student brainstormed when she decided to write about her father. The student made her first line in the left-hand column. Then, once she could think of nothing else, she went back to see if any items reminded her of other characteristics of her father. These she wrote in the right-hand column.

six feet tall, brown hair	dark eyes
good sense of humor	likes to play practical jokes
sensitive to problems I bring to him	
	willing to help me to accomplish any goals I set for myself
jogs every morning before work	muscular, lean, great shape for his age!
doesn't mind helping with housework	willing to sweep, dust, scrub, etc.
crazy about golf	prefers to play rather than watch
likes to read and go to movies	In short, a great guy!

Writing Assignment 3–4:
Brainstorming Ideas I

Form an image in your mind of your room at home, your dormitory room, or some other room you have strong feelings about. Make a brainstorming list of all the details of the room you can remember. What furniture is in it? What colors do you see? What little items catch your eye? What about the room is known only to you? What is out of place?

Study the following student sample for ideas on how you might use your brainstorming list for writing a passage on a room.

My Room

My room is usually clean, but when I left this morning, it was so messy that my dog wouldn't come in. My pink silk robe and pajamas were thrown across my unmade bed. My slippers were lying there in the middle of the floor, and I hate to admit it, but the floor was covered with big gobs of lint. Off to the right, my bureau top was piled high with caps from lotions, old empty bottles, hair curlers, deodorant, and many purses. And finally, my closet was overflowing with dirty clothes left over from last week and maybe even the week before. When I think of my room, it makes me glad I am not there.

Now plan your passage. Here are some suggestions:

1. In your first sentence, state when you were last in the room and summarize its general appearance in a word or two.

2. Choose at least five things that stand out for you as you think of the room.

3. Decide on some method for ordering your writing. Will you describe the room from left to right, from right to left, or from the most eye-catching features to the least eye-catching ones?

Using your brainstorming list, write a passage of at least 100 words on the room. Describe the details as precisely as possible. In your last sentence, give the one word or expression that best describes how the room makes you feel.

Writing Assignment 3–5: Brainstorming Ideas II

The telephone, automobile, airplane, and computer have all been celebrated as major technological advances in this century. Which one of these has contributed most to life in the modern world? Use brainstorming techniques to write a brief passage of 150–175 words arguing for one of these as having made the greatest contribution to modern life. If you would prefer to argue for a different choice than these, you may.

Before you begin, read the following sample, which argues, only half humorously, for the refrigerator as having contributed most to modern living.

> The late nineteenth and twentieth centuries have witnessed a number of fabulous inventions, but the modern refrigerator, that cool repository of sandwich meats, leftovers, and sodas, has got to rank first as making the most important contribution to modern living. That may sound exaggerated, but without the refrigerator, this society would face constant health problems from spoiled foods, and we would have more food thrown away as garbage than we do now. The refrigerator has also changed the work force, freeing up mothers to shop and store food when it is convenient and to make up meals ahead of time for their families. Without that ability, a lot of women would not work during the day, but would instead stay home, going to the market for fresh meat and vegetables and then spending all day in the kitchen to prepare the night's meal. It's easy to praise the telephone or the automobile for the changes they make in our lives, but the refrigerator is one of those essential things that we would literally be worse off without. Milk, green leafy vegetables, cold ripe apples and oranges, ice cream, leftover salsa, bottles and jars of condiments, wonderful cheeses, puddings and Jell-O, Snapple and Budweiser—they're all at home, right at our fingertips, and all thanks to the refrigerator. Nothing else has made modern life better for us.

Now decide which invention—the telephone, automobile, airplane, or computer—has contributed most to modern living. When you have decided upon your choice, you are ready to start the writing process.

Gather Your Ideas and Information: First, begin to jot down your thoughts. As quickly as you can, without stopping to think twice, use the left-hand column on this page to write down every way you can think of that the technological development you chose has indeed contributed to our lives more than others. *Don't censor your thoughts!* Express them all—creative, silly, brilliant, stupid, beautiful, ugly. If you bog down, see if any features you have already listed suggest new ones.

After you have filled the left-hand column, review it to see if the items there remind you of anything else or if you can be more specific about what you have already put down. Add these new ideas to the column at the right.

_____   _____

_____   _____

_____   _____

_____   _____

_____   _____

_____   _____

Working in a Group

Because one thought often inspires another, brainstorming works well when you do it with other people. Now share your most original ideas with the rest of the class. A volunteer can write the ideas on the blackboard. As you hear what others have come up with, you will think of new ideas for your own list. Write these down as well.

_____   _____

_____   _____

_____   _____

_____   _____

_____   _____

_____   _____

Analyze Your Ideas and Information: Review your brainstorming list to see what you have discovered about your topic. What ideas relate to each other?

Are any too isolated or unique to be useful? Have you listed ideas that show why the technology you chose is responsible for making our lives better? Are some items on the list more essential than others? See if you can add anything to the list to make it more detailed or convincing.

Identify Your Main Point: Use the analysis you performed about your choice of technology to decide what your main point is. Your main point may be simply a statement that the telephone, let's say, has made the greatest contribution to modern living, or you may wish to phrase the main idea in a way that makes it more interesting, as in the first sentence of the sample piece on page 38 about the refrigerator.

Plan Your Writing: Here are some suggestions for writing your passage:

1. State clearly the main idea and your choice of the most important technological development in the first sentence.

2. Describe at least four main features of this technology and tell how it has affected modern life. Include examples to illustrate these features and the effect you identify.

3. Decide on some order to discuss your ideas. You may decide to move from the smallest to the largest or most impressive features, or from the least to the most important.

Write: Following your plan and using the ideas from your brainstorming list, write a paragraph or two describing why the technology you chose has made the greatest contribution to modern life.

Revise and Edit Your Writing: Read your finished draft over carefully when you have completed your passage, paying attention to the order of your ideas and the clarity of your sentences. Look carefully for any needed changes in grammar, punctuation, or spelling.

Writing Assignment 3-6:
Brainstorming Ideas III

Use brainstorming techniques to write a passage that describes five or more characteristics of an object without ever naming it. Choose something that is not too large, preferably something you could hold in your hands or arms.

Before you begin, study the following samples for ideas about ways to describe your own object.

A Riddle

It is huge, dark brown, inexpensive, and people say it weighs a ton. It is also at times the family joke. Everyone cannot get over the fact that it contains so many different things. My husband has often said that if our country were bombed, our family would survive on the contents of this object. It contains headache pills, stomachache pills, and backache ointments, and if you dig deep enough, you can even find dental floss for those once-a-year emergencies. It contains chewing gum, a date book, a mini-umbrella, a checkbook, and several other essential items.

What Am I?

I am to be admired for what I am. I grow old and die along with the seeds of life. People love me and those who give me. I bring life to dull and shady corners. I bring warmth and smiles to the hearts of my owners. I dress up major dinners and decorate great celebrations. I am the color of a blush and must be seen only, for if I am touched, I will fall to pieces. What am I?

After studying the samples, use the steps of the Writing Process to write your description of an unnamed object.

Gather Your Ideas and Information: Brainstorm a list of all the characteristics of the object you want to describe. List as many characteristics as you can without paying any attention to their significance or obviousness.

Analyze Your Ideas and Information: Look over the list you generated to see which details provide the most *exact* clues about the nature of the object. Your audience should be able to guess the object by paying close attention to your choice of language and details. (However, delete or ignore characteristics that too obviously give away the object's identity. For example, if you are describing your grandmother's teeth that sit by the bed at night, do not characterize them as something she uses to bite with.)

Identify Your Main Point: The main point of your riddle passage may be stated or implied, but it should describe the dominant impression you want to convey about the object. Thus the main characteristic of the object described in "A Riddle" might be the comical fact that it seems to contain almost everything. You will need to make sure that all the details and language in your description accurately and fairly represent the object and your main point about it.

Plan Your Writing: Plan the language and arrangement of details in your passage. Group similar characteristics together so that your description moves from one feature of the object to another in a logical order—for example, outside to inside, least common to most common uses, color to shape to weight.

Write: In a passage of at least 100 words, describe your object as accurately as possible without explicitly giving away its identity. Use comparison to indicate qualities such as size, shape, or color ("bigger than an orange but smaller than a basketball," for example). Include enough details to be descriptive but not so many that you will confuse your reader.

Revise and Edit Your Writing: Reread your draft to see if it is clear and understandable. Are all the parts in the most effective order? Have you used specific language and adequate descriptive words? A thesaurus or dictionary can supply excellent synonyms or a variety of exact word choices. Are your grammar, spelling, and punctuation correct throughout?

When you have finished writing your passage, read it to members of the class to see if they can guess your object. You are playing a game with your audience here: You want to make your riddle hard enough to challenge and even stump them, but plausible and accurate enough so that they can make the connection instantly if you have to tell them the answer yourself. In this assignment especially, audience feedback is a sure measure of your success as a riddler.

Writing Assignment 3–7: Brainstorming Ideas IV

Use the brainstorming method to gather ideas and information on one of the following topics:

1. The ideal wife or husband
2. Your most unusual teacher
3. The most generous person you know
4. The most exciting sport you know about
5. The vacation spot you would most recommend

Now use the steps of the Writing Process to compose a passage of about 150 words on the topic you have selected:

Gather your ideas and information

Analyze your ideas and information

Identify your main point

Plan your writing

Write

Revise and edit your writing

Let us now turn to a third technique that experienced writers use to generate ideas.

Clustering

In her book *Writing the Natural Way,* Gabrielle Rico explains the method she devised to help her students get in touch with the creative, inventive part of themselves. Rico calls the part of ourselves that is always trying to be logical and put things in the right order the "Sign mind." The other, creative part of ourselves that is longing to express our well-hidden imagination and artistic ability she calls the "Design mind." Rico's Sign mind, very much like Auden's Watcher at the Gate, controls, judges, and supervises. To get out from under this watchdog, who tends to strangle our creative impulses in their early stages, Rico suggests the strategy she calls *clustering* as a way of giving your playful, curious Design mind free rein to generate ideas.

Begin with a nucleus word circled on an empty page. Then go with any connections that come into your head, writing each down in its own circle. Connect each new word or phrase with a line to the previous circle. "As you cluster," Rico warns, "you may experience a sense of randomness or, if you are somewhat skeptical, an uneasy sense that it isn't leading anywhere. . . . Trust this natural process, though. We all cluster mentally throughout our lives without knowing it; we have simply never made these clusterings visible on paper."

Here is how two students used the technique of clustering. The first student started with the nucleus word *computer*, as shown by the diagram on page 44.

The Value of a Computer

A medium-priced home computer system including basic components like the computer itself, a black-and-white monitor, and some kind of printer can cost at least $1,000 or more. I can assure you, though, that the advantages of owning a computer far outweigh the initial costs. Word-processing capability alone makes a computer worth having. With word processing you can do everything from writing essays for your English class to creating good-looking résumés for job applications. Writing on a computer, you can compose faster, rewrite, and make corrections, plus format your material more attractively than on a typewriter. And the computer gives you a way to store writing, too, which is handy for journals and any creative writing you do for personal pleasure. Your computer can even store recipes, keep bank account balances, help do your income tax, and let you play a variety of videolike games, all in your own home. You can also get a device called a modem, which will let you talk to your computer when you are away from home or make contact with the numerous computer clubs and electronic bulletin boards used by thousands of other computer owners. Don't bother getting a dog. In today's world, the computer is clearly your best friend.

In this clustering sample, the writer began by recording thoughts, feelings, experiences, and information that came into her mind in connection with the nucleus word *computer*—that is, when she could not think of any more to write along one clustering path, she simply returned to the nucleus word and began in a new direction. Before beginning, she thought she would be writing about the way a computer worked, but to her surprise each path pointed her toward the uses of a home computer. Notice that she did not use everything from her clustering in the passage.

In the second clustering sample, the writer began with the word *fear*, as shown by the diagram on page 45.

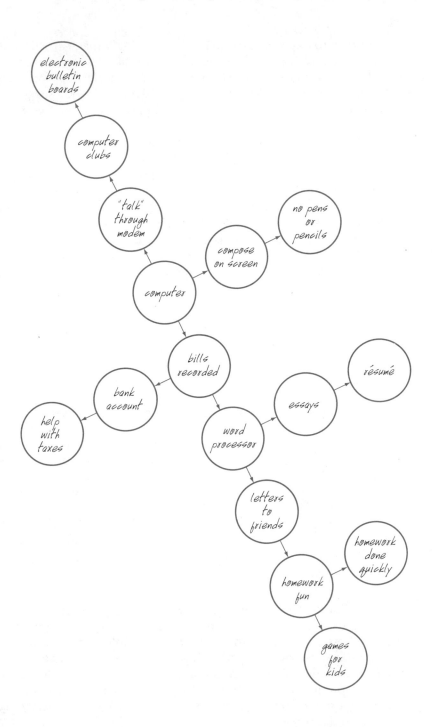

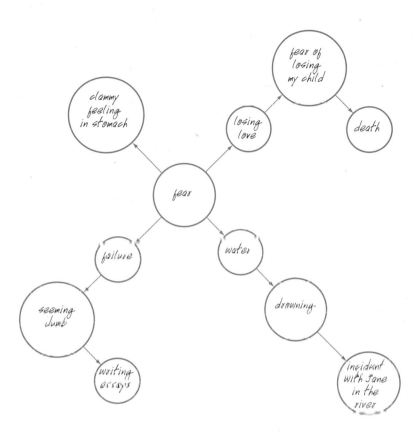

Fear

    To me, being afraid is associated with loss—loss of love, loss of pride, loss of life. When I was a child, my sister Jane and I nearly drowned in the Calcasieu River. While we were playing a game called "dragons," Jane was pulled into the undertow and reached out to me, the clumsy nonswimmer. I tried to help her, and soon we were both fighting for air, for life, wondering if this was what it would be like to die. Luckily, some people on the shore saw us and pulled us out in time. Since that day my greatest fear is of dying.

Notice that the writer focused most of his passage on one of the paths in the cluster, the near-drowning incident. In the first sentence, however, he generalized about fear, mentioning the different things fear meant to him. For this passage he used three of his four clustering paths.

Writing Assignment 3-8:
Clustering I

First, select someone you know well—a parent, your best friend, your girlfriend or boyfriend, your spouse—as your topic for clustering. Write the person's name, circled, in the middle of a blank piece of paper; that will be your nucleus word. Next, write down all the thoughts and associations about the person that come to mind. Do not censor any thoughts—just keep jotting them down. When you exhaust one set of possibilities, return to the nucleus word and begin again with a new string of associations. When you have clustered several connected thoughts, write a passage based on your cluster. Revise your passage using what Rico calls your "Sign mind" (and what Auden calls your "Watcher at the Gate"). The whole process, clustering and writing the passage, should take no longer than half an hour.

Now look at what you have written. Did clustering help lead you to any significant insights or important observations you might have overlooked if you were simply writing "off the top of your head"? How does clustering compare, as a technique, with focused free writing and brainstorming? Could it help with analyzing as well as gathering your ideas and information—that is, in making connections between ideas and expanding your train of thought? Discuss your experiences of this assignment with your classmates.

Writing Assignment 3-9:
Clustering II

Choose one of the following words or phrases as your nucleus, and use the suggestions for clustering to record whatever comes to your mind in association with the nucleus. When you finish, write a passage describing what the word or phrase means to you.

Remember to let your creative side take over as you cluster. The idea is to play with your thoughts and writing possibilities. The topics are intentionally broad and abstract to allow you plenty of freedom in giving your passage a focus and making it concrete.

Fear
Summer (fall, winter, spring)
Happiness
Romantic love

Use your clustering diagram as a guide in analyzing as well as gathering your information and ideas as you carry out the steps of the Writing Process:

Gather your ideas and information

Analyze your ideas and information

Identify your main point

Plan your writing

Write

Revise and edit your writing

Remember to use what Rico calls your Sign mind in revising your passage.

Discussing Your Response to Ideas with Others

Many students find that talking about a topic with classmates or friends is the best way to develop ideas for writing. Such discussions also can stimulate free writing, visualization, brainstorming, and clustering.

Writing Assignment 3–10:
Discussing Your Response to Poetry

In this assignment you will be asked to discuss your response to one or more of the poems on the following pages. These poems were chosen for this assignment because they use effective language and poetic form to call forth both ideas and emotions from the reader. First, read each of the poems carefully to yourself at least twice; focus on the ideas and feelings each of the poems evokes from you. Next, to help gather ideas and information for writing, discuss the poems with others and talk over your ideas for writing a response.

As you write the various pieces of writing assigned in this text, it is important to reflect on how you feel about the subject matter and at times to explain your feelings to your readers. Responding to the following poems should be a good way to practice these techniques. Notice, however, as you read the poems, that the writers manage to convey their feelings without using such conventional "feeling" words as *hate, happiness,* or *sadness.*

James Dickey, a well-known poet, once wrote this about poetry: "The first thing to understand about poetry is that it comes to you from outside you, in books or in words, but that for it to live, something from within you must come to it and meet it and complete it. Your response with your own mind and body and memory and emotions gives the poem its ability to work its magic; if you give to it, it will give to you, and give plenty."

Read the following poems carefully, and name the feeling or feelings each poem evokes in you. You will notice that the poems included here do not always follow standard grammatical rules. That is because poets claim the right to use non-standard constructions, such as fragments, in their writing in order to convey ideas and feelings that the use of standard grammar and punctuation cannot express.

The following poem was written by an immigrant from Cuba. After you have read this poem and the one that follows it, try to describe the attitude of each of the speakers.

Nobody Knows My Name

I'm tired
dead anonymous tired
of getting mail addressed
to all those people I never was:

Gustazo	Peres
Gustavio	Penley
Gary	Porris
Gus	Perry
Gustaf	Pirey.

Nobody here knows my name.
This would never have happened in Havana.

Gustavo Pérez Firmat

Girlfriend

My girlfriend does not like my wife
Because she is older than my wife
and because my wife is who she is
Though she is my wife no longer
Even though I still call her my wife
Because she is my wife, the only one
I ever had, whereas my girlfriend
Who lives with me as a wife
Is not my wife but my girlfriend
And probably won't take another
Name until there is someone
Else around to take over hers.

Robert Gelasco

As you read the following poem, notice how the poet uses language to create images and reinforce meaning. What is the speaker's attitude about the events described in the poem? How has the speaker's attitude changed?

Those Winter Sundays

Sundays too my father got up early
and put his clothes on in the blueblack cold,
then with cracked hands that ached
from labor in the weekday weather made
banked fires blaze. No one ever thanked him.

I'd wake and hear the cold splintering, breaking.
When the rooms were warm, he'd call,
and slowly I would rise and dress,
fearing the chronic angers of that house.

Speaking indifferently to him,
who had driven out the cold
and polished my good shoes as well.
What did I know, what did I know
of love's austere and lonely offices?

Robert Hayden

As you read the next poem, ask yourself if it is primarily about blacks rising out of oppression. Or could it be about any minority group or any individual person? On the other hand, could it be mostly about women? Is it human nature to begrudge other people their victories?

Still I Rise

You may write me down in history
With your bitter, twisted lies,
You may trod me in the very dirt
But still, like dust, I'll rise.

Does my sassiness upset you?
Why are you beset with gloom?
'Cause I walk like I've got oil wells
Pumping in my living room.

Just like moons and like suns,
With the certainty of tides,
Just like hopes springing high,
Still I'll rise.

Did you want to see me broken?
Bowed head and lowered eyes?
Shoulders falling down like teardrops,
Weakened by my soulful cries.

Does my haughtiness offend you?
Don't you take it awful hard
'Cause I laugh like I've got gold mines
Diggin' in my own back yard.

You may shoot me with your words,
You may cut me with your eyes,
You may kill me with your hatefulness,
But still, like air, I'll rise.

Does my sexiness upset you?
Does it come as a surprise

That I dance like I've got diamonds
At the meeting of my thighs?

Out of the huts of history's shame
I rise
Up from a past that's rooted in pain
I rise
I'm a black ocean, leaping and wide,
Welling and swelling I bear in the tide.

Leaving behind nights of terror and fear
I rise
Into a daybreak that's wondrously clear
I rise
Bringing the gifts that my ancestors gave,
I am the dream and the hope of the slave.
I rise.
I rise.
I rise.

Maya Angelou

Working in a Group

In small groups, discuss all four of the poems. The following suggestions may be helpful.

1. Reread the poem you are discussing. Perhaps someone will agree to read it aloud.

2. Discuss what the author is trying to say to you in the poem. For the time being, withhold your own response to the poem. Ask the following questions about the poem:

What lines best capture the meaning of the poem?
What is the message of the poem?
What feeling does the poet convey? Anger? Sadness? Hate? Happiness? Arrogance? Hopelessness?

3. Discuss your reactions to the poem:

What colors does the poem remind you of?
What pieces of music?
What would you like to say back to the author of the poem, or to any of the people in the poem?
What one word best describes how you felt as you read it?

Write a passage in two parts on one of the poems using the following questions to develop organizing principles for each part. (These two units, *paragraphs*, will be discussed in detail in the next chapter.)

1. *Part (paragraph) one:* What is the author trying to say in the poem? How does he or she say it? What images or pictures does the poet want you to see? What feeling is conveyed? What line says it best?

2. *Part (paragraph) two:* What would you like to say to the author or any of the people in the poem? Why? How does the poem make you feel? Does the poem relate to your own experiences or the experiences of someone you know? Explain.

Writing Assignment 3–11:
Writing a Poem of Your Own

Because poets must select their words very carefully, as well as control the length and form of their sentences, writing your own poetry provides an excellent way to develop your skills as a writer. To complete this assignment, begin by reading the essay "How to Write a Rotten Poem with Almost No Effort" by Richard Howey on this and the following pages. Although Howey pretends to demonstrate only how a "rotten" poem is written, you will find his method is not only fun to try, but can also be a surprisingly effective way to create a very fine poem.

Start by reading Howey's essay and then follow his directions for writing a poem. For each step in Howey's directions, experiment with different lines until you have one or two that satisfy you; then go on to the next step until you have enough lines for your poem. When you have one poem completed, try another. Try your hand at writing a poem using rhyme. You may find that you can write several small poems using Howey's technique or that you can use the method to create a poem even longer than four lines.

When you have completed at least one poem by following Howey's directions, share your work with other students in the class. Read your poem aloud to your classmates, and ask them to do the same with their poems. What were you each trying to say in your poem? Which lines work best? Do you agree that Howey's method can actually lead to writing better than "rotten" poetry?

How to Write a Rotten Poem
with Almost No Effort

So you want to write a poem. You've had a rotten day or an astounding thought or a car accident or a squalid love affair and you want to record it for all time. You want to organize those emotions that are pounding through your veins. You have something to communicate via a poem but you don't know where to start.

This, of course, is the problem with poetry. Most people find it difficult to write a poem so they don't even try. What's worse, they don't bother reading any poems either. Poetry has become an almost totally foreign art form to many of us. As a result, serious poets either starve or work as account executives. There is no middle ground. Good poets and poems are lost forever simply because there is no market for them, no people who write their own verse and seek out further inspiration from other bards.

Fortunately, there is a solution for this problem, as there are for all imponderables. The answer is to make it easy for everyone to write at least one poem in his life. Once a person has written a poem, of whatever quality, he will feel comradeship with fellow poets and, hopefully, read their works. Ideally, there would evolve a veritable society of poet-citizens, which would elevate the quality of life worldwide. Not only that, good poets could make a living for a change.

So, to begin. Have your paper ready. You must first understand that the poem you write here will not be brilliant. It won't even be mediocre. But it will be better than 50% of all song lyrics and at least equal to one of Rod McKuen's best efforts. You will be instructed how to write a four-line poem but the basic structure can be repeated at will to create works of epic length.

The first line of your poem should start and end with these words: "In the ——— of my mind." The middle word of this line is optional. Any word will do. It would be best not to use a word that has been overdone, such as "windmills" or "gardens" or "playground." Just think of as many nouns as you can and see what fits best. The rule of thumb is to pick a noun that seems totally out of context, such as "filing cabinet" or "radiator" or "parking lot." Just remember, the more unusual the noun, the more profound the image.

The second line should use two or more of the human senses in a conflicting manner, as per the famous, "listen to the warm." This is a sure way to conjure up "poetic" feeling and atmosphere. Since there are five difference senses, the possibilities are endless. A couple that come to mind are "see the noise" and "touch the sound." If more complexity is desired other senses can be added, as in "taste the color of my hearing," or "I cuddled your sight in the aroma of the night." Rhyming, of course, is optional.

The third line should be just a simple statement. This is used to break up the insightful images that have been presented in the first two lines. This line should be as prosaic as possible to give a "down-to-earth" mood to the poem. An example would be "she gave me juice and toast that morning," or perhaps "I left for work next day on the 8:30 bus." The content of this line may or may not relate to what has gone before.

The last line of your poem should deal with the future in some way. This gives the poem a forward thrust that is always helpful. A possibility might be, "tomorrow will be a better day," or "I'll find someone sometime," or "maybe we'll meet again in July." This future-oriented ending lends an aura of hope and yet need not be grossly optimistic.

By following the above structure, anyone can write a poem. For example, if I select one each of my sample lines, I come up with:

In the parking lot of my mind,
    I cuddled your sight in the aroma of the night.
I left for work next day on the 8:30 bus.
    Maybe we'll meet again in July.

Now that poem (like yours, when you're finished) is rotten. But at least it's a poem and you've written it, which is an accomplishment that relatively few people can claim.

Now that you're a poet, feel free to read poetry by some of your more accomplished brothers and sisters in verse. Chances are, you'll find their offerings stimulating and refreshing. You might even try writing some more of your own poems, now that you've broken the ice. Observe others' emotions and experience your own—that's what poetry is all about.

Richard Howey

Analyzing the Material You Have Gathered

Once you have begun to feel comfortable with the various techniques for generating ideas for writing on assigned topics—free writing, focused free writing, visualization, brainstorming, clustering, and group discussion—the next step in the Writing Process is to focus on *analyzing your ideas and information*—that is, sorting out what you came up with and deciding how to make the best use of it.

As you've already discovered in your previous writing assignments, analyzing your ideas and information means examining the odds and ends you've collected with a practical, analytical eye. Very often the problem of "having nothing to write about" is really one of not knowing how to use the ideas and information you already have at hand. Sifting, sorting, and determining the relative importance of the ideas you have collected *before you plan and write* will help you determine whether or not you need to collect more information or simply restate your topic to focus on what you really want to say.

Writing Assignment 3-12:
Analyzing Focused Free Writing

Return now to the passage you wrote for Writing Assignment 3-2 (page 34), the most unpleasant event you have ever lived through. As noted, the free writing you did was a kind of on-the-job collecting of material. Now you can move to *analyzing your ideas and information* by thoughtfully examining what you put down there. Ask yourself which items stand out as important to the overall story you are trying to tell. Which go together, and which seem unrelated to any of the others? Would you include anything more now that you had omitted while writing? Begin to narrow down the ideas and information to make the general topic—the unpleasant experience—more specific. How could you order this material? Would a good title help you get started?

Use brainstorming and clustering techniques to impose some order on your material. List the main ideas, as in brainstorming, or diagram their connections, as in clustering.

Identify Your Main Point: After analyzing the ideas you generated, you need to determine the main idea of your focused free writing. For this assignment, your main idea should clearly state some kind of conclusion about a negative experience that later proved to be positive. For instance, the sample might produce a main point such as this: "The difficulty I had at first communicating with my deaf cousin Sharon turned into a rewarding personal experience as I began to learn sign language."

Plan Your Writing: Using your focused free writing and your stated main point as the starting points, plan the order of a new passage on the same subject. Identify each central experience or set of ideas, and decide the best order in which to arrange them. Where would your story most effectively begin? Which details should you include, and which should you eliminate, to best enhance your main idea? How will you wind up your passage? Would your main idea be most effectively placed at the beginning or the end? Notice that the student author of the sample organized her focused free writing chronologically. She began by describing her first feelings about being in Oregon, moved through what she did during the summer, and ended by looking toward the future.

Write: Write a new, expanded passage of about 300 words that discusses an unpleasant experience that later proved positive. Keep your main point in mind, and include as many examples and details as a reader would need to understand and believe you. Keep the following suggestions in mind as you write:

1. Be willing to add to, delete, or change any of the material in your focused free writing.

2. Move your reader into the story as quickly as possible. You might want to begin by saying, "I started out my last year in high school with a broken leg and a grade point average that even embarrassed my dog."

3. Use transition sentences between related ideas wherever possible (see Chapter 4, pages 63–65 and Chapter 5, pages 83–84, for examples). If you were describing in one sentence how much money your car was costing you, you might follow it with a transition sentence such as this: "Not only was my car costing me a fortune, but so were my meals."

4. To conclude, be sure to tell your reader what you learned from this experience.

5. Give your passage a title. Keep it short.

Revise and Edit Your Writing: When you finish the first draft of the passage, revise and edit it as necessary. Check all grammar, punctuation, and spelling.

Writing Assignment 3–13:
Analyzing Journal Material

Look over some of the entries you have been making in your journal (see Chapters 1 and 2). Choose a passage to develop into a finished piece of writing. Then analyze what you have by (1) listing ideas/events/information in order of importance or, if events, in chronological order or (2) clustering them as you practiced in Writing Assignments 3-8 and 3-9. Do you have enough material? Is anything missing? Does more material need to be gathered to make a complete picture?

   Once you have completed this task, continue with the steps of the Writing Process:

   Identify your main point

   Plan your new passage

   Write your new passage

   Revise and edit your new passage

Compare your final effort with your original journal entry. You will probably discover a considerable improvement—in presentation, depth, and effectiveness—in your revised version. If possible, read the two versions to your classmates and gain their impressions as well.

The Writing Process

GATHER your ideas and information
ANALYZE your ideas and information
IDENTIFY your theme or main point
PLAN your writing
WRITE
REVISE AND EDIT your writing

4

Identifying Your Main Point

- **Paragraphs and Topic Sentences**
- **Essays and Thesis Statements**
- **Transitions Between Paragraphs**

THE PREVIOUS CHAPTER focused on the first two activities of the Writing Process—*gathering* your ideas and information and then *analyzing* your ideas and information—along with various techniques for accomplishing them. Taken together, these two activities lay the foundation for determining *what* you want to say about your material (*identifying* your main point) and *how* or in what order you want to say it (*planning* your writing). This chapter will teach you more about how to formulate your main point and will introduce some important tools to order your ideas: the thesis statement, the paragraph, and the topic sentence.

All writing is meant to communicate ideas, usually ordered to support and develop a main idea or argument about a subject to an audience. Deciding on the central focus of your ideas or argument can be the most important activity in the writing process. Before you begin to write, therefore, you need to examine all your ideas and identify one message that includes whatever general conclusion, observation, argument, or opinion you want to make about them. Once you have decided what that message is, you must express it in writing and develop a discussion that explains and supports it.

Making a final statement of your central viewpoint or argument on a subject is a continual process of focusing and refining your ideas through the first three activities of the Writing Process:

Gathering your ideas and information

Analyzing your ideas and information

Identifying your main point

Determining your main point or argument involves compressing your thoughts on a subject to a single main idea expressed in one sentence, called a *thesis statement.* This sentence must be general enough to sum up your thinking on the subject, to state what you want to say or prove to your audience, and to channel your ideas into a meaningful discussion. You might visualize the progress of your ideas through the prewriting, writing, and postwriting stages as sand running through an hourglass, as shown in the illustration on the following page.

As you can see, identifying your main point is crucial in transforming the mass of raw material you gathered into an ordered, consistent, effective piece of writing. This main point you have decided on during the prewriting stages of the Writing Process will become the thesis statement of your finished essay. The thesis statement, or main argument of your essay, will be explained and supported by a series of sentences grouped into the natural line breaks we call *paragraphs.* You will find that paragraphing is a valuable tool in separating and ordering ideas and information to develop and support your essay's thesis statement.

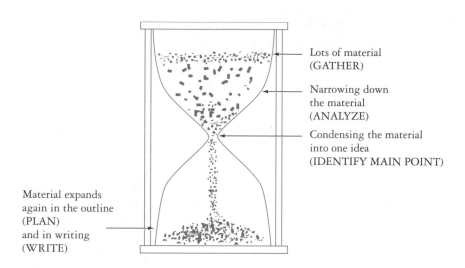

Lots of material
(GATHER)

Narrowing down
the material
(ANALYZE)

Condensing the material
into one idea
(IDENTIFY MAIN POINT)

Material expands
again in the outline
(PLAN)
and in writing
(WRITE)

The Paragraph and Its Topic Sentence

A *paragraph* is a group of related sentences that discuss and elaborate a single, complete idea. A paragraph usually contains a *topic sentence* that expresses its main idea and determines its content. A topic sentence orders a paragraph in the same way that a thesis statement or main point orders your essay as a whole. Thus you will find that identifying the main point of your paragraph is much the same activity as identifying the main point of your earlier passages.

The following sample is a strong paragraph because its content explains and supports the central idea expressed in the first and second sentences—that the only lasting ambition of the young Mark Twain and his friends was to work on one of the steamboats that traveled up and down the Mississippi River.

> When I was a boy, there was but one permanent ambition among my comrades in our village on the west bank of the Mississippi River. That was, to be a steamboatman. We had transient ambitions of other sorts, but they were only transient. When a circus came and went, it left us all burning to become clowns; the first minstrel show that ever came to our section left us all suffering to try that kind of life; now and then we had a hope that, if we lived and were good, God would permit us to be pirates. These ambitions faded out, each in its turn; but the ambition to be a steamboatman always remained.

In this paragraph, taken from his *Life on the Mississippi,* Twain lists all the lesser ambitions he and his friends briefly cherished as a way of emphasizing the main one: to be a steamboatman. The paragraph ends by returning to the original point, closing the circle.

As a development of a single idea, a paragraph can stand by itself or serve as part of a sequence of related paragraphs. You may frequently have to write a single-paragraph essay to answer, for example, discussion questions on exams, to give a brief account of a personal experience, or even to write a short memo at work. At other times you will want to write several paragraphs on a single topic.

As already noted, each paragraph you write should have an organizing principle, called a *topic sentence,* that determines and unifies the content of the paragraph. This central, main idea of the paragraph should be expressed as a complete sentence stating the idea. Subsequent sentences should support the main idea by providing details and examples. In the following sample paragraph about learning to drive a car, the student writer has made the topic sentence the first sentence of the paragraph. Notice how all the details in the paragraph relate to and further explain the general statement announced in the topic sentence.

> Teaching me to drive a car must have cost my father a good deal of money and patience. The first time I got behind the wheel of our stickshift Toyota, I let the clutch out too soon and sent the car jerking and bouncing forward until it hit the curb on the other side of the street. My father, who was seated next to me, kept saying, "Put on the brakes! Put on the brakes!" but I couldn't remember where they were. Another time, when he was teaching me to parallel park, he stood on the sidewalk and cautiously directed me between his own car and my brother's. I squeezed in so close to my father's car that I got nervous about hitting it, stepped on the gas by mistake—and knocked the rearview mirror off his car as I zoomed past. I guess the worst day was when I backed out of the driveway and ran straight into my grandmother's brand new Chevrolet. My father paid for the repairs. All he said to me was, "I hope you learn to drive soon—<u>very</u> soon!"

Be sure to express your topic sentence in the most effective way you can. It should be a single, complete sentence that clearly expresses your main idea in the form of a conclusion, observation, or opinion. Although most topic sentences will evolve as simple, direct statements of what you want to say, paying attention to the following points will help you to state your topic sentences effectively.

Write a General and Complete Sentence: Because it consists of a summary, observation, or opinion based on a number of ideas or instances, a topic sentence should be general enough to be explained or supported with further discussion. Do not make the mistake of confusing a topic sentence with a subject or title of an essay. A phrase such as "My Chemistry Lab" could be either a subject or a title for writing, but it is not a topic sentence. Only a full statement, such as "My chemistry lab is like a scene from a zany comedy film," qualifies as a topic sentence because it is a complete sentence and general enough to be developed with supporting discussion.

The topic sentence is most often a statement, but it can also be posed as a question—for example, "What makes my neighborhood so special?" In this case, the content of the paragraph would develop the topic sentence question by directly discussing things that make the writer's neighborhood special. However, you should use topic sentence questions sparingly since they do not focus ideas as clearly as direct statements do. Regardless of the form, be sure that all your topic sentences are full, complete sentences (see Chapter 22).

Avoid Intentional Statements: You also need to avoid writing *statements of intention,* sentences that announce what the paragraph will contain. A typical statement of intention might be "In this paragraph I will show what real friendship means." Because they only hint at a subject without stating a main idea about it, intentional statements are not topic sentences, nor do they even belong in the paragraph. You should revise such statements to offer a general idea or opinion that the rest of the paragraph can develop or explain further. A topic sentence statement about the subject of friendship might be "Friendship means giving time to those you care about."

Narrow the Focus: Writing an effective topic sentence means avoiding vague wording that only hints at the main idea. A topic sentence like "Playing tennis can be difficult" is too general to be developed in a single paragraph and too obvious an idea to promise much content of interest. After all, almost anything you can think of could be described as difficult. Even though a topic sentence such as "Last week I learned about what makes a good tennis serve" might work in some cases, it is nonetheless vague and delays our discovery of the real idea. The topic sentence should say more directly what the author means, such as "Last week I learned that a good tennis serve takes practice as well as cunning."

Be Simple and Direct: When in doubt about how to word your topic sentence, let this dictum be your guide: *Avoid elaborate, complicated statements if you can.* The brief topic sentence of the following paragraph, "Talk TV," is a complete sentence that clearly narrows the subject focus and effectively expresses the main idea of the paragraph:

> Rather than promoting new understanding and the potential for change, Talk TV actually perpetuates social stereotypes. As represented by such shows as Jerry Springer and Rikki Lake, for example, talk programs regularly draw upon the poor, the uneducated, and the already socially exploited for their content. In doing so, these programs reinforce existing stereotypes about virtually every segment of society, depicting minorities as violent and irresponsible, homosexuals as sexually outlandish, and teenagers as hormone-driven rebels and parent-despising ingrates. Negative gender stereotypes are perpetuated in nearly every segment, with males depicted as smug, sexual con-artists and women portrayed as weak, self-disapproving, and in constant, desperate competition with "the

other woman" for male sexual approval. As a result, Talk TV programs appear to justify existing social prejudices by giving audiences the illusion that they know and understand even more about particular kinds of people.

Write in Your Own Voice: Your topic sentence, like all your writing, should sound like you. That is, it should not be laboriously twisted into language you may think sounds more "official" but is actually contrived and hard to understand, such as:

> The major characteristic of Madeline Foster that stands out most is her competitiveness, which one can surely observe in her work and in her play.

A simple statement such as "Madeline Foster's most outstanding characteristic is her competitiveness" is more natural and effective as a topic sentence.

Support the Topic Sentence with Details and Examples: No matter how well you have written it, a paragraph consisting only of a topic sentence would not be of much use to your audience. It could not explain your reasons for having that idea or opinion, nor could it offer support for what you claimed about the subject. Without further development and support, even an appropriately worded topic sentence such as the one just given about Madeline Foster fails to communicate its full meaning and prove its validity. What does the writer mean by Madeline's "competitiveness"? At what? Shown when and how? What other characteristics does Madeline possess, and to what degree? How are we to judge whether competitiveness is actually her "most outstanding characteristic" unless we are given supporting information?

Having decided how you want to state the topic sentence, you should develop the rest of the paragraph with details and examples. These will further clarify the topic sentence and convince your audience that your conclusion, observation, or viewpoint about the subject is a sound one. Here is a student paragraph in which examples both explain the meaning of the topic sentence—a grandfather's lifetime love of the navy—and support its claim:

Topic sentence

My grandfather's experience in the U.S. Navy during World War I seemed to stay with him all his life. I remember how proudly he used to show off the dark blue tattoo on his right forearm, with the dates of the war, 1914–1918, printed below a picture of a battleship riding a wave at sea. After he retired, he was always telling stories about storms at sea or how the ships he served on managed to avoid being torpedoed by enemy submarines. He never missed a movie on television if it was about ships and navy men, and the annual Army-Navy football game was practically a sacred event to him. My grandfather used to say he had only two great loves in his life. The first was the navy, and the second was my grandmother, whom he sometimes jokingly referred to as "the Admiral."

Maintain Paragraph Unity: Once you have determined it, the topic sentence of your paragraph tends to commit you to include certain details and exclude others. When each detail and example in a paragraph relates to and fully supports the topic sentence, the content of the paragraph is *unified.* The preceding paragraph about a grandfather's attachment to the navy is a unified paragraph. There should be *unity of content* in all good paragraphs, whether written singly or as parts of an essay.

No doubt the writer of the preceding paragraph knew many other facts about his grandfather, facts that may have been jotted down during brainstorming or clustering activities. For instance, the writer may have recalled that his grandfather had been born in New York City, that he had once worked on a ranch, and that he enjoyed playing chess. However, these facts are not relevant to the specific purpose of this paragraph, which was to explain how the grandfather's naval experience remained part of him all his life. Because they were not part of the general idea stated in the topic sentence, the writer correctly omitted these ideas when he wrote the paragraph. By carefully selecting the details of the paragraph, the writer supported his topic sentence well and kept the paragraph unified.

Place the Topic Sentence Effectively: Topic sentences can be stated almost anywhere in a paragraph, although they nearly always occur at the beginning. Coming early in the paragraph, usually first, the topic sentence announces the theme of the paragraph and what its details are intended to show the reader. Study the sample paragraphs provided on pages 58 and 60 to see how effectively the topic sentences signal the content by appearing first in the paragraph.

Here is a paragraph in which the topic sentence occurs as the second sentence. (The first sentence is a *transition* that links this paragraph to a discussion of widespread drug use in a preceding paragraph. Transitions will be discussed in detail later in this chapter.)

Topic sentence

> With all the legal restrictions placed upon law enforcement agencies, it may seem that the police have become powerless to combat drugs. In fact, however, current drug-law enforcement procedures are getting much tougher and promising good results. Just last week, for instance, local police departments in our area began using federal laws with specifically stricter penalties to arrest and prosecute drug sellers doing business in or around a school. In addition, the recent "zero tolerance" practice by police—of immediately impounding cars or boats anytime drugs are found in them—has greatly reduced small-scale local use and made big-time dealers cut back on importing drugs by boat. In California, the use of a battering-ram type of vehicle to allow police quick entry into heavily fortified "crack houses" has been very controversial but also hugely successful.

You can also place the topic sentence at the end of the paragraph so that it serves as a climax or summary of what has preceded. The topic sentence of the following paragraph summarizes all the material that precedes it.

Believe it or not, John actually had his car stolen twice in the last year, once after he had just installed a new radio and speakers worth over $400. Without a car, he was late to work so often he finally got fired. Now he has no job at all. Then last week he hurt his back trying to carry his television set into a repair shop. He had to pay forty dollars for a visit to the doctor, and his TV set was a total loss: He dropped it down the stairs when his back went out. John has the worst luck of anyone I know.

Topic sentence { *(marginal note opposite paragraph above)*

There are no exact rules about where or how to state a topic sentence in a paragraph, but placement of the sentence should not be so subtle that your reader misses it. For example, you should avoid burying the topic sentence in the middle of the paragraph. Topic sentences placed there tend to get lost. In a short paragraph with a very obvious main idea, it may be possible to leave the topic sentence "understood," but generally it is not wise to do so. Both you and your reader need to know what the main idea is, and omitting the topic sentence can leave one or both of you with only a vague idea of the central point of the paragraph.

Maintain Paragraph Coherence: Your readers need to know where the ideas of a paragraph are taking them. They need to know when new ideas begin and when they end. Paragraphs have *coherence* when the ideas between sentences and other paragraphs relate clearly to each other in such a way that the reader can move smoothly from point to point. You can give your paragraphs coherence by *using transitions and repeating key words.* A *clincher statement* at the end of a paragraph (see pages 65–66) lets the reader know that the discussion in the paragraph has concluded.

Provide Transitions: As mentioned in Chapter 2 (page 26), *transitions* are words and phrases that show how sentence ideas relate to each other. Transitions act as verbal signposts to guide your reader's attention to the movement of ideas from sentence to sentence. Notice how the underlined transitions in the following paragraph signal the connecting of ideas between sentences:

Each one of us can make a more productive effort to cut down on the use of fossil fuels in this country. To begin with, all of us can start reducing gas and oil consumption by driving only when we have a real need. That won't be easy, I know, but we have to start somewhere. In addition, we can begin car-pooling to work once or twice a week, and we can also buy smaller cars with better gas mileage. Another way to reduce our fuel consumption would be to use less gas and electricity at home. How many times, for example, have you walked out of a room and left the lights or the television on when no one else was there? Furthermore, why not use a microwave to cook that baked potato in seven minutes instead of the forty minutes it usually takes in a traditional gas oven? I'm not suggesting everybody can do all of these things, of course. I'm positive, however, that each of us could start immediately to do some of them or other things to cut down on our use of limited fossil fuels.

As you can tell from this sample paragraph, transition words and phrases can serve a variety of purposes. Some of the most common are these.

To show relation in time:

after, before, during, meanwhile, then, eventually, next, when, suddenly, previously, gradually, finally

To show relation in space:

next to, beside, alongside, with, near, in front of, behind, inside, outside, to the left, to the right

To give an example:

for instance, for example, thus, specifically, as an illustration

To show a causal relationship:

since, because, due to, so that, consequently, therefore, as a result, hence, thus

To join ideas:

also, and, moreover, in addition, furthermore, first, second, third, . . .

To contrast ideas:

but, yet, still, nevertheless, nonetheless, however, on the other hand

To compare:

similarly, likewise, just as

To conclude:

finally, in conclusion, in brief, in summary

If you make more than one point in a paragraph, you can help your reader follow what you are saying by writing effective *transition sentences.* Here are examples of transition sentences within paragraphs. (Transition sentences *between* paragraphs of an essay are discussed in the next section.)

TOPIC SENTENCE 1
Elena Rodriguez has overcome her great handicap. (The writer first explains what the handicap is.)

TRANSITION SENTENCE
But Elena has learned to deal with her handicap and can do just about anything she wants to do. (The writer now explains exactly what she has learned to do.)

TOPIC SENTENCE 2
Today I realized that some people like me more than I like myself. (The writer explains what he learned.)

TRANSITION SENTENCE

Lately I have been very down on myself, feeling pretty depressed. (The writer next explains the nature of the depression.)

TRANSITION SENTENCE

But today I was surprised to find out that some people actually do care about me. (Here the writer introduces the next part of the paragraph.)

TRANSITION SENTENCE

The first surprise came when I received a letter from my father telling me how much he missed me. (The writer briefly explains what his father said.)

TRANSITION SENTENCE

The next surprise came when my math tutor told me that she liked working with me. (The writer explains.)

TRANSITION SENTENCE

But the best surprise came when I went home and found two friends waiting for me, ready to take me out to dinner. (The writer explains.)

Use Repetition: Besides using transitions, another effective way to create co herence in your writing is by *repeating* nouns, pronouns, and other key words or phrases. Notice how the underlined elements are repeated throughout the following two paragraphs to connect ideas:

There is more to the cost of a college education than just tuition. Take textbooks, for example. They can increase the cost of an education substantially, especially for math or science courses, where the price of the average text can run as high as $40. Besides textbooks, there are also incidental costs like parking (up to $50 a year), lab fees ($30 to $70 a semester), and student body fees ($30 a semester). I won't even mention what food and housing add to the bill for going to college.

This is not to say, however, that the cost of getting a college education is not worth paying. Besides the future financial gains college can offer, there is also the personal sense of feeling proud of one's knowledge of the world and its people. College is worth all that it costs. The only bill not worth paying is the one for the cost of ignorance.

Signal the Conclusion: You can provide the finishing touch to organizing your ideas in a paragraph by signaling the end of the paragraph with a *clincher statement*. Such a statement gives you the chance to make one parting shot, so to speak, before winding up the discussion in a given paragraph. It also sends a clear signal to your reader that you have completed the discussion. In fact, you can think of the end of the paragraph as the end of a conversation and let your final sentence flow naturally from what you have just said.

The best conclusion to a paragraph—and the best clincher statement—is a *brief* one. The last sentence of the paragraph should sound like the end of your discussion, not the beginning of another. A good clincher statement grows out of the context of the paragraph it concludes and neatly wraps it up:

Hiking the canyon was exciting, but next time I'll try riding a burro.

When I weigh the difficulties against the delights, reading Faulkner's *The Sound and the Fury* was still well worth the effort it cost me.

And just remember: If the environment is in trouble, so are we.

I now believe that if I can build a dog house, anyone can.

The conclusion of the multiparagraph essay "United We Roll" on page 76 also offers an example of ending with a clincher. You can review the sample paragraphs provided earlier in this chapter for others.

Exercise 4-1

In the blank spaces after each of the following possible subjects for writing, compose an appropriate topic sentence that could be developed into a fully unified paragraph.

1. Television sitcoms

   _____

   _____

2. High school friends

   _____

   _____

3. Going to school while holding down a job

   _____

   _____

4. Computers

   _____

   _____

5. The worst way to travel

   _____

   _____

Writing Assignment 4–1:
A Paragraph

Write a single paragraph in which you describe someone you know. Try to base your description on an outstanding or memorable characteristic of your subject. Use the Writing Process activities to plan and write your paragraph.

Gather Your Ideas and Information: Write down all the characteristics of this person that come to mind. In what way does he or she seem unusual or especially remarkable? Are there any consistent patterns in this person's nature or behavior? Use any of the free-writing, visualization, brainstorming, or clustering techniques you practiced in Chapter 3 to help you generate ideas for writing about your subject.

Analyze Your Ideas and Information: Study all the material you have gathered about this person, and decide which ideas can be grouped together, which ideas are irrelevant to your description, and whether you need more information before continuing. If you have put down lots of relevant ideas, decide which of them are the most important in describing your subject.

Identify Your Main Point: Ask yourself what *main point* or *dominant idea comes to mind* out of all this information when you think of the person. Is he or she timid? Aggressive? Religious? Does the person spend more time with animals than with people? Does the person have very strange eating habits? Exactly what is it that stands out the most when you think of this person? Write a topic sentence that states the main idea you have about this person's outstanding characteristic.

Plan Your Writing: Plan the order of details and examples in your paragraph, their relevance to the topic sentence, and the placement of the topic sentence.

Write: Write your paragraph, beginning with the topic sentence. As you develop the paragraph, be sure to use appropriate transitions between the points you are making. You may want to reread the sample transitions earlier in this chapter to see how other students have used transitions in their compositions.

Revise and Edit Your Writing: Revise and edit your completed paragraph, paying particular attention to these points:

1. Did you write a *topic sentence* that states the main idea of the paragraph? Did you avoid making a statement that announces what the paragraph is about? (For example, you do not need to say, "I am now going to write about my friend Melva Lee"; see the discussion of intentional statements on page 60.)

2. Did you support your main idea with enough *details* so that your reader will understand—and believe—the point you are making about your subject? If you have already used effective details, can you use more?

3. Did you move from point to point smoothly by using *effective transitions?*

4. Did you end with an appropriate sentence—*a clincher statement* so that your reader will know you are through?

You may find that you need to add, change, or delete several sentences to make your paragraph work. Or you may find that you must begin all over again. The more you revise, the more you will learn about writing. (You will learn more about revising your work in Chapter 6.)

Here is the first draft of a paragraph on an experience a student had on a certain day. An evaluation of the paragraph and the revised paragraph follow.

A New Stereo (first draft)

This is a paragraph about why I felt a little sad and guilty today when my parents gave me a new stereo. When I receive nice presents, I always think about how much I have and how little my mother had growing up. When my mother was a girl, the other children made fun of her because of her shabby clothes. They laughed at her also because of how she lived. She had never owned a bike, but when she was eleven years old, she got one for Christmas. It wasn't brand new, but to her it seemed like the best thing in the world. After the holidays she returned to school hoping the other girls would notice her bike. A girl named Tammy asked my mother what she was doing with <u>her</u> old bike. Tammy said that her father had taken it to a place where poor people buy secondhand things. She was standing in a group of four, and all the girls began to laugh at my mom and the gift she was so proud of. My mom never went to classes that day.

Evaluation

1. The topic sentence announces what the paragraph is about. Since such an announcement is unnecessary, rewrite the topic sentence.
2. The story about the bike gives excellent details, but can you give more? For example, can you describe the shabby clothes? Can you say more about *how* your mother lived?
3. The sentences flow together smoothly. The word *also* helps join the first example of your mother's humiliation with the second. Even though you give three examples of why people laughed at your mother, you do not need to say *one example, a second example, a third example.* The paragraph is clear and less awkward the way it is written.
4. You need to bring the paper to a close with a clincher statement.
5. When you expand the details, you will probably need two paragraphs. Where would be a good place to begin the second paragraph?

A New Stereo (revised)

Revised topic sentence

My parents gave me a new stereo today, but instead of feeling happy, I felt a little sad and guilty, as I always do when I receive nice presents. I always think about how much I have and how little my mother had growing up. When my mother was

Detail

a girl, the other children made fun of her because of her shabby clothes. Her dresses were often rumpled and hung on her like limp pillowcases. She had to take

Detail

whatever secondhand clothes she could get at the thrift shop. The other children also laughed at her because of her home. She lived with her brother and sister in a one-room shed in the back of their uncle's house until the day she married my father.

New paragraph for longest example

My mother had never owned a bike, but when she was eleven years old, she got one for Christmas. It was not brand new, but to her it seemed like the best thing in the world. After the holidays she returned to school hoping the other girls would notice the bike. A girl named Tammy asked her what she was doing with _her_ old bike. Tammy said that her father had taken it to a place where poor people buy second hand things. She was standing in a group of four, and all the girls began to laugh at my mom and the gift she was so proud of. My mom never went to classes

Clincher statement

that day. I wish I could go back in time and give my mom the stereo she and my dad gave me today.

When you write the final version of your paragraph, keep in mind the following points:

1. When you are writing by hand, indent the first line of each paragraph about one and one-half inches from the left; when you are typing, indent the first line five spaces.

2. Except for the indented first line of each paragraph, keep your left-hand margin completely straight.

3. Do not divide a word at the end of a line if you can avoid it (your right-hand margin does not need to be straight). However, if it is necessary, divide the word between _syllables_ (see Chapter 19.5). If you are not sure where the syllables begin and end, consult a dictionary.

Writing Assignment 4-2:
Turning a Passage into a Paragraph

Choose one of the assignments you completed for Chapters 1, 2, or 3, and turn the passage you wrote into a bona fide paragraph. First, evaluate your passage by writing your answers to the four questions on pages 67–68. (You will find that the "main point" you stated in these assignments will usually serve as your topic sentence.) Then rewrite your passage as an indented paragraph, but be willing to add, change, or delete several sentences or even to start over if that seems necessary. As you revise, follow the rules for paragraph form. Your revised paragraph should be about 200 words.

The Essay and Its Thesis Statement

Essays are longer compositions made up of two or more paragraphs that discuss, illustrate, and support a central idea. Often the purpose of an essay is to express an opinion or argument.

The content and structure of an essay is controlled by the *thesis statement* or *thesis* (from the Greek, meaning "position"), a single sentence announcing the topic of the essay and the writer's position on that topic. Like the topic sentence of a paragraph, the thesis statement announces the main point you are making about the subject of the essay. Just as the topic sentence expresses the central idea of a paragraph, the thesis statement contains the main idea of an essay.

You can see the importance of the thesis statement in controlling the form and content of an essay in the following student sample. The assigned topic of the essay was "a job I enjoyed."

Center Street Market

I left high school over six years ago, and I have had a number of interesting and even well-paying jobs since then. I have worked at car washes and at a cemetery, as a deck hand on a yacht, and for over a year on an oil rig off the New Jersey coast. For six months I worked as a magician's assistant—appearing, then disappearing and reappearing in and out of boxes in clouds of colored smoke. That was a great job, and I learned a lot of wonderful tricks which I can still do. The best job I ever had, though, was working for a man named Gus at the Center Street Market.

Thesis statement

I was nineteen when Gus hired me as a sort of all-around helper and clerk. My duties included everything from checking groceries, cutting meat, and setting up produce displays to watching through two-way mirrors to catch shoplifters. I was never bored. Was someone needed to change one of the big neon lights in the parking lot? That was me. Take the weekend cash receipts (several thousand dollars) to the bank? That was me. Drive a truck to the warehouse to pick up a few hundred ten-pound bags of sugar? Me. I got so I enjoyed my time at work more than my time away from it.

Topic sentence

Of course, none of that would have been possible if I had not had a person like Gus as my boss and the store's owner. He was a very generous and caring person, and he made me and everyone else feel we were more like members of a family than just employees. I remember how he always addressed me as "my boy"—"Jimmy, my boy, how are you today?" or "Help yourself to a candy bar or something, my boy," he would say. He always remembered everyone's birthday with a card and a ten dollar bill, and even when business was slow he kept everybody working. When I told him I had to quit to go to college full time, he gave me two weeks extra pay and lent me the store truck to move my belongings to an apartment nearer campus.

Topic sentence

Working at the Center Street Market was not the highest paying job in the world, but it was still one of the most personally rewarding. I learned a lot of things

Topic sentence

working there that I've been able to use elsewhere, like how to handle money, drive a fork lift, or just talk to people. Also, I appreciate the fact that my boss was also a good friend. Whenever I go back to say hello to Gus and the others at the market now, he always says, "How's college, my boy? Want a candy bar or something?" What more could a person ask from an ex-boss?

Notice that the thesis statement appears at the end of the first paragraph and narrows the focus of the essay to the discussion that follows. Each of the paragraph topic sentences offers a specific example of the thesis, which has stated a general idea or opinion that the rest of the essay supports.

Writing an Effective Thesis Statement

Your thesis statement for an essay is the same as the main point you have been identifying in your writing assignments so far. It will evolve from thinking about a subject and selecting a focus from the various ideas and pieces of information you gather. The focused free-writing, brainstorming, and clustering techniques you studied in Chapter 3 are useful tools for collecting ideas for a thesis statement. These techniques can help you discover what you want to say about a topic. (Chapter 5 will discuss *planning,* how all the pieces might fit together to support and develop the thesis of the essay, in greater detail.)

Frequently, you must invest a lot of thought to come up with just the right statement, and you will probably find that this statement has to be revised several times as your essay takes shape. Allowing yourself enough preliminary time to arrive at a good thesis *before* you begin writing your essay can save you much frustration and dead-ending down the road.

How you state your thesis is important because the wording of this statement determines the content of your essay and shapes your reader's expectations of what is to follow. The thesis statement "Motorists without car insurance endanger themselves, their passengers, and you" can help the writer organize the content of an essay. It also can alert the reader to the order in which points will be discussed. Of course, not all thesis statements can be phrased this way, and you need to be careful about settling for a too superficial or too mechanical way of thinking about a topic. In general, a good thesis statement has the same qualities that a good topic sentence has: It is a complete sentence; it is general but to the point; and it sounds direct and convincing, not contrived.

Here are some major points to keep in mind as you compose the thesis statement for your essay.

Keep Your Thesis General but Focused: Like the topic sentence for a paragraph, your thesis statement should be broad enough to generate ideas and details to write about, but narrow enough to keep a focus. Avoid theses that are so general that they would require you to write about everything related to your topic or that are so watered down that they seem vague and artificial:

WEAK

Aunt Kathleen was a very interesting person.

STRONGER

Aunt Kathleen was poor but proud.

WEAK

The Joy Luck Club is a fascinating book.

STRONGER

The Joy Luck Club is a story of tenderness and courage.

On the other hand, you will want to make sure that the thesis statement you create is broad enough to give you enough ideas to elaborate on:

TOO NARROW

Laguna Niguel is forty miles south of Los Angeles.

A statement of simple fact cannot be developed enough to serve as a thesis statement.

BETTER

Laguna Niguel is an expensive city in which to rent an apartment.

State an Opinion, a Position, or an Argument: A *thesis* is literally the same as a *proposition,* a statement to be defended in an argument. The thesis statement must convince the reader. It should insist on a position, express an opinion, or, in general, state an argument. Factual statements do not express ideas for argument or further discussion and so are not suitable as thesis statements. "Laguna Niguel is forty miles south of Los Angeles" is a purely factual statement. Notice the differences between the following:

STATEMENT

Mike is someone I play basketball with.

ARGUMENT

Mike is a tough opponent in basketball.

STATEMENT

Cheryl has worked at the city library for over a year.

ARGUMENT

Cheryl's job at the city library has changed her personality.

STATEMENT

White Castle is a famous rock group.

ARGUMENT

White Castle's lyrics put them in the literary vanguard of rock groups.

The thesis statement, like the topic sentence, should never be a statement of intention such as the following:

WEAK

In this essay I will describe three ways to improve study habits.

WEAK

This essay will discuss the large numbers of unemployed persons in this country and the growing need to provide better health care for them.

Such statements should be rewritten to express an opinion or argument, as in the following:

STRONGER

Improving study habits requires honesty and commitment.

STRONGER

State and federal governments need to provide better health care for the large numbers of unemployed persons in this country.

State Only One Major Idea: The thesis statement should express the single idea you will prove to the reader. A good essay often will have secondary purposes, but they should not compete with the main point. The student in the last example given may intend, among other things, to discuss the *numbers* of unemployed people in this country. However, the main point is that state and federal governments *should provide better health care for them.*

Thesis statements with two or more ideas should be revised to focus only on one, or the ideas should be combined to present a single central idea. Here are some examples:

WEAK

The federal government should take steps to make cigarette smoking illegal and should actively seek nuclear disarmament.

STRONGER

The federal government should take steps to make cigarette smoking illegal.

or

STRONGER

The federal government should actively seek nuclear disarmament.

Alternatively, both ideas could be combined in a sentence like this:

STRONGER

The first two priorities of the federal government should be to make cigarette smoking illegal and to seek nuclear disarmament.

Exercise 4-2

Mark the following sentences *W* for weak thesis statement or *S* for stronger thesis statement. Be able to say why you answered as you did.

_____ 1. The reading texts we used in my elementary school taught us to dislike reading.

_____ 2. Capital punishment should be abolished, and long jail sentences should be shortened.

_____ 3. John Steinbeck's *Of Mice and Men* is a story about maintaining hope when there is none.

_____ 4. In this essay I will describe three types of high school teachers.

_____ 5. The drivers in Washington, D.C., must be the worst in the nation.

_____ 6. My boss, Mrs. Viola Wright, is nice.

_____ 7. Learning to write well is largely a matter of developing self-confidence, and the same thing is true of reading.

_____ 8. My two sisters are as different as any two people can be.

_____ 9. I will describe discrimination against women, first in the United States and then in Russia.

_____ 10. The only difference between my cat and me is that she has four legs and I have two.

Exercise 4-3

Write thesis statements expressing a position on the following topics. (Be sure to write in complete sentences.)

1. Your favorite relative

   _____

   _____

2. A well-known celebrity

   _____

   _____

3. Drunk driving

   _____

   _____

4. Tattoos

_____

_____

5. The women (or men) on your college campus

_____

_____

6. Single-parent families

_____

_____

7. Saturday nights

_____

_____

8. Religion

_____

_____

9. Divorce

_____

_____

10. Something that is unfair and should be changed

_____

_____

 ## Writing Assignment 4-3:
Constructing an Essay from
a Thesis Statement

Write an essay of two or more paragraphs based on one of the ten thesis statements you composed in Exercise 4-3. Chapter 5 will explore the planning and
writing of longer essays. For now, use the suggestions for the single paragraph in
writing your essay. However, note that the first paragraph of an essay should point
to what the essay is about. The beginning sentences of succeeding paragraphs
should both introduce those paragraphs and relate to the other paragraphs in the

essay. (In this text, these sentences are called *transition sentences between paragraphs.*)

Here is a student essay that started from a single thesis and was too long to be written in one paragraph. Notice how the writer used transition sentences to introduce his paragraphs. They are very much like the transitions you have been studying that introduce points within a single paragraph. Notice also how the writer developed his points with details and how he brought his essay to a close.

United We Roll

A person in a wheelchair faces many barriers. Some of them can be overcome, but some cannot. I have noted a few of both kinds of barriers around our city and even experienced a few myself.

One barrier we wheelchair users face every day relates to transportation. Although there are a few buses equipped for wheelchairs, they are not dependable. They run only on certain streets in the city, and the hoisting equipment does not always work. Even if a person overcomes the problem of getting from place to place in a wheelchair, that person must then worry about getting up on the sidewalks. I have had the experience of actually turning over, upside down, trying to wheel over a curb on French Street. I was not hurt, but the experience was very embarrassing.

Another barrier to the wheelchair user is the stairs in front of the public buildings downtown. No one should be deprived of entering a public building. Some of these buildings do not even have elevators, and I know of one in which a person has to go up a flight of stairs to get on the elevator. (This shows just how intelligent people can be.) Stairs and wheelchairs do not go together very well.

The worst barrier of all, however, and the meanest one, is the occupational barrier. When wheelchair users go looking for a job, they often get discouraged. Nine times out of ten, employers do not give wheelchair users a chance to prove themselves. I can do a job just as well as the next person, but I, too, have difficulty finding work. Last summer I filled out an application for a job as a tow-truck dispatcher at a tire shop. The shop manager told me that the job had been filled by someone else. Later I found out that the manager was still looking for someone to fill the opening. I went back to the shop and again asked the manager for the job, but again he told me that the position had been filled. People in wheelchairs are a minority, and minority groups are often discriminated against.

These are only a few of the many barriers that wheelchair users face. Someday we will break through these barriers. We need everyone's help, but first we must organize ourselves. I have already thought of a good slogan for wheelchair users: Divided we stall; united we roll.

Now write an essay from the thesis statement you have selected, using the activities of the Writing Process:

Gather your ideas and information

Analyze your ideas and information

Identify your main point

Plan your essay

Write your essay

Revise and edit your essay

As part of the revision process, be sure to check the organization and content of your paragraphs. Have you used transition sentences to link your paragraphs? Has your essay developed your thesis statement sufficiently? Did you end your essay effectively—that is, with the same kind of clincher statement you used to end your paragraphs—or does it simply stop? With this assignment as your introduction, you will be ready to explore the art of planning and writing essays in greater detail in Chapter 5.

GATHER your ideas and information
ANALYZE your ideas and information
IDENTIFY your theme or main point
PLAN your writing
WRITE your essay
REVISE AND EDIT your essay

5

Planning and Writing Your Essay

- **Transitions Between Paragraphs**
- **Introduction, Body, and Conclusion**
- **Titles**

LIKE ANY PIECE of writing, an essay requires careful planning to be successful. If you have ever put together anything complicated—cut and sewn your own clothes, assembled a new bicycle, or thought out a complicated committee project for your school or community—you know how important planning can be and how many needless steps good planning can save. Putting an essay together out of all the ideas and information you have gathered on a topic requires good planning, too.

Significantly, *planning* is the last of the Writing Process activities you perform before actually beginning to write. All the prewriting activities you have focused on so far, that is,

Gather your ideas and information

Analyze your ideas and information

Identify your main point

are concerned with having something to say, and knowing how you want to say it, *before you begin to write*. If you do not know what you want to say or where best to say it as you begin to write, you will spend a lot of frustrated time and effort trying to find out. Performing these activities first will give you the confidence and the solid groundwork you need to write your essay effectively.

You will also find that *planning*, like the other Writing Process activities, is an ongoing affair. Most writers plan and replan almost continually as they compose a longer piece of writing. Because many ideas and connections can be discovered only during writing, such replanning is a natural part of the writing process. However, good preparation can reduce the need to repeat the planning activity and can save time and effort later.

Planning Your Essay

Planning the organization of an essay means deciding on the order in which you want to present your ideas. As you get ready to make a plan of the essay you want to write, you may find that the manner in which you analyzed the ideas and information you collected may have already provided an informal structure for your essay. Or your *thesis statement*—the main point you have identified—may itself suggest the order in which to discuss different aspects of your topic.

The following are three common methods of ordering the content of an essay:

1. *From the least important to the most important ideas.* This sequence usually means that the real substance of your essay comes not early on, but later, where the most significant ideas get the fullest treatment. Sometimes this kind of organization is used to present ideas in an order of *climax,* in which you build step by step to your main point, which concludes your essay.

2. *From the general to the particular.* In this approach, you present general ideas on the topic and then develop or support your main point through particular examples. (You also can use the opposite order, *particular to general.*)

3. *Narration, description, comparison and contrast, classification,* and *cause and effect.* You may decide to organize your essay by following the structure implied by these methods of essay development, which will be discussed in Chapters 7, 8, and 9.

Making an Outline

Outlines are the traditional planning tool in writing an essay. Some writers balk in the face of a formal outline; others rely on it completely. You may find that you prefer the more informal preparation provided by techniques such as brainstorming and clustering. However, many writers find that making some kind of outline for their essay helps order the content and helps identify potential problems before they write.

An *informal outline* can be as simple as listing the major ideas in the order you plan to discuss them, or it may use the topic sentences from each planned paragraph as a blueprint from which to work. For example, an informal outline listing the topic sentences from the sample essay "Center Street Market" in Chapter 4 (pages 70–71) might look like this:

Thesis: The best job I ever had was working for a man named Gus at the Center Street Market.

1. I was never bored. (First paragraph)

2. Gus was a very generous and caring person. (Second paragraph)

3. It was one of the most personally rewarding jobs I ever had. (Third paragraph)

More complete *formal outlines* are also valuable for planning essays, especially longer forms, such as research papers. Some writers prefer making a formal outline *after* they write in order to check the organization or to provide an overview for their readers.

Formal outlines can be written in either sentence or topic form, and they should follow these two general guidelines:

1. Every level of ideas should be paired. (Thus every I has a II and perhaps a III; every A has a B and perhaps a C; every 1 has a 2 and perhaps a 3, and so on.)

2. Ideas on the same level should be expressed in the same grammatical form. (Thus, the headings "check groceries," "cut meat," and "set up produce" each begin with verbs.)

Here is a formal outline for "Center Street Market":

Thesis Statement: The best job I ever had was working for a man named Gus at the Center Street Market.

I.   My duties
   A.   In the store
      1.   Check groceries
      2.   Cut meat
      3.   Set up produce
      4.   Watch customers

   B.   Out of the store
      1.   Change neon lights
      2.   Take cash to bank
      3.   Drive to warehouse

II.   My boss
   A.   Generous
      1.   Birthdays
      2.   College

   B.   Caring
      1.   Family atmosphere
      2.   Friendly greeting

III.   The rewards
   A.   Experience
      1.   Handle money
      2.   Drive a fork lift
      3.   Talk to customers

   B.   Friendship

Now read a finished student essay that was written using the activities of the Writing Process outlined in this text. Answer the questions that follow, and see if you can reconstruct the writer's organizing principle in the spaces provided.

My Home in the Country

When I think of the sights, sounds, and smells of our place in the country, it makes me wish I were there right now. I have been living in the high-rise student dormitory for the last few months and have heard nothing but the screaming sirens, screeching tires, roaring motors, and other boisterous sounds of the city.

There are many beautiful things to see around my home, for instance, blue and white cranes wading in ponds and dipping their heads in the water to catch fish, frogs, and other things to eat. In the spring, when the farmers are beginning to prepare the ground for planting, white egrets swoop down behind the tractors to prey on bugs and insects harmful to crops. These egrets, along with white cranes, water turkeys, and various other birds, come each spring and nest in large cypress trees.

In addition to these sights, deer run across the fields; you can see their tails sticking up and the whiteness of the hide underneath shining brightly. Also, squirrels jump and play games in the tiptops of the trees. There is the large red squirrel with his half-rust, half-fire color and big fuzzy tail. There is also the elite gray squirrel, who must think he is a smart little rascal because he is so clever at racing up and down the trees.

The changing of the seasons announces itself in the color of the lush green crops and the green woods. When the crops ripen and the fall steals the life from the trees, there is a beautiful blending of brown, gold, and rust colors. An old shack nearby hardly seems to notice the death and later the rebirth of the crops.

Also, my home is surrounded by sounds, such as all those birds I have been describing, cawing and chirping, making one wonder if they have a distinct language of their own. Oil wells stand in the distance, with their "pop-pop-pop-pow" repeated over and over. It seems as though that sound will go on indefinitely. At nightfall, the crickets produce their chirping, which combines with the deep bellowing and croaking of the bullfrogs, sounding like beautiful music.

Finally, distinctive smells surround my home. My favorite smell is the indescribable scent of rain as it beats down on the raw earth after the soil has been plowed. There are also the bad smells, such as trash burning or a skunk that has emitted his device of self-defense. But when I get homesick, I miss those smells, too.

My father tells me I should learn to like the city as much as I like the country, but as my description here may suggest, I have a long way to go.

Questions for Discussion and Writing

1. The student (a male) gathered a lot of details for his paper. Did he use too many details? What particular detail stood out for you?
2. What is the thesis statement (the one sentence that says what the essay will be about)? Did the student accomplish his purpose in the essay? Explain.
3. In developing his paper, the student tried to build each paragraph on a controlling idea, an organizing principle. For example, the organizing principle for the second paragraph was the birds he can see around his home. What is the organizing principle of the other paragraphs in the body of the essay? (The *body* is simply the main part of the essay; it is the essay minus the introduction and conclusion.)

Paragraph 1: Introduction (includes thesis statement) _____

Paragraph 2: Things to see, especially birds _____

BODY { Paragraph 3: _____

Paragraph 4: _____

Paragraph 5: _____

Paragraph 6: _____

Paragraph 7: Conclusion _____

4. Would you prefer to live in the city or the country? Why?

Transition Sentences to Join Paragraphs

Your analysis of the student essay "My Home in the Country" demonstrates the importance of ordering paragraphs in planning your essay to achieve a coherent whole. All your paragraphs should be connected as smoothly as possible by transition sentences, as shown in the diagram on the next page. This first principle of essay writing can serve as a general blueprint for planning any essay you may write.

Transition sentences that join paragraphs have three functions: (1) to connect a paragraph with the previous paragraph, (2) to point to the content of the new paragraph (here it functions as the topic sentence of that paragraph), and (3) to help carry out the thesis statement. Keep these functions in mind, but remember that the main purpose of the transition sentence is to help the reader move *smoothly* from point to point. (*Note:* You will often come up with the best transition sentences when you revise your paper; see Chapter 6.)

Here are examples of transition sentences that might be used to carry out the following two thesis statements:

THESIS STATEMENT 1

When I think of the <u>sights, sounds,</u> and <u>smells</u> of our place in the country, it makes me wish I were there right now.

TRANSITION SENTENCES

There are many beautiful things to <u>see</u> around my home.

You can experience the seasons of the year by <u>watching</u> . . .

Also, my home is surrounded by <u>sounds</u> such as . . .

Finally, distinctive <u>smells</u> also surround my home.

Notice how the underlined words in the thesis statement connect with the underlined words in the transition sentences.

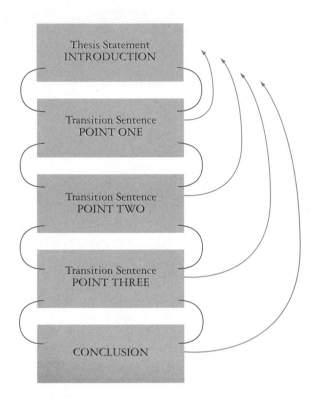

THESIS STATEMENT 2

You can tell what time it is by the various noises in my neighborhood.

TRANSITION SENTENCES

I never have to use an alarm clock to wake up because at six o'clock each morning the train comes <u>clanging</u> by.

In the early afternoon, the children from Craft Elementary School <u>shriek</u> for a full hour as they pour out of their "prison."

By six o'clock in the evening, most of the men are home from work and are <u>banging</u> on their cars as they try to repair them.

About eleven o'clock each night, just as things begin to get quiet, the Urban Decay Band next door starts practicing its <u>loud rap music</u>.

Notice how the underlined words in the transition sentences connect with the thesis statement. Clanging, shrieking, and banging are all disturbing noises, to say nothing of the loud rap music played at eleven at night.

Writing Assignment 5-1:
Writing an Essay from a Plan

Write a paper of 300 to 500 words on your own neighborhood or another one with which you are very familiar. Use all the activities of the Writing Process as carefully as possible, but concentrate especially on your writing plan (suggestions are given under "Planning Your Essay").

Before you begin, read the following sample of student writing on this topic and answer the questions about it.

My Home in Wilmington Heights

When I think of the sights, sounds, and smells of my neighborhood, it makes me wish that I were living somewhere else instead of Wilmington Heights. I have lived in this neighborhood all my life. When my family first moved here, the area was very pleasant and the apartments were recently built. The lawn was well cut, and the environment was clean. But things have changed.

There are no beautiful things to see. The project consists of brick apartments, which have faded in color. Outside, there is only a limited amount of grass. The grounds consist mostly of dirt. The streets have large holes and are covered with glass. If you are trying to avoid getting a flat tire, please do not visit. Many people pile up trash on the sidewalk, which is a sight to see. You can see paper flying all around on windy days.

There are no nice sounds to hear. You may hear gunshots when people are fighting. People frequently use obscene language. Children are constantly playing and making noise with their bicycles and skates. Most of the parents call their children without using their names, using words I do not enjoy hearing. At night and during the day, it is very disturbing hearing police sirens and trains passing across the tracks. I really wish my neighborhood would quiet down.

There are no pleasant things to smell. You smell mostly the scent of marijuana. Guys walk the street and stand in hallways smoking dope. At times there are foul odors from trash burning and from urine, and sometimes there is no smell at all.

What I like most about my neighborhood is that the people in my building and I get along well. Even though I am not satisfied with the area in which I live, I am very comfortable inside our apartment. I feel as though I have most of the things I want inside my home, regardless of what is seen, heard, and smelled outside.

Questions for Discussion and Writing

1. What details stand out for you? What else would you like to know?
2. What information does the student include in the introduction besides the thesis statement? Is it effective? Why?
3. In her conclusion, the student makes a different point from what she has been saying. What is it?

4. The first sentences in paragraphs two, three, four, and five are transition sentences. They are meant to join the paragraphs. Are they effective?
5. If you were describing this neighborhood to someone else, what would you say about it?

   Now you are ready to begin your essay. Use the activities of the Writing Process, with special attention to *planning* your essay.

Gather Your Ideas and Information: First, brainstorm, cluster, or visualize to gather ideas and information about the neighborhood you are going to write about. (Later you can fill in any gaps by closely observing your neighborhood in person with a pencil and paper in hand.)

1. Imagine yourself across the street from your home or someplace where you can get a good view of everything going on in the neighborhood. Conjure up a vivid picture of the neighborhood. Become aware of every detail before you. In the left-hand column below, write down *every* detail that you see. Do not censor your thoughts. Take above five minutes.

   _____   _____

   _____   _____

   _____   _____

   _____   _____

   _____   _____

   _____   _____

   _____   _____

2. To test just how precise your details are, share some of them with the class or with your instructor. Now go back and make your more general observations as exact as possible, this time writing in the right-hand column above. For example:

   blue car parked in front   *baby-blue '94 Ford*

   _____   *with 2 flat front tires,*

   _____   *rusty fenders, for sale*

   green hedge   *10' high green hedge hiding porch*

   yellow cat   *yellow-and-white striped cat*

   _____   *prowling over turf as if he*

   _____   *were somebody*

3. You are still at the spot where you can see everything in the neighborhood. Only now imagine that you cannot see, but have a keen sense of hearing. Become aware of everything you might hear over the course of a day— horns honking, mothers calling their children (what are their exact words?), boys arguing over a baseball, and so on. Make use of your skill in recording a conversation, using the space below. Again, use the left-hand column.

_____

_____

_____

_____

_____

_____

_____

4. Share some of your list with the class or check it with your instructor. In the right-hand column above, make your observations even more precise. For example:

Mother calling son to dinner — *Mrs. Sims bellowing, "Charles, get in here right now before I come after you with the cattle prod."*

church bells — *church bell ringing every hour*

5. Imagine that you now have a superior sense of smell. You are still at the same place. Write down everything you might smell in the neighborhood in the course of a week—fumes from automobiles, your neighbors' cooking, burning trash, garbage, cows, newly cut grass, and so on. Make your observations as precise as possible.

_____

_____

_____

_____

_____

_____

6. If someone were to ask you how you felt about the neighborhood, how would you answer?

_____

_____

_____

_____

_____

Analyze Your Ideas and Information: Sit back, with pen in hand, and read over the information you have gathered so far and ask yourself what you think. Which detail is most interesting to you? Which items are closely related? Which items will you probably not want to use? How might you order the material? Write notes to yourself. Now might be a good time to reread the student samples at the beginning of this section for ideas on how you might use your information. Write notes to yourself. Be ready to add to your list if you notice any gaps.

Identify Your Main Point: Try to say in one sentence what you really want to tell your reader about the neighborhood you are writing about. Writing an effective thesis statement usually takes several attempts. But for this essay, keep the following suggestions in mind as you try to come up with a thesis statement that is just right.

     1. Does your thesis statement include your opinion about the neighborhood?

     2. Is it narrow enough in scope so that you will not have to write about everything?

     3. Is it at the same time broad enough so that you will have enough material on which to write 300 to 500 words?

Here are some examples of thesis statements from successful papers:

The various noises in my neighborhood indicate the time of day as accurately as any clock. (In this paper, the student uses each paragraph in the body to discuss a different type of noise heard at different times during the day.)

Tourism and tourists make life in Grant's Beach forever fascinating. (The student discussed the colorful shops and beautiful scenery that attract so many interesting people to her town every summer.)

To see what my neighborhood is like, just pull up a chair outside the Poplarville General Store and watch the people coming and going. (The student wrote first about women carrying large bundles, then the farmers drinking colas, and finally the children carrying book bags.)

My neighborhood is a picture of multiculturalism. (The writer described the abundant variety of nationalities, races, and cultures in her neighborhood.)

At night my neighborhood becomes a sad and scary place to live. (The student described the junkies, arguing couples, homeless people, and shootings that become increasingly disturbing at night in his neighborhood.)

Experiment with your thesis statement until you get it just right, and then write it below:

Plan Your Essay   Study the following suggestions for planning an essay, and then make an informal outline for your neighborhood paper. Your plan need not be rigid. The best plan is the one that helps you say what you want to say. You may need to change it once you begin your essay.

   1. Your outline should help you develop your main point. Here are two examples:

THESIS STATEMENT 1	You can tell what time it is by the various noises in my neighborhood.
POINT 1	How it is noisy in the morning.
POINT 2	How it is noisy in the early afternoon.
POINT 3	How it is noisy in the late afternoon.
POINT 4	How it is noisy at night.
THESIS STATEMENT 2	My neighborhood is overrun by young people, but I enjoy them all.
POINT 1	The five Reed children are in and out of everyone's house.
POINT 2	The eleven- and twelve-year-old groups play catch football every afternoon of the week.
POINT 3	The Mushroom Cloud on the corner is a teenage hangout.

2. Your outline should be consistent; that is, each major point should fit in with the other major points. Here are two examples of abbreviated outlines whose points fit together:

I.	Introduction	I.	Introduction
II.	Sights in the neighborhood	II.	Neighborhood in the fall
III.	Sounds in the neighborhood	III.	Neighborhood in the winter
IV.	Smells in the neighborhood	IV.	Neighborhood in the spring
V.	Conclusion	V.	Neighborhood in the summer
		VI.	Conclusion

Which of the following abbreviated outlines are not consistent? Apply this test: Which of the things (organizing principles) is not like the others?

OUTLINE A	**OUTLINE B**	**OUTLINE C**
I. Introduction	I. Introduction	I. Introduction
II. Most eye-catching features	II. Neighborhood as viewed from the left	II. One example that illustrates the purpose
III. Next-most eye-catching features	III. Neighborhood as viewed straight ahead	III. A second example that illustrates the purpose
IV. Crime in the neighborhood	IV. Neighborhood as viewed from the right	IV. Why I like my neighborhood
V. Conclusion	V. The people in the neighborhood	V. Conclusion
	VI. Conclusion	

3. It may be helpful to you to let your outline reflect the paragraph divisions in your essay. This way you can name the organizing principle of each paragraph in the outline itself. The student who wrote an essay on his country home (pages 81–82) set up his outline as follows:

Paragraph 1: Introduction

Paragraph 2: Things to see, especially birds

Paragraph 3: Things to see, especially animals

Paragraph 4: Things to see, especially vegetation

Paragraph 5: Things to hear

Paragraph 6: Things to smell

Paragraph 7: Conclusion

In deciding how to divide your essay into paragraphs, be sure you have enough information to develop each paragraph fully. The paragraphs in the body of your essay should probably run between 50 and 100 words each. In the preceding out-line, the student divided the category "things to see" into three paragraphs, each of which turned out to be over 50 words, but he described "things to hear" in one paragraph, which turned out to be about 100 words.

4. The introduction and conclusion should be designated in the outline as separate paragraphs, even though they may be short (fewer than 50 words).

5. Under each major point in your outline, include enough notes so that you will have before you, as you sit down to write, the details and other information necessary to support your point. If you cannot think of enough details, perhaps you need to rework your outline, changing your major points. The student who wrote the paper on his home in the country wrote detail into his outline in the following way:

PARAGRAPH 1   Introduction
_____
                (organizing principle)

                Thesis statement, how long in the city, contrast with the country
_____
                (detail)

PARAGRAPH 2   Things to see, especially birds
_____
                (organizing principle)

                cranes in ponds, white egrets behind tractors, nests, birds eating bugs
_____
                (detail)

                harmful to crops
_____

Write your outline for your essay about the neighborhood in the space pro-vided below. For a paper of between 300 and 500 words you will probably need five to seven paragraphs, including an *introduction,* a *body,* and a *conclusion* (to be discussed in detail in the next section). Include in your introduction such information as where you live, how long you have lived there, your thesis state-ment, and anything else that will capture the reader's attention. Develop the body of the essay with paragraphs that support the thesis statement with ex-amples and details. If you cannot think of a conclusion in the outline step, do not worry. The best conclusion often comes to you after you have written the rest of the paper.

PARAGRAPH 1   Introduction
_____
                (organizing principle)

_____
                (detail)

_____

PARAGRAPH 2   _____
(organizing principle)

_____
(detail)

_____

PARAGRAPH 3   _____
(organizing principle)

_____
(detail)

_____

PARAGRAPH 4   _____
(organizing principle)

_____
(detail)

_____

PARAGRAPH 5   _____
(organizing principle)

_____
(detail)

_____

PARAGRAPH 6   _____
(organizing principle)

_____
(detail)

_____

PARAGRAPH 7   **Conclusion** _____
(organizing principle)

_____
(detail)

_____

Check your outline with your instructor before going on to the next step.

Write Your Essay: As you write, keep in mind the following suggestions:

1. Use smooth transition sentences to connect your paragraphs (see pages 83–84).

2. Avoid words that are redundant—that is, words that repeat what you have already said.

3. Avoid the passive voice (see Chapter 17).

4. If you have stated a point clearly in one sentence, you need not repeat the same idea in another sentence.

5. Let your conclusion flow naturally from what you have said. Make sure your reader knows you are through.

Revise and Edit Your Essay: Evaluate your essay by asking these questions:

1. Did the thesis statement meet the criteria given on pages 71–73?
2. Did each paragraph help to carry out the thesis statement?
3. How can I better support each major point with more or different details?
4. Did I repeat myself unnecessarily at any time?
5. Did the conclusion effectively bring the essay to a close?

Now revise and edit your essay. Be alert for two errors that often appear with this assignment: verb agreement and fragments (see Chapter 16 for verb agreement and Chapter 22 for avoiding fragments).

Share Your Writing: Read your papers in a small group, and discuss the questions listed under "Revise and Edit Your Essay" after each person reads.

Writing Your Essay

In this chapter we have focused on the planning activity for writing a full-length essay with paragraphs. Now let us examine the actual writing itself—the grand event for which you are ready once you have established a thesis for your essay and a plan for putting it together. So far, you have practiced a variety of techniques for writing spontaneously, getting words on paper rapidly and fluently. *Good* writing, however, is usually not a product of the first, the second, or even the third try. Therefore, even though you will want to "get something down" as your rough draft, be prepared to allow long periods of time for writing your essay, and expect as well to go through several drafts.

However, do move ahead as you write. Make revisions and changes as you go along, but do not let yourself get completely bogged down in any one difficulty you may encounter. The important thing is to keep your momentum going, trusting yourself (and the preparation you have invested) to go back and forth, adding, deleting, or strengthening as you perceive the need.

Every essay has three main parts: an *introduction,* a *body,* and a *conclusion.* Each of these parts plays a special role in framing your ideas in the essay. You will need to consider the function of each of these parts as you write your essay.

Writing the Introduction

Although it is not absolutely necessary to do so, most writers prefer to write the introduction of their essay first so that they can follow their own sense of logic and whatever outline they have made. The first paragraph of the essay should serve as the introduction and state the thesis, unless you choose to follow a plan in which your thesis statement comes as the *climax* of your essay (see page 79). The introduction of a very long essay might be more than a single paragraph, of course, and the thesis statement, even when it is not a climax, can be postponed until it is properly introduced. Generally speaking, however, an introduction does *introduce* the topic; it does not become a separate discussion by itself.

Use the following guidelines when you write an introduction:

1. Unless your instructor gives you other directions, include your thesis statement in your introduction. Place it at a point where it is most effective—usually either the first or the last sentence of the introductory paragraph. If it is a catchy thesis statement, such as "My neighborhood is so noisy it disturbs the dogs," use it as the first sentence.

2. Include enough background information so that your reader will be able to put your essay in some context. For example, the essay "Center Street Market" in Chapter 4 uses the introduction to provide the reader with background about the author's other jobs and establishes a basis for his preference for the one he describes.

3. Include anything else in your introduction that will stimulate your reader to continue to read. One effective way to begin an essay is by telling an anecdote. If you were writing about how a student's life is a difficult one, you might begin with a short example that illustrates your point.

Writing the Body

As you move into the body of your essay, using details and examples to support your thesis and paragraph topic sentences, you also will need to give thought to the length of your paragraphs. A very short paragraph often signals a lack of detail or discussion, and a too lengthy one may be the result of wandering away from the topic sentence.

There are no definite rules about paragraph length, although "longer than one sentence and less than a page" is an old saying that is still generally true. The average paragraph is about 50 to 150 words long, depending on how much you have to say and on your strategy as a writer.

Your paragraph might be shorter than 50 words if you want to achieve emphasis or greater readability by organizing ideas into smaller units of discussion. Newspapers and business letters use short paragraphs for these purposes. However, be careful about overusing this tactic. Too many brief paragraphs can scatter the discussion by cutting short the development of your ideas and making the page itself look monotonous to the reader.

Paragraphs that are too long also can be a problem, for the writer as well as the reader. Any long paragraph, even one slightly under 200 words, tends to be weightier and more full of ideas than the norm and consequently requires more attention from the reader. A paragraph that approaches a fully typewritten page exhausts the reader and usually has lost its own focus.

Although paragraphs of 200 to 250 words can sometimes be very effective, you should usually divide one of this length into two or more smaller paragraphs, each with its own topic sentence. Luckily, dividing a long paragraph into two or more of manageable size is not a difficult thing to do. You will find that the content of any overblown paragraph will usually fall into two or more distinct sections all by itself. Make sure that each new paragraph has an appropriate topic sentence and that all paragraphs are linked by transitional words or sentences (see pages 83–84).

Keep in mind that writing a good paragraph is not a strictly mechanical process. You should try to vary the lengths of your paragraphs to provide variety as well as a visual sense of the unfolding of your ideas. As a general rule, a good paragraph offers enough discussion to justify its length and to keep the reader interested in what you are saying. Whenever you write, stay alert to the lengths of individual paragraphs, giving attention both to your own purposes and to the needs of your readers.

Remember to connect your paragraphs with transition sentences, as discussed earlier in this chapter, always keeping in mind the overall direction of your essay and the conclusion you are aiming for.

Concluding Your Essay

In every essay you write, you must make sure your reader knows you have come to the end of what you want to say. Like your introduction, your conclusion will usually—but not always—be shorter than the other paragraphs in the body of your essay. If your conclusion is just one sentence long, however, you may want to hook it onto the last paragraph.

Like the clincher statement that signals the end of the discussion in a paragraph, the conclusion of your essay should *sound* like an ending—not like a beginning or, more commonly, like an abrupt halt in midstream. Your concluding statements will usually come naturally to you in your own voice, much as you would end a telephone conversation. For example:

But at least I learned one thing from all this: Everybody gossips.

Despite all the cuts and bruises, I'd go rock climbing in Arizona again anytime.

The "good old days" were not so good after all.

Until we can guarantee its improvement, television should simply be outlawed.

Besides bringing your essay to a graceful end, you may want your last paragraph to include one of the following features:

1. *A contrasting idea.* The student who wrote the paper on living in Wilmington Heights (page 85), for example, used the conclusion to show what she *did* like about her home after writing the rest of the essay about what she did not like about it. If you were writing about sad or difficult times, you could use your last paragraph to note that not *everything* was bad, beginning perhaps with a sentence like "But not everything was disappointing during those years."

2. *A statement of the significance of your topic.* When you finish making your points about why something is true, you may want to bring your reader up-to-date, spelling out what it all means. One student described the highlights of her fifth-grade year in her essay and then wrote the following conclusion, explaining the significance of what had happened to her that year:

> These experiences were important to me then, and they are still important to me. I continue to play the trumpet, first chair in concerts, and in the school marching band. Mary and I are still best friends. And would you believe, I still play baseball every chance I get?

If you were writing an essay about why sex education should be taught in high schools, you might conclude with a statement on the difference it would make to young people if your ideas were accepted.

3. *A call to action.* If you are arguing for a belief, you may want to ask your reader to join with you in trying to remedy a certain problem. For example:

> The best way for us to conserve energy is to make a decision—right now—that we will cut down on our driving, use less heat, and, if possible, insulate our homes.

> If you agree that capital punishment should be abolished, write your state and congressional representatives today.

4. *A summary.* Beware of this one. You will not need to repeat *each* point that you made in a separate sentence. Summary endings are useful if each point can be expressed in a word or two and if the summary takes only a single sentence. Most important, the conclusion should incorporate the idea expressed in the thesis statement without repeating it word for word. For example, an essay with the thesis statement "My cousins in Denver could not resist a chance to gossip about anyone—including me" might conclude like this:

> By the time I returned the next summer, everybody in town knew about my mistake with the fake money. I was reminded of it wherever I went, and I finally learned to laugh about it, too. I don't know which of my cousins told the story first, but now it hardly matters. I certainly learned something about gossip, though: Rich or poor, male or female, young or old—everybody likes to gossip, and that includes family members most of all.

Titling Your Essay

Unless your instructor gives other instructions, write titles for all your paragraphs and essays. You may want to wait until you have completed your essay before you give it a title.

Here are some suggestions for composing titles:

- Make your title relate to the main idea of your paper.
- Try to pick a title that stimulates interest in your subject.
- If possible, keep your title short: one to six words. Usually the title should not be a whole sentence.

Always follow these rules in writing titles:

1. Do not underline or put quotation marks around your title when it appears at the top of your paragraph or essay.

2. Always capitalize the first and last word and every other word except

   Articles (*a, an,* and *the*)
   Short prepositions (such as *of, on, in,* and *for*)
   Short conjunctions (such as *and, but,* and *or*)

Here are some examples of properly capitalized titles:

The Ghost of the Plantation   The Truth About Frogs
When I Was Very Young   The Curse of My Childhood
An Experience on the Road   Pranks and Punishments

Using the preceding guidelines, explain why each word in these titles was either capitalized or not capitalized.

Writing Assignment 5–2: Writing an Essay with an Introduction, a Conclusion, and a Title

Write an essay of 300 to 500 words on the topic "Those Were the Days," using each activity of the Writing Process. Before writing your essay, review the preceding sections on transitions, introductions, conclusions, and titles. Also, before you begin, read the following two student samples and answer the questions about them.

Sample A: Those Were the Days

The friend I can remember best from my childhood is Curtis Johnson. I met Curtis Johnson in Children's Hospital when I was there in 1989, but I have not seen him since. Even though we had our bad times as well as our good times, I will never forget Curtis.

I entered Children's Hospital a year after my family had moved to this country from Cuba. Curtis used to come up to me and talk about many things. At first I would never talk because I did not speak English, but later I learned how to speak English in the hospital. There was a school room in the hospital, and every day the teacher, Mr. Manuel, would show me flash cards with different letters and words on them. Pretty soon I began to speak a little English. I started communicating with Curtis, and he would talk to me as though I were a native-born American. I think that is why I picked up English so fast. Curtis and I started hanging around each other. I depended on him, and he depended on me. I cannot use my legs, and he does not have arms.

Curtis and I did everything imaginable together. We played games, went to parties, chased all the female volunteers, hunted blue jays with slingshots in the park near the hospital, set up squirrel traps, and played tricks on people. The best times we had were when we tried to talk to pretty volunteers. Here were a couple of young punks, one ten and the other eleven, trying to make it big with girls seventeen and older. Curtis had a line that would get them every time. It went something like this: "Hi, my name is Curtis; I'm from Turtle Creek. Have you ever heard of it?" Then Curtis would drop something on the floor on purpose, knowing that the girl would feel sorry for him and pick it up. When she reached down, Curtis would stand near her. The moment she stood up he would kiss her smack on the lips. He tried to get me to do it a few times, but I did not have the nerve. With my luck, the girl would probably have slapped me. We did many things that were fun and sometimes got into trouble doing them.

Every now and then Curtis and I would get into fights. Our worst brawl happened one day when I had a visitor who brought me some chocolate-chip cookies. When my visitor was leaving, I escorted her out. When I returned, all my cookies were gone. Curtis had cookie crumbs on his lips, so I asked him, "Curtis, did you eat my cookies?" He said no. Then I said, "You're lying!" He answered, "Are you calling me a liar, Rudolfo?" I said, "Yeah, you are a liar." That started feet kicking and fists swinging. To make a long story short, Curtis gave me a good beating with his feet. It was a real back-alley brawl with flying books, flying toys, and flying people (mainly me). We both got punished for three weeks.

During that time we made up and became good friends once again. I often wonder what Curtis is doing now.

Questions for Discussion and Writing

1. What is the thesis statement? Is it effective? Is the student successful in carrying it out?
2. What is the organizing principle of each paragraph?
3. Look at the transition sentences that introduce the second, third, and fourth paragraphs. Could any of them have been written more effectively?
4. One of the best ways to develop your paragraphs is by giving examples. What examples does this writer give? What points do they illustrate?

5. Does the student give enough background information in the introduction for you to put his paper in some context?
6. Is the conclusion effective? Would you like the writer to say more? If so, what?
7. What might be a more exact title for this essay than the one the student used?

Sample B: A Rose for My Father

I was twelve years old when my father died. I came home from the store on a Sunday morning at about ten o'clock and got the news. I had lost someone I loved, my father.

As I walked up to our front door, I saw many people standing around in our house. I wondered what was going on because everyone was crying and whispering. I just knew something had happened. When my mother's best friend, Marcia Tilden, told me that my father had died, I cried and cried. At first it was hard for me to believe. We had eaten breakfast together earlier that morning. Marcia told me he had a heart attack. When they took him out to the car to go to the hospital, he died.

That was one of the worst days of my life. Everybody in the house was weeping. I remember how all my aunts, uncles, and friends gave us their sympathy and brought us plates and plates of food. It was late that night before everyone left. I cried the whole night and wondered how much I was going to miss my father.

The funeral was at Illinois Funeral Home on North Clairborne Avenue, November 25, 1986. All the family was ready for the funeral, except me. I did not want to go because I knew this would be the last time I would see him. When I finally got to the funeral home, Mother and I said a prayer together. After we finished praying, the funeral director closed the casket. The chauffeur then drove us to the cemetery, where the preacher prayed and the people sang sad hymns. After all the family and friends had left, I picked a rose from the basket of roses nearby and dropped it on the casket. "Good-bye, Daddy," I said. "I will miss you. I love you very much."

Adjusting to life without him was not easy. I was too frightened to sleep in my bed, so I slept at my friend's house as much as I could. About six months after he died, I finally began to sleep in my bed, but I often woke up screaming. It was hard to grow up without my father. I had no one to help me with my homework, nobody's back to jump up on for rides. Now that I am older I have accepted his death, and I am going to try to make my father proud of his daughter.

Questions for Discussion and Writing

1. The student is writing about an event that was very sad for her. Was she able to convey her sadness without sounding too emotional? Do you feel the sadness with her? If so, what did she say that made you feel that way?
2. What examples did the student give as she developed each paragraph?

Now you are ready to begin your essay.

Gather Your Ideas and Information: Using brainstorming or clustering techniques, bring back past memories from the years you were between the ages of six and eleven or twelve—your elementary school years. You may want to ask your parents or others who knew you then to help you fill in any information gaps.

1. As you think about yourself when you were in elementary school, what comes to mind when you hear the word *home?* Do not censor your thoughts. Write down everything! (If you are using the clustering method, use *home* as your nucleus word.)

    _____

    _____

    _____

    _____

    _____

2. What comes to mind when you think of the schools you attended during those years? (If you are using the clustering method, use *schools* as your nucleus word.)

    _____

    _____

    _____

    _____

    _____

3. Who were your best friends during those years? Write down one or two things that stand out about each of them. (If you are using the clustering method, use *friends* as your nucleus word.)

    _____

    _____

    _____

    _____

    _____

4. What setbacks (accidents, illnesses, deaths, parents' divorces, and the like) did you experience in those years? (If you are using the clustering method, use *setbacks* as your nucleus word.)

    _____

    _____

_____

_____

_____

5. What special times do you remember (birthdays, awards, victories, vacations, and the like)? (If you are using the clustering method, use *special times* as your nucleus.)

_____

_____

_____

_____

_____

Analyze Your Ideas and Information: One of the tasks of this activity is to narrow down the information you have gathered. Of the five categories, pick the one that you would find the most meaningful (or fun) to write about. Look at the information you listed under the other headings and see if any of it relates to the category you have chosen. If so, add that information to the list, and add any other information you can think of. Use the blanks that follow.

_____

_____

_____

_____

_____

_____

_____

Sit back and look at this revised list. What stands out? Which things relate to each other? How can you begin to give an even more narrow focus to your topic? Which things can be eliminated from the list? What information gaps can your parents or someone who knew you during those years help you fill in? At this point it may be helpful to reread the student samples on pages 97–99.

Identify Your Main Point: You began with a very large topic, your elementary school years; you then narrowed it down to one of five subtopics—home,

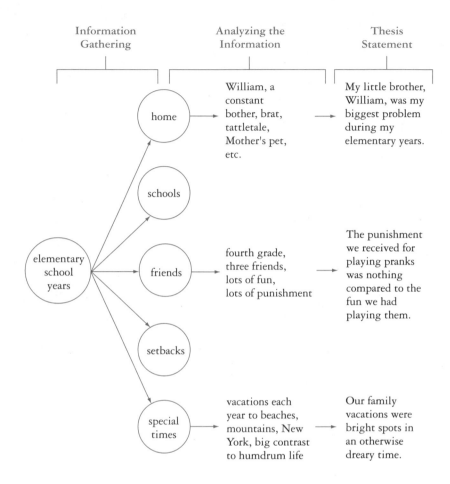

school, friends, setbacks, or special times; and you have now begun to give a more narrow focus to the subtopic. Next you will need to narrow down the subtopic even more and say in *one sentence* what you will try to show in your paper. The diagram above gives examples of this process.

The thesis statement should not be simply a statement of what your essay is about, as these attempts at thesis statements are:

WEAK

In this essay I will write about my three best friends from the fourth grade.

WEAK

This essay is about the various vacation trips my family made when I was in elementary school.

Instead, include within your thesis statement your *opinion* about the topic. Your thesis statement should challenge you to be persuasive. The two thesis statements could be revised as follows:

STRONGER

The punishment we received for playing pranks was nothing compared to the fun we had playing them.

STRONGER

Our family vacations were bright spots in an otherwise dreary time.

Now you have to write convincingly to persuade your reader that the fun you had with your friends really was worth the punishment or that the vacations you and your family had really were bright spots in years that were otherwise dreary.

The diagram on the previous page shows how you can move from information gathering to your thesis statement. Here are some more examples of effective thesis statements for this assignment. In each, the writer must convince the reader of something.

The hard times of my youth were also times of great learning. (The writer must not only describe the hard times but also show *why* they were occasions of great learning.)

The hobbies I became interested in at ten years old changed my life. (The writer must both describe the hobbies and show *how* they changed her life.)

Whenever Mike, Tommy, Bean, and I are together, we begin to talk about and long for the good old days at Libson Elementary. (The writer must show just *why* he and his friends long for the good old days. What made them so memorable?)

Even though we had our bad times as well as our good times, I will never forget Curtis Johnson. (The writer must not only describe the good and bad times but also *make the reader believe* that his relationship with Curtis Johnson is unforgettable.)

Write your own thesis statement for this assignment in the space provided, and then check it with your instructor.

_____

_____

_____

Plan Your Essay: In the space provided, write an informal outline for your paper that effectively carries out your thesis statement. If you have difficulty making enough points and filling in enough detail, perhaps you need to rewrite your thesis statement. Your essay should probably consist of four to seven paragraphs. Study the instructions in this chapter on writing introductions, conclusions, and titles.

_____

(your title)

PARAGRAPH 1   **Introduction (include thesis statement)** _____

(organizing principle)

_____

(detail)

_____

PARAGRAPH 2   _____

(organizing principle)

_____

(detail)

_____

PARAGRAPH 3   _____

(organizing principle)

_____

(detail)

_____

PARAGRAPH 4   _____

(organizing principle)

_____

(detail)

_____

PARAGRAPH 5   _____

(organizing principle)

_____

(detail)

_____

PARAGRAPH 6   _____

(organizing principle)

_____

(detail)

_____

PARAGRAPH 7   <u>Conclusion</u>

(organizing principle)

_____

(detail)

_____

Before moving to the next step, check your outline with your instructor.

Write Your Essay: As you write, keep in mind the following suggestions:

1. Most of your essay will probably be written in the past tense. If you switch to the present tense, make sure you have a legitimate reason for doing so.

2. Let your sentences flow into each other as smoothly as possible.

3. Give your sentences variety. Write compound, complex, and simple sentences (see Chapter 21).

4. If you have stated a point clearly in one sentence, do not repeat the idea in another sentence that says just about the same thing.

Revise and Edit Your Essay.   Evaluate your essay by asking these questions:

1. Did the thesis statement express an opinion?
2. Did each paragraph help carry out the thesis statement?
3. How can you better support each major point with more or different detail?

Now, using your evaluation, revise and edit your essay. Look especially for two errors that often appear with this assignment: verb-tense errors and run-on sentence errors.

1. *Verb tense.* Be careful to give regular verbs a *-d* or an *-ed* ending when they refer to action in the past. Watch out especially for those verbs whose endings are hard to hear:

She seem<u>ed</u> less nervous now.

He help<u>ed</u> us all more than he knew.

If you have any problem at all with irregular past-tense endings, check the list of irregular verbs in Chapter 17. Watch out especially for those that are often missed, such as

She <u>began</u> her work on time that day.

He <u>laid</u> his pen on the table and refused to write.

It <u>cost</u> more last year than it costs this year.

2. *Run-on sentences.* Be careful not to run your sentences together. In telling of events in the past, many of your sentences will be closely related in content. The more closely related they are, the easier it is to run them together (see Chapter 22.2).

INCORRECT

A family friend from across the street came over, he saw what had happened and rushed me to the hospital.

CORRECT

A family friend from across the street came over. He saw what had happened and rushed me to the hospital.

INCORRECT

I was finally admitted by the nurse, she x-rayed my arm in different positions.

CORRECT

When I was finally admitted by the nurse, she x-rayed my arm in different positions.

Share Your Writing: Read your essay to an audience composed of a small group of your classmates, and make use of the evaluation questions under "Revise and Edit Your Essay" as each essay is read. Next, exchange essays with one other person, and proofread the essay you receive. Be sure to check with your classmate before writing any changes on the essay.

If class time does not permit small-group discussions, share this and later essays you write with a classmate outside class when possible. It makes good sense to read your essay to the people for whom it was written and to listen to their essays as well. It is also a good practice to exchange essays for proofreading and editing. In this ongoing exchange with your classmates you will gain valuable feedback on several levels about how effectively you have communicated.

Writing Assignment 5-3: Writing an Essay

Write another essay of 300 to 500 words on the same topic, "Those Were the Days," but this time focus on your high school years (or some other four-year period in your life).

GATHER your ideas and information
ANALYZE your ideas and information
IDENTIFY your theme or main point
PLAN your writing
WRITE your essay
REVISE AND EDIT your essay

6

Re-Visioning Your Essay

- *STSOE*
- *Revising and Editing*
  Paragraphs and Essays

THE WORD *REVISION* means "re-seeing," that is, looking at your writing with fresh eyes to see how it can be improved. When you revise your work, be willing to change, delete, and add to material you have already written. If you can see that your essay is not working and probably cannot be overhauled in its present form, be willing to start over, perhaps with a different topic.

Editing, as you have already seen, means paying attention to the mechanics of punctuation, spelling, and grammar. It also means checking word choices for accuracy and effectiveness, and it means using varied and effective sentence forms. Many writers edit, as well as revise, while they are writing. However, all writers learn that they must read a final draft at least three times before they can feel sure that the basic components of the essay are what they should be—and this includes catching and correcting typing errors.

Some students resist the revising and editing activity because they see it as extra work or as an admission that they did not write well enough in their drafts. However, revising and editing are *an integral part of the writing process,* not just an extra ingredient added to it. All writers—students and professionals—revise and edit their work, just as engineers or welders check their work thoroughly and call others in to examine it before even considering pronouncing it finished. Writing is a difficult and challenging craft; mastering this art form takes a great deal of practice and reworking.

"Re-visioning," however, can be an enjoyable and rewarding activity in the writing process if you approach it in just this spirit—that is, as a tool for reconsidering what you have said and how you have said it. As you develop your revising and editing skills, you will learn to ask yourself increasingly better and more focused questions about your work, both during the process of writing and afterward.

STSOE: Revising Paragraphs

A handy framework for evaluating your writing, whether a paragraph or an entire essay, covers the following points: *subject, topic, supporting details, organization,* and *editing,* or *STSOE* for short. Let's first apply the STSOE approach to revising paragraphs.

Subject: Is your paragraph on the *subject* you intended to write about or were assigned?

Topic Sentence: Did you include a *topic sentence* that points your reader toward the subject matter and main idea of the paragraph? Did you avoid writing a topic sentence that is vague, contrived, or a statement of intention?

Support: Did you *support* your idea with enough *details* so that your reader will understand—and believe—what you are saying? If you have already included effective details, can you provide more?

Organization: Check to see that details are *organized* in an appropriate order, such as chronological, general to particular or vice versa, least to most or most to least. Did you move from point to point smoothly by using effective transitions? Did you end with an appropriate sentence so that your reader will know you are through—a *clincher statement?*

Editing: Have you edited the paragraph for grammar, spelling, and punctuation?

A Sample Revision

Here is the first draft of an interview with Tom Jackson, owner of Doughnut King, a small doughnut and coffee shop. An evaluation of the paragraph and a revised version follow.

The Doughnut King (first draft)

Tom Jackson, the owner of Doughnut King, says he loves the doughnut shop business and will probably stay in it for the rest of his life. Tom is fifty-one years old and has had several business careers in the past, including running a pet store, owning an auto shop, repairing televisions and radios, and even being a nightclub singer. Tom says the only thing he does not like about owning Doughnut King is not being able to resist his own products, he has gained over twenty pounds since the place opened two years ago. Toms' shop is named Doughnut King because that is what his friends started calling him as soon as they found out he was going to open a doughnut shop. Tom makes a variety of unusual doughnuts that people cannot get anywhere but Doughnut King. Because of this, he does not worry about the competition from other doughnut places.

Revision Evaluation

Subject: The paragraph fulfills the assigned interview subject, as indicated by the use of *says* to show that what we are told is not the author's comments but a summary of Tom Jackson's own words.

Topic Sentence: The topic sentence successfully points to the subject of the paragraph. It mentions Tom and how he likes his work. But the topic sentence is not supported by the paragraph's content because we are not shown what things make Tom like his work so much.

Support: The facts about Tom's other businesses are interesting details that tell us more about him and help us appreciate his love of the doughnut shop business. Before you get into what businesses Tom was in previously, however, you first need to support more fully the idea that he *likes* his present one.

The "variety of unusual doughnuts" Tom makes is not listed or described.

In the last sentence, the use of the word *this* is vague. Combine the sentence with the preceding one to make both more specific.

The mention of "other doughnut places" should be more specific to indicate why they would not produce a variety of doughnuts to compete with Tom's.

Organization: The third and fourth sentences interrupt the discussion of why Tom likes his present business. Move these sentences to a later point in the paragraph, after you have first supported the topic sentence more.

Details in the paragraph seem to be arranged in a general to particular order, but that order is not apparent yet. Subordinate more details to the topic sentence or to other ideas that they illustrate.

No *clincher statement* appears at the end to signal that the discussion is completed.

Editing: The apostrophe in Tom's name is incorrectly placed (see Chapter 20.3 on the use of the apostrophe).

Too many sentences start with "Tom" or a form of "Tom." Rewrite some sentences to achieve more variety in style.

Also, there is a comma splice in the third sentence (see Chapter 22.2 on avoiding comma splice errors).

The Doughnut King (revised version)

Tom Jackson, the owner of Doughnut King, says he loves the doughnut shop business and will probably stay in it for the rest of his life. Tom is fifty-one years old and has had several businesses in the past, including running a pet store, owning an auto shop, repairing televisions and radios, and even being a nightclub singer. He likes the doughnut shop best, though, because it gives him working hours he enjoys and a chance to meet people over a friendly product, coffee and doughnuts. He also likes being creative. Since he makes a variety of unusual doughnuts like Grape Bars, Lemon Spikes, and Chocolate Creamers, Tom says he does not worry about competition from traditional or chain-owned doughnut places. Naming his shop Doughnut King was Tom's own idea. Friends started calling him that as soon as they found out he was going to open a doughnut shop. The only thing Tom does not like about owning Doughnut King is not being able to resist his own products. He says he has gained over twenty pounds since the place opened two years ago, and he blames it all on the Blueberry Cream Cheese Delight—his own beloved creation.

Writing Assignment 6-1:
Revising a Paragraph

Use the STSOE revision and editing method to evaluate the following paragraph. Then rewrite the paragraph according to your evaluation. Feel free to make up whatever details seem necessary.

Officer Mary Kennedy

When officer Mary Kennedy is not patrolling the streets for crime, she works as a recruiter for the Greenville Police Force. She was the first female police officer with whom I actually sat down and talked, she spends most of her day on the look-out for crime. Usually, things are quiet, but every now and then she finds herself in dangerous situations. Officer Kennedy seems angry that so many people in our city say such critical things about the police force. She says that on the whole the Greenville police do an excellent job. Officer Kennedy was born in Ohio, but she moved here when she was nine years old. Her father is a television repairman. Besides patrolling the streets, Officer Kennedy tries to recruit young men and women for "The Force," as she calls it.

STSOE: Revising an Essay

Once you have gained confidence revising paragraphs using the STSOE framework, the task of re-visioning a whole essay should no longer seem quite so daunting. After you have written your first or second draft of an essay, let it sit for a while and then evaluate it—ask yourself honestly how well the essay works overall. Then move to specifics. Although every essay you write will present unique problems of content that you must address, you can still apply the STSOE guidelines you used for revising paragraphs to the larger scale of your essay.

Subject: Is your essay written on the appropriate subject? Does it address the topic you intended or were assigned to write about? If it is an examination essay, did you answer the question that was asked and all its relevant parts? Has anything been omitted that should be included—or vice versa?

Thesis: Is the thesis statement or the topic sentence for each paragraph clearly expressed and appropriately placed? Does it say what you wanted it to say, and does its wording accurately reflect the ideas expressed in the paper? Is the thesis kept prominent throughout the beginning, middle, and end of your essay?

Support: Have you developed the thesis of your essay and its supporting topic sentences with specific details and examples? Do the topic sentences relate to the thesis? Is each topic sentence supported with enough relevant details? Should you provide more explanations or examples?

Organization: Is the content of your essay organized in an effective way? Can you define that order (for example, least to most, general to specific)? Do the organization and content of the essay present a clear introduction, body, and conclusion? Are paragraphs an appropriate length, and are there useful transitions throughout?

Editing: Have you carefully checked all spelling, punctuation, and grammar? Are there any especially unusual things to be concerned about in this essay (quotation marks, verb tense, italics, the spelling of a repeated, important word)? Are sentences written in effective, varied forms (simple, compound, and complex)? Have you used good vocabulary throughout? Would adding certain adjectives or adverbs make your ideas clearer? Have you avoided extra, unnecessary words and words that repeat the same meanings (for example, "*really* tall," "*expensive* Cadillac")?

While you are evaluating your essay, show it to a friend to see if he or she understands what you meant to convey. Ask your friend to state the thesis or main idea and to give evidence of what made the essay convincing or unconvincing. As you evaluate the essay yourself, follow the STSOE steps outlined. Make notes directly on the essay, on another sheet of paper, or both. The rewrite the essay. While you are rewriting, you may want to make even more changes.

A Sample Revision

The following is a student's response to an assignment to "write about the value of the kinds of movies or books you enjoy." The essay is in its later draft stages, but the student and teacher agreed that the paper needed revising and editing before it would be acceptable as a final draft. An evaluation and a revision of the paper follow.

A Defense of Science Fiction (unrevised draft)

After the movies "Star Wars" and "E.T." became so popular, a lot of people started paying more attention to the role of science fiction in film and literature. Many of my friends who had never before thought they would enjoy any science fiction suddenly found themselves reading authors like Ray Bradbury and Isaac Asimov, major science fiction authors whom I have appreciated for years. What my friends found out in their reading was something I and millions of others have known for a long time—that science fiction offers a lot of good things you won't find elsewhere.

Science fiction is not just an escape from present, current reality. It actually treats it in a fresher way so that you begin to pay more attention. A story that has Earth people and strange, alien creatures living and socializing together can be a valuable way to make someone think about how people of different races could get along on this planet today. The movie "Star Wars" has an example of this.

I like the way science fiction also raises other questions that relate to things here on Earth and during our century. Some stories centered on the question of who owns and controls outer space, just like here on Earth we argue about who owns the oceans. Sometimes in science fiction space is governed by a federation of countries and planets, just like our United Nations. And just like now, there is always one group who does not belong to the federation and wants to control everything itself. The way the problems are resolved in these stories is often enlightning about how we solve or could solve some of our problems about governing the oceans. Religion is also a problem. Do martians have religion? Should we teach them one of ours? Which one?

I guess the best thing about science fiction for me is what it says about how people will live in the future. Science fiction says that things like a completely computerized home environment may actually be possible. We may someday be zooming back and forth to Europe and the United States in our own private rocket ships. And medicine will have found cures and ways to treat all the major illnesses affecting us now. I think that science fiction assumes these kinds of things are possible, it plants the seeds for someone to figure out how to make them happen.

My friends have gained a lot of respect and admiration for science fiction since they started reading it. I know you will, too.

Revision Evaluation

As you evaluate this sample essay, remember to use the STSOE guidelines for revision evaluation.

Subject.   The essay correctly addresses the assigned subject. Although it was not necessary to do so, the writer was able to choose a topic that managed to address both parts of the assigned subject, movies and books.

Thesis: The thesis statement, "Science fiction offers a lot of good things you won't find elsewhere," needs to be focused more sharply. "A lot of good things" and "elsewhere" are too general. Each paragraph in the essay has an appropriate topic sentence that relates to and supports the thesis statement. The topic sentences are effectively placed at the beginnings of the paragraphs to introduce and order the ideas that follow.

Support: The example of earth people and aliens in the second paragraph is a good one, although "living and socializing together" could be made more meaningful with specific examples. The *this* in relation to the movie *Star Wars* is too vague: What specific things happen in the movie to show earth people and aliens getting along together?

The third paragraph is interesting. It could be made more detailed by mentioning some specific examples of stories that deal with the government of outer space and by being more specific about some of the kinds of problems we have here on earth in managing the oceans. The example of religion on Mars is a fascinating one, but what is the "problem" about religion—on earth or in science fiction? The subject of religion and science fiction needs more discussion to make it meaningful. The writer probably has a lot to say about this subject; perhaps it needs to be treated in a separate paragraph.

The fourth paragraph is generally a good one, although the author should spell out which "major illnesses" he has in mind.

The last paragraph is too brief and does not relate very well to what has been previously said. The paragraph needs to summarize the ideas of the essay more explicitly.

Organization: The essay has good organization, proceeding by examples in a kind of least to most important order. Because the topic sentence of paragraph 3 really also states the ideas of paragraph 2 in a more general way, perhaps it ought to come first.

Editing: A few things need correcting in this essay. The "so popular" in the first paragraph implies a "so popular that . . ." construction that is not intended. The word *so* should be deleted. Titles of movies, like titles of books, are underlined or written in italics, not put in quotation marks. The movie titles should be written as *Star Wars* and *E.T.*

In the second paragraph, saying "present, current realities" is redundant. Since both adjectives mean basically the same thing, eliminate one of them.

In paragraph 3, the verb <u>centered</u> is in the wrong tense; it should be <u>center</u>. The word *enlightning* in paragraph 3 is misspelled; it should be *enlightening.* Finally, *Martians,* like the names of all people of a country (or planet), should be capitalized.

The fourth paragraph has a comma splice between two sentences: "I think that science fiction assumes these kinds of things are possible, it plants the seeds for someone to figure out how to make them happen." The writer needs to put a period between the sentences or rewrite them, perhaps combining and condensing ideas into one sentence.

Here is the revised version of the essay.

A Defense of Science Fiction (revised draft)

After the movies Star Wars and E.T. became popular, a lot of people started paying more attention to the role of science fiction in film and literature. Many of my friends who had never before thought they would enjoy any science fiction suddenly found themselves reading authors like Ray Bradbury and Isaac Asimov, major science fiction authors whom I have appreciated for years. What my friends found out in their reading was something I and millions of others have known for a long time— that science fiction offers new ways of looking at realities in our own time, as well as those which may be <u>possible in</u> the future.

I especially like the way science fiction raises questions that relate to things here on Earth and during our century. Some novels, such as one called <u>Small World</u> by Stephen Jackson and another titled <u>Dark Space</u> by Marjorie Sands, center on the question of who owns and controls outer space, just as here on Earth we argue about who owns the oceans. Sometimes in science fiction space is governed by a federation of countries and planets, just like our United Nations. And as is typical of politics and world government here on Earth, there is always one group who does not belong to the federation and wants to control everything itself. The way the problems are resolved in these stories is often enlightening as to how we could solve some of our problems relating to governing our own planet.

As you can see, science fiction is not just an escape from present reality. It actually treats reality in a fresher way so that you begin to pay more attention. A story that has Earth people and strange, alien creatures living and socializing together can be a valuable way to make someone think about how people of different races could get along on this planet today. The movie Star Wars has an example of this when all the different types of weird and exotic aliens are drinking and socializing in a bar together.

Religion is another subject that science fiction deals with in new ways. Do Martians have their own religion? Should we teach them one of ours? Which one? These questions are explored in novels like The Stars Have Always Been and The Infinite Infinite by Jonathan Brent. Some of the situations discussed parallel what goes on today in our debates about which church is right or whether or not we should teach evolutionary theory.

The most appealing thing about science fiction for me is what it says about how people will live in the future. Science fiction says that things like a completely computerized home environment may actually be possible. We may someday be zooming back and forth to Europe and the United States in our own private rocket ships. And medicine will have found cures and ways to treat major illnesses like cancer and heart disease that affect us now. I think that because science fiction assumes these kinds of things are possible, it plants the seeds for someone to figure out how to make them happen.

My friends have all gained a new respect for science fiction since they found out that it is more than a lot of wild fantasy. Like me, they have grown to appreciate the way it deals with problems and situations that are similar to those we have today on Earth and may face in the future. No doubt they also enjoy dreaming about how much better life may be for all of us—thanks, perhaps, to science fiction itself.

Writing Assignment 6–2:
Revising an Essay

Using the STSOE guidelines outlined in this chapter, revise the essay you wrote for Writing Assignments 5-2 or 5-3 ("Those Were the Days") in Chapter 5. Review the revision evaluation of "A Defense of Science Fiction" if you need further guidance in performing your revision.

PART II

Structuring Your Writing

In Part I you learned how to draw on your own experiences and use the Writing Process to create well-organized and effective paragraphs and essays. Part II will take you one step further by teaching you how to write different types of essays that are more sophisticated but just as easy to write, once you learn how.

In Part II you will learn to write essays that demonstrate your ability to do the following:

- Describe and narrate
- Use examples
- Compare and contrast
- Classify information
- Illustrate a process
- Discuss a cause and its effect

In writing any of these types of essays, you will use the steps of the Writing Process that by now have become so familiar.

The Writing Process

GATHER your ideas and information

ANALYZE your ideas and information

IDENTIFY your theme or main point

PLAN your essay

WRITE your essay

REVISE AND EDIT your essay (STSOE)

7

Describing and Narrating

ONCE YOU HAVE practiced using the activities of the Writing Process to compose your essays, you will want to build on this foundation by learning more sophisticated writing skills. This chapter will show you how to use techniques of *description* and *narration* to enhance your writing. These techniques represent valuable tools for organizing as well as expressing the content of your essay, as you will see when you begin incorporating them into your writing assignments.

The Art of Describing

Here is the way the writer Robyn Davidson, author of *Desert Places,* describes the Great Victoria Desert in her trek with camels across the western wastelands of Australia:

> Soon after leaving Tempe, I crossed a wide river-bed, slapping my bare feet on hot river pebbles and soft sticks and delighting in the crunch of glittering sand between my toes. Then I saw my first sandhills. This country had had bushfires through it the previous season which had been followed by heavy rains, so the colors of the landscape were now brilliant orange, jet black and sickly bright lime Day-glo green. Whoever heard of such a desert? And above all that, the intense hot dark blue of a perennially cloudless sky. There were new plants everywhere, tracks and tracks I had not noticed before, patches of burnt bushes sticking up like old crows' feathers from wind rippled ridges, new bush foods to be searched for and picked. It was delicious new country, but it was tiring. The sand dragged at my feet and the repetition of the dunes lulled me into drowsiness when the first excitement wore off. The stillness of the waves of sand seemed to stifle and suffocate me.

A good description paints a vivid picture for your reader of a person, place, object, or action, a picture that conveys your overall impression or feeling about what you are describing as well as its specific features. Description makes an author's perceptions *live* in the reader's imagination.

In fact, description is a vital skill in any situation where you need to convey your impressions or understanding of a certain topic to others. In a college literature class, you may be asked to describe George and Lennie's dream in John Steinbeck's *Of Mice and Men,* not only to demonstrate your understanding of its meaning but to help others understand as well. In a history class, you may need to describe both the historical events and the cultural ambience of the reign of Louis XIV of France; in a science class, the structure of an atom; in a music appreciation class, the rhythms of a contemporary rap artist. Inside or outside the classroom, description is one of the most important communication skills at your disposal. In this chapter you will learn some methods for enhancing your powers of description.

Objective and Subjective Description

When we describe, we usually present more than just facts—we are also communicating our feelings or ideas about how something or someone looks, moves, sounds, tastes, or smells. Communicating the bare facts is known as *objective description.* Communicating our personal impressions of what we are describing is known as *subjective description.*

An objective description of the Great Victoria Desert might read as follows:

> A barren or desolate area, especially a dry, often sandy region of little rainfall, extreme temperatures, and sparse vegetation.

This, in fact, is the American Heritage Dictionary definition of *desert,* and it is as valuable a description, in scientific and factual terms, as Davidson's is in subjective terms. Objective and subjective descriptions serve equally important roles in communication. The kind of description you use in your writing, objective or subjective, will ultimately depend on your audience: Are you writing for a group of scientists or for a chemistry class? Are you writing a literary interpretation for a literature class? Are you communicating information to a business group, or are you writing a personal letter to a friend? All these factors of audience and purpose will influence the amount of subjective and objective description you employ in your writing.

In most situations, however, a good descriptive passage will be one that combines both approaches, objective and subjective. That is, it will present enough concrete details to provide a factual foundation (objective) at the same time that it reveals the author's own attitude (subjective) toward what he or she is describing. The following paragraph from Michael Herr's *Dispatches,* an account of the author's experiences in the Vietnam War, describes the sensations of night in a jungle surrounded by hostile forces:

> There were times at night when all the jungle sounds would stop at once. There was no dwindling down or fading away, it was all gone in a single instant as though some signal had been transmitted out to the life: bats, birds, snakes, monkeys, insects, picking up on a frequency that a thousand years in the jungle might condition you to receive, but leaving you as it was to wonder what you weren't hearing now, straining for any sound, one piece of information. I had heard it before in other jungles, the Amazon and the Philippines, but those jungles were "secure"; there wasn't much chance that hundreds of Viet Cong were coming and going, moving and waiting, living out there just to do you harm.

Herr's paragraph gives us an objective sense of this jungle and the wildlife it contains—"bats, birds, snakes, monkeys, insects"—but it also communicates the ominous feeling behind the sudden silence that falls, the dread of wondering what "you weren't hearing" out there, the possibility of an enemy attack rendered subjectively more frightening by the fact that, when silence reigns, there are no objective signals for hearing such an attack whatsoever.

Dominant Impressions

There is no precise formula for the amount or type of concrete detail a descriptive paragraph ought to contain. However, the details you include should add up to a *dominant impression*—your overall sense of, or feeling about, your subject. Any description other than a purely objective one should convey that dominant impression by means of a succession of carefully selected objective and subjective details. A good description conveys a unified impression as much by what it omits as by what it includes. For example, notice how author Stephen King in his horror novel *'Salem's Lot* uses carefully selected details to convey a dominant impression of foreboding surrounding an abandoned house:

> It was huge and rambling and sagging, its windows haphazardly boarded shut, giving it that sinister look of all old houses that have been empty for a long time. The paint had been weathered away, giving the house a uniform gray look. Windstorms had ripped many of the shingles off, and a heavy snowfall had punched in the west corner of the main roof, giving it a slumped, hunched look. A tattered no-trespassing sign was nailed to the right-hand newel post.

The boarded-over windows, weathered paint, and no-trespassing sign are *objective* details that contribute to a scary effect. The overall "look" of the house King describes as "sinister," "uniform gray," and "slumped, hunched," all of which are *subjective* impressions. He does not include such details as the square footage of the house, the type of concrete used in the sidewalk outside, or the species of plants growing in the yard. None of these details, even if accurate, would have contributed to the "haunted house" effect he is seeking to create.

In writing a descriptive paragraph, you will find it helpful to state your dominant impression in the topic sentence. Doing this will help you, as author, decide which details to include as you write. The topic sentence also sums up the main point of the description for your reader. For example, a student writing about her first visit to an expensive perfume shop in New York found that her dominant impression was the effect that all the smells and colors had on her senses. This idea became her topic sentence in the descriptive paragraph she wrote about this experience:

> My first visit to The Perfume Mine on Adams Avenue left my senses reeling. Upon entering, I could actually feel the thickness of the various perfume smells hit my face, the way you might feel a gust of warm air against your skin. Wonderful, delicious smells were everywhere. Turn in one direction and you find yourself breathing the thick scent of lilac; turn around and you are greeted by vanilla or sandalwood, or musk, or jasmine, rose, carnation, or one of dozens of fragrant spices. Everywhere you look there are perfume decanters of every size and shape: square bottles with long necks, rounded bottles with spiraled tops, tiny perfume flasks, or expensive decanters with heavy crystal lids. Hundreds of small glass atomizers of red, black, purple, green, blue, or a mixture of colors seem to be scattered all over the store like shining, fragrant flowers. It was all so overwhelming that I could not decide whether I was more impressed by what I saw or by what I smelled.

The descriptive language and abundant detail paint a vivid picture of the author's experience. The rich mixture of visual and olfactory impressions also conveys the writer's strong interest in her topic, another factor that is visible (or strikingly absent!) in everything you write. Your personal involvement in a subject communicates itself to your readers in many ways, not the least of which is the quantity and quality of telling details you are able to generate.

However, a description should not be so personal that it ignores or distorts the reality of what you are describing. You must take care to make your descriptions sufficiently precise and accurate for your reader to be able to recognize or understand what you are talking about. If Robyn Davidson had stated only that the monotonous sand dunes of the desert made her sleepy, or if Stephen King had simply remarked that the old house had a "sinister look" and omitted all mention of boarded-up windows, weathered wood, and no-trespassing signs, we would not be inclined to accept these subjective impressions by themselves. Similarly, if the writer of the paragraph about the perfume store had said only that there were "many kinds of smells in the shop," she would not have truly *described* the store at all. Her description of specific smells—lilac, musk, jasmine—and the variously shaped bottles paints a much more complete picture and helps us understand why she reacted to the store the way she did. The fact that all three writers supported their dominant impressions with a successful balance of general and particular, objective and subjective, detail allows us not only to visualize what they are describing, but to *believe* in their responses as well.

The art of good description takes practice and attention. The following four guidelines can help you refine your descriptive skills.

Gather and Analyze Details: First, jot down as many impressions of your topic as you can, either by firsthand observation or by thoughtful reflection and/or visualization. Although you want to avoid inserting irrelevant details, think of the important ones as elements in a painting: The more you present, the more complete you make the picture for your audience. For example, you might use brainstorming to generate and then analyze these details to come up with a dominant impression about the Mississippi River in the summer.

Changes color day and night
Moves silently around bridges and landings
Fog at night and mornings
Bends and wrinkles like a snake

Focus Your Description on a Dominant Impression: Now *involve* yourself in the details you have gathered on your subject, either by direct observation or by thoughtful reflection and/or visualization. Then state your dominant impression in a single sentence. (As discussed in Chapter 4, this statement will be a topic sentence if you are writing a paragraph and a thesis statement if you are writing an entire essay.) Here are some sample dominant impressions that could be developed either as paragraphs or essays:

> The Mississippi River has an unearthly, quiet kind of beauty in the summer.

> Miss Jackson looked and acted more like a professional nurse than anyone I had ever met.

> A Harley-Davidson motorcycle is a work of art.

Use Exact Language: Avoid vague, imprecise, or slang words when you are writing descriptions. Make a decision about the words you use: As you proofread and then revise your essay, look at each word separately to see if you have chosen it well and are saying what you want to say. Instead of writing "a truck," for example, write "a red Toyota pickup"; instead of "several things," write "a cup full of paper clips, two small boxes of rubber bands, a roll of postage stamps, and a dictionary"; instead of "freaked out," write "excited," "astounded," "angry," or "out of control." (Notice how slang words tend to be highly general; one word may stand for a variety of conditions. For this reason, it is a good idea to avoid slang in your writing.)

Use Comparisons Whenever Possible: You can enhance your descriptions by comparing what you are describing to something else. There are two basic ways to make comparisons: You can make an indirect comparison by using a *simile*—that is, saying something is *like* (or the *same as*) something else—or you can make a direct identification by using a *metaphor,* saying that your subject *is* something else. One student used a simile to describe a sloppily dressed friend who "looks like a load of laundry." Another said her hiking companion was "as slow as a tired turtle." If the second student had said her companion "*was* a tired turtle," she would have been using a metaphor instead of a simile.

Do not settle for using similes and metaphors you have heard many times before. Instead of saying "He was as thin as a rail," one student wrote "He was as thin as a capital I." Instead of saying that the ice on a pond was "as smooth as glass," one student wrote "The frozen ice pond looked like Grandmother's cloudy, cracked bureau mirror." The use of such similes and metaphors can make your descriptions rich and original.

Review the sample paragraphs presented earlier to see how their authors managed to write successful descriptions by incorporating these four basic guidelines.

Writing Assignment 7–1:
Objective and Subjective Description

Write two separate descriptive paragraphs using selected details to illustrate and support your dominant impression. Write the first paragraph using *objective* description. Write the second paragraph using *subjective* description. Unless your instructor tells you otherwise, you should write on the same topic for each paragraph.

First select your topic from this list:

- A mountain, lake, or other natural feature near where you live
- A memorable party you attended
- A memorable meal (good or bad)
- An important material object in your life
- The downtown area of your town or city
- The campus or physical setting of your college or university

Write your paragraph by following the activities of the Writing Process and the guidelines given here for each activity.

Gather Your Ideas and Information: Involve yourself in your topic as much as you can for this assignment. Go to the place you are writing about, or otherwise acquaint yourself as fully as possible with your subject. Study closely the object of your description. Take notes, trying to distinguish between the *objective* and *subjective* observations you are making. Practice focused free writing, visualization, brainstorming, or clustering to generate ideas and help your observations take shape on paper.

Analyze Your Ideas and Information: Review the notes you made to see what features of your subject stand out most. Have you left out any significant details? What attributes seem to be either connected or more important than others?

Identify Your Main Point: What stands out most for you about your subject? Identify your *dominant impression,* and state it as a topic sentence for your paragraph. Does it seem to sum up the major ideas and information from the first two activities? If you were writing an objective description of the Mississippi River, your topic sentence might be "The fourth longest river in the world, the Mississippi River is an impressive water system that stretches from northern Minnesota to the Gulf of Mexico." The topic sentence for a subjective description might be "The Mississippi is a ribbon of life that weaves through the hearts of all who live along its banks."

Plan Your Paragraph: Make a logical plan for your paragraph by deciding on the order in which you will present details to your reader. When you write a description, it is usually best to establish a point of view from which you present your subject. If your first version of this paragraph is to be an objective description, then it might be helpful to think of yourself as a television camera moving from point to point. If you were describing the Mississippi River, for example, you might start at its point of origin and follow the flow of the river southward. If you were describing your car, you could move from the outside (the overall shape, color, bumpers, tires) to the inside (upholstery, dashboard, radio). You might describe a computer first in very general terms ("a Rincon 340T") and then focus on specific details as your camera "eye" moves in for a close-up ("two black slots for the disk drives"). Be sure you decide which details you will use to support your topic sentence and develop your dominant impression.

Write Your Paragraph: Keep your topic sentence (your dominant impression) in mind as you write. Include specific details, and provide transition and directional words such as *next to, to the right of,* or *in addition to* so your reader can follow your description. Use exact words, including making comparisons with original similes or metaphors that enhance your descriptions. (You can review the definitions and use of simile or metaphor on page 123.)

Revise and Edit Your Paragraph: Check to see that your description is either objective or subjective as you intended and that a reader can follow your discussion easily. Have you maintained a consistent point of view and used enough transitional words to guide your reader? Have you presented details that develop the dominant impression as it is stated by your topic sentence? Have you used exact, vivid words in your description and avoided vague and general phrases?

Using the STSOE guidelines for revision, review each of the following areas of your essay:

Subject: Have you followed the assignment? Is your objective paragraph predominantly objective? Is your subjective paragraph predominantly subjective?

Topic Sentence: Does your topic sentence state a dominant impression that the rest of the paragraph supports and explains?

Support: Did you support the topic sentence with enough details? Are all the details and examples relevant to the topic sentence?

Organization: Have you described your subject's characteristics in the best possible order? Is the topic sentence effectively placed? Is there a sense of conclusion in the final sentence?

Editing: Review the paragraph for corrections in grammar, punctuation, and spelling. Use a dictionary to check the accuracy, as well as the spelling, of any unfamiliar adjectives you may have included in your description. Besides giving the definition and spelling of a word, a good dictionary also will give *synonyms* (words of similar meanings) for many words. A *thesaurus* is a reference book consisting entirely of synonyms and *antonyms* (words of opposite meanings). Ask your instructor to recommend a complete dictionary and perhaps a thesaurus.

Writing a Descriptive Essay

In pieces of writing that are longer than a paragraph, description usually occurs in combination with other devices, such as narration or argument. Occasionally, however, description itself will be the major tool you use in writing about a topic.

You may write a *descriptive essay* to paint a subjective picture of the kind of neighborhood or general environment in which you grew up. This technique also might be appropriate if you were writing an objective essay about the paintings of the Italian Renaissance or, equally, the geology of a specific mountain range. To a great extent, whether or not your essay is *descriptive* depends simply on how much description you use to present and support your ideas.

In preparation for Writing Assignment 7-2, read the following student essay and note the way it uses description to convey its main idea about the Vietnam Veterans Memorial in Washington, D.C.

The Vietnam Veterans Memorial

Visiting Washington, D.C., last summer, I was eager to see everything I could, starting with the Capitol itself and working my way to the National Air and Space Museum. I had of course heard about the Vietnam Veterans Memorial, but since no one in my family had taken part in that conflict, seeing the memorial did not rank any higher than several other sights on my list. I have since realized, however, that the fame of the Vietnam Veterans Memorial is well deserved. After viewing the long list of names engraved in its black marble walls, I now understand why so many find the memorial a fitting and powerful tribute to those who died in the Vietnam War.

The Vietnam Veterans Memorial is located at the western end of Constitution Gardens, a ten-acre parklike area that was appropriately chosen for its peaceful, natural beauty. Here broad pathways wind gracefully beneath oak trees that border spreading green lawns and tidy gardens of flowers and bushes. Amidst all this natural scenery, the memorial itself is an imposing sight. Although commonly referred to as "the Wall," it is actually two walls made of polished black granite, each about 250 feet long and roughly ten feet high, that meet in a V. Inscribed on the walls in the chronological order of their owners' deaths are the names of the nearly 60,000 soldiers who were killed in the Vietnam War.

The angular black walls of the memorial are imposing, but the seemingly endless rows of the names of the dead are what affect viewers the most. People stand in front of the Wall for hours at a time, slowly reading the names, touching them, tracing their outline with their fingers. One man I watched moved along the Wall, stopping every few feet to photograph some of the names. A woman and her child, a girl about six or seven years old, were busy placing small bouquets of roses along the wall, apparently choosing places at random. Although I knew no one who had served in the war, I found the names pulling at me, too. Once I began reading them, I kept on, overpowered by their number. I felt obliged to give every name the tribute of being read and contemplated for what it represented. By the time I was ready to leave, I understood why thousands of visitors leave something—flowers, photographs, poems, and other mementos—at the Wall: Their tributes are testimony to a new understanding of the tragedy of the Vietnam War, of any war, and of what war costs.

Washington, D.C., has a number of beautiful, inspiring monuments, but none of them compare to the Vietnam Veterans Memorial in their ability to stir emotions. I doubt anyone can view the Wall without feeling a mixture of pride, grief, and tears all at once. I feel a little guilty that I had not planned to see the Vietnam Memorial sooner on my visit to Washington, but I am grateful now for the chance I had to experience firsthand its powerful beauty and meaning.

Writing Assignment 7-2:
A Descriptive Essay

Keeping in mind the model of the preceding essay, write a brief descriptive essay of your own about your neighborhood, your college campus, or a place you have visited that you think of as memorable. Include a thesis statement that suggests a dominant impression about the place you describe, and give details and examples that help your reader visualize the subject. Remember to use the Writing Process and the STSOE guidelines for revision as you prepare your essay:

Gather Your Ideas and Information: Using brainstorming or listing techniques, jot down details and the dominant impression you have of your subject.

Analyze Your Ideas and Information: Read over the information you have gathered to see which items are the most significant. Add more items if you think you need them

Identify Your Main Point: State your dominant impression about the subject as a single sentence.

Plan Your Essay: Allow for several paragraphs of description, and be sure they include enough details about your subject. Decide whether you want to devote several sentences or whole paragraphs to describing each part of your subject.

Write Your Essay: Pay attention to detail and use concrete language as you write. Make your conclusion say something significant about the subject or what you have written about it.

Revise and Edit Your Essay: Use the STSOE guidelines to revise and edit your essay.

The Art of Narrating

Whether it is written or told aloud, a *narrative* is simply a story that describes an event or a series of closely related actions. One of our great American writers, Flannery O'Connor, wrote this about telling stories: "There is a certain embarrassment about being a storyteller in these times when stories are considered not quite as satisfying as statements and statements not quite as satisfying as statistics; but in the long run, a people is known, not by its statements or its statistics, but by the stories it tells" (*Mystery and Manners*).

In the following paragraph from her memoir *Woman Warrior,* the writer Maxine Hong Kingston narrates the story of a young girl being visited by a ghost:

> She did not know whether she had fallen asleep or not when she heard a rushing coming out from under the bed. Cringes of fear seized her soles as something alive, rumbling, climbed the foot of the bed. It rolled over her and landed bodily on her chest. There it sat. It breathed airlessly, pressing her, sapping her. "Oh, no. A Sitting Ghost," she thought. She pushed against the creature to lever herself out from underneath it, but it absorbed this energy and got heavier. Her fingers and palms became damp, shrinking at the ghost's thick short hair like an animal's coat, which slides against warm solidity as human flesh slides against muscles and bones. She grabbed clutches of fur and pulled. She pinched the skin the hair grew out of and gouged into it with her fingernails. She forced her hands to hunt out eyes, furtive somewhere in the air, but could not find any. She lifted her head to bite but fell back exhausted. The mass thickened.

However, a writer can tell all kinds of stories, not just make-believe ones. In its simplest terms, narration gives a chronological account of *what happened,* such as when a newspaper reports on a forest fire or summarizes the events of a baseball game. To explain a theory, a physicist may narrate a hypothetical account of how our solar system was formed. Historians narrate their reconstructions of past events. In the paragraph that follows (taken from his autobiography, *Giant Steps*) basketball star Kareem Abdul-Jabbar narrates the story of how, as a very young and inexperienced player, he first discovered the hook shot that was to help make him a legend in later years:

> One day I stumbled upon a strange and delightful experience, kind of like that exciting yet amazingly unexpected feeling you get when you know, quite definitely, that you've entered puberty. In the first half, I was in the game, which was already unusual, and a rebound fell my way near the right of the basket. I fumbled with it, trying to conquer the dribble, and it almost got away. Finally, with a guy from the other team at my back, I looked over my shoulder, saw the basket, turned into the lane, and with one hand put up my first hook shot. It missed. Hit the back rim and bounced out. But it felt right, and the next time I got the ball I tried it again. Neither of them went in, but I had found my shot. At halftime my teammates, surprised that I had showed some coordination, encouraged me to practice it, and from then on, whenever I got into play I would shoot it. Nobody showed me how; it came naturally.

Like all writing that tells a story, this paragraph uses blow-by-blow narration not simply for its own sake, but in the service of a main point. If you think about it, most stories you tell have a point you want to get across—why you broke up with someone you were seeing and what happened afterward; why a certain relative is strange and what he or she has done lately to prove it. These stories and others like them are narratives with a main point to illustrate.

As you will discover, narration and description are devices that often work together in writing. The difference between them is that description is basically *static*—that is, it tells how things are at a specific point in time. Narration, on the other hand, proceeds chronologically, recounting what happened or what someone did, usually presenting each action or event as it occurred in sequence. In a narrative paragraph, you will find it helpful to state your main point as the topic sentence. The events you describe in the paragraph will explain, develop, or further support that main point.

The important thing to remember when you narrate a series of events is that your story should have a point. Without the topic sentence stated in the first sentence, this narrative would mean very little to a reader. As with all stories, the "so what?" factor—the point of your narrative—is essential for your readers' interest and understanding alike. After they have finished reading your narration, you do not want your readers to ask "So what?" or "Why bother?" In a narrative paragraph, the answer to "So what?" is the stated or clearly implied topic sentence. In a narrative essay, it is the thesis statement.

Writing Assignment 7-3:
A Narrative Paragraph

Write a paragraph that uses narration to illustrate or further develop the idea expressed in its topic sentence. First read the following sample. Here is how one student used narration to support a topic sentence about learning to read:

> Even if they happen when we are very young, we often remember in great detail those events that continue to affect our lives for years after they occur. I recall being five years old and waiting on our old green and white living room couch for my mother to make time to read a new comic book to me. Though I had by then been introduced to a few principles of reading in my first-grade classroom, the few words I could spell out and pronounce had never seemed to have much application anywhere but at school. I relied on pictures and the reading skills of others for my enjoyment of books. On that day, however, I remember getting impatient and leafing through a new "Spiderman" comic book alone. Out of boredom and curiosity, I first began translating the letters for "POW!" and "WHAM!" into sounds in my head. The next thing I knew, I was doing the same for other words, piecing one or two together here and there on the page and gradually getting a vague sense of what was being said. I wasn't reading every word, but I do remember a kind of excited awakening of meaning like I hadn't felt before. I've read ever since. Twenty-five years later, I still remember that day.

Now select one of the following topics on which to write your paragraph, or develop one of your own:

- A time I made a new friend
- A time I was lied to
- When my best effort paid off

- A time I had a brush with death
- The most surprising experience I ever had
- How my family (ancestors) came to this country

Use the Writing Process activities and the suggestions that follow to write your paragraph.

Gather Your Ideas and Information: Begin by thinking about one of the topics listed or one that you have selected, and focus on the specific episode in your life it relates to. Try focused free writing as a way of narrating chronologically the series of events that makes up the "story." Start by writing down the topic and the event you selected on a piece of notebook paper. Write as much and as fast as you can about the experience. Do not worry about making sense or using good grammar or punctuation; just put down what comes into your head. Write for about five minutes or until you complete the paragraph.

You also could use brainstorming to generate the material for your narrative. For example, if you were writing about "A time I had a brush with death," you might have something like this in your two columns of material:

falling off the cliff at Preston Beach	hiking with Jack; slipped; falling; concussion; unconscious for a week; hospital a month; missed school, missed friends

You could use this material as an outline for identifying your main point—that is, what did this close call *mean* to you ultimately?—and for planning your paragraph before you begin to write it.

Analyze Your Ideas and Information: Have you narrated your story fully enough to give a complete picture of what happened? Have you included all the relevant details and actions? Is the experience you selected appropriate to demonstrate the topic? Look over what you have recorded to see what the message of your experience might be.

Identify Your Main Point: Write down a topic sentence that sums up what point your story, as sketched in your focused free writing and brainstorming, seems to be moving toward.

Plan Your Paragraph: Decide on the order of the events you want to narrate and where in the paragraph (at the beginning or at the end) you might best place your topic sentence. Will you want to comment on the action you are describing, or will the narrative be clear enough by itself? Do you have enough details? Are they all relevant to your main point as expressed in the topic sentence?

Write Your Paragraph: Now write, taking care to include needed transition words (see pages 63–65 for review) to link each step of the experience you describe.

Revise and Edit Your Paragraph: As you look over what you have written, ask yourself these questions: Have you pared your narration down to its essentials, or does your story ramble? Have you painted a clear picture for your readers of what actually happened? Is your main point demonstrated? Use the STSOE revision guidelines to revise and edit, and refer to Chapters 15–22 for help with grammar, punctuation, and spelling.

Writing a Narrative Essay

As in your practice paragraph in Writing Assignment 7–3, your main goal in writing a full-length narrative essay is to tell in detail a story that has one main point. You will find that keeping this goal in view can be a little trickier in a longer piece of writing than it is in a paragraph.

In writing your own longer narration, you will want to keep the following points in mind:

1. Make sure you write a story, not reflections on a story. If you were in an automobile accident and went to see a lawyer about it, your lawyer would ask you to tell exactly what happened, not give your view on reckless driving or on how right you were and how wrong the other driver was. When you write your story, it is appropriate to use your introduction to give background information and your conclusion to discuss the significance of the story for you, but most of your essay should be an account of exactly what happened.

2. For short essays, choose to write about events of limited duration that take place in an hour, half a day, or at most a day. Do not tell your reader what happened last summer or during the three weeks you worked at Sammy's Salmon Camp. Pick *one* event from last summer or *one* event from your work at the camp that illustrates what it was like.

3. In writing narration, you often discover the main point of the story as you write. Be willing to revise your essay until you make the point you really want to make. By the time you write the final draft, however, you should have a main point or thesis in mind, although you may decide not to state it outright anywhere in the essay.

4. When possible, choose to write about an event in which conflict is present. Conflict is the stuff powerful stories are made of. Here are four kinds of conflict you can develop in a narrative:

Conflict between people. If you are writing about a disastrous canoe trip during which you and your friends argued heatedly about whether to stop and make camp or paddle to the next campsite, describe the argument.

Conflict between an individual and the environment. Perhaps one of the reasons the canoe trip was a disaster was that it rained and turned much colder. Write about the conflict between the canoe party and the forces of nature.

Conflict within yourself. Perhaps you really did not want to go on the canoe trip in the first place, knowing that there would be bad weather, but you went because your friends put a lot of pressure on you. Write about the conflict within yourself between doing what they wanted you to do and what you wanted to do.

Conflict between an individual and society. Sometimes it is appropriate to write about how an individual fights with society. In such cases you may want to show how one person refuses to go along with what everyone else does.

5. Make use of your skills in presenting detail and, when it helps your story to come alive, recording dialogue.

Writing Assignment 7-4: A Narrative Essay

The following essay, Paula Poundstone's "Be Like Gandhi," uses narration to demonstrate the way an experience on the street can lead to greater understanding of oneself and others. After reading the essay and discussing the questions that follow it, write about an experience that taught you something important about yourself or others.

There is no God. At least, I'm practically certain there isn't. I don't believe there's a heaven or a hell either, so I don't really know what makes me want to be a good person, but I do, in the worst way.

I want to be a good person, and I want to be considered a good person, which may, technically, undermine the legitimacy of my goodness. According to the movie, Gandhi didn't want a big fuss made over him. Of course, I also read that when Gandhi lived in the ashram be believed that all of the children there were all of the adults' responsibility. So when one of the kids would screw up, Gandhi would fast, feeling it was in some way his failure as well. Imagine watching "The Partridge Family" one night instead of doing division problems 1 to 20 on page 41 in your math book and having your dad not eat as a result. Even my mother, who used to say, "Your ass is my meat," may have had a better technique. Still, Gandhi's overall record of goodness was better than my mother's, so I do try to use him as a role model.

I'm aware that my efforts are much smaller than Gandhi's. He liberated India; I let people in in traffic. I smile and say, "Hi," when I see people on the street. Sometimes, when I do so, mothers draw their children nearer to them and pick up their pace walking past me. It's difficult for me to tell if I'm actually doing good. I need a sign. If I let someone in in traffic and they wave, I feel so good. If someone lets me in in traffic I always wave, because I want them to feel good, too. I'll follow them until they see me wave. Sometimes they feel threatened, and I wish I had a button on the steering wheel so I could unhonk. Just a couple of days ago I let three cars in ahead of me in traffic and the guy behind me got mad. I think that's why Gandhi walked so much.

I knew a guy in San Francisco who everyone thought was a saint. He "worked with kids." I'm always suspicious of such a vague description of someone's deeds. Fagin worked with kids. Someone in the airport once approached me with a sign asking for money for "the kids." I asked what he did with the money. He had that long rap that people soliciting often have, the one where, when you realize they're not gonna take a breath, you just sort of tune out. When I tuned back in, I heard him mumble something about taking "the kids to Vegas to show them the ills of gambling and sex." I swear it. I gave him the dollar anyway, because it struck me as so funny.

Anyway, the guy in San Francisco was the kind of guy who secretly wanted the world to suck so he could be seen fixing it. When he'd ask how I was, I'd say, "Fine," and he'd say, "Really?"—like he was hoping I'd reconsider and have a big breakdown right in front of him.

I used to think if I was a good person I would feel good. I give money to about 30 different organizations. Not only do my efforts feel like spitting in the ocean, but each contribution invites stronger appeals for more money that grow exponentially. For the most part I trust that these needs are real and I don't begrudge their requests, but it doesn't feel at all good.

Each request for money comes with a redundant newsletter describing how much worse the situation has become since I sent my last check—the religious right is mobilizing; the Klan is marching; libraries are closing; our fundamental rights are under increasing attack; fires have finally been put out, causing flooding; AIDS continues to ravage despite the most recent dance-a-thon; the NRA has bought the Congress, which has subsequently banned logic; the most recent attempt at campaign-finance reform has been defeated; and farmers are being particularly cruel to chickens this month. I feel like I spend half my life tearing the plastic windows out of their business envelopes so they can go in the recycle pile. When I see the mailman I well up with tears.

Once, on my way into a record store, a couple of street guys asked for spare change. One of them said he needed money to feed his dog. I didn't have any spare change, so I said I'd catch them on my way out. But I forgot to get change. Although I do want to be a good person, I'm not quite there yet, so, when I didn't see these guys right away, I was relieved. It's such an internal wrestle: I didn't want to encourage their downfall, but, on the other hand, they were hungry, and I was just in the store looking to buy a blues tape to cheer me up after opening the mail. Mentally, I had myself in a full nelson, when they appeared at the car to remind me of my promise. Assuming they were together, I gave the guy with the dog $20. He hustled across the parking lot while the other guy flew into a little lecture. He said, "Naw, man, that ain't right. Pops is just gonna take that money and go buy alcohol." I felt sort of trapped, at first apologetic and then pissed. I said, "I'm sorry, I thought you were togeth—you mean, he lied to me about the dog!"

I never want to say it too loudly, but I'm beginning to have a helpless feeling. I'm not saying I condone it, but I see why rich people like to build fences around their property. I know after I watch "MacNeil/Lehrer" and "Life and Times" (a PBS show discussing Los Angeles issues), I almost frantically turn to "Murder, She Wrote." With this helpless feeling comes a compelling desire to turn away. I don't think I'll ever be rich enough to totally shut out the uglier side of the world, but if I am not very vigilant, I might become one of those people who does not let people in in traffic.

Questions for Discussion and Writing

1. Is Gandhi an appropriate role model for Poundstone? What attributes of his does she admire and want to imitate the most? Are there any she chooses to ignore? Why?

2. What does Poundstone do to be a "good person" in her life? Do you agree that these actions make her a good person? Why or why not?

3. Review Poundstone's encounter with the two men who asked her for money. What do you think they wanted the money for? Do you think Poundstone should have given them money?

4. What lesson did Poundstone learn from her experience on the street?

5. Have you had an encounter with people asking for money on the street? How do you react in such situations? Why?

Choose Your Topic: Using the brainstorming method, name as many events from your past as you can think of in which you learned something important. The following categories should help you think of such events:

1. A time you learned that not all promises should (or would) be kept
2. A time you learned a bitter lesson
3. A time you learned something important about the opposite sex
4. A time you learned never to do a certain thing again
5. A time you learned to take care of yourself
6. A time you learned that mothers (or fathers) are not always right (or wrong)
7. A time you learned what it is like to deal with the police
8. A time you learned to "grin and bear it"
9. Some other time you learned something important to you
10. A time something you did helped someone else learn something important

Analyze Your Ideas and the Information: Ask yourself the following questions:

    1. Where is the conflict in the essay? How can I develop it?
    2. Where is the essay going? What is it really about?
    3. What dialogue might I use in my narrative? (Although dialogue is not essential, it often helps make a story come alive for the reader.)

Identify Your Main Point: The narrative is one kind of writing in which the thesis statement is often not revealed until the middle or the end or is even left out altogether. But you should know where you are headed in your narrative and what you want to accomplish. Thus you should have a thesis statement in mind, even though it may not be expressed. Look over the work you have done so far and write your thesis statement here:

_____

_____

_____

One way to prepare your thesis statement for this assignment is simply to fill in the blanks in the following sentence:

    I learned _____ the time_____ _____

_____

    A thesis statement for Poundstone's essay could be "I learned that sometimes doing the right thing isn't the best thing to do." (Once you begin to write, you may find that you need to change your thesis statement and start your essay again.)

Plan Your Narrative: Write an informal outline that will help you accomplish your purpose. If you quote a conversation with several exchanges, you may not be able to set up your outline in the usual paragraph form because you will have to begin a new paragraph each time the speaker changes. Instead, let each episode within the event you are writing about constitute one of the main points in the body of your outline. You will want to use the information-gathering worksheet as you write your outline.

    You may want to use the introduction to place the event you are writing about in a larger context by mentioning other events that led up to it. You also may want to use the conclusion to show the significance that the event had for you.

Write Your Narrative: As you write, make sure you are telling the whole story. Your narrative should have a beginning, a middle, and an end. Also, make sure you are not going off in directions that take you away from your thesis. If you can build suspense into your narrative, do so. If possible, emphasize conflict. Concentrate on using detail and, when it seems helpful, dialogue. Finally, be careful to give your sentences variety.

Revise and Edit Your Narrative: Evaluate your essay by asking the following questions:

1. Did you tell what happened, or is your story mostly reflections on what happened or what could have happened?
2. Did you keep the main point of the story before you throughout the essay? If not, where did you go off in another direction?
3. Did your story take place within a short period of time? If not, what was the time span?
4. Did your sentences flow smoothly into each other, or were they choppy? Did you use too many *and*s and *then*s to connect sentences and clauses?

Now revise and edit your essay, using the STSOE guidelines. Watch especially for the following errors, which often show up in narrative essays:

1. Run-on sentences (See Chapter 22.2.)
2. Tense confusion (See Chapter 17.)
3. Errors in punctuating dialogue (See Chapter 20.7.)

The techniques of description and narration you learned in this chapter also can be applied in other types of essays, especially when you need to discuss more than one item or event at a time or show the relationship between objects, events, or ideas. Objective and subjective descriptions also can be combined to enhance your treatment of your subject, and both description and narration can make general ideas more understandable to your readers. These techniques make the persons, actions, objects, or ideas you write about come alive, even when you use them in essays that are not primarily narrative or descriptive. Chapters 8 and 9 will show you how to write essays using organizing principles that are different from those discussed in this chapter, but narration and description can play a large role in these and many other writing contexts as well.

The Writing Process

GATHER your ideas and information
ANALYZE your ideas and information
IDENTIFY your theme or main point
PLAN your essay
WRITE your essay
REVISE AND EDIT your essay (STSOE)

8

Writing with Examples, Comparison and Contrast, and Classification

BESIDES DESCRIPTION AND narration, writers have other tools at their disposal for developing and expressing their ideas. This chapter will explore three ways of presenting and explaining ideas and information:

- Citing examples, a technique that offers your reader particular illustrations of a general idea or principle
- Comparing and contrasting, which points out similarities and differences
- Classifying, which groups a number of items into like categories or classes

Like a house, an essay can be put together using a variety of tools. As you study how to incorporate these three new techniques into your essay writing, you will discover yourself also using description and narration when presenting ideas to your readers.

Examples

An *example* functions as a representative of a group as a whole; it is a selected instance that makes an abstract idea concrete and familiar. By itself, *cold weather* is an abstract idea until you offer examples of what you mean by this term: "ten degrees below zero" or "freezing rain and icy winds." In your writing you will often find yourself making general statements such as "I had a rough day" or "The concert was wonderful." These statements remain abstract and ungrounded unless you cite specific examples of what you consider a "rough day" or a "wonderful concert"—examples, incidentally, that demonstrate that your definition of these concepts may not be the same as someone else's. Differences in individual values and judgment make it important that you anchor all your conclusions in the concrete evidence on which they were based. One writer might explain the first statement this way:

> I had a rough day. The Mercedes refused to start, and I was late for my appointment with my personal trainer.

Another writer might exemplify it this way:

> I had a rough day. My mother had a heart attack, and I spent the afternoon waiting outside the intensive care unit.

As these two versions show, general statements alone cannot communicate much meaning unless you develop them with plenty of examples.

Examples strengthen your discussion by illustrating and defining general statements more completely for your reader. If you write "The cab driver entertained us," you need to explain how, exactly, he or she entertained you by citing an example or two. These concrete details make your statement more specific and anchor it in reality:

> The cab driver entertained us by whistling little songs and telling funny stories about Boston's past.

Here is how the mystery writer Raymond Chandler uses examples to expand on the idea that a hot desert wind affects human behavior in unexpected ways:

There was a desert wind blowing that night. It was one of those hot dry Santa Anas that come down through the mountain passes and curl your hair and make your nerves jump and your skin itch. On nights like that every booze party ends in a fight. Meek little wives feel the edge of the carving knife and study their husbands' necks. Anything can happen. You can even get a full glass of beer at a cocktail lounge.

Once you have grown accustomed to providing your reader with specific examples of your general statements, you will want to use these examples in the most effective way possible. Here are some helpful guidelines for incorporating examples into your writing:

Use Examples to Support a Main Idea: Examples help develop your point of view by providing specific instances that support, illustrate, or more precisely define the ideas in your topic sentence or thesis statement. Here is how Joyce Carol Oates, a well-known writer and critic, effectively offers specific examples to support her point that money has lured retired boxers back into professional fighting:

Topic sentence

Example

Other examples

Example

Money has drawn any number of retired boxers back into the ring. The most notorious example is perhaps Joe Louis, who, owing huge sums in back taxes, continued boxing well beyond the point at which he could perform capably. After a career of seventeen years he was stopped by Rocky Marciano—who was said to have felt as upset by his victory as Louis by the defeat. (Louis then went on to a degrading second career as a professional wrestler. This, too, ended abruptly when 300-pound Rocky Lee stepped on the forty-two-year old Louis's chest and damaged his heart.) Ezzard Charles, Jersey Joe Walcott, Joe Frazier, Muhammad Ali—each continued fighting when he was no longer in condition to defend himself against young heavyweight boxers on the way up. Of all heavyweight champions, only Rocky Marciano, to whom fame and money were not of paramount significance, was prudent enough to retire before he was defeated.

Use Examples to Strengthen Content: Examples also help your reader because they make your writing meaningful and convincing. Notice how general—and also how unconvincing—the following paragraph is.

My parents mean the most to me because of what they have given me. Without the help of my mother and father, I would not be where I am today, nor would I be the kind of person I have become. Although each of my parents gave me different kinds of gifts in my life, I know that they both gave me a lot to be grateful for in my personal, educational, and career development. They also helped me learn other important things like appreciating others and valuing myself. I also know that my parents are probably the biggest reason I am here at this college today.

Despite the many statements about the writer's parents, this paragraph stays too general and tells almost nothing about its subject. The author has given no examples of *how* her parents have helped her or *what* they have taught and given her. Expanded with examples, the same thoughts could be expressed more meaningfully as follows:

> My parents mean the most to me because without the help of my mother and father, I would not be where I am today. My mother stopped working when I was born so she could give me as much of her time as possible. When, at the age of six, I was unable to learn to read, she sat for hours with me after school and in the evenings to give me the help I needed. We could not afford music lessons, so my mother taught me herself to play the piano and sing. Because of her, I am today working my way through college by singing with a small professional chorus. My father taught me to hold my own opinions and to speak up for myself. When the wrong man asked me to marry him, I said no—and proudly waited until Phil, my husband today, got up the nerve to ask me. Both my parents taught me to respect other people and to care about them, no matter how different they may be. Today I am at this college pursuing a career in medicine, a choice undoubtedly governed by what their gifts to me have meant all these years.

Offer Specific Examples: Keep your examples as specific as possible. A specific example offers a particular instance rather than a more general one. "Fruit" is a general example of *food,* but "an apple" is more specific than both. Although general examples often have their place in writing, offer your reader specific examples as much as you can. If you write "Many professional athletes, such as heavyweight champions, have returned to sports after retiring," make your general example of "heavyweight champions" more specific by writing instead "Many professional athletes, such as heavyweight champions Joe Louis and Muhammed Ali, have returned to sports after retiring." Well-chosen, concrete examples clarify a topic sentence or other general statement by providing your reader with specific illustrations that add interest and content to what you write.

Cite Enough Examples to Support Your Idea: The number of examples you will need to support general statements varies, but *enough to support the main point* (the topic sentence or thesis statement) is a good rule to keep in mind. How many is enough? Although a single example is rarely enough (because it may represent a unique case), two to three examples in a paragraph are adequate. An essay may require three to four extensively developed examples. With these numbers, you can support your main point and provide interesting content for your reader.

However, the real key to deciding how many examples to offer comes from understanding what you are trying to demonstrate. The more challenging your idea is to your reader, the more concrete evidence you will need to support it. Obviously, some ideas require fewer examples than others. An assertion such as "Freeway traffic is terrible in the afternoon" needs only a few instances for support because most people are sufficiently familiar with the topic to agree with this statement. In such a case, your supporting examples would be used more to *illustrate* your claim than to prove it. A statement such as "Animals are more intelligent than humans," on the other hand, requires several examples, both to show what you mean by "more intelligent" and to convince your reader.

Anytime you seem to be describing *all* or *most* of a category, you will clearly need several representative examples. Demonstrating that (all) "animals are more intelligent than humans" or that (all) "politicians rarely deliver what they promise" would require numerous examples. One or two examples are too small a sampling to support either statement. If you have only a few examples to offer, revise the statement of your main point, such as "Many animals seem as intelligent as humans" or "Some politicians do not deliver what they promise."

Use Examples Accurately: The examples you offer your reader should accurately represent the general idea you want to illustrate or support. If you argued in your topic sentence or thesis statement that "college students today know very little about the Vietnam War," you would need to discuss a representative number of students as examples to support your claim. In supporting such a claim, simply citing the lack of knowledge expressed by your friends Carolyn and Jason is not enough. They alone cannot accurately represent all or even most other college students today because that category includes a wide range of people. Even if you examine the evidence for your idea and still conclude that Carolyn and Jason are typical in their lack of knowledge about the Vietnam War, you need to prove this conclusion to your reader by citing other examples.

Play Fair with Your Reader: If you claim that "teenage marriages are usually successful" and then cite a few cases to demonstrate that fact, you would be arguing a point that is statistically untrue. Do not make such a statement and then support it by providing examples of a few exceptional teenage marriages that succeeded. Instead, you should restate your argument in fair and more accurate terms by saying "Teenage marriages can sometimes be successful." In this case, you could offer several examples to back up your position, and you would be playing fair with your reader.

Put Your Examples in the Best Order: Although all your examples should be equally representative, it is also wise to think about their most effective order. You can avoid a confusing pattern of examples by arranging them in a least-to-most order. You do this by starting with the least complicated or least important examples and moving into the larger, more developed, and significant ones as your discussion progresses.

The following paragraph demonstrates such a least-to-most order of examples:

Least important example {   Many politicians do not keep the promises they made during their election campaigns. The last mayor we had promised he would write a column in the local newspaper every week, but he never did. Last June three of the five current city

Most important example

council members told the voters they would not allow the airport to be expanded to accommodate more air traffic. Despite their promises, new runways and larger maintenance facilities are now under construction. Worse yet, our own governor guaranteed he would reduce the crime rate within a year of taking office. He's been governor three years now, and crime has risen by over 16 percent.

You may find other patterns of ordering examples effective for different purposes. In a narrative, for instance, examples usually appear chronologically. Sometimes an important example appears first in a paragraph or essay to introduce the subject and gain the reader's attention. In general, however, a least-to-most order keeps building your reader's interest and gives the last, most striking, or most important example the greatest impact.

State Your Examples Effectively: Try to avoid using such phrases as *for example* to introduce the examples you give. Such expressions can be easily overused, especially if your paragraph or essay offers several examples. Simply offering an example usually makes your strategy clear to the reader. The examples that follow show how varying your style or punctuation can help you avoid repetitious use of *for example* or *for instance:*

WEAK

Henry was a downright thief. For instance, he stole my wallet and a new jacket when he was here.

STRONGER

Henry was a downright thief. He stole my wallet and a new jacket when he was here.

WEAK

Richard has several means of transportation available. For example, he's got a bicycle, a car, two motorcycles, an old Chevrolet truck, and a horse named Frisco.

STRONGER

Richard has several means of transportation available: a bicycle, a car, two motorcycles, an old Chevrolet truck, and a horse named Frisco.

WEAK

She dreamed of traveling and wanted, for example, to go to China, Russia, and Egypt after she finished college.

STRONGER

She dreamed of traveling, wanting to go to China, Russia, and Egypt after she finished college.

The following sample student essay shows how to incorporate these suggestions. As you read the essay, notice the way each paragraph contains specific examples that support and illustrate the topic sentence as well as the essay's thesis statement.

A Student's Life

Contrary to the popular idea that most students have an easy life of just going to classes, parties, and football games, getting a college education is not all fun and games for everyone. When my aunt Mary decided last year to go back to school to get her B.A. in psychology, she still had to take care of two children, look after a house, and maintain a good, active relationship in her marriage. I do not see how she has had the needed time to do her homework. Can you imagine trying to write an essay and having to take care of two children, ages four and six, at the same time? Or what if your husband wants to go to see a movie on the weekend you have a major exam to study for? Naturally, Aunt Mary is constantly faced with having to decide which should get the highest priority for the day: the house, the family, or homework. For people like my aunt, being a housewife, mother, and student are three major jobs in one.

Going to school is no easier for my friend Sue Laporte, either. The other day she was complaining to me about her teachers expecting too much from her. Sue is majoring in accounting and has a tremendous amount of homework in her courses. But in order to attend college, she also has to keep a job. To add to her burden, Sue's mother works, leaving Sue to babysit her younger brother and sister after school each afternoon. Sue works three nights a week from six to ten P.M., and by the time she gets home, showers, and generally settles down for the night, it's around eleven o'clock. It is not unusual for her to sit up studying until two or three in the morning. Sue's schedule allows her very little time for herself right now. But she has decided to commit herself to a few years of misery so she can later enjoy what she jokingly refers to as the "laughs of luxury."

Another friend, José Morales, is attending the University of Colorado on a scholarship, which means he must keep his grades at a certain average. He is majoring in chemical engineering, carrying a total of seventeen units, and playing baseball. Because José's scholarship does not pay for everything, he also needs to work a few hours a week at a part-time job in the student bookstore. Some days he attends school, practices baseball, goes to work, and then comes home to do several hours of homework. He gets up at six-thirty every morning and usually goes to bed very late. How he manages to keep up a good grade point average with all he does is a mystery to me.

I guess dedication is the secret these people share in getting themselves through college. I'm sure they have their moments of doubt about what they are trying to achieve. No wonder they want to graduate: What better way to start enjoying an easier life?

Questions for Discussion and Writing

1. How effective is the introduction of this essay? What are its strengths and weaknesses? Should the writer have included other material? If so, what kind?
2. How do the transition sentences that begin the third and fourth paragraphs serve to carry out the thesis statement?

3. What major examples does the author give to support the thesis? Are these examples sufficiently explained? Why or why not?
4. How effective is the conclusion? Explain how the last paragraph serves or fails to serve as a clear *conclusion* to the discussion.

Writing Assignment 8–1:
An Example Essay

Choose one of the thesis statement topics that follow to write an example essay of several paragraphs in length. First, select the most exact words you can think of to complete the following sentences. Then choose one of these sentences as the thesis statement for the example essay you will write.

1. My college could improve service to students by _____

    _____

2. Getting a good part-time job requires _____

    _____

3. Most television soap operas _____

    _____

4. I usually procrastinate when _____

    _____

5. I know of several good marriages between people who _____

    _____

6. Children's television programs today are _____

    _____

7. Most of my past (or current) teachers could be described as _____

    _____

8. My philosophy about driving is _____

    _____

9. My friends and I have a number of ways to _____

    _____

10. The biggest mistake a student can make is _____

    _____

Now follow the activities of the Writing Process to complete your example essay:

Gather your ideas and information

Analyze your ideas and information

Identify your main point

Plan your essay

Write your essay

Revise and edit your essay (STSOE)

Comparing and Contrasting

When you develop and support your ideas with examples, you are offering your readers instances that are equally representative. However, it is often necessary to show how two things are alike through *comparison* or how they are different through *contrast*. These methods can be used when you want to persuade your reader that one thing is superior to another. They also can be used to show that two things are alike or different in unusual ways.

Much of our thinking is based on comparison and contrast. When we say a house is big, we mean it is big in relation to other houses. The same house is quite small when compared with a skyscraper or a large industrial plant. When we note that someone is wearing a ring with a small diamond, we are contrasting the size of this diamond with large diamonds or perhaps other precious stones. The same stone may be very large when contrasted with another, smaller diamond, such as one used for the tip of a phonograph needle. The words we use to describe objects, people, or events are often meaningful only when we compare and contrast those objects, people, or events with others in their category. (You can compare and contrast large and small diamonds, or diamonds and sapphires, but not diamonds and apples.)

Many essays assigned in college call for this method of discussion. In a sociology class, you might be asked to compare the political views of white-collar workers with those of blue-collar workers. In a political science class, you might need to contrast communism as practiced in Cuba with communism in the People's Republic of China. In a biology course, you may compare meiosis with mitosis. In fact, anytime you have to decide how two things are alike, or how they are different, or how one is better than the other, you will be using comparison and contrast.

The following paragraph demonstrates how techniques of comparison and contrast can be combined to show likeness and differences in the ways that stars and planets give off light.

Night Lights

As you look up into the sky at night, you may wonder whether the different individual points of light you are seeing are stars or planets. Both appear to shine, and
planets as well as stars exhibit colors ranging from white to slightly orange. Only stars
actually generate their own light, however. The light from a star is generated by constant nuclear reactions and the resulting release of energy. As a star begins to age
and cool, its colors shift toward red. This is why in a telescope the hottest stars appear blue, the cooler ones yellow, and so on. Unlike stars, planets do not generate
light. Their brightness results from light being reflected off their surfaces from stars
such as our own sun, the star closest to us. Stars appear to twinkle because, since
they are literally light-years away from us, atmospheric disturbances such as air cur-
rents interfere with our viewing and make their light seem unsteady. Planets, on the
other hand, are much closer to us than stars. Consequently, their light is subject to
less interference and appears more regular.

Your main purpose in comparison and contrast writing is to show how two
people, two places, or two things are alike or different. As the sample paragraph
demonstrates, to compare and contrast effectively, you must pay careful attention to the organization and selection of your material. You may find the following guidelines helpful in writing paragraphs and essays using comparison
and contrast.

Compare and Contrast Similar Items: First, choose only two things for
your comparison and contrast; use classification (discussed later in this chapter)
to compare and contrast three or more things. However, you also need to select
comparable items to compare and contrast. Two things are comparable if they fit
into the same category and are related in some way; for example, cars and buses
are both in the category *highway transportation,* and dogs and cats are both in
the category *common household pets.* Cars and buses are both forms of transportation, so they are comparable. Cars and computers, however, are not in the
same category and so could not be usefully compared with each other.

Even if they fall into the same broad category, things too similar or too far
apart in likeness cannot be usefully compared or contrasted. Pink roses and red
roses would not provide a very lively subject for comparison and contrast; dogs
and roses, though both living organisms, would be equally unpromising. However, you can use comparison or contrast to show your reader *unexpected* or
previously unknown similarities or differences: how snowboarding and skate-
boarding require similar skills, for example, or how our galaxy, the Milky Way, differs from another galaxy.

Compare and Contrast to Make a Point: Comparing and contrasting are
methods of developing or supporting ideas but are not ends in themselves. When
you compare and contrast two things, you need a reason for doing so. This reason
is your main point, expressed either as a topic sentence of a paragraph or as a thesis statement of an essay. If you want to tell your reader that Indian elephants are

usually domesticated and African elephants are not, you must have a main point to make, such as "Not all elephants are suitable for domestication."

As you compose your comparison or contrast discussion, keep your main point prominent. Although you may need to state certain general facts about your subjects, keep such information to a minimum. You should focus primarily on either the similarities or the differences indicated in your topic sentence or thesis statement. Points of comparison or contrast that are known to common sense, are trivial, or are irrelevant to the main point should be omitted from your discussion.

State Your Main Point Effectively: You might be tempted to begin your paragraph by simply stating that you will compare or contrast two people, places, or things. The better way to begin is to state an opinion and imply a similarity or difference between the two things you are comparing or contrasting. For example, do not say that you will show similarities or differences between life in the suburbs and life in the city or that "life in the city is different from life in the suburbs." Instead, offer an opinion as you compare or contrast the suburbs and the city. Here are several ways you could express a main point and the comparison it implies in a paragraph or essay:

> Life is easier in the city than in the suburbs.

> The city is full of excitement, but the suburbs are boring.

> Life in the suburbs is surprisingly similar to life in the city.

Plan and Write Your Comparison and Contrast: There are two methods for organizing and writing a comparison or contrast discussion.

Method A: After introducing the two topics and stating your main point, first write completely about one topic and then write completely about the second. In a paragraph, you should finish with a clincher sentence; in an essay, end with a conclusion paragraph.

One student organized the following paragraph about his sister and himself by using Method A:

Anne and Jack

My sister Anne and I will probably never agree on what we want in a movie. She is convinced that to be any good, a movie has to have some of her favorite stars in it, like Eddie Murphy, Tom Cruise, or Barbra Streisand. Next, she wants an exotic setting for the film's story. If the story takes place somewhere she has never been— Honolulu, Paris, Mozambique, even Philadelphia—Anne just knows she wants to see it. Anne says she wants movies to inspire her about people and what they can accomplish in the world, or else teach her something about life and its worth. Her favorite film is The Joy Luck Club, in which the famous European actress France Nuyen costarred. I don't care much about the stars because I value special effects more than anything. I also want entertainment in my movies, and that means interesting characters, exciting plots, or maybe humor. I like to get involved with a film so that I jump in my seat when I get scared or cheer when the good guys finally win. My favorite movie is RoboCop 3. I probably don't even have to tell you what Anne thought of it.

This paragraph has a very simple organization. First, Jack presents Anne's taste in movies, then his own preferences. Notice that in Method A each item about the first subject is *matched* to or *contrasted* with a similar item about the second. The sequence of items is also the same for each person:

ANNE
Main attraction is big stars
Also likes distant settings
Responds to inspiration or lessons
Favorite movie: The Joy Luck Club

JACK
Main attraction is special effects
Also likes good entertainment
Responds to imaginative involvement
Favorite movie: RoboCop 3

Method A allows you to present all the relevant details of one subject and then the relevant details of the next. This method is usually most effective in paragraphs or short essays in which your discussion provides the reader with a complete picture of each subject for comparison. In a long essay using this method, readers would have to refer back to previous pages to keep the separate points of comparison about each topic in mind.

Method B: Unlike Method A, this method allows you to compare or contrast each similar point for both subjects as you proceed in your discussion. If you used Method B to organize the paragraph about Anne and Jack, the outline for it would look like this:

Topic Sentence: My sister Anne and I will probably never agree on what we want in a movie.

I. Main attraction
    A. Anne: big stars
    B. Jack: special effects

II. Second attraction:
    A. Anne: distant settings
    B. Jack: good entertainment

III. Response
    A. Anne: likes inspiration and lessons
    B. Jack: likes to feel involved

IV. Favorite movie:
   A. Anne: The Joy Luck Club
   B. Jack: RoboCop 3

Here is Jack's paragraph about his sister and himself using Method B:

Anne and Jack

My sister Anne and I will probably never agree on what we want in a movie. She is convinced that to be any good, a movie has to have some of her favorite stars in it, like Eddie Murphy, Tom Cruise, or Barbra Streisand. I'm different. I don't care much about the stars because I value special effects more than anything, which is why I liked Star Trek: The Movie so much. Anne also wants an exotic setting for the film's story. If the story takes place somewhere she has never been—Honolulu, Paris, Mozambique, even Philadelphia—Anne just knows she wants to see it. I, on the other hand, want entertainment in my movies, and that means interesting characters, exciting plots, or maybe humor. Finally, Anne says she wants movies to inspire her about people and what they can accomplish in the world, or else teach her something about life and its worth. Her favorite film is The Joy Luck Club, in which the famous European actress France Nuyen costarred. I like to get involved with a film so that I jump in my seat when I get scared or cheer when the good guys finally win. My favorite movie is RoboCop 3. I probably don't even have to tell you what Anne thought of it.

Method B offers the advantage of allowing your readers to compare specific likenesses and differences throughout the discussion. In a short paragraph, however, this pattern of organization can sometimes make for a choppy, back-and-forth discussion. When you compare this version with that written according to Method A, you will see that Method B may require some extra content to keep the discussion balanced and additional transition words or sentences to keep the paragraph flowing. Whether you are writing a paragraph or an essay, make sure that you use appropriate transitions to guide your reader whenever you use Method B.

Writing a Comparison and Contrast Essay

The following two essays are Method A and Method B versions of writing comparison and contrast. As you read and study them, note how each method is used to organize and present details.

Method A: Two Medical Jobs

Detail

Thesis statement

I have worked both as an x-ray technician in a hospital and as an assistant in a private physician's office. Most people probably think working in a small, quiet doctor's office would be preferable to working at a hospital, but it is not. After working in both places, I'll take the hospital any time.

98

Topic sentence

Detail

Detail

Detail

Detail

Topic sentence

Detail

Detail

Detail

Detail

Conclusion

Surprisingly, the doctor's office where I used to work was either always deadly dull or fast-paced and hectic. The doctor was frequently out of the office, causing tiresome delays until he returned from hospital rounds or a hospital duty. Because the office was run to make a profit, the work was rushed, and I was not able to take my time with each patient. It was like an assembly line. "Get 'em in, and get 'em out," I was told. Lunchtime was a problem, too. If I did not bring my lunch, I had to go to a fast-food restaurant that was expensive and served terrible food. There were no fringe benefits, no health insurance, no reimbursement for uniforms, not even free parking. The worst thing was that I not only had to do x-ray work, but also practically everything that had to be done—from answering the phone to bringing the doctor coffee.

In the hospital, where I am working now, I am also very busy, but the job is more satisfying. I work with many patients and doctors. Since the hospital is a nonprofit organization, no one makes me hurry, and I am able to take my time with each patient. I talk with the patients and learn from their medical history. I do not feel as though I am the only person doing the work because the staff is large enough to share all the work required. Also, the doctors are nice and compliment us often on a job well done. There are other good things, too, like the fact that lunchtime is no longer a problem. The cafeteria is convenient and the prices are reasonable. Parking costs employees only fifty cents a day, and as long as I continue to work full time, my health insurance is fully paid. The best thing about the job is that I am not given a lot of extra work. All I am required to do is x-ray the patients and show a lot of interest in each of them.

I am glad I had the chance to experience both places of work because now I know which is more fulfilling.

Questions for Discussion and Writing

1. Does the author successfully support the thesis statement? Can you think of a more effective way of phrasing the thesis statement?
2. Read the essay aloud to see if it has been smoothly written. Are the details incorporated effectively enough that they do not sound like a list?
3. Is the transition sentence at the beginning of the third paragraph effective? Should there be other "reminders" of the work in the doctor's office in the third paragraph? Or does the parallel structure allow the reader to think of both jobs together?
4. Should the author have added any details to the introduction? If so, what details?

Exercise 8–1

In the spaces provided, list the details in the second and third paragraphs of the essay "Two Medical Jobs" to see if they are successfully presented in a parallel manner.

Paragraph 2	*Paragraph 3*
1. _____	1. _____
2. _____	2. _____
3. _____	3. _____
4. _____	4. _____

The following essay by Tom Wolfe, "Columbus and the Moon," illustrates the similarities between the early years of the National Aeronautics and Space Administration (NASA) space program and the voyages of Christopher Columbus. As you read this piece, notice the way Wolfe uses the *point-by-point comparison* method to organize his ideas.

Method B: Columbus and the Moon

The National Aeronautics and Space Administration's moon landing 10 years ago today was a Government project, but then so was Columbus's voyage to America in 1492. The Government, in Columbus's case, was the Spanish Court of Ferdinand and Isabella. Spain was engaged in a sea race with Portugal in much the same way that the United States would be caught up in a space race with the Soviet Union four and a half centuries later.

The race in 1492 was to create the first shipping lane to Asia. The Portuguese expeditions had always sailed east, around the southern tip of Africa. Columbus decided to head due west, across open ocean, a scheme that was feasible only thanks to a recent invention—the magnetic ship's compass. Until then ships had stayed close to the great land masses even for the longest voyages. Likewise, it was only thanks to an invention of the 1940's and early 1950's, the high-speed electronic computer, that NASA would even consider propelling astronauts out of the Earth's orbit and toward the moon.

Both NASA and Columbus made not one but a series of voyages. NASA landed men on six different parts of the moon. Columbus made four voyages to different parts of what he remained convinced was the east coast of Asia. As a result both NASA and Columbus had to keep coming back to the Government with their hands out, pleading for refinancing. In each case the reply of the Government became, after a few years: "This is all very impressive, but what earthly good is it to anyone back home?"

Columbus was reduced to making the most desperate claims. When he first reached land in 1492 at San Salvador, off Cuba, he expected to find gold, or at least spices. The Arawak Indians were awed by the strangers and their ships, which they believed had descended from the sky, and they presented them with their most prized possessions, live parrots and balls of cotton. Columbus soon set them digging for gold, which didn't exist. So he brought back reports of fabulous riches in the form of manpower, which is to say, slaves. He was not speaking of the Arawaks, however. With the exception of criminals and prisoners of war, he was supposed to civilize all natives and convert them to Christianity. He was talking about the

Carib Indians, who were cannibals and therefore qualified as criminals. The Caribs would fight down to the last unbroken bone rather than endure captivity, and few ever survived the voyages back to Spain. By the end of Columbus's second voyage, in 1496, the Government was becoming testy. A great deal of wealth was going into voyages to Asia, and very little was coming back. Columbus made his men swear to return to Spain saying that they had not only reached the Asian mainland, they had heard Japanese spoken.

Likewise by the early 1970s, it was clear that the moon was in economic terms pretty much what it looked like from Earth, a gray rock. NASA, in the quest for appropriations, was reduced to publicizing the "spinoffs" of the space program. These included Teflon-coated frying pans, a ballpoint pen that would write in a weightless environment, and a computerized biosensor system that would enable doctors to treat heart patients without making house calls. On the whole, not a giant step for mankind.

In 1493, after his first voyage, Columbus had ridden through Barcelona at the side of King Ferdinand in the position once occupied by Ferdinand's late son, Juan. By 1500, the bad-mouthing of Columbus had reached the point where he was put in chains at the conclusion of his third voyage and returned to Spain in disgrace. NASA suffered no such ignominy, of course, but by July 20, 1974, the fifth anniversary of the landing of Apollo 11, things were grim enough. The public had become gloriously bored by space exploration. The fifth anniversary celebration consisted mainly of about 200 souls, mostly NASA people, sitting on folding chairs underneath a camp meeting canopy on the marble prairie outside the old Smithsonian Air Museum in Washington listening to speeches by Neil Armstrong, Michael Collins, and Buzz Aldrin and watching the caloric waves ripple.

Extraordinary rumors had begun to circulate about the astronauts. The most lurid said that trips to the moon, and even into earth orbit, had so traumatized the men, they had fallen victim to religious and spiritualist manias or plain madness. (Of the total 73 astronauts chosen, one, Aldrin, is known to have suffered from depression, rooted, as his own memoir makes clear, in matters that had nothing to do with space flights. Two teamed up in an evangelical organization, and one set up a foundation for the scientific study of psychic phenomena—interests the three of them had developed long before they flew in space.) The NASA budget, meanwhile, had been reduced to the light-bill level.

Columbus died in 1509, nearly broke and stripped of most of his honors as Spain's Admiral of the Ocean, a title he preferred. It was only later that history began to look upon him not as an adventurer who had tried and failed to bring home gold—but as a man with a supernatural sense of destiny, whose true glory was his willingness to plunge into the unknown, including the remotest parts of the universe he could hope to reach.

NASA still lives, albeit in reduced circumstances, and whether or not history will treat NASA like the admiral is hard to say.

The idea that the exploration of the rest of the universe is its own reward is not very popular, and NASA is forced to keep talking about things such as bigger communications satellites that will enable live television transmission of European soccer games at a fraction of the current cost. Such notions as "building a bridge to the stars for mankind" do not light up the sky today—but may yet.

Questions for Discussion and Writing

1. Make a list of the points of comparison that Wolfe's essay makes about NASA and Columbus's explorations. Which point gets the most development in the essay? Why?

2. What is Wolfe's purpose in comparing NASA's efforts with respect to the space program and Columbus's voyage? Is the comparison worth making?

3. What is Wolfe's attitude about the "spinoffs" NASA publicized to gain support for the space program? Can you think of other benefits from space exploration that have been realized since Wolfe wrote his essay in 1979?

4. Identify the transitions Wolfe uses in his essay and point out where they appear. Would the essay be improved with more transitions? If so, which ones, and where should they occur?

5. What is the thesis statement for this essay? Is it effective? Suggest different wording of your own for the thesis.

Writing Assignment 8-2:
A Comparison and Contrast Essay
(Method A or B)

Write a comparison and contrast essay of four to six paragraphs about any two of the following paired subjects. Choose your topic by listing pairs of possible subjects on a separate piece of notebook paper. Place your possible subjects opposite each other, as this first example shows:

1. Two jobs I have held

   _____   _____
                    (job A)   (job B)

2. Two relatives or friends I know well
3. Two places I have lived
4. Two famous athletes in the same sport
5. Two houses of worship or religious centers
6. Two famous singers or musicians
7. Two opposing political candidates
8. Two popular magazines covering the same subjects
9. Two teachers I have known
10. Two very different styles of dress

After you have completed listing the possible pairs for comparison or contrast, choose one pair for your essay topic.

Now use the activities of the Writing Process and the suggestions that follow to plan, write, and revise your comparison and contrast essay.

Gather Your Ideas and Information: On a separate working page, brainstorm to generate ideas about the pair of subjects you selected. First, make two separate columns. Then, in the left-hand column, write down everything that comes to mind when you think of the first subject in your comparison. In the right-hand column, write down everything that comes to mind when you think about the second subject. Try to think of specific examples as well as descriptive details.

Next, connect similar items. In brainstorming for the first sample, the student wrote the following details and connected similar items in the comparison with numbers:

Work in the Hospital	Work in the Doctor's Office
lots of doctors	one doctor
good lunches	had to do many jobs
time for patients	(bring coffee, answer phone)
nonprofit organization	no parking
hospitalization insurance	"Get 'em in" and "get 'em out"
good parking	
professional treatment	

Now go back over your list and think about the items you did not connect. See if you can think of a detail that corresponds with an unconnected item and add it to your list. In the example given here, three items in the left-hand column were not connected. The student added the following to the right-hand column to correspond to those items:

good lunches	poor lunches in fast-food restaurants
nonprofit organization	everything for a profit
health insurance	no health insurance

Analyze Your Ideas and Information: Look over both lists and identify the most important items. Which items might be grouped together, and which items might be omitted? Which of the two subjects in your comparison do you prefer? Why? Has your preference changed in recent months or years? If so, you may want to write in your essay about the reason for this change.

Identify Your Theme or Main Point: On your work page, write a thesis statement that compares or contrasts your two subjects. Name both subjects of the comparison and contrast in your thesis statement, and state your opinion of the two subjects when you think of them together.

Here are some examples of suitable thesis statements for a comparison and contrast essay:

Shopping without money can be more exciting than shopping with money.

No twins could be more opposite than Joanne and Christine.

High school teaching was related to our experience, but college teaching is focused on the theoretical.

Bill Walton was a good basketball player, but Kareem Abdul-Jabbar was great.

My children see me as serious, but I am actually full of fun.

Plan Your Essay: Using the criteria given here, choose either Method A or Method B to organize your essay. Use examples to support and develop your thesis statement. On a separate piece of paper, outline your essay according to either Method A or Method B.

If you use Method A, the beginning of your outline would look like this:

_____

(your title)

_____

PARAGRAPH 1   *Introduction, including thesis statement*

_____

(detail)

PARAGRAPH 2   *Organizing principle (item 1)*

1. _____
   (detail)

2. _____
   (detail)

3. _____
   (detail)

PARAGRAPH 3   *Organizing principle (item 2)*

1. _____
   (detail)

2. _____
   (detail)

3. _____
   (detail)

And so on. You will need to plan as many paragraphs and details in the paper as your ideas call for.

If you choose to follow Method B in organizing your essay, the beginning of your outline will look like this:

_____

(your title)

_____

PARAGRAPH 1   *Introduction, including thesis statement*

_____

(detail)

PARAGRAPH 2   *Organizing principle*

_____

(item 1) (detail)

_____

(item 2) (detail)

PARAGRAPH 3   *Organizing principle*

_____

(item 1) (detail)

_____

(item 2) (detail)

As with Method A, you should plan as many paragraphs and details as the material in your brainstorming list indicates. Be sure to use examples and descriptive details with each item.

Write Your Essay: Although a comparison and contrast paper is highly structured, your writing does not have to sound rigid or contrived. Use either Method A or Method B to structure your essay, write clear transitions, and make your constructions parallel wherever possible. Remember, though, that you are speaking to your readers through your writing, so make sure it flows smoothly.

Revise and Edit Your Essay: Evaluate your paper by asking the following questions:

1. Did you express an *opinion* in your thesis statement? What was it?
2. If you used Method A, did you present your details in a parallel manner?
3. If you used Method B, check the transitions in the middle of the paragraphs in the body of the paper. Do they help the reader move easily from the first subject in your comparison to the second?

4. When you read the paper aloud, does it sound like you? If not, where in the essay does the writing not sound like you? Why not? Can you revise it so that it does?
5. Now revise your entire paper by using the STSOE guidelines.

Writing Assignment 8-3:
A Comparison and Contrast Essay
(Method A or B)

Choose another topic from the list provided for Writing Assignment 8-2. Write a second comparison and contrast essay with the organizational method that you did not use in Writing Assignment 8-2. (If you used Method A to organize your essay for Writing Assignment 8-2, use Method B this time.)

Follow the suggestions in Writing Assignment 8-2 to write your essay.

Classifying

Classifying is a means of organizing. When you *classify*, you place different items into separate categories so that all items sharing a certain characteristic are grouped together. The yellow pages of a telephone book list restaurants according to the kinds of food they serve—Mexican, French, Italian, Chinese, Indian, and so on. A future bride or groom might classify various wedding guests as friends of the bride, friends of the groom, and friends of both the bride and groom. A video store classifies its hundreds of titles under headings such as new releases, musicals, horror, sci-fi, adult, drama, or adventure. In short, people use classification any time they need to organize or separate items into convenient groupings.

Classification as a writing technique organizes items included in a large, broad category into smaller, separate categories according to their similarities. Let's say you decide to review your home library to find a way of organizing all the various books you own. You might classify the *kinds of books* you have in the following manner:

Textbooks	*Reference Books*	*Books for Pleasure*
Algebra II	*Webster's Dictionary*	*A Tale of Two Cities*
Handbook of English	*World Atlas*	*The Adventures of*
Beginning Spanish	*Guide to Synonyms*	*Huckleberry Finn*
Using Computers		*Lost Planets*
		Clan of the Cave Bear
		Poetry for Today
		Of Mice and Men
		The Color Purple
		The Kitchen God's Wife

Like comparison and contrast, classification identifies some items as similar and others as different. As you can see from the example, classification allows you to place items that share a certain characteristic together within separate categories, in this case "textbooks," "reference books," and "books for pleasure."

Although there is no one way to classify anything, observing certain steps and criteria can help you avoid problems in using this technique in your writing. You may find the following guidelines helpful in learning how to classify:

Start with a Principle of Classification: When you decide on a subject or area that you want to classify into convenient groupings, the first step is to select a *principle of classification* by which to organize the items included in that subject. In the example of the books in your home library, the principle of classification is the *kinds of books* you own. This principle guides the grouping of all the different books into the categories of "textbooks," "reference books," and "books for pleasure." If you wanted to classify your books by a different principle of classification, you could adopt one of the following categories: *how they were acquired, how often they are read,* or *how much they cost.*

As these examples demonstrate, a subject may be organized according to more than one principle of classification. However, you cannot classify your books by what kinds they are and by how much they cost *at the same time.* Use only one principle of classification each time you classify—to organize items by more than one principle of classification would only leave everything as mixed up as when you started. The principle you choose to classify items depends on your purpose.

State the Principle of Classification at the Beginning: Always inform your reader of the principle of classification you are using at the beginning of your classification paragraph or essay. If your principle of classification, for example, was *kinds of friends,* you might begin by stating, "Although everyone has different kinds of friends, mine fall into three groups." If your principle of classification in a discussion about grades was *ways to study for a test,* you might want to say something like "Several good ways to study for a test include. . . ."

Classify by Categories: Once you have decided on a principle of classification for your subject, you should arrange the items included by that principle into *classification categories.* In the example given earlier, using *kinds of books* as a principle of classification produced the classification categories of "textbooks," "reference books," and "books for pleasure." If you chose one of the other principles of classification suggested, you would have an entirely different group of classification categories. Depending on whether you used *(1) how they were acquired, (2) how often they are read,* or *(3) how much they cost* as principles of classification, your books would be grouped into the following categories:

Books I Purchased	Read Often	$5–$15
Books Given to Me	Occasionally Read	$15–$25
Books I Borrowed	Never Read	$25 and Over

As these examples show, the classification categories you generate should fit together logically and should occur in the same or parallel forms.

Include Appropriate Classification Categories: When you decide on the categories for your classification, be sure to include all the essential, obvious ones. Try not to omit categories or include any that are not consistent with your principle of classification. For example, leaving out "reference books" while classifying the *kinds of books* you own would make the classification incomplete. At the same time, including a category such as "magazines" would be inconsistent with the other categories and the principle of classification, kinds of books. Finally, make sure that your categories do not overlap: Adding a category titled "nonfiction" would include books already classified under "textbooks" and "reference books." Remember that the purpose of classification is to separate items, not to mix them in new ways.

Including too many categories in a classification discussion can force you to treat each of them superficially. If you find you have too many classification categories to discuss in a single composition, you may find it necessary to revise your principle of classification. In classifying the books you own, for instance, you might decide that the principle of classification *how much they cost* generates too many categories. On the other hand, you may want your classification discussion to include mention of several expensive books that you own. Changing to a different principle of classification, such as *valuable books,* can generate fewer classification categories that still fit your needs: "expensive books," "very useful books," and "irreplaceable books."

The following paragraph demonstrates a principle of classification and appropriate classification categories as a way of organizing a discussion of neighborhood gangs. The author uses *types of neighborhood gang members* as a principle of classification. He then develops the paragraph by naming three classification categories and illustrating each of them with descriptive examples.

Neighborhood Gangs

Principle of classification

Classification categories

Example

Example

Example

Many people do not realize that the members of most neighborhood gangs are not equally involved in or dedicated to the gang. Most neighborhood gangs are composed of three different kinds of members, ranging from spontaneous members, to occasionally active members, to a few hardcore, active leaders. The spontaneous members are those who just happen to be around the gang at a particular time, like someone who may be visiting a friend, who is temporarily recruited by the gang, or who is just interested in a single, particular activity at the time. The other group of gang members, the occasionally active ones, belong more out of pride than real interest. They like being known as part of a gang, and they join in gang activities when they have to in order to give their membership with the gang credibility. The last type, the hard-core members, are consistently active as a gang. They are the most dangerous because they lead the others into performing unlawful activities out of their own self-interests and as a way of unifying the gang with a sense of shared guilt.

Use Your Main Point to Identify Categories: In your topic sentence or thesis statement, give your overall view of the individual classification categories.

Remember that a topic sentence or thesis statement is an *opinion* to be supported or explained. Avoid classification statements such as "There are four kinds of soap operas" or "Snakes, lizards, and turtles are the three most common kinds of reptiles." Instead—just as in writing a description—generate a subjective statement that reflects a dominant impression of your subject. Here are three sample thesis statements that offer subjective views on college teachers:

> Although most of our teachers seem interested in students, others seem either indifferent or downright hostile.

> Teaching ability has little to do with whether the teacher is a graduate assistant, an instructor, or a full professor.

> Teachers vary in using too much or too little structure, although most use just the right amount.

Make Full Use of Examples: You must be particularly careful in classification writing to describe each category fully so that your reader sees why it has been included in the classification. Let's say that your principle of classification is *types of friends* and that one such type is "fun-loving." If you identify your friend Shirley as fun-loving, give examples of her behavior to show that you have put her in the correct category.

When possible, present details for each category in a way that parallels the details in other categories.

Inexperienced Teachers	*Moderately Experienced Teachers*	*Highly Experienced Teachers*
1. The way they lecture	1. The way they lecture	1. The way they lecture
2. The way they test	2. The way they test	2. The way they test
3. The way they deal with students	3. The way they deal with students	3. The way they deal with students
4. A particular example	4. A particular example	4. A particular example

As much as you can, you should present the same number of details for each category you describe.

Use Transitions Between Categories and Examples: As you write your classification paragraph or essay, use transitions to introduce categories and to compare or contrast them. As a general rule, the transition sentences that introduce each category should parallel each other.

TOPIC SENTENCE OR THESIS STATEMENT

In spite of the large number of pitchers in the major leagues today, there are basically only three types.

TRANSITION SENTENCE

The first type of pitcher relies on his fastball.

TRANSITION SENTENCE

The next type of pitcher uses the curveball all he can.

TRANSITION SENTENCE

The last kind of pitcher throws the screwball.

These transition sentences are roughly parallel because each begins with a type of pitcher followed by a description of what kind of pitch he throws.

Whenever you can, avoid transitions that are too monotonous or expected. Counting (*first, second, third,* . . .) is useful in longer essays, but marking transitions in only this way for your reader can make your writing boring. Use variation to introduce your classification categories:

TOPIC SENTENCE ON THESIS STATEMENT

I have several good reasons for going to the library every night: I like to browse, study, socialize, and nap there.

TRANSITION SENTENCE

I go there to browse because I like the surprise of discovering an unexpected good book.

TRANSITION SENTENCE

Naturally, I also go to the library to study.

TRANSITION SENTENCE

Whenever I get tired of browsing or studying in the library, you will find me socializing with friends.

TRANSITION SENTENCE

If I get tired of doing all the above, my favorite activity in the library is to curl up in a big chair for a nap.

Writing a Classification Essay

Classification essays include three main components: a *principle of classification,* appropriate *classification categories,* and their descriptive *examples.* The classification essay gives you space to thoroughly develop examples, make comparisons, and analyze the subject for your reader. The following sample essay demonstrates the major components of a classification essay.

Unwanted Campers

I was a forest ranger for sixteen years and got to know a lot about how people act when they are away from home. Although most people you meet while camping are delightful to know, there are a few you want to avoid all you can when you camp. Some types of bad campers, like the two I call the City Camper and the Helpless One, are just plain annoying; another, whom I call the Destroyer, just does not belong in the woods.

The City Camper is the most irritating type to be around. This kind of camper thinks it is somehow a sign of cleverness to have all the luxuries of home when he camps—and to display them proudly every chance he gets. He will probably drive up in a truck loaded down with everything from a portable barbecue to a miniature Ping-Pong table. While everyone else is cooking stew or roasting hot dogs over a fire, he is the one who drives into town and brings back a pizza from the local deli. He is also the one whose portable radio blasts all day and night, and who ignores your irritated stare by turning up the volume. I remember a camper like this at Yellowstone National Park one year. He actually had an old green overstuffed chair he had brought with him to lounge in all day. At night, he watched a portable television set that he had also brought with him. I am sure he must sometimes have forgotten that he was even in the woods.

Another kind of camper, what I call the Helpless One, is just the opposite of the City Camper. The Helpless One never comes prepared with anything. He drives up to a campsite in his small sports car like he is just stopping to check out the view. The next thing you know, he pulls a single blanket out of the trunk, stares long and hard at the heavy jacket or sweater you are wearing, and then asks if it gets cold at night. He has soon borrowed that jacket or sweater, as well as your axe, some firewood, and maybe your lantern in case he wants to go down by the lake while you are just sitting around your camp. Being humane, you will of course ask him to share your food, since he did not bring any of his own and because you get tired of his watching you eat without him. Fortunately, the Helpless One usually leaves after one night, perhaps because he hopes to find someone even more generous than you at the next campground.

These two types are mere pests compared to the camper who thinks the forest is there to destroy, however. The Destroyer treats the woods like a mischievous child treats a toy he cannot operate: Unable to enjoy it, he decides to wreck it all he can. The Destroyer spends the day chopping trees and even road signs to pieces for firewood or tearing up and down the hillsides in his four-wheel-drive vehicle. At night he gets drunk around the campfire because he does not know how to make use of or appreciate where he is. The Destroyer's campfire roars just inches beneath low, overhanging trees, ready to ignite a blaze that could burn down the entire woods. The odd thing is, the Destroyer often boasts about how at home he is in the woods and how much he enjoys camping. Yet you will see him carving his name into a tree or beating down cattails with a stick every chance he gets. Beer cans litter his campsite. After he has left, I think even the forest breathes a sigh of relief.

What makes people like this come to the woods in the first place? My guess is that they do not come to the woods for any reason at all, except they are bored with staying at home. I would even bet that the City Camper, the Helpless One, and the Destroyer are just as irritating, in different ways, to their neighbors back in the city.

Questions for Discussion and Writing

1. What is the thesis statement of this essay?
2. What is the principle of classification?
3. What categories make up this classification? Do the classification categories fit together logically?
4. What transitions does the author use between and within paragraphs?
5. How accurate does the author's description of the campers seem to you?

Writing Assignment 8-4:
A Classification Essay

Write a classification essay of five to seven paragraphs. First, for the topics listed here, fill in as many blanks as possible. Choose classes that fit together.

1. Types of college men or women

   _____   _____

   _____   _____

2. Types of mothers or fathers

   _____   _____

   _____   _____

3. Types of teachers in your college or high school

   _____   _____

   _____   _____

4. Types of problems elderly people or teenagers face

   _____   _____

   _____   _____

5. Types of pitchers in baseball, quarterbacks in football, or athletes in another sport.

   _____   _____

   _____   _____

6. Types of social classes in America or your native country (Try to focus on specific behaviors or traits, such as dress.)

   _____   _____

   _____   _____

7. Types of television series

_____   _____

_____   _____

8. Types of people in your neighborhood

_____   _____

_____   _____

9. Types of police officers, nurses, doctors, or other professionals

_____   _____

_____   _____

10. Types of music played on AM or FM radio stations or the types of music *within* a certain class, such as country music

_____   _____

_____   _____

11. Types of bosses

_____   _____

_____   _____

12. Types of opinions on subjects such as death, drugs, sex, or love

_____   _____

_____   _____

Discuss your classifications with others and check them with the instructor to see if they meet the criteria given on pages 157–161. Choose one topic to write on or generate a topic of your own.

Gather Your Ideas and Information: Brainstorm for details to describe and examples to illustrate each of the classes or divisions of the subject area you have chosen. In your brainstorming, include your opinions: what you like, what you do not like, what is most and least worthy of praise, and so forth.

Class One	*Class Two*
_____	_____
_____	_____
_____	_____
_____	_____
_____	_____

_____   _____
_____   _____
_____   _____
_____   _____

Class Three   *Class Four (Optional)*

_____   _____
_____   _____
_____   _____
_____   _____
_____   _____
_____   _____
_____   _____
_____   _____

General Brainstorming on the Topic

_____   _____
_____   _____
_____   _____
_____   _____

Analyze Your Ideas and Information: Have you chosen the best way to classify your material? Or do you need to rearrange your material in different classes? Check the information that is most important. What might you leave out? What might you add?

Identify Your Theme or Main Point: In one sentence, state your views on all the classes when considered together.

_____

_____

Here are some examples of thesis statements for the topics listed above:

All nurses perform valuable services.

We sometimes forget about the many problems elderly people face.

Of all the music played on AM stations, I like country music the most.

The chief petty officers run the Coast Guard.

Each type of boss is a tyrant in his or her own way.

The unusual teenager is the one who does not have serious problems.

Plan Your Essay: In outlining your essay, first try to make the transition sentences parallel to each other; second, try to present the details and examples in each paragraph in the body of the essay so that they are parallel to the details and examples in the other body paragraphs.

_____

(your title)

PARAGRAPH 1   Introduction _____

_____

(detail)

PARAGRAPH 2   _____

(transition sentence)

_____

1. _____   4. _____
   (detail and examples)

2. _____   5. _____

3. _____   6. _____

_____

PARAGRAPH 3   (transition sentence)

_____

1. _____   4. _____
   (detail and examples)

2. _____   5. _____

3. _____   6. _____

PARAGRAPH 4   _____

(transition sentence)

_____

1. _____   4. _____
   (detail and examples)

2. _____   5. _____

3. _____   6. _____

PARAGRAPH 5 _____

(transition sentence)

_____

1. _____   4. _____
   (detail and examples)

2. _____   5. _____

3. _____   6. _____

PARAGRAPH 6 **Conclusion** _____

_____

(detail)

Write Your Essay: Like the comparison and contrast essay, the classification es-say is highly structured. As you make use of the suggestions for parallel transitions and details, be careful not to lose sight of the main task, which is to say what you want to say in your writing. As you write, avoid sentences that begin as follows:

There are three types of . . .

The three types of problems are . . .

The trouble is that when you go to name the types, your sentences often become long and unwieldy, as shown below:

The three types of problems elderly people face are that their children often desert them, they live on a fixed income and every time the cost of living goes up they lose money, and many elderly people have illnesses or at least they cannot get around very well.

Simply say in your introductory paragraph that elderly people face many prob-lems. Each time you begin a new paragraph in the body of your essay, introduce one of the problems, as the example here demonstrates:

Elderly people face many problems. . . .

Many elderly people are lonely; often their children have deserted them. . . .

Another problem many elderly people have to deal with is living on a fixed in-come, which means that every time the cost of living goes up they lose money. . . .

Many elderly people also face the problem of not being able to get around very well. . . .

Revise and Edit Your Essay: Use the STSOE guidelines and ask yourself the following questions:

1. Did you state your opinion in your thesis statement?
2. Did you present your detail and examples in a roughly parallel way?
3. Did the classes of things you chose to write about fit together?

The Writing Process

GATHER your ideas and information
ANALYZE your ideas and information
IDENTIFY your theme or main point
PLAN your essay
WRITE your essay
REVISE AND EDIT your essay (STSOE)

9

Writing About Process ("How To") and Cause and Effect

How to Write a "How To"

Writing about a process is often called "how to" writing because you are explaining to a reader how to do or make something or you are describing the series of steps that make up a specific activity or process. In a college political science class, for example, you might be asked to explain, step by step, how a bill is enacted into law in the United States. In a biology class, you might be asked to describe the process of photosynthesis. In an education class, you might be asked to formulate a sequence of activities you would use to teach a blind person to ride a bus.

Writing about a process resembles writing a narrative because both types of writing are based on a chronological sequence—both, that is, describe events or actions as they unfold in time. When you write a narrative, you present events in the order in which they happened. When you write a process essay, you tell how to do or make something one step at a time from beginning to end.

You will find that, even more than with other types of writing, the art of explaining a process demands that you write succinctly—yet your writing also must be clear enough to guide your reader through all the necessary steps. Include descriptive details, personal anecdotes, and background and incidental information only to the extent that they contribute to explaining the process you are writing about. Keep your language simple and direct. The whole focus of your discussion must stay on the process itself, from beginning to end.

Think about the last set of instructions you read on a package label. These simple directions, which tell you how to do anything from cooking frozen green beans to assembling a computer, are models of process writing. The following directions for preparing a rather massive barbecue offer a good example of this most basic level of process writing:

> Here is how to barbecue enough meat for feeding 600 persons:
>
> Dig a pit about 16 feet long, 8 feet deep, and 8 feet wide. Cover the bottom with cobblestones or firebricks, and build an oak fire on this base. After six hours the coals should be ready for cooking. Hang a heavy wire netting half way down the pit; place the meat (cut roast size) on the matting. Lay wooden planks across the top, snugly butted together. Cover these with heavy canvas and seal the edge of the canvas and any steam jets with a layer of dirt. Let the meat roast for about six hours. This pit has the capacity for two prime beef two-year-old steers when prepared for barbecuing.

You should note that even though the writers of this sample (the editors of *Sunset* magazine) present the process with no introduction, you should open your own process description with a topic sentence or thesis that includes more than the bald statement "This is how you. . . ." For example, compare how the Danish writer Isak Dinesen (the pen name of Baroness Karen Blixen) presents her description of coffee-growing in her famous memoir, *Out of Africa:*

Coffee-growing is a long job. It does not all come out as you imagine, when, yourself young and hopeful, in the streaming rain, you carry the boxes of your shining young coffee-plants from the nurseries, and, with the whole number of farm-hands in the field, watch the plants set in the regular rows of holes in the wet ground where they are to grow, and then have them thickly shaded against the sun, with branches broken from the bush, since obscurity is the privilege of young things. It is four or five years till the trees come into bearing, and in the meantime you will get drought on the land, or diseases, and the bold native weeds will grow up thick in the fields—the black-jack, which has long scabrous seed-vessels that hang on to your clothes and stockings. Some of the trees have been badly planted with their tap-roots bent; they will die just as they begin to flower. You plant a little over six hundred trees to the acre, and I had six hundred acres of land with coffee; my oxen dragged the cultivators up and down the fields, between the rows of trees, many thousand of miles, patiently, awaiting coming bounties.

In this paragraph, the step-by-step information supports Dinesen's opening thesis: "Coffee-growing is a long job [that] does not all come out as you imagine." At the same time, she describes vividly and in sequence the tasks and hazards of the coffee-growing process. However, the primary goal of "how to" writing is to convince your readers that they could perform all the steps in the process just by following your directions. You will want to put more emphasis on the process itself than on your opinion about it, and for this reason, your topic sentence or thesis statement will usually be brief and simple.

No matter how familiar you may be with the process you undertake to write about, you will be surprised to find how much vital information you may leave out in your written description. Use the following guidelines to ensure that your process writing is effectively presented and *complete:*

Be Clear: Know who your audience will be, and keep this in mind while you are writing your "how to." Ask yourself if your readers could actually do what you are showing them how to do if all they knew of the subject was what you had written. Always break your process down into steps and define all terms that might be unclear to your audience. If, for example, you are writing to your class about how to master the skill of editing, you will need to define *editing* if the class has not yet talked about what it is.

Plan to Describe All Necessary Steps in Sufficient Detail: As you plan and write your process description, you can make sure that you have included all the steps in the process by following this procedure: First, start by brainstorming all the steps you can think of. Second, arrange these steps in their proper order. Third, visualize yourself performing the process. If you find in doing this that you omitted any steps, add them to your list.

Even a relatively simple process could conceivably be broken down into dozens of steps and substeps. How thoroughly should you divide the process? If you are writing a paragraph, you will probably have space enough only to list the major steps in the process. If you are writing an essay, you can probably divide each of the larger steps into smaller substeps for your readers. The number of *essential* steps involved in your process may determine whether you need to describe it in a paragraph or in an essay.

Describe Materials and Equipment Needed to Perform the Process: As you are identifying the steps in your process, make a point of listing all the materials and equipment necessary to complete them. Your process may require anything from a hammer and nails for mending an old fence to a quiet room, comfortable chairs, and a desk for studying with a friend. You should mention these items at the beginning of your discussion. If you are explaining how to make your favorite dish, for example, you will want to list all the ingredients first. If you are describing how to give a haircut, you must name the kinds of scissors and combs to have on hand. Never overestimate your readers' knowledge of the tools necessary to perform a given process. After all, if they knew that much about it, they would not need you to explain it. (However, use common sense, too. If you are explaining how to shoot free throws in basketball, you do not have to tell your readers that they will need a ball and a court.)

Give Advice, Too, Whenever Necessary: Besides telling your readers the tools they will need and the steps they must follow to complete a process, you may be obliged to offer advice as well. Think about those steps in your process where your reader may require special guidance or suggestions. If you are writing about haircutting, you may need to alert your readers to the specific hazards of cowlicks on some heads of hair and give them some tips on dealing with the problem if it arises. If you are describing a program for losing weight, you may need to encourage your readers with advice on the rewards of meeting long-term goals over giving in to short-term gratification.

   Useful tips do more than save a beginner time and frustration—they can also make the difference between success and failure when performing a process. Whenever you can, anticipate your readers' need for encouragement, a warning, or useful advice.

Use Transitional and Directional Words: In a process discussion, transitional and directional words do more than simply guide the reader; they also help to separate the steps of your process from other comments or advice. Here is how one student effectively described how to cook pasta by interweaving the directive words and phrases *then, also, next, while the pasta cooks,* and so on between various steps.

> Cooking great pasta is easy. The best way is to fill a big pot with 4 to 5 quarts of water and heat the water to a full, rolling boil. Then add a little salt, about a teaspoon. If you have any, also put in about one or two teaspoons of peanut or vegetable oil. The oil not only keeps the pasta from sticking together; it also prevents the water from boiling over the edge of the pot. Next, add the pasta a little at a time,

slowly, so that the water continues to simmer. The water will return to boiling once all the pasta has been added. While the pasta cooks, occasionally stir it with a wooden fork or spoon to keep the pieces separated. Be sure the utensil is wooden: A metal fork or spoon gets very hot and could burn you; plastic ones bend or melt in the hot water. The pasta is cooked when it's <u>al dente</u>, that is, "firm to the tooth." How will you know if it's <u>al dente?</u> Taste it. That's the only way!

However, be sure to vary your transitional words. Counting through too many steps ("Seventh, you unscrew the lid . . .") or presenting a series of sentences each opening with *Then* is a device that quickly becomes tedious to your readers.

Avoid "Recipe Language":   Because its language is lively and natural, the paragraph about cooking pasta demonstrates good style. As you write, give attention to presenting the process to your readers in an appropriate style. For instance, avoid a shorthand style of "recipe language" that may omit either words or standard grammatical constructions:

POOR
Use trowel to smooth cement until dry.

BETTER
Use a trowel to smooth the cement until it is dry.

POOR
Sign application and mail immediately.

BETTER
Sign the application and mail it immediately.

Address Your Reader Directly: An effective way of writing about a process, when appropriate—not, for example, when you are describing how a bill is enacted into law—is to talk to your readers as if they were following your instructions on the spot. In the body of your discussion, address your readers in the second person, as *you:* "When you glue . . . ," "Use your fingers to . . . ," "Put the lid on. . . . " Note that when you give instructions directly, the *you* is often understood: "Hold the handle down tightly. Now turn the latch." "Avoid spilling." Use meaningful transitions or directional words throughout to show that you are still directing your readers' performance of the tasks: "After you have finished cutting the bias . . . ," "The next step is to . . . ," and so on.

Writing Assignment 9-1:
A Process Paragraph

Write a paragraph of about 200 or more words that describes to your reader a process that you understand well. Select one of the following topics for your paragraph, or devise a topic of your own.

1. How to test-drive a car
2. How to dress well inexpensively
3. How to pick a ripe watermelon
4. How to buy a stereo
5. How to change a tire
6. How to housebreak your dog
7. How to find a job
8. How to enjoy a pizza
9. How to find a girlfriend (or boyfriend)
10. How to polish your nails

Now use the activities of the Writing Process and the accompanying suggestions to plan, write, and revise your paragraph.

Gather Your Ideas and Information: On a piece of notebook paper, brainstorm about your topic. Start by making two columns. List the steps involved in the first column; list the materials needed in the second. However, do not be too concerned about the order in which ideas occur to you. Just write down the various elements as you think of them. Now try to visualize the process as you would actually perform it in real life. Doing this will help you think of more steps to write down.

Analyze Your Ideas and Information: Now look over what you have written. Have you identified all the steps? Are they in the correct order? If not, think about how to rearrange them. What extra advice will your readers need to carry out these instructions? Check your list of materials and tools for this process. Have you included everything? Which steps require which items?

Identify Your Main Point: What point can you make about this process? Is it easy, complicated, frustrating, tiring, or challenging? State an opinion about the process that your discussion will support. Statements such as "Buying a good horse takes patience" or "Setting up an aquarium is easier than you think" would be appropriate. Be sure to state your main point in a single sentence.

Plan Your Paragraph: Decide whether the topic sentence would be most effectively placed at the beginning or the end of your paragraph. If you offer advice for this process, where will you fit it in the discussion?

Write Your Paragraph: Write your paragraph, including any necessary transitional or directional words and phrases. Avoid using "recipe language" and too many numbered steps.

Revise and Edit Your Paragraph: Use the STSOE guidelines to revise and edit your paragraph.

Writing a Process Essay

Not all processes can be explained clearly in a single paragraph or two. How to play tennis, how to plan a large dinner party, what steps to take to win a national election, how cocaine enters the country and then gets distributed, and how reforestation takes place after a major fire are examples of processes requiring more than a few hundred words to be of use to anyone. For subjects such as these, you will want to write a complete essay so that you can discuss the process and all its components as completely as possible.

Break a Complex Process into Simple Steps: The key to writing about larger, more complex processes is to break them down adequately into their component steps. First, think of each of the major steps involved in your process and write them down. Then divide each of these steps into smaller, less complicated steps. If you need to, reduce these smaller steps into even smaller ones, and so on. Break down any step in the process that your reader may not understand without the greater detail that substeps provide.

Let's say you are describing the process of driving a stick-shift car to someone who has never driven. You should divide an action like starting the engine, for example, into its necessary smaller steps: (1) making sure the car is in neutral, (2) inserting the key in the ignition, and (3) turning the key. However, notice that the first of these steps—making sure the car is in neutral—will need to be broken down still further for your beginning driver. You will need to tell him or her to put the car in neutral by stepping down on the clutch and then moving the gearshift.

You should plan your process essay by grouping related steps together in a chronological order. If you are writing about how to succeed in a job interview, for example, you might decide that one important step, "Research the company you might work for," is actually composed of several smaller steps, such as talking to present employees, reviewing end-of-the-year reports, and touring the facility. Each of the smaller steps would require a detailed explanation of its own. Check the sequence of steps you have identified, and shuffle the steps as necessary until you have them arranged in the correct order.

As you write your essay, you may find that certain steps require a whole paragraph or groups of paragraphs for a proper explanation. Other steps, large or small, may best be lumped together in a single paragraph or two.

Introduce Your Process Discussion Effectively: The first paragraph of your process essay, besides including your thesis statement, should probably state why it is important to do or make the thing you are explaining or to follow the process you are describing. You also may want to mention your own background or qualifications for giving directions about the process. One student began her essay as follows:

> If you want to decorate your living room for a special occasion, try making a flower arrangement. I have worked at a florist shop for the last three years and have discovered what a nice touch a flower arrangement can add to a room. You will see just how easy it is to arrange flowers.

Like any essay, your process essay needs an appropriate thesis statement. The thesis for a process essay should indicate what you are going to explain and also state an opinion or judgment about it. In the sample, the student not only announced that she would describe how to make a flower arrangement but also stated that arranging flowers was easy. She has thus set herself two goals in her essay: first, to explain the steps of flower arranging, and second, to persuade the reader to accept her point of view—namely, that flower arranging is easy. If she had a different point of view about the process, she would need to state her purpose differently, perhaps in one of these versions:

Creating a good flower arrangement can transform your day.

Arranging flowers is a difficult but satisfying art.

Read the following process essay to see how its student author divided the process of changing the oil in a car into major steps and introduced his discussion by talking about the importance of the subject. As you read the essay, ask yourself if you could change the oil in your car by following the instructions. You may even want to try doing it!

How to Change the Oil in Your Car

With prices as they are today, people are trying to figure out all kinds of ways to economize. As a result, many Americans want to learn how to do simple maintenance on their own cars. Changing your own oil is a way you can save money. If you were to take your car to a garage for an oil change, you would find that a mechanic would charge you about fifteen dollars and maybe keep the car for a whole day. What many people do not realize is that you can change the oil yourself for about eight dollars and fifteen minutes of your time. So for those who do not know how to change the oil in their car, here is how it is done.

To begin, you will need to gather all the necessary equipment. You will need a jack, a blanket or a creeper to lie on, a wrench to fit the nut on the oil pan, an oil filter wrench, a bucket to catch the oil, an oil filter, and new oil. Ask a salesperson at an auto supply store to help you pick out the right wrenches, oil filter, and oil. You will regain the cost of all these items through the money you save by changing your own oil a few times.

When you have all your equipment, start your car and let the engine run about five minutes to get the oil warm. Turn the motor off and put on the emergency brake. Then put the car up on blocks, jacking it up just high enough so that you can fit under it without any trouble. Before you get under the car, make sure that the bucket, the wrenches for the oil pan nut, and the oil filter are all close by. If you have a creeper (a small wooden platform on wheels), use it to slide under the car, but if you do not, throw an old blanket on the ground to prevent your clothes from getting dirty.

Once you are under the car, look for the oil pan, behind the radiator, under the engine block. At the corner of the pan there is a nut about one-half inch wide. Put the bucket under the nut and loosen it. Be careful because the oil may be hot. After the nut is off, let the oil drain into the bucket for about five minutes. Put the nut back on and make sure it is tight.

Now look for the oil filter. It is next to the oil pan and is about the size of a man's wrist. It should be only hand tight, but if not, use the oil filter wrench to take it off. Some oil will still be in the filter; let it drain. Now you have the option of either keeping the old filter or using the new one. (You should change the filter at least every other oil change.) If you decide to put on the new filter, take a little of the old oil and rub it on the rubber gasket around the filter to make a better seal. Tighten the filter only hand tight as you screw it in.

Finally, to put fresh oil in the engine, raise the hood and look on the side of your engine for a cap that screws into the engine block. It usually says "oil." Take the cap off and put the right amount of oil in your engine, usually four or five quarts. After the oil is in the car, open the door on the driver's side and start the engine without getting in the car. (It's still up on jacks, remember.) Run the engine for a few minutes and examine the nut and the oil filter to see if any leaks have formed. If not, turn off the engine, lower your car from the jack, and put the equipment away.

That's all there is to it. As you can see, changing your own oil is not difficult at all, and it can save you money.

Questions for Discussion and Writing

1. Identify the steps involved in changing the oil on a car. Were the larger steps sufficiently broken down into smaller ones?
2. What materials and tools does the essay indicate are needed to change a car's oil?
3. What advice does the author of this essay offer the reader? Are there any places where more advice would have been helpful?
4. Identify transitional and directional words used in the essay.

 ## Writing Assignment 9-2:
A Process Essay

Write a process essay of six to eight paragraphs in length. Use this page to choose your topic by brainstorming as many specific topics as you can under the following headings. Suggested sample topics are provided for the first five headings.

   1. How to do something related to automobiles—how to jump-start the engine

     _____   _____

     _____   _____

   2. How to do something related to sports—how to win the half mile

     _____   _____

     _____   _____

   3. How to do something relating to homemaking—how to make a blouse

     _____   _____

     _____   _____

4. How to do something relating to music or art—how to write a song

_____   _____

_____   _____

5. How to do something relating to pets—how to train a rabbit

_____   _____

_____   _____

Or consider brainstorming about one of these topics:

6. How to teach a child to swim
7. How to succeed (or not succeed) in the military
8. How to survive in college
9. How to make your first million
10. How to spend a rainy weekend
11. How to catch a big fish
12. How to plan a party
13. How to make friends with a stranger
14. How to buy a car
15. How to cut your own hair

Now use the activities of the Writing Process and the accompanying suggestions to plan, write, and revise your essay.

Gather Your Ideas and Information: This is probably the most important step in a process essay. On a lined piece of notebook paper, draw a line to make two separate columns. In the left-hand column, make a list of the steps your reader must do or follow to perform what you are describing.

Next, look at each step carefully to see if you need to include additional steps, steps within steps, or steps between steps. Write these in the right-hand column. Remember to keep your directions simple but clear.

Now look over your list and see what equipment or materials your reader will need. Write these items down in a separate list on your paper.

Analyze Your Ideas and Information: Decide what steps you can group together so that you will not have too many small segments or paragraphs in your process essay. Make sure that your list of equipment and materials is complete. Plan a strategy for handling vocabulary. Are there any terms you will need to define? What steps will be particularly hard to explain? Should any steps be deleted?

Identify Your Main Point: Write a thesis statement that identifies and states an opinion about the process you will describe. Here are some sample thesis statements for other process papers:

Preparing for a hiking trip can be almost as much fun as the trip itself.

Giving your dog a bath is a more complicated operation than you might think.

You have to be very careful when you are charging a battery with jumper cables.

Plan Your Essay: Decide what you will include in your introduction, and then group the individual steps in a logical way. Decide if you will discuss equipment or material in the introduction or the body. Will you need to mention these items again later in the paper? Plan to have at least one paragraph for each major step in the process. On your planning page, list the step and details included in that major step under each individual paragraph heading.

Write Your Essay: As you write, try to be perfectly clear. Be sure to use transitional and directional words and phrases such as "Start by . . . ," "After . . . ," "Then . . . ," and so on. Remember that you are *talking* to a reader, not just making a list. Avoid "recipe language" and a monotonous "First . . . , second . . . , third . . ." way of listing to introduce each step.

Revise and Edit Your Essay: Read your draft over to make sure that the process you have described is clear and complete. Use the STSOE guidelines to be sure you have completed everything in the paper as you intended. Also ask yourself the following questions:

1. Is every step of the essay clear? If not, where is it not clear? What can I do to make it clear?
2. Does my purpose statement tell readers what I want to say about the topic?
3. Does the paper sound choppy when I read it aloud? If so, at what point do I notice the choppiness? How might I correct it?

   When checking your grammar, watch for two kinds of errors that often appear in this type of essay—pronoun shifts and run-on sentences.

■ *Pronoun person shifts.* Do not change the person of a pronoun within the same sentence unless you have a valid reason for doing so. (See Chapter 18.5.) What is the error in the following sentence?

   One has to walk very slowly, breathing deeply, if you are going to make it to the top.

■ *Run-on sentences.* You cannot join two sentences or independent clauses with *then* or *next* only, but you can join them with a comma and the conjunction *and* or with a semicolon. (See Chapter 22.2.) The following is a run-on sentence. Correct it.

   First, you make a white sauce, then you begin slowly adding water.

How to Write About Cause and Effect

When you write about a process, you are describing a sequence of actions or events that brings about a specific result. Similarly, when you write about cause and effect, you are also describing events that produce a result. Process writing and cause-and-effect writing differ mainly in their emphasis. Process writing focuses mainly on describing the *sequence* of events leading to the result. Cause-and-effect writing focuses on *why* one event causes another event to occur. When you write about cause and effect, you are concerned with relationships among actions and events—how one action creates, destroys, changes, or influences a second to produce a specific outcome.

In his memoir *Hunger of Memory,* Hispanic writer Richard Rodriguez, a native Spanish speaker, describes the surprising effect that learning to speak English had on him.

> After English became my primary language, I no longer knew what words to use in addressing my parents. The old Spanish words (those tender accents of sound) I had used earlier—*mamá* and *papá*—I couldn't use anymore. They would have been too painful reminders of how much had changed in my life. On the other hand, the words I heard neighborhood kids call *their* parents seemed equally unsatisfactory. *Mother* and *Father; Ma, Papa, Pa, Dad, Pop* (how I hated the all-American sound of that last word especially)—all these terms I felt were unsuitable, not really terms of address for *my* parents. As a result, I never used them at home. Whenever I'd speak to my parents, I would try to get their attention with eye contact alone. In public conversations, I'd refer to "my parents" or "my mother and father."

Like Rodriguez, we all use cause-and-effect analysis as a way of understanding events in our daily lives. Sometimes we know that an event will lead to something, but we are uncertain about what that something may be. For instance, you might know of a couple having marriage problems and not be sure of the outcome of those problems. In cases such as this, we know a cause but not its effect (or effects). In other instances, we may know of the effect (or effects) in advance of the cause (or causes). You may know that your tropical fish are sick (an effect), for example, but you may not know why (the cause). If you change the filter in their tank and notice a rapid improvement, you have probably determined the cause of their illness.

Cause

Because effects are usually more observable to us than the factors that produced them, many cause-and-effect analyses focus on causes. The idea of causation can be expressed in several ways: *why* the Civil War was fought, the *reasons* your friend Mary joined the Army, your *motivation* for going to college, what *brought about* the changes in a law, *what makes* a person commit a crime, what *produces* nuclear fusion.

Writers use causal analysis to describe why one person, event, or situation affects another or brings about a certain result. You will need to consider causes in your college courses when you are asked to write about the origins of the Russian Revolution or to tell why volcanos suddenly erupt after centuries of inactivity. Educators try constantly to determine what motivates some students to enjoy learning and others to drop out of school early.

Effect

Like a cause, an effect also can be described in various ways: the *consequences* of waiting too long to study for a test, the *outcome* of a lawsuit, the *results* of expanding commercial air traffic, a *development* arising from new environmental concerns, the *product* created by the process of clear thinking. Although some effects are known to us, they may require still better understanding or more emphasis because of their importance. In a science course, you may need to explain what effect ultraviolet light has on human skin; in an animal husbandry class, you may have to discuss the consequences of overfeeding certain livestock. We study unknown effects in order to understand their influence and potential as causes of other effects. A few years ago, the governments of several nations combined efforts to study the effects of industrial chemicals on the earth's ozone layer. The resulting research will undoubtedly lead to major changes in every country's use of industrial chemicals.

Types of Causes and Effects

Causes and their effects can be classified as either *immediate* or *remote*. To say that the fact that your car ran out of gas in the middle of traffic was caused simply by lack of gasoline would be leaving out other possible causes. What about the fact that the last gas station you passed was closed? Couldn't your own tendency to take risks (and thus knowingly let the gas level get low) also be a contributing factor? And what other consequences besides simply running out of gas are involved in this situation? You may block other cars or cause an accident; you may be late to class and miss a test; you may decide to be more careful in the future. To understand the full range of causes and effects in any given situation, you must analyze that situation thoroughly.

Immediate and Remote Causes: An *immediate cause* takes place just before a result emerges and is directly responsible for making that result occur. An immediate cause of your being in a restaurant may be to get something to eat, or it may be the result of wanting a job as a server. The fact that your car ran out of gas would be an immediate cause of your being late to class.

A *remote cause* is further removed from the effect it generates and may have a more profound importance than do immediate causes. Whereas the immediate cause of your being late to class may be that your car ran out of gas, the remote cause may be your lifelong habit of taking chances or not planning ahead.

Causes have degrees of immediacy and remoteness. For example, your habit of taking chances is a *more* remote cause of running out of gas than the fact that a nearby gas station was closed:

Running out of gas {

Remote Cause	More Remote Cause
Closed station	Taking chances

Immediate and Remote Effects: An *immediate effect* follows directly after an event, such as when your car suddenly comes to a halt because of lack of gasoline. A *remote effect,* on the other hand, comes long after its cause and after any immediate effects. Months after you run out of gas, you may find that your final grade in the class is lower because you missed an important lecture.

Immediate and remote effects also usually differ in their nature and seriousness. Smoking a cigarette has the immediate effect of increasing pulse rate, raising blood pressure, and decreasing appetite. But smoking also has the long-range effect of increasing one's chance for heart and lung disease. A negative effect like a large number of traffic accidents at an intersection near your house may have the remote positive effect of helping to get a traffic signal installed. Even seemingly unimportant events have immediate and remote consequences that may differ. For instance, dropping and breaking a glass produces a negative immediate effect, but it also produces a positive remote effect if it reinforces a sense of caution in other areas of your life.

Like causes, effects may be more or less immediate or remote in comparison with each other:

Immediate Effect	Remote Effect	More Remote Effect
Increased pulse	Shortness of breath	Heart and lung disease
Raised blood pressure		
Drop in appetite		

Cigarette smoking { (braces linking to the Immediate Effect column)

Using the Concepts of Immediate and Remote Causes and Effects: You should consider analyzing your topic to identify immediate and remote causes and effects during the prewriting activities of the Writing Process. Then, as you narrow your topic, you can determine how you will focus the discussion.

Usually your subject and purpose for writing will determine the extent to which you discuss either immediate or remote causes and effects. For example, the fact that someone dented your car's fender in a public parking lot is usually the only concern your insurance company will have in processing your claim. Remote causes such as lack of other parking spaces or the dense population of people and cars in your city would be irrelevant to understanding the cause of your accident. In this case, you are concerned only with providing the immediate cause (and immediate effect) of the accident.

More often, however, you will need to introduce the concepts of causes and effects as a way of developing a full and interesting discussion. Include those elements in your discussion that your reader will need to understand the topic fully. For instance, if you wanted to present the causes for your friend Douglas's sudden weight gain, you would start by describing his habit of eating pizzas or chocolate sundaes every day after classes. These are the *immediate causes* of his weight gain. However, your analysis would not be very useful if you stopped there. Considering the *remote causes* of the weight gain—low self-esteem, the recent loss of a girlfriend, an inherited tendency, or a lack of outside activity—also would be necessary for your cause-and-effect analysis to have practical value. Identifying the *remote effects* that being overweight can have on his personality and health also would be useful as a way of indicating the seriousness of the problem you are analyzing.

Patterns of Cause and Effect: Describing causes and effects accurately for your reader requires understanding how they occur and how to explain them clearly. There are several cause-and-effect patterns to consider when you analyze the relationship between an event and its cause or result:

- A single cause with a single effect:

  The heavy traffic made me late to work.

  The earthquake cracked the plaster on my wall.

- A single cause with multiple effects:

  The storm damaged crops, flooded roads, and caused schools to be closed.

  Exercise strengthens the heart, reduces blood pressure and stress, and helps you lose weight.

- Multiple causes with a single effect:

  Pruning and feeding roses regularly will produce more blooms.

  High blood pressure, stress, obesity, and lack of exercise all contribute to heart disease.

- Multiple causes with multiple effects:

  Drunk driving and speeding are the two biggest reasons for accidents and deaths on the highway.

  An unstable economy, lack of food and clothing, and a complete mistrust of the government led to riots in the capital and strikes in all the factories.

Notice that each of these statements of cause-and-effect patterns also could be used as the topic sentence for a paragraph or the thesis statement of an essay.

Causal Chain: In a *causal chain,* the individual causes of the effect or effects are linked to each other. The first cause produces the second, the second leads to the third, and so on. The causal chain may be *circular* in its pattern, such as when a company facing lower profits lays off several employees and then because of fewer employees produces less, a consequence that further lowers profits and leads to the laying off of more employees.

A causal chain also might be *successive,* whereby each effect becomes the cause for the next. The following paragraph describes a chain of successive causes.

Once Mike got promoted to production manager, his ambition increased. He went back to college for a master's degree in business administration and then used the degree to get a job with Smith & Taylor, a large manufacturing firm. His experience there gave him the expertise to start his own company three years ago, and he used the profits from that company to start two additional manufacturing plants and a retail store in Chicago.

Exercise 1

On a separate sheet of paper, list possible immediate and remote causes and effects for the following situations. When you have completed your responses, discuss them with your classmates. A sample response is provided here for the first situation.

1 The immediate and remote effects of taking a required class in art appreciation

IMMEDIATE
Satisfying graduation and transfer requirements; filling up your course load

REMOTE
Greater lifelong awareness of art and artists; feeling more self-assured around others who discuss art; background for a hobby someday; encouraging your children to like art

2. The immediate and remote effects of losing your wallet or purse
3. The remote causes of an argument with a friend
4. The remote effects of having learned a second language as a child
5. The immediate causes of a high grade-point average
6. The immediate and remote causes of someone not voting in political elections
7. The immediate and remote effects of someone not voting in political elections
8. The immediate effects of a law forbidding rock music
9. The remote causes of drug use in society
10. The remote effects of drug use on society

When you write about a cause-and-effect relationship, remember that you do not have to identify *every* cause and effect. In many cases, such comprehensiveness would be boring for your reader because it would provide unnecessary information. Your job is to think thoroughly and honestly about the causes and effects that you identify and then to explain their relationships to your reader. The following suggestions will help you decide which causes and effects are best to include in a given discussion:

Avoid Illogical Reasoning: Cause-and-effect relationships must be stated logically. That is, you should not misinterpret the relationship between a cause and its effect. One common kind of illogical reasoning is called *post hoc ergo propter hoc* (Latin for "after this, therefore, because of this"). This error in reasoning occurs when you notice that event *A* happened before event *B* and therefore assume that *A caused B.* Let's say it rained last Thursday morning and you also were fired from your job on Thursday afternoon. The first event (rain) happened before the second event (your getting fired), but the rain in the morning did not cause you to get fired.

Beware of mistaking an *associated condition* with either a cause or an effect in a given situation. You have to demonstrate the cause-and-effect relationship between events before claiming one caused or resulted from the other. If you claim that "U.S. foreign aid has caused the people in countries that receive aid to lose their self-respect," you must show that it is foreign aid that is responsible for this perceived condition. It is possible that the people in countries receiving U.S. foreign aid have indeed lost their self-respect. However, this loss may have resulted from causes other than U.S. foreign aid.

State the Cause and Effect as Your Main Point:　Your topic sentence or thesis statement should clearly state the relationship between causes and their effects. You do not always have to say boldly, "*A* causes *B,*" but your wording should indicate it. Here are some sample cause-and-effect statements that could serve as topic sentences for paragraphs or as thesis statements for essays:

> Requiring completion of a writing course during the first year of college will improve students' academic success.

> Ultimately, the lack of discipline disgusted her, and she left the college for good.

> Off-road vehicles are destroying our wilderness.

> We will not have a successful basketball season without Coach Winterford.

Order Causes and Effects Effectively:　Discuss causes and their effects in the order that makes them clearest for your reader. As a general rule, begin with the known and work to the less known. This tactic gives your content development. For example, if you are discussing a known effect such as a sudden increase in the numbers of students unable to get textbooks for their classes, start by describing that effect and then go into the probable cause for this unusual situation. Begin a discussion of oil pollution with known causes and occurrences; then focus the majority of your content on the immediate and remote effects.

Other ways to order content include treating causes and effects chronologically, such as when you first describe the causes of a water shortage and then explain its consequences. Another method of discussing cause and effect is by listing them in an increasing order of importance, treating the lesser causes of a water shortage first, then discussing the next most important causes, then the next, and so on. You could also begin with the most important causes and then discuss the less important ones before you discuss the effect of all of them. Whichever way you choose, be sure to consider the best order for your material during the planning stages of your writing or arrange parts effectively while you write. This way, you can determine the most effective order for your content.

Writing Assignment 9-3:
A Cause-and-Effect Paragraph

Write a cause-and-effect paragraph on one of the following topics (note that you will be writing primarily about either the causes or the effects):

1. Why you began or did not begin smoking cigarettes (causes)
2. The effects of moving to another city (effects)
3. What makes a certain store your favorite place to shop (causes)
4. What happened to change your attitude or feelings about another person (causes)
5. What factors brought you to the college you now attend (causes)
6. Why you practice a given sport or hobby (causes)
7. Events that have improved or damaged your self-assurance lately (causes)
8. The consequences that dropping out of college now would have for you (effects)
9. The impact a recent movie had on you (effects)
10. What ruined your last social engagement (causes)

Use the activities of the Writing Process to plan, write, and revise your cause-and-effect paragraph:

Gather your ideas and information

Analyze your ideas and information

Identify your main point

Plan your paragraph

Write your paragraph

Revise and edit your paragraph (STSOE)

Writing a Cause-and-Effect Essay

When you have a subject containing causes and effects that require a good deal of explaining, you will find the essay more suitable than the paragraph for developing your ideas. An essay provides the space to develop examples that illustrate cause-and-effect relationships more completely than a paragraph. For this reason, you will want to make sure that you have chosen a topic suitable for an essay.

Selecting the Right Topic for a Cause-and-Effect Essay: Not all cause-and-effect situations are equally easy to write about. A topic such as "What Causes Genius?" may require a fair amount of library research, whereas "Why I Am Me" is probably far too general to produce a good discussion. Topics that deal with the causes of major social problems such as AIDS or the effects of worldwide hunger are certainly appropriate for a cause-and-effect essay, but do not forget that they also require adequate time for research and planning.

Be sure not to overlook more familiar and personal subjects for writing. A topic such as "Why I Left Home" or "When I Quit Playing College Basketball" can offer wonderful insights for an excellent cause-and-effect paper. It is usually best to choose a topic that you can easily divide into the categories of cause and effect. If you were brainstorming about why you urged your family to move from Vermont last year, you might list the following:

Tired of the cold winters
Wanted to go to college out of state
No good part-time jobs there
Want to live near the seacoast
Farm too much work
No strong personal ties to worry about

Once you begin to isolate several separate causes (or effects) for a subject, you have probably discovered a suitable topic.

Finally, when selecting your topic for a cause-and-effect essay, be sure to think in terms of *cause and effect* and not *process*. Remember that a process essay traces *how* something is done; a cause-and-effect analysis shows how one thing *causes* another. The same topic can sometimes be discussed with either approach: "How to Catch Trout" (process) or "What Makes a Trout Bite?" (cause-and-effect) would overlap in content, but their emphases and methods of development would be very different. Instead of providing a step-by-step description of how to fish for trout, the cause-and-effect essay stresses the influence of one element of trout fishing on another.

The following essay by Nicole Noyes, a medical doctor, shows how cause-effect analysis can be effective in making an argument.

Why Human-Cloning Research
Should Not Be Banned

by Nicole Noyes, M.D.,
with Isabel Burton

I'm a fertility expert. My job revolves around finding new ways to bring life into this world. But when news broke last February about the birth of a sheep named Dolly, the world's first successful clone of an adult mammal, even I shuddered. My knee-jerk reaction was to call it a very bad idea.

Like the rest of the world, I needed time to digest this futuristic-sounding concept. Eerie questions came to mind: Would cloning do away with the awesome mystery of natural reproduction, in which two people's genes are combined into something new, unique, and wonderful? Would clones become a commodity, with scalpers hawking Cindy Crawford carbon copies at $10,000 a head?

Still, while cloning fully developed people may be something we never want to implement, banning the pursuit of the research and technology that makes cloning a possibility would be detrimental to all of us.

For starters, my own research is exploring a revolutionary new fertility technique that could enable an infertile woman to have a child who would carry her genes. In theory, it involves removing the nucleus (where all the genetic information is stored) from a woman's unproductive egg and transplanting it into a donor's healthy egg (whose own nucleus has been extracted), fertilizing the altered egg with sperm, and then allowing the embryo to develop normally. This procedure, called nuclear transfer, uses the very same techniques, and originates from the very same findings, as cloning. But unlike cloning, it produces a person like you and me, with genes from two separate parents . . . not a carbon copy born of only one person's DNA. Yet because of the similarity in technology, what could be the only chance for some couples to have a child who is genetically their own may be prohibited by the government.

Nor are infertile women the only people who stand to lose out from a ban. Already, scientists are working on how to use cloning to manufacture human skin, a medical breakthrough that will greatly benefit burn patients. Researchers also speculate that the same technology can be used to generate bone marrow for leukemia and Hodgkin's disease sufferers. And eventually, we may have the ability to clone whole organs, which means eliminating the need to be placed on long waiting lists for donors.

But here is the main point: In scientific research, one idea sparks another, and every time we set out to accomplish a new goal, it leads to countless additional findings. In other words, you can't get from A to Z without exploring the middle ground, and it's precisely that middle ground which inevitably opens the door to yet another world of discovery.

Think about the first time we put a man on the moon. True, the actual event probably didn't benefit you directly. But you needn't look any farther than your own car to find extralight, extrasafe metals that are just one of the everyday benefits derived from NASA's space research. Likewise, pursuing the study of human cloning may spin off not only some of the previously mentioned medical breakthroughs but others as yet undreamed of. And it may be that such discoveries could be achieved without the birth of a single fully cloned human being. But slap a ban on the research and progress stops.

So am I ready to stare a Xerox of myself in the face? Probably not. But I am prepared to use the building blocks of cloning to break new medical ground. And each time I meet a couple anticipating the procedure that will allow them to have their own genetic child, my resolve is reaffirmed.

Questions for Discussion and Writing

1. What is Noyes's thesis for this essay and where is it stated?
2. Identify the effects Noyes claims would result from banning cloning research and technology. What other effects might she have discussed?
3. What immediate and remote causes and effects are discussed in the essay?

4. What reasons (causes) do people have for opposing the pursuit of cloning research and technology? What reasons does Noyes mention?
5. What elements in the essay establish Noyes' credibility? After reading the essay, did you change your position on cloning?

Writing Assignment 9–4: A Cause-and-Effect Essay

Write a cause-and-effect essay of several paragraphs in length about any one of the topics listed below. Feel free to adapt any topic to a more personal or more objective approach as it suits you. Or write on a topic of your own, if you wish.

1. Why you gave up a habit or an activity that once played an important role in your life
2. What makes people drop out of college
3. The deterioration of neighborhoods
4. Literacy skills in children
5. Doing volunteer work
6. Why most Americans avoid learning a foreign language
7. Why a certain cartoon strip is popular
8. The popularity of a certain music group
9. The extinction of a certain species of animal
10. The loss of a childhood illusion or fantasy

As you select a topic, give some thought to how much information you may need to develop it. Depending on your approach, the topics will vary in the amount of personal experiences or outside examples they will require. Select a topic that interests you.

Once you have a topic, you may need to narrow it. If you chose topic 4, for example, you would want to select a specific group of children, such as urban ghetto children of the United States. If you chose topic 2, you might want to narrow "people" to yourself or a close friend.

Now use the activities of the Writing Process and the suggestions that follow to write your essay.

Gather Your Ideas and Information: Use brainstorming techniques to generate cause-and-effect ideas about your topic. Begin by writing the name of your topic at the top of a separate sheet of paper. Make two separate columns on the page, labeling one column "Causes" and the other "Effects." Now begin listing as many items as you can in each column. Do not worry if you confuse "Causes" as "Effects" or vice versa. Just put down your ideas as they come to you. Try to write at least six to eight causes and effects.

Analyze Your Ideas and Information: Look over what you have brainstormed in your lists of causes and effects. If you have put some things in the wrong column, move them to the correct one. Be sure you have listed at least all the major causes and effects. Mark your causes and effects as either "immediate" or "remote." Do any of them duplicate or overlap each other? Do you need to brainstorm more items for any of your lists? Decide which pattern your ideas follow. Have you identified a single cause with multiple effects or multiple causes with a single effect? Can you explain the *relationship* between the causes and their effects? In what order do these causes and effects occur? Which are major, and which are minor?

Identify Your Main Point: Write a thesis statement for your cause-and-effect essay. Be sure it is a single sentence and that it suggests cause and effect.

Plan Your Essay: Arrange your discussion of causes and effects in the best order. You may decide to start with the effects and then explain the causes, or the other way around. If it helps, plan to organize your material in most-important to least-important order. Use a chronological sequence if that works best for your topic and your way of writing.

Write Your Essay: Write your cause-and-effect essay. Begin by introducing your topic and including your thesis statement. Be careful of illogical fallacies as you explain causes and effects, and use specific examples as often as you can to illustrate ideas and support your topic sentences. Make sure you have adequately distinguished between immediate and remote causes and effects in your discussion.

Revise and Edit Your Essay: Use the STSOE guidelines to revise and edit your essay.

1. Is every step of your essay clear? If not, where is it not clear? What can you do to make it clear?
2. Does your purpose statement tell your readers what you want to say about your topic?
3. Does your paper sound choppy when you read it aloud? If so, at what point do you notice the choppiness? How might you correct it?

When you are proofreading, ask yourself if you have given variety to your sentence structure. Have you used a good balance of simple, compound, and complex sentences? (See Chapter 21.)

The Writing Process

GATHER your ideas and information
ANALYZE your ideas and information
IDENTIFY your theme or main point
PLAN your essay
WRITE your essay
REVISE AND EDIT your essay (STSOE)

10

Notes on Writing Essay Exams and In-Class Essays

YOU HAVE ALREADY practiced various types of spontaneous writing as one of the many activities involved in an orderly process of planning, writing, and revising an essay. However, you will often find yourself in situations where you must deliver your best writing effort in a one-draft, time-limited performance. How can you apply the Writing Process activities you have been learning here to such high-pressure situations? This chapter will explore the ways you can display your writing and thinking skills to best advantage on essay examinations and in-class essays.

Writing Essay Examinations

Essay examinations are a fact of college life. You may have taken one to enter your present college, to get into an English class, or as a requirement in one of your other college courses. Whether they are whole papers written in class or test questions that require a paragraph response, essay examinations offer you the opportunity to express your mastery of a subject—to apply, synthesize, compare, or describe ideas from your own perspective. They represent a chance for you to demonstrate not only your recollection of facts and details, but also your complete understanding of how all the parts of a topic fit together. Your audience here is just one person—your instructor—to whom you must demonstrate your understanding and application of the course material.

Like all writing assignments, essay examinations and in-class essays require that (1) you know your subject and (2) you write effectively about it. What sets essay examinations apart from other types of writing is the requirement that *you must write in the classroom and usually without notes for a very limited amount of time.* And it is this very time and performance requirement that presents the most difficulty for many student writers. However, your experience with the Writing Process will give you a built-in advantage in meeting this challenge because the key to success on a timed, in-class essay lies in preparing in advance and planning a good writing strategy. As in your regular essay writing, you will find it helpful to follow the activities of the Writing Process when preparing for and writing in-class essays and exams.

Gather Your Ideas and Information: Because most essay exams are announced ahead of time, you can prepare at home by reviewing all materials you have from the course, including the course syllabus, any handouts, past quizzes or exams, and your notes from class lectures and readings. Also be sure to review your textbook for the course. You may find it helpful to compare the arrangement of material in your text with the structure of the course content or lectures. Take notes on all your reviewing.

Analyze Your Ideas and Information: Study all your review materials carefully to detect any patterns of emphasis, categories of ideas or information, and dominant trends. Look for connections among the various materials. Study and be able to define key terms and concepts, especially those which are used and applied repeatedly. Think about the concepts and facts your instructor emphasized most in class lectures and discussions.

Identify the Main Point(s):   After you have thoroughly reviewed and analyzed the class materials, try writing your own test questions. Imagine you are writing the key question or questions for the material covered by the test. Compose one or several possible essay questions that you think would best test students' understanding of the material. Then take fifteen or twenty minutes to write a response to one of your own questions.

Performing this exercise gives you an overview of the material and will help you identify ahead of time what subjects the test may cover. It will also alert you to your own weaknesses in your grasp of the material. Formulating and writing down your own ideas on a subject helps you see connections and make comparisons ahead of time.

Plan: Successful test taking has two components. First, plan to prepare yourself physically as well as mentally. Writing a timed in-class essay or test can be an exhausting experience. You should guard against being too tired to think well or proofread for material you have left out. Don't cram. You will write better and think more clearly with a good night's sleep before the exam. Do not go to the exam hungry, either. Plan to be at your personal best, mentally and physically, when you sit down to write your essay exam.

Second, when you are actually in the classroom and preparing to write, plan to use your time in the most efficient way possible. Students often lose points on exams because they waste time not knowing how to begin or how to follow through on their preparations. Use the following guidelines to plan your response before you begin writing:

1. *Read and answer the essay question.* Many good students do poorly on essay exams by not responding to what was asked or by answering only half the question. When you take an exam, begin by reading the entire essay question carefully from start to finish.

As you read, pay attention to what you are being asked to do. Most essay questions include words like *explain, describe, compare, analyze, define, trace,* and *identify* as part of the directions. Be sure that your answer does all that the question's directions call for. If you are asked a question such as "Identify and explain the various means by which radioactive rays can be detected in a laboratory," remember that you have two tasks: *to identify* and *to explain.* An answer that does not identify *and* explain will not be sufficient.

For this reason, as you read the question a second time, circle, underline, or otherwise mark all key terms in the directions and in the question itself. For example, you might mark key terms in the following question for a world history examination this way:

(Explain) the role of Confucianism in China [during the T'ang, Five Dynasties, and Sung periods of rule in China,] (accounting) in each case for its rise or decline in influence. 25 points

Such notation emphasizes for you the three major elements you will need to think about as you answer:

a. *Instruction words* that tell you what kind of writing to do ("Explain" and "account")

b. *The subject* you are to write about ("the role of Confucianism" and "its rise or decline in influence")

c. *Any context or special limits of the subject* (Confucianism during the T'ang, Five Dynasties, and Sung periods)

To be adequate, your answer needs to focus on and include these three elements.

2. *Plan your response time.* Because you will have only a certain amount of time for an essay exam, you need to plan how much time to devote to each question or part of the test. Some students prefer to begin with questions they know they are prepared for, leaving more difficult ones for later. Others like to tackle the hard ones first, reserving more time for the answers they know well. Either technique is fine, but be sure you give real thought to what you are doing and why. Remember, you want to answer *all* the questions as fully as you can. Concentrating on one or two and not having time for others could cost heavily in overall points. Plan how much time you will need for each part of the test, giving more time to more heavily weighted questions. Allow yourself enough time to read quickly over your essay before handing it in.

3. *Plan your essay.* Although you will not have time to make a complete outline of an essay answer, you should jot down major ideas before you write and the sequence in which you plan to discuss them. If you were asked to compare the development of identical and fraternal twins for a biology essay examination, you might jot down notes like these before you began to write:

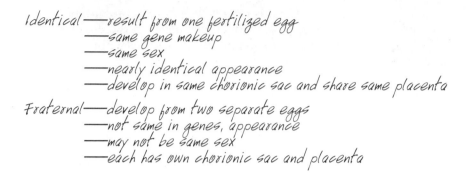

A rough list like this one (or any similar plan of ideas) will keep you on track as you write. It will also serve as a guard against forgetting important points once you start writing.

Write: Write your essay examination as efficiently and effectively as you can. Write as clearly as you can, and neatly cross out mistakes as you write. Your instructor will not expect a polished draft, only a legible one that makes sense and clearly communicates your major points. For this reason, you will need to make use of all the good writing skills that you can.

Begin your essay answer by writing down your thesis statement right away. This gets your essay started quickly and sets you on course for answering the question. Some students like to use the language of the essay topic itself to make their thesis statement and begin their essay response. Thus the topic "Name and describe the major types of galaxies in our universe" could be turned into this thesis statement and transitional sentence: "The three major types of galaxies found in our universe are the elliptic, spiral, and irregular-shaped galaxies. The most common of these, the elliptical galaxies, are usually small. . . ." Like all good thesis statements, this one is direct and focused and immediately gives the audience (in this case, your instructor) the information he or she is judging you on. Just as in your other writing, you should avoid vague and contentless openings such as "I will now describe the major types of galaxies in our universe."

In the body of your essay, organize your ideas around topic sentences that clearly reflect the thesis statement with which you have opened. Offer as many specific examples as you can, remembering that in the context of a test they serve as a way both of showing what you have learned and of supporting your general statements. Use such transition words and phrases as *on the other hand, for example,* and *consequently* to indicate relationships between your ideas and examples. Punctuate clearly and correctly.

Revise and Edit: Once you have finished your essay, *do not try to recopy* it. Recopying takes valuable time away from writing a good response. However, do take a few minutes to read over your essay quickly before handing it in. First, make sure that you have answered all the questions you were supposed to and that you have followed the directions correctly. Check for spelling errors, especially the names of people or any special terms. Look at the punctuation and grammar as you read your responses, and make any necessary corrections. Finally, be sure your name is on your essay. You will want to get credit for the good work you have done.

Exercise 1

Analyze each of the following essay exam questions to determine what your best response would be. For each question, do the following:

1. *Circle* the instruction words that tell you what kind of writing you are being asked to do.
2. *Underline* the subject you are asked to write about.
3. *Bracket* any context or special limits of the subject.

Here is a sample question analysis:

Describe the events of the Berlin Blockade (June 24, 1948, to May 17, 1949) and the lesson it taught the USSR [about the question of Germany's unification]

1. Compare Shakespeare's play *King Lear* with the Aristotelian concept of tragedy.

2. Define what is meant by the term *expanding universe,* and explain its significance to theories of space travel and the discovery of life on other planets.

3. Trace the rise of the women's suffrage movement in the United States from 1850 to the present.

4. In discussing at least two representative artists from each school, distinguish between the two art movements of "Expressionism" and "Impressionism."

5. Explain the process by which a *valley glacier* first forms and then later produces the effect called *alpine glaciation.*

Writing In-Class Essays

Use the same strategies to prepare for an in-class essay as you would for an essay exam. You can use the activities of the Writing Process even more directly when you are writing a single full essay than several one- or two-paragraph responses to test questions.

Sometimes the topic for an in-class essay is announced ahead of time. Knowing the topic in advance allows you to perform all the prewriting activities of the Writing Process—*gather your ideas and information, analyze your ideas and information, identify your main point,* and *plan your essay*—just as you would in writing an essay on your own time. A further helpful tactic is to write your introduction ahead of time as well. Writing a good introduction is often the most difficult and time-consuming part of writing an essay. If you have composed an introduction ahead of time, you will know exactly how to begin your essay when you sit down to write in class. As the example about the galaxies given in the preceding section shows, a one- or two-paragraph essay can be effectively introduced with one or two sentences. If you are writing an in-class essay of more than three paragraphs, you will probably need a separate paragraph for your introduction.

If the in-class essay topic is not announced ahead of time, you can prepare by reviewing class material for likely topics and by keeping the activities of the Writing Process firmly in mind as you sit down to write. Use the procedure described for essay exam questions to organize your preparation. If you will be writing an in-class essay for an English class in which you have no course materials to review and the emphasis will be placed entirely on your writing proficiency, practice timed writing on topics of your own choice, using Writing Assignment 10–1 as a model.

Writing Assignment 10–1:
An In-Class Essay

At home or in class, allow yourself fifty minutes *total* to plan, write, and review an essay on the topic "What I Want My Life to Be by the Year 2005." Use *all* the activities of the Writing Process during the fifty minutes, but plan to allot specific amounts of time for your prewriting, writing, and review activities.

In the next class meeting, share your essay and your responses to the limited-time framework with your classmates. Do you find it harder or easier to write under pressure? Did you discover after the time was up that you omitted important material? Did you find yourself spending too much time on one or another of the activities of the Writing Process? How would you plan to redistribute the amount of time you spent on each of the activities over the class hour? Becoming aware of your own habits can help you change and improve your responses in all test-taking and time-specific writing situations.

PART III

Writing with Outside Resources

You studied the art of essay writing in Parts I and II by writing about ideas and information you drew from within yourself or from the people and places around you. As you progress in college, however, you will be asked more and more to write on topics that you cannot understand solely on the basis of your own experience. Thus you will need to find outside resource material that will help you in these areas. In Parts I and II, for example, if you were asked to write about a relative or friend, probably all you had to do was bring to mind a picture of that person and recall some of your experiences with him or her. However, if you are asked to write about your opinion on capital punishment, affirmative action, or drunken driving, you will need to learn more about these issues before writing your essay; you will need to know the facts and what experts think about the issues even though you may already have strong feelings about them yourself.

Part III will help you find and understand resource material that you can use in your writing. Chapter 11 focuses on developing your reading skills and techniques for summarizing the material you read. Chapter 12 shows you how to find resource material in the library and stresses the importance of doing what comes naturally—namely, reading for pleasure. Chapter 13 shows you how to write an argument essay. And Chapter 14 introduces you to techniques for writing a research paper.

The Writing Process

GATHER your ideas and information

ANALYZE your ideas and information

IDENTIFY your theme or main point

PLAN your essay

WRITE your essay

REVISE AND EDIT your essay (STSOE)

Reading and Summarizing

- *Reading to Summarize Material:*
  The SRR Method
- *Writing Summaries*

READING IS A habit-forming experience that brings unexpected benefits in many other areas. You will find that the more widely you read, the better you will write. This is a learning process that takes place automatically and painlessly without your even noticing it. Reading helps you learn how words fit together to make strong sentences. It greatly increases your vocabulary and general knowledge. Reading also helps you learn how to analyze a subject and order your thoughts.

The further you progress in college, the more you will need to incorporate outside sources into your writing. Sometimes you can gather the best information on a topic by interviewing others who have had firsthand experience with your subject, sometimes by taking notes in class, and sometimes by watching the news or a documentary on television. However, your main source of ideas and information will be printed matter: textbooks, library books, and periodicals. To gain the most from your sources, you need to be able to read with facility and understanding.

This chapter focuses on how to grasp the main points of what you read and how to summarize them. The ability to give a concise, accurate account of a writer's thoughts is one of the most valuable writing skills you can acquire. In your college classes you will often have to summarize reading materials: in taking an essay exam, for example (see Chapter 10), or in compiling information from many sources for a research paper (see Chapter 14).

Summarizing is also an essential ingredient in many kinds of essay writing besides research papers. You often summarize your own thoughts when you write a conclusion to an essay. A summary also can serve to inform your reader about any subject before you begin to discuss it in detail. The summary is especially useful in writing an argument essay (see Chapter 13). Before you argue for your own point of view on a certain subject, you may wish to summarize the essential points of an article or book on the same subject.

To write effective summaries, you need to read the material carefully with good comprehension. If you do not have a good reading method, try out the suggestions in the following section. This reading technique is known as the *SRR method:* *S*kim, *R*ead, and *R*eview.

Reading to Summarize Material: The SRR Method

Just like the act of writing, the act of reading consists of more than simply reading. The SRR reading method is actually three separate activities: skimming, reading, and reviewing. Follow these activities carefully and see if your reading comprehension improves.

Skim the Material

1. Try to pick out the main idea of the piece you are reading. Often you can find it in the title or the first paragraph.

2. Try to determine the organizational method that the author is using. For example, is the piece organized as cause-and-effect writing? Identifying this method would help you identify the causes and effects presented, thus allowing you to determine the author's point.

3. Look for definitions and difficult words that you must understand if you are to understand what follows. Look them up in the dictionary if necessary, and jot their meanings in the margin.

4. Skim all the subheadings. They will help give you an overview of the material.

5. Read the first (and sometimes second) sentences of enough paragraphs to allow you to know the general subject. Reading the last sentence of each paragraph will help provide a context for the next.

6. If something confuses you, stop and try to figure it out. If you still do not understand, move on.

7. Read the last paragraph or two.

8. Jot down the main point of the material on a piece of notebook paper. Also, write several questions that emerge from your skimming. When you read the material closely, be sure to answer these questions.

Read the Material Thoroughly

1. Underline the main ideas. When possible, summarize the main points in the margin. (If you own the book, write all over it if this will help you learn.)

2. Relate the material to your own experience when possible. Make notes that name the experience the material reminds you of.

3. Write down questions to ask your instructor or another student on any important points that you do not understand.

4. Look up words that you do not understand in the dictionary. Keep a list of new words and their definitions.

Review the Material

1. Without looking back, ask yourself: What was the main point of the material? What ideas were presented to back up the main point? Write these down.

2. If you cannot answer these questions, review the material and read over your notes.

Now try out these techniques in the following exercises.

Exercise 1

Using the SRR method, read the article "Workplace Wiles" from *Psychology Today* (May 1989). The following sample of underlining and notes in the margin will give you an idea of how to make notes as you read:

preen—to dress up in a fussy way
Machiavellian—a crafty or clever person
charm—used to influence both
Men use their charm more than women—main point.

Of the men, 22% said they <u>preen</u> to get ahead, while only 14% of the women admitted to doing so. And who are the <u>Machiavellians</u> in the workplace? Again, 22% of the men—but only 15% of the women—admit they resort to manipulation to achieve their aims. Almost 40% of the men turn on the charm to influence <u>bosses</u> or <u>coworkers</u>, compared to 29% of women.

Now read the complete article, adding underlining and notes of your own as you proceed.

Workplace Wiles:
Who Uses Beauty and Charm?

by "M. R."

"I use my personal appearance to my advantage in getting things accomplished on the job."

If that statement brings to mind miniskirts and make-up, you've got another think *(sic)* coming. Men are a lot more likely than women to say they use their looks to get their way at work

In fact, men report using a variety of influence tactics more often than women do, according to a recent study by psychologist Andrew DuBrin of the Rochester Institute of Technology. More than 300 men and women in fields from education to retail sales told him what methods they use to get what they want.

Of the men, 22% said they preen to get ahead, while only 14% of the women admitted to doing so. And who are the Machiavellians in the workplace? Again, 22% of the men—but only 15% of the women—admit they resort to manipulation to achieve their aims. Almost 40% of the men turn on the charm to influence bosses or coworkers, compared to 29% of women.

What's happened to eyelash batting, kerchief dropping and other stereotypical female strategies of persuasion? DuBrin acknowledges that women might deny using such techniques because they have been accused of doing just that.

But women, wishing to be judged on brains and qualifications rather than on looks and charm, says DuBrin, may aim instead to influence others with assertiveness or reason. Men, whose place in the world of work has never been questioned, probably don't worry as much about using whatever tactic it takes to get ahead on the job.

Questions for Discussion and Writing

1. What is the main idea of "Workplace Wiles"? Where is the main idea stated in the article?
2. What is the purpose of the quotation at the start of the article?
3. What words did you need to look up in the dictionary as you read the article? How do words like *wiles, preen, Machiavellian, manipulation,* and *stereotypical* contribute to the author's attitude about people using their appearances to get things accomplished on the job?
4. What details does the author use to support and illustrate the article's main idea?
5. What is the effect of the author's including Andrew DuBrin in the article? What use does the author make of this person in explaining the article's material?

Exercise 2

Use the SRR method to read the article "Fear of Dearth" by Carll Tucker. As with Exercise 1, use underlining and notes to make your reading more effective, as in this example:

dearth—insufficiency, lack
tedious—dull, boring
conducive—helpful
vistas—views

Summary: Jogging doesn't offer enough to think about.

Fear of Dearth

I hate jogging. Every dawn, as I thud around New York City's Central Park reservoir, I am reminded of how much I hate it. It's so <u>tedious</u>. Some claim jogging is thought <u>conducive</u>; others insist the scenery relieves the monotony. For me, the pace is wrong for contemplation of either ideas or <u>vistas</u>.

Fear of Dearth

by Carll Tucker

I hate jogging. Every dawn, as I thud around New York City's Central Park reservoir, I am reminded of how much I hate it. It's so tedious. Some claim jogging is thought conducive; others insist the scenery relieves the monotony. For me, the pace is wrong for contemplation of either ideas or vistas. While jogging, all I can think about is jogging—or nothing. One advantage of jogging around a reservoir is that there's no dry shortcut home.

From the listless looks of some fellow trotters, I gather I am not alone in my unenthusiasm: Bill-paying, it seems, would be about as diverting. Nonetheless, we continue to jog; more, we continue to *choose* to jog. From a practically infinite array of opportunities, we select one that we don't enjoy and can't wait to have done with. Why?

For any trend, there are as many reasons as there are participants. This person runs to lower his blood pressure. That person runs to escape the telephone or a cranky spouse or a filthy household. Another person runs to avoid doing anything else, to dodge a decision about how to lead his life or a realization that his life is leading nowhere. Each of us has his carrot and stick. In my case, the stick is my slackening physical condition, which keeps me from beating opponents at tennis whom I overwhelmed two years ago. My carrot is to win.

Beyond these disparate reasons, however, lies a deeper cause. It is no accident that now, in the last third of the twentieth century, personal fitness and health have suddenly become a popular obsession. True, modern man likes to feel good, but that hardly distinguishes him from his predecessors.

With zany myopia, economists like to claim that the deeper cause of everything is economic. Delightfully, there seems no marketplace explanation for jogging. True, jogging is cheap, but then not jogging is cheaper. And the scant and skimpy equipment which jogging demands must make it a marketer's least favored form of recreation.

Some scout-masterish philosophers argue that the appeal of jogging and other body-maintenance programs is the discipline they afford. We live in a world in which individuals have fewer and fewer obligations. The work week has shrunk. Weekend worship is less compulsory. Technology gives us more free time. Satisfactorily filling free time requires imagination and effort. Freedom is a wide and risky river; it can drown the person who does not know how to swim across it. The more obligations one takes on, the more time one occupies, the less threat freedom poses. Jogging can become an instant obligation. For a portion of his day, the jogger is not his own man; he is obedient to a regimen he has accepted.

Theologians may take the argument one step further. It is our modern irreligion, our lack of confidence in any hereafter, that makes us anxious to stretch our mortal stay as long as possible. We run, as the saying goes, for our lives, hounded by the suspicion that these are the only lives we are likely to enjoy.

All of these theorists seem to me more or less right. As the growth of cults and charismatic religions and the resurgence of enthusiasm for the military draft suggest, we do crave commitment. And who can doubt, watching so many middle-aged and older persons torturing themselves in the name of fitness, that we are unreconciled to death, more so perhaps than any generation in modern memory?

But I have a hunch there's a further explanation of our obsession with exercise. I suspect that what motivates us even more than a fear of death is a fear of dearth. Our era is the first to anticipate the eventual depletion of all natural resources. We see wilderness shrinking; rivers losing their capacity to sustain life; the air, even the stratosphere, being loaded with potentially deadly junk. We see the irreplaceable being squandered, and in the depths of our consciousness we are fearful that we are creating an uninhabitable world. We feel more or less helpless and yet, at the same time, desirous to protect what resources we can. We recycle soda bottles and restore old buildings and protect our nearest natural resource—our physical health—in the almost superstitious hope that such small gestures will help save an earth that we are blighting. Jogging becomes a sort of penance for our sins of gluttony, greed, and waste. Like a hairshirt or a bed of nails, the more one hates it, the more virtuous it makes one feel.

That is why *we* jog. Why *I* jog is to win at tennis.

Writing Summaries

Writing a summary of an article, a chapter, or a book is like writing about your dominant impression of a photograph or painting. You state the work's main idea, and then you describe briefly the major supporting points for that idea. In writing a summary, your goal is to convey as accurately as possible the full sense of the original, but in a more condensed form for your reader. You will have to make decisions about which details of the original to include and which to omit from your summary, and you will have to give attention to possible limits on length.

Suggestions for Writing Summaries

The following suggestions will help you write effective summaries of outside sources:

Identify the Main Idea: Identify the main idea of the material, and state it in your own words in a sentence or two. If your outside source is a paragraph, the main idea will probably be stated as a topic sentence. If your source is an essay or article, look for a thesis statement.

As with any paragraph or essay, all or most of the source's content will support and illustrate the main idea. Don't assume that the opening sentence of the original always states the main idea, which can be expressed indirectly at the beginning or delayed until the end. If you have trouble deciding on the main idea of the original material, write a one-sentence summary of each of the paragraphs you've read until the main idea begins to emerge. Be sure that your statement is the main idea of the entire work, not just of one paragraph or section of it.

List Supporting Details: Find and list the details that support the main idea. Analyze this list to find similarities, and then group similar supporting details. If there are too many supporting details to give in your summary, remove the least important ones and then the next least important ones until you have the right number. You should include as many supporting details as the length of your summary allows.

Write an Outline of the Material: Make an outline that includes information about your outside source, the main idea of the material, and the supporting details you plan to discuss. The basic information about your source should include its title, the author's name, date, and general content. If the source is an article or chapter in a magazine or book, give the title of the magazine or book as well. Be sure that your outline shows how the author of the original supports the main idea. Arrange the individual points in the outline in a logical order such as least to most important, most to least important, or chronological order. The order you decide on does not have to be the same as the order in the original.

Here is a sample outline for the Tucker article on jogging in the preceding section:

First Paragraph
Title, author, general content
Main point: why we jog even though it is boring

Second Paragraph
Reasons people jog
    —health
      —to "get away"
        —gives a sense of responsibility
      —holds off dying

Third Paragraph
Main reason for jogging
our fear of using up everything
Why Tucker jogs

Write the Summary: Use the following guidelines whenever you write a summary of an outside source:

1. *Cite your source in your first sentence.* Name the author and the work you are summarizing, and give general information about the topic. Put quotation marks around titles of articles, essays, and short stories; underline titles of magazines, books, and newspapers. For example.

> In his essay "Fear of Dearth," Carll Tucker begins by stating that he dislikes jogging because it does not give him anything to do or think about—except jogging.

2. *State the author's main idea in the next sentence or shortly thereafter.* "He believes most people would agree that jogging is boring, but he also thinks there may be several reasons why people jog anyway." (Note that the first name of the author is dropped after it is given once.)

3. *Be brief.* Remember that you are writing the summary to reduce the original material to its main points. You may want to use direct or indirect quotations, but do not get bogged down by extensive quoting. (Suggestions and rules for quoting appear on pages 253-257.) It may help to put the original reading material aside while you are writing the summary. This way, you will be less likely to retell everything.

4. *Write the summary in your own words, not the words of the author.* Not only will this be much better writing practice for you, but it also will help you avoid *plagiarism,* which is the use of the words or ideas of another as though they were your own. If you need to use the exact words of the author, the proper way to do so is by using direct quotations.

5. *Do not offer your opinion in the summary itself.* It is sometimes appropriate to write an additional paragraph or more in which you give your response to the material you are summarizing. Generally, however, you should present only the author's views in the summary. The summary should be as objective as possible, although stated in your own words.

6. *Divide summaries of 200 words or more into two or more paragraphs.* A lengthy summary will be clearer to your reader if you divide the material into more than one paragraph. Try to organize the summary logically so that supporting points that are related stay together. The organization pattern you decide to follow—least to most important, most to least important, or chronological—may offer logical places to divide your summary.

Here is how you might write a three-paragraph summary of the Carll Tucker article on jogging:

Why We Jog

Title and author
Main point

> In his essay "Fear of Dearth," Carll Tucker begins by stating that he dislikes jogging because it does not give him anything to do or think about—except jogging. He believes most people would agree that jogging is boring, but he also thinks there may be several reasons why people jog anyway.

Some reasons for jogging

> One reason people jog, says Tucker, is for their health; others jog to get away from themselves or difficult situations at home. He goes on to say that economics is surely not one of the reasons people jog, but admits that people may jog because it gives us a sense of responsibility in a world that does not ask much of us. Another reason is that we fear mortality and use jogging as a means to hold off dying for a while.

Main reason for jogging—
direct quotation

Tucker's reason for jogging

> But the deepest reason people jog, according to Tucker, is out of fear of using everything up—the earth, its natural resources, and ourselves. We jog, says Tucker, as a way of paying a penalty for all our excesses—"a sort of penance for our sins of gluttony, greed, and waste"—and because we feel better for doing so. However, he insists, <u>he</u> jogs to win at tennis.

Revise and Edit the Summary: As you are evaluating, compare your summary with the original and ask yourself these questions: Have I conveyed the important points as briefly as possible? Have I rephrased the words of the author without altering his or her original meaning? Notice that since you are writing a summary of another writer's material, the STSOE steps you use for your own writing will not apply. Revise the summary according to the preceding guidelines, making sure that you have given general information about your source, stated the author's main idea, written briefly, stated the material in your own words, and presented only the author's views. If your summary is over 200 words, revise by dividing it into two paragraphs. Edit your summary by checking spelling, grammar, and punctuation.

The article below about playgrounds of the future is followed by a sample summary. After reading both selections, note the way the writer of the summary has selected details and organized the summary to maintain brevity.

Playgrounds of the Future:
They Ain't Got Swing

by Kendall Hamilton and Patricia King

On a sunny Sunday afternoon, seventh grader Josh Hartley is helping to build a wet-sand dam at Jack Fischer Park in his hometown of Campbell, Calif. A 6-year-old "reinforces" the dam with twigs. Another presses a button that floods a concrete channel with water, to test the structure's mettle. The barrier holds. "It's pretty cool," says Hartley. "You feel like you've accomplished something." The 13-year-old prefers this brand-new playground to more traditional ones, with their "rusty old stuff" that sheds paint chips and burns fingers after a few hours under the sun. The slides at Jack Fischer are plastic, and their impact zones are cushioned with special wood chips to ensure soft landings. That's important to Hartley, whose sister cut her chin when she fell from a climbing structure at another park. You won't find monkey bars or a Jungle Gym at Jack Fischer. And come the year 2000, you'll have a hard time finding them anywhere in California.

The state is the first in the country to mandate compliance with federal safety recommendations. Some long-beloved fixtures—monkey bars among them—will bite the dust, and others such as swings, slides and seesaws will have to be scaled down or modified. Traditionalists scoff at what they see as undue protectionism, but activists say changes are long overdue. About 150,000 children a year wind up in emergency rooms with playground injuries, and 15 or so die. Seymour Gold, professor of environmental planning at the University of California, Davis, says studies place playgrounds among the five greatest hazards to children in the nation. "That's serious, when you're up there with chain saws and ladders."

New and safer playgrounds are still evolving, but some trends are already clear. First, says designer Jay Beckwith, equipment will be lower to the ground. No more 20-foot-tall corkscrew slides. Merry-go-rounds, where kids kept whirling "until they threw up," could also trap children underneath, says Beckwith, so they're out. Old-style seesaws are giving way to spring-loaded ones so you can't "jump off and have your friend's eyeballs come out of his head." Heavy animal-shaped swings look like fun, but they routinely flatten passing toddlers. Even conventional swings are on the wane. "Swings are going to be very scarce, and high swings are going to be gone," says Beckwith. Mandated "fall zones" are so large and the surfacing required beneath them so costly that most parks don't have the space or money for more than a few. Writing a check for $10,000 to pad the area around two swings is no fun for civic officials.

But will the new playgrounds be any fun for kids? Designers are devising alternative fixtures, like Jack Fischer Park's water channel, but to some it just isn't the same. Marin County day-care assistant Kristen Eldridge, 25, has a "major problem" with the new rules. "I had seesaws and monkey bars when I grew up and I'm fine, and generations before us were fine," she says. "Parents are just getting too busy to take time to watch their kids." Terry Norton, an irked mom who fired off an op-ed piece to the San Francisco Examiner, says the new rules will create "plastic-bubble childhood for kids. Let them get out there and bang against hard things. It's reality."

But parents of children who bang against hard things often file lawsuits. It is this hazard, as much as nanny-minded legislators, that's driving the changes. Besides, "you're still going to break your arms and fingers," says Susan Goltsman, a Berkeley, Calif., playground designer. The new rules are aimed at eliminating deaths, she says, not minor injuries. And some of the new stuff is catching on. "Usually you get dirty and everything, but I think it's fun," says Josh Hartley of his park's water channel, which may not be dangerous but certainly offers a taste of reality. Budding civil engineers learn what it's like to work with bossy colleagues, and even the occasional conspiracy is hatched. "Let's go terrorize my brother," says one boy, proving that there are some childhood hazards that no amount of padding can eliminate.

Summary

"Playgrounds of the Future," by Kendall Hamilton and Patricia King, discusses the fact that California is the first state to require compliance with federal safety recommendations for safer playground equipment. The new rules will mean the end of some traditional playground fixtures such as monkey bars, merry-go-rounds, and eventually even swings. The changes arise from the 150,000 injuries and some 15 deaths a year that result from accidents on playground equipment. Interest in preventing such injuries or deaths, as well as avoiding lawsuits, is behind the push for new designs in playground equipment, with an emphasis on safety first. Some parents are resisting the changes, saying children should have access to the traditional kinds of equipment and claiming children are being overprotected. State safety concerns and fear of lawsuits are prevailing, but it's likely children at play will always find ways to take risks.

This summary keeps as much of the original content as necessary to convey its major ideas. As you can tell from this condensed version of the original, writing a summary of any length or purpose first requires careful reading and understanding of the source material.

 ## Writing Assignment 11–1

As you read the following reading selection, "Is Sex All That Matters?" by Joyce Garity, notice the way she uses summary to tell about others and to provide examples to her readers.

Read the selection carefully, using the SRR reading method described in this chapter. Then, using the suggestions for writing a summary, write a two or three paragraph response to Garity's article. In the first paragraph of your essay, summarize the article. State the main idea and explain the author's reasons for holding the point of view she does. In the second paragraph, state your response to Garity's ideas. Begin your second paragraph with something like this: "Garity is correct when she argues that . . ." or "Garity is mistaken when she argues. . . ."

Somewhere in your essay, practice using direct quotation. See pages 253–257 for suggestions and rules for using this technique.

A few years ago, a young girl lived with me, my husband, and our children for several months. The circumstances of Elaine's coming to us don't matter here; suffice it to say that she was troubled and nearly alone in the world. She was also pregnant—hugely, clumsily pregnant with her second child. Elaine was seventeen. Her pregnancy, she said, was an accident; she also said she wasn't sure who had fathered her child. There had been several sex partners and no contraception Yet, she repeated blandly, gazing at me with clear blue eyes, the pregnancy was an accident, and one she would certainly never repeat.

Eventually I asked Elaine, after we had grown to know each other well enough for such conversations, why neither she nor her lovers had used birth control She blushed—porcelain skinned girl with one child in foster care and another swelling the bib of her fashionably faded overalls—stammered, and blushed some more. Birth control, she finally got out, was "embarrassing." It wasn't "romantic." You couldn't be really passionate, she explained, and worry about birth control at the same time.

I haven't seen Elaine for quite a long time. I think about her often, though. I think of her as I page through teen fashion magazines in the salon where I have my hair cut. Although mainstream and relatively wholesome, these magazines trumpet sexuality page after leering page. On the inside front cover, an advertisement for Guess? Jeans features junior fashion models in snug denim dresses, their legs bared to just below the crotch. An advertisement for Liz Claiborne fragrances shows a barely clad young couple sprawled on a bed, him painting her toenails. An advertisement for Obsession cologne displays a waif-thin girl draped stomach-down across a couch, naked, her startled expression suggesting helplessness in the face of an unseen yet approaching threat.

I think of Elaine because I know she would love these ads. "They're so beautiful," she would croon, and of course they are. The faces and bodies they show are lovely. The lighting is superb. The hair and makeup are faultless. In the Claiborne ad, the laughing girl whose toenails are being painted by her handsome lover is obviously having the time of her life. She stretches luxuriously on a bed heaped with clean white linen and fluffy pillows. Beyond the sheer blowing curtains of her room, we can glimpse a graceful wrought-iron balcony. Looking at the ad, Elaine could only want to be her. Any girl would want to be her. Heck, *I* want to be her.

But my momentary desire to move into the Claiborne picture, to trade lives with the exquisite young creature pictured there, is just that—momentary. I've lived long enough to know that what I see is a marketing invention. A moment after the photo session was over, the beautiful room was dismantled, and the models moved on to their next job. Later, the technicians took over the task of doctoring the photograph until it reached full-blown fantasy proportions.

Not so Elaine. After months of living together and countless hours of watching her yearn after magazine images, soap-opera heroines, and rock goddesses, I have a pretty good idea of why she looks at ads like Claiborne's. She sees the way life—her life—is supposed to be. She sees a world characterized by sexual spontaneity, playfulness, and abandon. She sees people who don't worry about such unsexy details as birth control. Nor, apparently, do they spend much time thinking about such pedestrian topics as commitment or whether they should act on their sexual impulses. Their clean sunlit rooms are never invaded by the fear of AIDS, of unwanted pregnancy, of shattered lives. For all her apparent lack of defense, the girl on the couch in the Obsession ad will surely never experience the brutality of rape.

Years of exposure to this media-invented, sex-saturated universe have done their work on Elaine. She is, I'm sure, completely unaware of the irony in her situation: She melts over images from a sexual Shangri-La, never realizing that her attempts to mirror those images left her pregnant, abandoned, living in the spare bedroom of a stranger's house, relying on charity for rides to the welfare office and supervised visits with her toddler daughter.

Of course, Elaine is not the first to be suckered by the cynical practice of using sex to sell underwear, rock groups, or sneakers. Using sex as a sales tool is hardly new. At the beginning of this century, British actress Lily Langtry shocked her contemporaries by posing, clothed somewhat scantily, with a bar of Pear's soap. The advertisers have always known that the masses are susceptible to the notion that a particular product will make them more sexually attractive. In the past, however, ads used euphemisms, claiming that certain products would make people "more lovable" or "more popular." What is a recent development is the abandonment of any such polite double-talk. Advertising today leaves no question about what is being sold along with the roasted peanuts or artificial sweetener. "Tell us about your first time," coyly invites the innuendo-filled magazine advertisement for Campari liquor. A billboard for Levi's shows two jeans-clad young men on the beach, hoisting a girl in the air. The boys' perfect, tan bodies are matched by hers, although we see a lot more of hers: bare midriff, short shorts, cleavage. She caresses their hair; they stroke her legs. A jolly gang-bang fantasy in the making. And a TV commercial promoting the Irish pop group The Cranberries blares nonstop the suggestive title of their latest album: "Everybody else is doing it, so why can't we?"

Indeed, just about everybody is doing it. Studies show that by the age of 20, 75 percent of Americans have lost their virginity. In many high schools—and an increasing number of junior highs—virginity is regarded as an embarrassing vestige of childhood, to be disposed of as quickly as possible. Young people are immersed from their earliest days in a culture that parades sexuality at every turn and makes heroes of the advocates of sexual excess. Girls, from toddlerhood on up, shop in stores packed with clothing once thought suitable only for streetwalkers—lace leggings, crop tops, and wedge-heeled boots. Parents drop their children off at Madonna or Michael Jackson concerts, featuring simulated on-stage masturbation, or at Bobby Brown's show, where a fan drawn out of the audience is treated to a pretended act of copulation. Young boys idolize sports stars like Wilt Chamberlain, who claims to have bedded 20,000 women. And when the "Spur Posse," eight California high school athletes, were charged with systematically raping girls as young as 10 as part of a "scoring" ritual, the beefy young jocks were rewarded with a publicity tour of talk shows, while one father boasted to reporters about his son's "manhood."

In a late, lame attempt to counterbalance this sexual overload, most schools offer sex education as part of their curriculums. (In 1993, forty-seven states recommended or required such courses.) But sex ed classes are heavy on the mechanics of fertilization and birth control—sperm, eggs, and condoms—and light on any discussion of sexuality as only one part of a well-balanced life. There is passing reference to abstinence as a method of contraception, but little discussion of abstinence as an emotionally or spiritually satisfying option. Promiscuity is discussed for its role in spreading sexually transmitted diseases. But the concept of rejecting casual sex in favor of reserving sex for an emotionally intimate, exclusive, trusting relationship—much less any mention of waiting until marriage—is foreign to most public school settings. "Love and stuff like that really wasn't discussed" is the way one Spur Posse member remembers his high school sex education class.

Surely teenagers need the factual information provided by sex education courses. But where is "love and stuff like that" talked about? Where can they turn for a more balanced view of sexuality? Who is telling young people like Elaine, my former houseguest, that sex is not an adequate basis for a healthy, respectful relationship? Along with warnings to keep condoms on hand, is anyone teaching kids that they have a right to be valued for something other than their sexuality? Madison Avenue, Hollywood, and the TV, music, and fashion industries won't tell them that. Who will?

No one has told Elaine—at least, not in a way she comprehends. I haven't seen her for a long time, but I hear of her occasionally. The baby boy she bore while living in my house is in a foster home, a few miles from his older half-sister, who is also in foster care. Elaine herself is working in a local convenience store—and she is pregnant again. This time, I understand, she is carrying twins.

Writing Assignment 11-2

The following reading selection, "Colleges Should Confer Degrees by Examination," was originally published in the *Wall Street Journal.* First read the article carefully, using the SRR reading method. Then reflect on why the author, Mark Kleiman, chose to publish his article in a business, rather than an educational, publication. Do you think his proposal has merit? How well would you succeed in studying for a college degree on your own?

Next, using the suggestions for writing a summary, write a three- to four-paragraph paper in response. In your first paragraph, summarize Kleiman's ideas and conclude with a thesis sentence stating your response. In the following paragraphs, support and develop the thesis by explaining the reasons for your response.

As you write, try to practice using direct quotation to present Kleiman's ideas in his own words. See the guidelines for using quotation on pages 253–257.

> Colleges and universities offer their undergraduate students two distinct commodities: an education (or rather the opportunity for one) and a degree. The offer is what antitrust lawyers call a "tie sale": They won't sell you the diploma unless you buy the whole package.
>
> As fall approaches and parents dig into their pockets (or apply to their banks) for the $15,000 a year it now costs to send a child to a "prestige" institution such as the one where I work, it's time to ask why the education-and-degree package shouldn't be unbundled. If a student can achieve on his own, and demonstrate to the faculty, knowledge and competence higher than, say, the median of a school's graduating class, why shouldn't he be able to buy a certificate testifying as much?
>
> Such a certificate—a B.A. by examination—would qualify its holder for employment, or for graduate or professional study, without costing him four years of forgone earnings plus the cash price of a small house. . . .
>
> There are three arguments for such a proposal.
>
> First, it would save resources.
>
> Second, it would make a valuable credential available to some who cannot now afford it, thus contributing to social mobility. (In addition to those earning their first degrees in this way, B.A.-by-exam programs at high-prestige schools might attract students who feel, often correctly, that their obscure sheepskins are holding them back.)
>
> Third, and more speculatively, it might free high-powered but unconventional high-school graduates to pursue a self-education more useful to them than any prepackaged education, without shutting themselves out of jobs and advanced-degree programs.
>
> There are two obvious objections. Those who took their B.A.s by examination might miss out on the opportunities college provides for social interaction and other forms of personal and intellectual development. It might also be said that, since no examination could capture the richness of an undergraduate education, B.A.s by exam would have incentives to become, and would in fact be, narrower and shallower than their eight-semesters-in-residence counterparts.

The first objection is probably true but not conclusive. Some who would choose the exam route over the regular undergraduate course would probably be wise not to buy the nonacademic attributes of college for fours years' income plus $60,000; others will not, in fact, choose the more expensive option, even if it is the only one offered.

To the second objection there are two solutions: high standards and resource-intensive examinations. A process lasting a month and costing $3,000 to administer and score, testing both general knowledge and competence in a major field, and involving written, oral and practical components and the preparation of a thesis or the equivalent, should suffice to evaluate breadth and depth at least as well as the current systems does. The interests of the group running an examination program would run parallel with those of the rest of the institution in keeping standards high, and the social and moral pressure to award degrees in borderline cases ought to be much less for exam students than for ordinary undergraduates. By setting standards for examination B.A.s above the median of the eight-semester graduates, an institution could ensure that the exam program raised the average education level of its degree-holders.

The price to candidates could reflect fully loaded cost plus a substantial contribution to overhead and still look like a bargain. To deal with the unwillingness of potential candidates to gamble several thousand dollars on their chances of success, it might make sense to administer a fairly cheap ($200) screening test and give anyone who passed a moneyback guarantee on the more thorough (and expensive) degree exam. The failure rate could be built into the price, or some insurance company might be willing to administer the screening test and sell failure insurance.

This proposal should not be confused with college credit for "life experience," "urban semesters" or other moves to substitute the pragmatic for the scholarly in undergraduate education. The point is to tie the degree more rather than less tightly to specific academic competence, to certify the result—an educated person—rather than the *process* leading to that result.

If this idea required a consensus in order to be tried out, it would never stand a chance. Fortunately, no such consensus is needed. All it takes is one undeniably first-rate institution willing to break the credential cartel.

 ## Writing Assignment 11-3

Write summaries of two magazine or journal articles listed in recent volumes of the *Readers' Guide to Periodical Literature* (discussed on page 220) under one of the following headings. (The exact wording of the topics may differ somewhat.)

AIDS	divorce	the poor
artificial intelligence	drug abuse	public schools
capital punishment	greenhouse effect	sexual ethics
civil rights	the Internet	space exploration

Once you have picked a topic, read through the list of titles of relevant articles, and choose several that interest you. Find them on the shelves or on microfilm, and decide which two you would like to write on. If your library carries the *Social Issues Resources Series (SIRS),* you may find the articles you would like to write on there (see page 222).

In writing your summaries, use the suggestions given in this chapter. For practice, use at least one direct quotation in each summary. In your first sentence, be sure to include the title of the article and the name and date of the publication in which it appears, as well as the author's name if it is given.

The Writing Process

GATHER your ideas and information
ANALYZE your ideas and information
IDENTIFY your theme or main point
PLAN your essay
WRITE your essay
REVISE AND EDIT your essay (STSOE)

12

Using the Library's Resources

As you sharpen your reading skills and grow confident in your ability to grasp main points and summarize, you will find yourself looking beyond your textbooks for ideas and information to incorporate into your college writing. You can almost always find the material you need on any given subject in your college library. The library is a valuable resource for books and magazines containing current information on an amazingly large range of topics. Your library's card and online catalogs are simple to operate and will show you how to locate exactly the information you need in books, periodicals, reference volumes, and microfilm.

This chapter gives suggestions for finding resource material in the library and offers several writing assignments that require library use. As you progress in college, you will be asked to use the library as the basis for research papers. But do not limit your use of the library to working on research papers. Use it also to locate books that you will read for pleasure, to find magazines that will keep you informed about national and international news, and to learn current information in areas of special interest to you: sports, fashion, auto mechanics, music, and so forth. Also use the library to find resource material for essays that you will write in English classes and other courses. You will probably be assigned many essays in college that are not full-length research papers but that will nevertheless require outside reading to gather information for them. More than likely, what you need to know for these essays can be found somewhere in your college library.

The library belongs to you, and you should learn your way around it as soon as possible. Check at the main desk to see if there is a handbook explaining where everything is. If you need assistance, do not hesitate to ask. Library personnel are there to answer your questions and help you find what you need. Many college libraries offer orientation tours and classes to acquaint students with the organization of the books and other items (records, documents, periodicals, and so forth). Even without a formal tour, however, you can learn where things are located simply by studying the library plan and taking a stroll. In particular, you will want to investigate the reference room and locate the major indexes mentioned in this chapter. These simple steps may save you hours of frustration and aimless wandering.

Finding Your Way in the Library

There are several main kinds of resources in the library that can help you find the things you need to know:

The Card Catalog: Most libraries have at least three kinds of collections: books, periodicals, and reference materials. Although most libraries today have online catalogs, traditional card catalogs are still used in many. The card catalog is a large cabinet full of many traylike drawers that is usually located near the main desk. Each book the library owns is cataloged three ways in the file: by title, author, and subject. The title card is filed alphabetically according to the title of the book. (Books are not alphabetized by *a, an,* or *the.* Look up the next word in the title.) The author card is filed alphabetically according to the author's last name. In addition, one or more cards are filed alphabetically according to the subjects treated in the book. If you know the author or the exact title of a book, you will be able to check quickly to see whether the library owns a copy. If you are looking for a book on a particular subject, such as gymnastics, solar energy, French cooking, or public education, use the subject index.

When you are using the subject index, you will often find cards that read "See" or "See also." For example, if you look up "America" in the subject index, the card may say "See United States." If you look up "public education," the card may say "See also Education, public." ("See also" means that you will find cards under both subject headings.) Students often make the mistake of looking up a common-language word like "Car," which will in fact be listed in the card catalog as "Automobile." If you cannot find any card on your subject, ask the librarian for help. Sometimes the author and title indexes in the card catalog will be combined; sometimes all three indexes will be combined.

When you find the card for the book you want, write down the entire *call number* (the number printed on the top left-hand corner). The number will look something like this:

F

279

.C49N4

or this:

191.9

S233

In the first call number, the *F* designation is from the Library of Congress classification system. The call number in this system always begins with a letter.

In the second call number, the *191* designation is from the Dewey decimal system. The call number in this system always begins with a three-digit number from 000 to 999. Depending upon a library's system for cataloging, books will be shelved either by numbers first (in the Dewey decimal system) or by letters first (in the Library of Congress system). For example, to find the example book using the Library of Congress designation, you first find the *F* stacks, and then you look for the shelves labeled *279.* Next you look for the books designated *.C.* Finally, you look for the particular book with the designation *.C49N4.* If you have trouble finding your book, ask the library staff for help.

The Online Catalog: If your library has an online computer catalog, you can use it to locate books by title, author, and subject. The online system can save you time and work because you can conduct your catalog search by entering information and commands at a computer terminal. If you enter a title, the terminal screen will show you all the books the library has with that title or titles similar to it. If you enter an author's name, the screen shows you all the books it has by that author. When you enter a subject, the screen displays the titles of books the library has on that subject.

The online catalog is also useful when you don't know all the information about a book. You can enter only part of a title or just an author's last name and still get a list of books to consult. For example, if you know only the first part of the title for a book titled *Exotic Medicines and Their Uses,* you could enter just the words *Exotic Medicines.* The online system will give you the book's complete title and the information you need to find it. Similarly, if you know only an author's last name, entering it will get you a list of all the library's books by authors with that last name.

Since the online catalogs in each library differ slightly in their operation and the assistance they provide, find out how your own library's system works and follow the directions provided for it.

Periodicals (Magazines, Newspapers, and Journals):　Often, you will want the very latest information about a particular subject, such as space travel, ecology, or nuclear power. Recent magazines are a good source for this information. You can find the latest editions of many popular magazines such as *Time, Newsweek, Scientific American,* and *National Geographic* in the magazine section of your library. You will also find many scholarly journals (usually shelved separately from the popular magazines), which contain more specialized articles on science, literature, philosophy, and art. Browse until you become familiar with the various periodicals your library receives.

Periodicals from previous years may be bound together in book covers, and then shelved in order by year, or they may be preserved on microfilm. (Microfilm is a film on which printed material appears, greatly reduced in size. You can view the microfilm of a magazine or newspaper by placing the film in a special viewer and advancing the film till it reaches the material you wish to read.) The best way to find particular articles is to use the large sets of indexes and bibliographies available in the reference room of your library.

An index that is especially valuable in locating articles in popular magazines is the *Readers' Guide to Periodical Literature.* It is bound in separate volumes by years and contains listings of articles from over 150 magazines. The articles are listed by both subject and author. Here is a sample entry from the 1998 volume of the *Readers' Guide:*

    Rap Music

       Taking the bad rap

       T. McCarroll

       Time 141:63 15 Mr '98

This entry tells you the following:

1. The article title: "Taking the bad rap"
2. The author: T. McCarroll
3. The magazine in which the article appears: *Time*
4. Location: volume 141, page 63 of the issue dated March 15, 1998

If any abbreviations confuse you, check the list of abbreviations and what they stand for at the beginning of the *Readers' Guide*. The magazine abbreviations are listed together. If you cannot find your subject listed, perhaps you are using a term different from the one used by the *Readers' Guide*. Ask for assistance, if necessary.

Another useful reference tool for finding recent articles of popular interest is called *Hot Topics: The Magazine Index*. This is an article-finding machine and accompanying booklet, usually located in the reference section of the library, that can provide you with a long list of articles on a given subject published over the last five years. The articles are listed both by subject and by author, using a format similar to that in the *Readers' Guide*. The advantages of this machine are its speed and the fact that it allows you to see several years' accumulation of articles on one subject at a glance. Ask the reference librarian to show you how to use the *Magazine Index*. It is a simple procedure and well worth your time.

If you need scholarly articles on subjects of historical or literary interest, however, the *Readers' Guide* and the *Magazine Index* are not likely to list them. To find an article on the writings of Mark Twain, for example, or one on the economic roots of the Great Depression, you should consult the *Humanities Index*. Organized much like the *Readers' Guide*, it lists scholarly articles pertaining to history and literature. For articles related to psychology, sociology, anthropology, political science, and economics, check the *Social Studies Index*. The library also will have a number of highly specialized indexes for more intensive research into a particular field. For instance, if you are looking for information for a paper on needed reform in our public schools, the *Education Index* would list many articles on the subject. Check with your reference librarian about these special indexes.

Whichever index you use, the next step is to see whether the library has the periodicals you need. The *Serials Directory*, usually located at the reference desk, lists all the periodicals the library receives and their call numbers. The catalog also will indicate whether the article you need is on microfilm or in bound issues of the periodical. Once you have found the periodicals you need, write down their call numbers and consult the general plan of the library to see where the back (older) issues are located.

Other Reference Tools: In addition to the indexes listed here, a few others may be especially useful in your research. The *Essay and General Literature Index* can help you find essays and chapters within books that relate to your topic, even if the title of the book gives no clue to this. This allows you to find valuable information that you would have missed if you had relied on only a quick glance at the card catalog. The *New York Times Index* is the chief guide to newspaper articles on any event of note since 1851.

One extremely helpful guide to recently published articles on social issues is the *Social Issues Resources Series (SIRS)*. Although often located in the reference room, this series of books is actually far more than a tool for locating information. Each volume contains dozens of reprinted copies of articles on subjects of social concern, written from many points of view. The volumes are continually updated as the library receives new articles. Using the *Resources Series* is quite simple. Each volume has a general subject heading: Abortion, Aging, Defense, Drugs, Religion, Schools, and so on. (The books are arranged alphabetically by subject.) An index at the front of each book breaks the subject into subdivisions so that you can easily locate the articles that are important to your study.

The reference shelves also contain many specialized dictionaries, as well as sets of encyclopedias. As with the other reference tools, these usually cannot be checked out of the library but are for reference room use only. Although the encyclopedia will probably be of limited use to you in writing college papers (it would be inadequate as a major source of information for a term paper, for example), it can be a good place to begin if you are not familiar with a topic. Many encyclopedia articles contain excellent background and statistical information on general areas. Many also supply you with a bibliography for further reading on a given subject.

Publications on Reserve: Some instructors put certain books and periodicals "on reserve." That is, they ask the library staff to make these publications available only to a particular class for short periods of time so that everyone has access to the material. Consult the library floor plan to find the location of the reserve section, or ask the librarian.

Exercise 1

Answer the following questions about your library:

1. What hours is the library open?

   _____

2. Check out a novel or an autobiography you think *you* will enjoy reading. (You might try one of the books suggested under "Reading on Your Own" at the end of this chapter.) Give the following information for your book:

   (a) Call number

   _____

   (b) Title

   _____

   (c) Author

   _____

(d) Publisher; place and date of publication

_____

_____

(e) Due date

_____

(f) Fine for each day the book is late

_____

3. If your name were in the card catalog, what name that is now in the catalog would come right before it?_____

4. Exactly where is the *Readers' Guide to Periodical Literature?*

_____

_____

5. Locate an article on public education in a recent volume of the *Readers' Guide.* Give the name of the article, the author, the periodical it appeared in, and the date it was published.

_____

_____

6. Does your library own *Hot Topics: The Magazine Index?* If so, ask the reference librarian to show you how to find a list of articles printed over the last five years on cloning. How many articles have been printed on this subject? Write the title and source (name of magazine, date, pages) of one such article.

_____

_____

7. Does your library own the *SIRS?* If so, ask the reference librarian to help you find the set of volumes, which will be labeled by subjects on their spines. Give the title of the first article in the volume on drugs.

_____

_____

8. Exactly where is the *Serials Directory?*

_____

9. According to the information in the *Serials Directory,* does your library subscribe to *Scientific American?* If so, what is its call number?

_____

10. In which volume of the most recent edition of the *Encyclopaedia Britannica* will you find an entry on African religions? What is the page number?

_____

_____

11. Using the *Humanities Index,* locate the title of an article on the writings of Edgar Allan Poe and write it here.

_____

_____

12. Of all the magazines your library carries, which are your favorites?

_____

_____

 ## Writing Assignment 12-1

In your library, locate the issue of *Newsweek, Time, Ebony, Life,* or *U.S. News & World Report* that came out the week you were born. Next, find a recent issue of the same magazine. Write a four-paragraph essay in which you compare and contrast one major difference between the older and the current issues. For example, you might want to compare advertisements, political coverage, or sports news.

1. In the first paragraph, give the title and date of each of the magazines you have selected. Include a brief description of the magazines, including the audience they address, their appearance, and their general contents. Include any other information that you feel will help acquaint your reader with the magazines. Then state a thesis that tells how the magazines differ in the one feature you have selected for comparison.

2. In the second and third paragraphs, describe the single major difference that you have selected. Starting with your second paragraph, use this method to compare and contrast the way the two magazines are different. First, describe how the topic you have selected for comparison and contrast is treated in the earlier magazine. Then, in your third paragraph, tell how the topic is treated in the more recent magazine. If it helps, refer to Chapter 8 for a review of how to compare and contrast.

3. In your fourth paragraph, write a conclusion (see pages 95–96) that comments on the single major difference you have shown in the two magazines. Your comments might offer an explanation of the difference or express your positive or negative feelings about it. Include a clincher statement (pages 65–66) to signal the end of your discussion.

Writing Assignment 12-2

Write summaries of two magazine or journal articles listed in recent volumes of the *Readers' Guide to Periodical Literature* (or your library's computer database) under one of the following headings. (The exact wording of the topics may differ somewhat.)

abortion	gene transplants	illiteracy
campus drinking	guns and children	marriage
college entrance exams	Hillary Clinton	tattoos
dolphins	the homeless	toxic waste dumps

Once you have picked a topic, read through the list of titles of relevant articles and choose several that interest you. Find them on the shelves or on microfilm, and decide which two you would like to write on. If your library carries the *SIRS*, you may find the articles you would like to write on there.

In writing the summaries, use the suggestions in Chapter 11. For practice, use at least one direct quotation in each summary. In your first sentence, be sure to include the title of the article and the name and date of the publication in which it appears, as well as the author's name if it is given.

Writing Assignment 12-3

Imagine that a very close friend has just been killed in an automobile wreck. The driver of the car in which your friend was riding was intoxicated. You are naturally extremely upset that such a thing has happened. Everyone has been saying that the death was such an unnecessary loss of human life. To help prevent other deaths or injuries from drunken driving, you decide to write the editor of your college newspaper to try to convince other students to think twice before they drink and drive or before they ride with someone who has been drinking.

Since you want to be as informed as possible when you write this letter, go to the library and read about drunken driving. Find pertinent articles in the *Readers' Guide* under the heading "Alcohol and automobile drivers" and in the *SIRS*, and read several of them. When you think you have done enough reading on the issue, write the letter to the editor. Here are some suggestions:

1. Begin your letter *Dear Editor:*

2. In the first paragraph, explain that your close friend has been killed because the driver of the car in which he or she was riding was intoxicated. Give a brief account of what happened.

3. In the following two or three paragraphs, describe how this unnecessary death points up the national problem of drunken driving. Use your library research to explain just how serious this problem is. Give the titles of the articles that support your findings, their authors, and the dates and names of the publications in which they appeared.

4. In your final paragraph, ask your fellow students not to drive after they have been drinking or not to drive with others who have been drinking. If you believe that additional laws need to be passed to help prevent drunken driving, you may want to state this as well, but be specific about the type of law or laws that you suggest.

 ## Writing Assignment 12-4

Imagine that you have just received a letter from your friend Emily, who is in her first year of college, where she lives in a dormitory. She has recently discovered that she is pregnant. Her parents do not know about the situation, and her boyfriend has distanced himself from her, although he has offered to pay for an abortion. Emily knows that if she has the child, she will have to drop out of college, go home to live with her parents, and get a job. She will have little chance of returning to college for years to come. Emily has always said that she did not think abortion was right, but now she faces giving up college and thus a professional career. Moreover, she knows that her parents are not likely to be supportive if she does go home to have the child. They will probably feel shamed and treat her unkindly, although she believes they will let her live with them during the maternity period.

Your friend sounds desperate in her letter. She asks for your advice, saying that you are the one person who can help her think clearly about the situation. Your task is to write her a letter and give her your opinion on whether she should have the abortion. Before you write the letter, however, you need to become as informed as you possibly can on this very important issue. Go to the *Readers' Guide* or *SIRS* in your library, and search for recent magazine and journal articles on abortion. Study them carefully. Also consult one or more of the encyclopedias in your library.

When you write to your friend, compose a friendly, personal letter giving her advice and explaining why you feel the way you do. You will probably not want to make reference to the reading you have done on the subject, but instead use it for background information. Remember that you are writing to a friend who needs help: She does not need to be lectured or scolded. (Also, assume that the boyfriend's detachment and the parents' insensitivity will not change. For most of the letter, address the central question: Should Emily have the abortion?)

Include with your letter—on a separate sheet—the research you did in the library. (Give the titles of the articles you consulted, their authors, and the dates and names of the publications in which they appeared.)

Reading on Your Own

When American author Richard Wright, in his book *Black Boy,* told his story of growing up in the midst of poverty and oppression in the first part of this century, he said over and over again that what enabled him to free himself from the bondage of his youth was, more than anything else, *reading*. Reading novels, especially, allowed him to enter new worlds and transcend the crippling world into which he had been born:

> Reading grew into a passion. My first serious novel was Sinclair Lewis's *Main Street*. It made me see my boss, Mr. Gerald, and identify him as an American type. I would smile when I saw him lugging his golf bags into the office. I had always felt a vast distance separating me from the boss, and now I felt closer to him, though still distant. I felt now that I knew him, that I could feel the very limits of his narrow life.

Although you may not face the same difficulties Wright faced in growing up, reading on your own can be just as liberating. Furthermore, the more you read, the better you will write. Without even thinking about it, you will learn how to give variety to your sentences, you will greatly increase your vocabulary, and you will learn to avoid mechanical errors.

The following books are popular among beginning college students. Read as many of these books as you can—and more.

The Adventures of Huckleberry Finn, by Mark Twain   Thought by many to be the "great American novel," this wonderfully funny yet deeply serious book tells of the adventures of Huck, a runaway teenager, and Jim, a runaway slave, as they float down the Mississippi River on a raft toward freedom.

Black Boy, by Richard Wright   This autobiography is an American classic, for it is the story of a person who triumphs even though everything seems to work against him.

Blue Highways, by William Least Heat Moon   This is the true account of a man who has lost his job and whose wife has left him. He buys a van, outfits it for travel, and takes off on a journey around the country in search of his own identity—and the best diners in America.

Bread Givers, by Anzia Yezierska   This is an autobiographical novel of a young immigrant growing up in New York City at the beginning of the twentieth century. If you or close family members are immigrants, be sure to read this novel. Even if you and your family are not immigrants, you will find it hard to stop reading this engrossing story.

The Catcher in the Rye, by J. D. Salinger   A long-time favorite among college students, this novel is the story of Holden Caulfield, a prep-school dropout, and his frantic search for meaning in a world where everything seems phony.

Clan of the Cave Bear, by Jean Auel   This is an amazing and beautiful long novel about a tribe of prehistoric Neanderthals who adopt a young girl named Ayla. Ayla is strange to the tribe but familiar to us because she is what we call a "human being."

The Color Purple, by Alice Walker   This is a novel about a badly abused young black woman who gradually learns how to take care of herself in a "man's world." It is also a book about the power of love to reconcile and change.

The Hunger of Memory: The Education of Richard Rodriguez, by Richard Rodriguez   This book is an Hispanic author's account of his childhood and struggles to fit into mainstream American life.

The Joy Luck Club, by Amy Tan   This is a story about a second-generation Chinese-American woman who tells about the lives of four Chinese women—her mother and her mother's three friends—and how they came to this country to begin new lives and leave past events and secrets behind them.

Love Medicine and ***The Beet Queen,*** by Louise Erdrich   These two novels are by a Native American writer who blends history and family saga.

The Member of the Wedding, by Carson McCullers   Frankie Addams, a twelve-year-old girl and the main character in this novel, is a member of no peer group and feels quite alone. Wanting desperately to belong to someone, she takes part in the plans for her brother's wedding, imagining that she will be with the bride and groom when they go away on their honeymoon.

The Natural, by Bernard Malamud   If you are a sports fan, you will enjoy this book. It is the story of a baseball star's rise and fall, beautifully told.

Never Cry Wolf, by Farley Mowat   A young zoologist is dropped off in the Yukon to spend a year alone, studying the habits of wolves. He meets a few natives living in the wilderness and encounters sport hunters; he also meets the wolves. He learns about the Yukon wilderness and about the wolves; he also learns about himself.

Of Mice and Men, by John Steinbeck   This is the story about the friendship of Lennie, a retarded giant of a man, and George, a ranch hand. It is also the story of a hope that will not die.

One Flew Over the Cuckoo's Nest, by Ken Kesey   This novel opens in a mental institution where Big Nurse has reduced her patients to passive robots. Then McMurphy, a brawling, fun-loving, highly intelligent rebel, appears on the scene and challenges Big Nurse's authority. Whether or not you have seen the film, be sure to read this novel.

The Woman Warrior: Memoirs of a Childhood Among Ghosts, by Maxine Hong Kingston   Part autobiography, part fiction, part legend, this fascinating narrative weaves Chinese and American stories into a single rich fabric.

To Kill a Mockingbird, by Harper Lee   This all-time favorite is the story of one person's willingness to stand up for what is right, even though his cause is unpopular.

Here are some other books that you might consider reading:

Fiction
Charlotte Brontë, *Jane Eyre*
Emily Brontë, *Wuthering Heights*
Kate Chopin, *The Awakening*
Ernest Hemingway, *For Whom the Bell Tolls* and *A Farewell to Arms*

Tony Hillerman, *Ghost Way*
Toni Morrison, *Beloved* and *Song of Solomon*
Mary Wollstonecraft Shelley, *Frankenstein*

History

Frances FitzGerald, *Fire in the Lake*
Stanley Karnow, *Vietnam*
Gore Vidal, *Lincoln*
Tom Wolfe, *The Right Stuff*

Science and Technology

Rachel Carson, *Silent Spring*
Loren Eiseley, *The Star Thrower*
Tracy Kidder, *The Soul of a New Machine* and *House*
Barry Holstun Lopez, *Arctic Dreams*
Lewis Thomas, *The Lives of a Cell*

Social Sciences

Barry Commoner, *The Closing Circle*
Michael Harrington, *The Other America*

Autobiography and Personal Experience

James Baldwin, *Notes of a Native Son*
Annie Dillard, *Pilgrim at Tinker Creek* and *An American Childhood*
Dian Fossey, *Gorillas in the Mist*
Beryl Markham, *West with the Night*
Scott Russell Sanders, *The Paradise of Bombs*
Richard Selzer, *Mortal Acts*
Scott Turow, *One L*

The Writing Process

GATHER your ideas and information
ANALYZE your ideas and information
IDENTIFY your theme or main point
PLAN your essay
WRITE your essay
REVISE AND EDIT your essay (STSOE)

13

Writing Persuasively

- **Forming an Argument**
- **Writing an Argument Essay**

230

IN MOST OF the essays you wrote in Parts I and II, you needed to persuade. You were asked to include your opinion on a topic in your purpose statement and then to support your opinion in the body of the essay. In this chapter, however, you will concentrate on using the combined techniques of persuasion and outside resources to write an argument essay. You will learn how to sway your reader of the validity of your position on a given subject by presenting a convincing argument and supporting it with relevant material drawn from your reading.

The ability to argue well is an invaluable writing and reasoning tool. Many college essays assigned in both English classes and other courses are arguments. For example, you may be asked to defend your point of view on why some historical event occurred, why the labor movement is or is not a constructive force in our economy, why authors present characters in novels in a certain way, why a poem is powerful, or why Plato was a greater philosopher than Aristotle.

The skills you learn in writing an argument also will help you in a practical way after college. Think of the many occasions when you might need to write a convincing argument. If you are concerned about a local or national issue, you may want to write a letter to your local newspaper or to your city council member or congressional representative. If you think your church, community organization, or children's school should do something differently, you can argue for your position in a letter to the appropriate official. The library contains a vast store of information that will help you think through your positions on various subjects and develop sound arguments to promote your point of view.

Forming an Argument

The exercises given here should help you prepare to write argument essays. Before you can convince someone else of what you believe on a topic, you must be quite sure that you know what you believe. As you reflect on a certain subject and discuss it with others, you may find that you actually believe something quite different from what you had thought you believed. If so, this is fine; some people call this process of changing one's opinions "growth." Also, it is important that you understand the positions held by those who disagree with you. You must learn to address these positions, as well as to state your own case.

Exercise 1

Let two opposite sides of yourself talk with each other about an important decision you have to make. Record the "conversation" and then revise it, using 300 words or more. What you have to do is to persuade *yourself* on a course of action. Here are some examples of a decision you may want to write about:

> I have a great job offer. Should I take it, or should I stay in college and finish my degree?

I think one of my brothers (or sisters) is developing a serious drinking problem. Should I talk with him (or her) myself or ask someone else to do so? Or should I do nothing?

I have a choice of two jobs: One pays a lot of money, but I do not think I would like it very much. The other sounds more interesting but does not pay nearly as well. Which one should I accept?

I broke off an important relationship. Now I think I have made a mistake. Should I try to reconcile with the person or just leave things as they are?

In choosing a decision to write about, make sure that it would be a difficult decision for you to make.

While having their internal "conversation" for this exercise, some students find that it helps to set up two chairs and to switch seats each time they argue for the other position. Argue as convincingly as you can for each point of view—that's the trick! Keep going back and forth between the two sides as long as necessary; just be sure that you finally make a decision. You might begin to record your "conversation" something like this:

For the twelfth time today I went to the phone, picked up the receiver, and dialed six of the seven numbers. I am dying to accept the job my uncle has offered me as the lead auto mechanic at his service station. He told me that I would start at fifteen dollars an hour and that with my military experience I should do terrific work.

One side of me has been saying "Oh, go ahead. You can go back to college anytime. What job could you get after college that would pay you more than ten dollars an hour? That's over thirty thousand dollars a year. Call your uncle and. . . ."

The other side has been saying "Hold it. Not so fast. All those years you were in the military you planned to go to college so that you would have many career possibilities to choose from. You have planned your whole life around going to college, and now. . . ."

Then the first side says, "Just think: Thirty thousand dollars a year! Why, I could buy. . . ."

When you revise your internal conversation, use the rules for recording dialogue on pages 28–30 and observe how they are used in the student sample on page 9. See Section 20.7 for more on how to use quotation marks.

Exercise 2

Have a class discussion about all the examples of public persuasion that you can think of. Include examples from persuasive advertising (from television, newspapers, magazines, and so forth), military recruiting, religious proselytizing, and political campaigning. Your instructor may want to ask someone to write these examples on the chalkboard. Which are most persuasive? With the class, carefully analyze *why* they are persuasive.

Choose one example of persuasion, and write a paragraph explaining why it is particularly convincing for many people. As an alternative exercise, choose a very persuasive political figure, and in a paragraph analyze why he or she is so influential. You need not agree with this person's point of view. In fact, it may help to choose someone with whom you do not generally agree. Revise your paragraph before turning it in to your instructor. If class time permits, share your paragraph in a small group to learn what others consider effective persuasion.

Exercise 3

Write a paragraph explaining how someone changed your mind on a particular issue or how you changed someone else's mind. Be sure to state exactly what the original position was and what caused the change. Logical arguments? Examples from experience? Appeals to morality?

Exercise 4

In preparation for this exercise, go to the library and read about capital punishment in an encyclopedia and in at least one of the articles indexed in the *Readers' Guide* or reprinted in the *SIRS*.

In class, divide into groups of no fewer than five and no more than eight students. Listed on the next page are five case situations in which someone was sentenced to die. After your instructor reads each case, indicate your reaction to the death sentence, not to the murder—ranging from absolutely wrong to absolutely right—by putting your initials in the appropriate box in the grid.

	Absolutely Wrong	Wrong	Slightly Wrong	Slightly Right	Right	Absolutely Right
CASE 1						
CASE 2						
CASE 3						
CASE 4						
CASE 5						

There should be no discussion until each person has responded to all five case situations. Then all participants should speak in turn about why they put their initials in the particular boxes. Be sure to discuss the underlying values that led to the decisions. Only after everyone has given his or her reasons for the decisions should there be general discussion.

The purpose of this exercise is to help you appreciate the degrees of right and wrong on particular issues and to help you understand why others may disagree with your opinion. (Your instructor may want to replace capital punishment with some other issue of social importance.)

Here are the five case situations:

CASE 1

A skyjacker has been sentenced to die after trying to steal a commercial plane and then killing one of the passengers. He claimed that his only objective was to call the world's attention to the plight of his badly oppressed people.

CASE 2

A woman has been sentenced to die after killing her husband in a fit of rage. She cried on the witness stand and said that she deserved to die and that she loved her husband.

CASE 3

An eighteen-year-old boy has been sentenced to die after shooting a grocery store owner who pulled a gun on him while the boy was robbing the store. This was the teenager's first major offense.

CASE 4

A prison inmate has been sentenced to die after killing a prison guard. He claimed that the guard was always harassing him. Some witnesses agreed. The prisoner was serving a sentence for simple assault and would have been re-leased in three weeks.

CASE 5

A paid gunman has been sentenced to die for killing three people. He was paid five thousand dollars to kill two of the victims and fifteen thousand to kill the third. He offered no defense at his trial, saying "It doesn't matter anyhow."

After the discussion, choose one of the case situations and write a paragraph explaining why you made the decision that you did. It may be most helpful to choose a situation that forced you to make a truly difficult decision because of your conflicting values about the case. In your paragraph you can thus write about all the reasons supporting, as well as opposing your position. Revise your paragraph before submitting it to your instructor.

Writing an Argument Essay

The purpose of the argument essay is to express your opinion on a particular subject. Acknowledge the complexity of the subject if you like, but state a definite opinion. Think of yourself as a member of a jury. Consider the arguments on both sides of the issue, but then cast your vote one way or the other.

If you are permitted to choose your own topic, always pick one that is important to you so that you can make your essay a real argument.

As you develop an argument essay, ask yourself what kinds of arguments would convince you of a certain point of view. You would probably not be convinced by emotional arguments or by general statements that were not soundly supported. Your reader is no doubt very much like you. In your writing, emphasize arguments that are calm, rational, and not overstated.

Take advantage of all the information-gathering resources at your disposal: Use brainstorming or clustering techniques, talk to others for ideas, and use the resources in the library such as encyclopedias, magazines, books, and newspapers (see Chapter 12).

State your position in the first paragraph. This will serve as your thesis statement.

Address the arguments on the other side of the issue somewhere in your essay. You want to avoid having your reader say "Yes, that sounds good, but. . . ." You will do much to reduce the impact of such a response if you address reasonable arguments made by the opposition. Sometimes you can best address the opposing arguments in your introduction, sometimes as you make each of your own arguments, and at other times in a separate paragraph, perhaps the second.

Use the various writing methods discussed in Part II:

1. *Description.* Your skills in observing detail and listening to dialogue will help you support your arguments. Fine points and concrete details convince; general and abstract statements do not.

2. *Narration.* Use your skill in telling a story to illustrate certain arguments. If you are arguing that sex education should be taught in high school, you may want to tell in one paragraph what happened to someone you know who was not properly educated in this subject.

3. *Examples.* Examples strengthen all arguments. In fact, many effective arguments are written as example essays. You first state your point of view; then you support it with three or four examples, using a paragraph or so for each one. You could write convincing essays on topics such as the following simply by giving examples:

Capital punishment sometimes takes innocent lives.

Disabled persons are often discriminated against.

_____ has perhaps the worst drivers in the country.
(name a city)

4. *Comparison and contrast.* If you want to give full treatment to the other side of an issue, the comparison and contrast structure may work best. Here you would give the opposing arguments in the second paragraph and then state your own arguments in the third. (Of course, you may need to subdivide each of these two paragraphs in the body of the essay.) If you choose this structure, whenever possible make your arguments parallel to the arguments of the opposition. For example:

Paragraph 2: *For Capital Punishment*	*Paragraph 3:* *Against Capital Punishment*
deters crime, why "an eye for an eye" now administered justly, examples	does not deter crime, why "To err is human, to forgive, divine" now administered unjustly, examples

5. *Classification.* The most common method for writing an argument is to give several reasons why something is right or wrong. Your skills in classifying material will help you arrange your arguments in a logical way.

6. *Cause and effect.* Showing the cause of a particular problem is essential in arguing for that problem's remedy. Similarly, demonstrating the effect something may have is the best argument for promoting or discontinuing its cause. Use cause-and-effect analysis anytime you want to show that *A* causes *B* or that stopping (or starting) *A* will affect *B* also.

In your introduction, consider telling why the issue under discussion is an important one. Also, consider ending your paper with a call-to-action conclusion.

Support your main points with logical arguments and, when appropriate, statistics, quotations from reading material, examples, descriptive details, and one-paragraph stories. Here are two logical arguments that could be made about the effect of capital punishment on deterring crime:

> Capital punishment is not likely to deter others from committing crime. Stop and think about it. What person is going to make a rational decision about whether to kill on the basis of possible punishment by death or life imprisonment? Both fates are terrible.

> Capital punishment is bound to reduce crime. If convicted murderers are executed, at least *they* will not kill again. Maybe ridding society of a few potential killers is reason enough to justify capital punishment.

Here are two other argument statements, this time on the issue of banning handguns:

> We should ban the possession of handguns by anyone except police personnel. No one else really needs a handgun in our society, not even hunters. Only criminals need handguns in order to commit crimes with them.

> We should control handguns better, not ban them completely. Most people who own handguns will never use them to commit a crime, and banning handguns won't stop criminals from using them, legal or not, to commit crimes.

Throughout your essay, keep your audience in mind. What will it take to persuade your readers that you are right?

Following are two selections expressing opposing points of view about the issue of "phased-in" driver's licenses. The first is an opinion published by the American Automobile Association (AAA). The second is a response to the AAA's article. As you read the two selections, notice how each writer states the argument and marshals evidence in support of it.

Phased-In Licenses Make Teen Driving Safer
by the American Automobile Association
(Copyright 1997, USA TODAY. Reprinted with permission.)

When it comes to worrying about the safety of their teen-agers, studies show that parents fear drug addiction the most. Only one in five realizes that driving is the No. 1 teen killer.

Such ignorance about the dangers of teen driving is deadly as more baby boomers turn over the car keys to their driving-age kids. More than 6,300 teens ages 15 to 20 died in crashes last year. Without changes, teen driving deaths are expected to jump to 7,500 by 2012.

Teens at Risk[1]

More than 6,300 teens ages 15–20 died in auto crashes last year, and 595,000 were injured. Drivers 15–20 comprise:

■ 7% of licensed drivers

■ 14% of driving fatalities

■ 20% of all crashes.

[1]Source: American Automobile Association

Leading Causes of Death, Ages 15–24[2]

Motor vehicle crashes: 31%

Homicide: 20%

Suicide: 14%

Other injuries: 9%

Cancer/heart disease: 3%

AIDS: 2%

[2]Source: 1995 preliminary data from National Center for Health Statistics

Studies show the majority of teen crashes are caused by a lack of experience. Because it takes up to three years of practice to become a skillful driver, several states are embracing a sensible solution: phasing in teen driving privileges.

This step-by-step approach to driver training, known as graduated licensing, recognizes that inexperienced teen drivers are going to make mistakes. Crash rates for 16-year-olds are three times as high as for 19-year-olds, according to the AAA.

So instead of granting full driving privileges to any teen who passes a quickie driving course and a road test, the programs gradually increase teens' driving rights as they become more skilled.

Ten states have enacted limited forms of graduated licensing, including bans on night driving and required practice time with adults. But the Insurance Institute for Highway Safety says that to reduce deaths, the laws should include a package of restrictions for drivers under 18, including:

A prohibition on recreational night driving—since 42% of teen driving deaths occur between 9 P.M. and 6 A.M.

Zero tolerance for alcohol use—because it is illegal for teens to drink.

Restrictions on chauffeuring other teens unless an adult is along—since 66% of teens killed in crashes are riders.

Required practice with adults—found to improve teens' driving skills.

One year after Ontario passed a similar graduated licensing law for all new drivers in 1994, government studies showed a 66% drop in 16-year-olds' accident rates.

The AAA has launched a nationwide effort to pass comprehensive graduated licensing laws in every state. And a "model" law awaits the governor's signature in California, the first to require a six-month wait before a young driver can carry teen passengers unless an adult is on board.

These laws won't stop young drivers from making dumb mistakes. Only age and experience can do that.

But by requiring teens to hone their skills under adult supervision, in the light of day, there's a better chance they'll be around to learn from their errors.

Train, Don't Tinker

by Todd Franklin

Spend a few minutes on the road and you'll realize that the driver education system in this country needs repair. Many drivers lack basic knowledge of driving courtesy, safe driving practices and crash-avoidance techniques.

The amount of training most teens receive before they drive is not sufficient, considering the dense and intense driving environment many of them will face. Most teens think "driver's ed" is a joke.

In some respects, they're right. Teaching young drivers when to use turn signals and how to parallel park is simply not enough.

Now there is a growing clamor for graduated driver-licensing programs. The concept is to gradually phase in driving privileges for new licensees as they "demonstrate growth in driving skills and responsible operation of motor vehicles." The misguided premise for graduated licensing programs is that time is a substitute for training.

Studies in California and Maryland have credited such programs with reducing teen accidents by 5%, which means they would reduce teen accident involvement from 20% to 19% nationally. This minuscule reduction in accidents is due to the fact that teen drivers are logging fewer miles because of the graduated licensing restrictions. It's quite likely that the barely detectable reduction

Source: The National Motorists Association.

in accident involvement will simply be transferred in the form of increased accidents to the next-higher age group.

We're glad to see a growing interest in reducing accidents involving teenagers, but the focus should be on improving driver training programs. Let's teach young people such things as driver etiquette, handling a car under adverse conditions and crash-avoidance techniques.

Graduated licensing programs will waste millions of dollars, complicate the lives of millions of families and provide new excuses for traffic tickets and insurance surcharges. The programs will serve the insurance industry, federal agencies and "safety" groups by lowering the exposure of these higher-risk drivers. However, these programs will do nothing to improve young drivers' skills and will have no meaningful effect on highway safety.

Questions for Discussion and Writing

1. Which selection did you find more persuasive? Why?
2. What was the most effective evidence or reasoning presented in each selection? What made it effective?
3. Does each selection address the arguments of the other side? If so, how? Do you think the opposing side's arguments were adequately addressed in each piece?
4. What arguments on the issue of phased-in driver's licenses can you think of that were not mentioned in either selection? Can you think of a reason the writers of these pieces did not include those arguments?

 ## Writing Assignment 13–1

The object of this assignment is for you to use the library to help you think through and support your views on a particular issue of national importance that is also a concern of yours. (Read Chapter 12 on using the library, if you have not already done so.) Then, after you have finished your research, write an argument essay of several paragraphs on the subject you have chosen.

Choose Your Topic: In your library, find a recent volume of the *Readers' Guide* and look up at least one of the following subjects:

animal rights
campus crime
charter schools
college entrance exams
drug abuse
gun control
the homeless

paramilitary organizations
same-sex marriages
seat belt laws
sexual ethics

Read through the titles of the articles that are listed under the headings, and read at least three articles on one of the topics. If they are not informative and thought provoking, try three more, and keep trying until you find the right articles. As you read, take notes. You also may want to summarize particular articles. It may be helpful to consult an encyclopedia for background information on your topic, but do not stop there.

As you study your subject, try to narrow it down so you will not be covering an issue too broad for a short essay. For example, if you are studying charter schools, you may want to write on the proposed voucher system, discipline problems, or required courses. If you are studying sexual ethics, you may want to write on faithfulness in marriage.

When you are ready, write a statement in which you take a position on an issue. Here are possible thesis statements on some of the subjects listed:

Same-sex marriages should be banned.
Society should insist on the rights of animals.
Seat belt laws infringe on individual rights.
Drugs are seriously damaging college sports.
The homeless cannot be ignored any longer.
At this time, the welfare system is the best we can devise.
Sex outside marriage is immoral.
Charter schools will destroy public education.
We can save the public schools.
Violence on college campuses has made getting an education hazardous.
This country should pass stricter laws controlling handguns.
Paramilitary organizations are a threat to national security.

Before you move on to the next step, check your thesis statement with your instructor.

Gather Your Ideas and Information: Think of as many reasons as you can why your position on the issue you have chosen is the right one, and write these reasons in the left-hand column below. Then think of all the arguments that could be made for other positions on the issue, and write these in the right-hand column. (This is a difficult but important step.) In addition to using the brainstorming and perhaps the clustering techniques to gather ideas, be sure to discuss the issue with others. Now read through the notes you have taken from your reading, and write down any information or quotations you may want to use. If you find that you need more information, go back to the library and explore your topic further.

Your Position   *Other Positions*

_____

_____

_____

_____

_____

_____

_____

_____

_____

_____

Relevant Information and Quotations

_____

_____

_____

_____

_____

_____

_____

_____

_____

_____

_____

_____

_____

_____

Analyze Your Ideas and Information: Looking at both sides of the issue, which arguments are valid? Which are weak? Exactly where do you stand on the issue now that you have had time to reflect on it with resource material in hand? Has your position changed since you began to think about the issue?

Identify Your Main Point: In an argument essay, the thesis statement is usually just a simple statement of what you believe. Any of the statements listed on page 240 could serve as a thesis statement. Be sure you state your thesis exactly as you want to defend it. You may want to qualify your statement to some degree, as follows:

> In spite of the strong arguments that can be made for teaching sex education in high school, I am against it.

> The advantages of teaching sex education in high school are greater than the disadvantages.

However, beware of qualifying your purpose *too much.* Take a position and argue for it. Too much qualifying will weaken your argument.

Plan Your Essay: Before writing an outline for your argument essay, review the various writing methods that are listed on pages 235–236. Can you best develop your essay by using examples, comparison and contrast, or simply by stating several reasons why your position is the correct one? As you write your outline, plan to address the reasonable arguments of the opposition. It may help you to reread the samples to see how those two writers outlined their essays. You may also want to read the two argument essays that follow.

Write Your Essay: As you write, keep reminding yourself of your audience. Is it your instructor and your class? The readers of your school newspaper? Or is it some other group? Also keep in mind the purpose of an argument essay, which is to convince your readers of the validity of your point of view. Would you yourself be convinced by your writing? Include at least one direct quotation in your essay.

Revise and Edit Your Essay: Using the STSOE method, evaluate your paper. Write a short paragraph, as though you were your instructor, commenting on the organization and style of the essay. Is it convincing? Why or why not? Now revise your essay. Finally, edit your writing.

Read the following arguments about whether or not doctors should assist patients in dying, and then complete the writing assignments that follow.

Should Doctors Be Allowed to Help Terminally Ill Patients Commit Suicide?

YES by Derek Humphry

It would be a great comfort to people who face terminal illness to know they could get help to die if their suffering became unbearable. All pain cannot be controlled, and it's arrogant for anybody to say that it can. Quality of life decisions are the sole right of the individual.

It's nonsense to say that death shouldn't be part of a doctor's job—it already is. We all die. Death is a part of medicine. One of a doctor's jobs is to write death certificates. So this idea of the doctor as superhealer is a load of nonsense. The fact is that it's not so easy to commit suicide on your own. It's very hard for decent citizens to get deadly drugs. Even if they do, there's the fear that the drugs won't work. There are hundreds of dying people who couldn't lift their hand to their mouth with a cup of coffee, let alone a cup of drugs. They need assistance.

Of course, people who are depressed or who feel they are a weight on their families should be counseled and helped to live. But you have to separate those instances from people who are dying, whose bodies are giving up on them. If you think there is a cure around the corner for your malady, then please wait for it. That is your choice. But sometimes a person realizes that her life is coming to an end, as in the case of my wife, whose doctor said, "There is nothing else we can do."

We're not talking about cases in which a depressed person will come to a doctor and ask to be killed. Under the law the Hemlock Society is trying to get passed, the doctor must say no to depressed people. A candidate for assisted suicide has to be irreversibly, terminally, hopelessly ill and judged to be so by two doctors.

NO by Daniel Callahan

If it's a question of someone's wanting the right to die, I say jump off a building. But as soon as you bring in somebody else to help you, it changes the equation. Suicide is legally available to people in this country. Just don't ask a doctor to help you do it. That would violate the traditions of medicine and raise doubts about the role of the physician.

One of my worries is that people will be manipulated by a doctor's suggesting suicide. A lot of seriously ill people already feel they're a burden because they're costing their families money. It would be easy for a family to insinuate, "While we love you, Grandmother, and we're willing to spend all our money and not send the kids to college, wouldn't it be better if . . . ?" There is no coercion there, but you build on somebody's guilt. We'd have a whole new class of people considering suicide who hadn't thought about it before.

Then, too, I don't believe that you could successfully regulate this practice. The relationship between the doctor and the patient begins in confidentiality. If they decide together that they don't want anybody to know, there is no way the government can regulate it. The presumption is that physicians would only be helping people commit suicide after everything else had failed to end their suffering. But a lot of people won't want to be that far along. None of the proposed regulations take into account a person who is not suffering now, but who says, "I don't want to suffer in the future. Let me com

mit suicide now." I can imagine a doctor who would say, "Yes, we're going to make sure that you don't have to suffer at all."

Derek Humphry is the founder of the Hemlock Society and author of *Final Exit,* a book advising terminally ill people on how to commit suicide. Daniel Callahan is a bioethicist and director of the Hastings Center, a medical ethics think tank in Briarcliff Manor, New York.

Writing Assignment 13–2

Go the library and find other sources that discuss the issue of doctor-assisted suicide. Be sure to check the *Readers' Guide* and the *SIRS.* Discuss the issue—and perhaps share the two selections above—with at least one other person. Then, using the Writing Process and the suggestions for writing an argument essay, write an argument of your own on the issue of doctor-assisted suicide. Where possible, include direct quotation in your essay. You can refer to the guidelines on using quotations on pages 253–258 for help.

Writing Assignment 13–3

Write a brief, half-page summary of one of the above selections on doctor-assisted suicide.

Writing Assignment 13–4

Read the following essay, "Gay Marriages: Make Them Legal," by Thomas B. Stoddard. Then write a 300 to 400-word response in which you state your agreement or disagreement with Stoddard's ideas. Before you begin writing, first jot down notes about Stoddard's major ideas and any response you may have to them. Use the resources in your campus library or elsewhere to learn more about this topic to support and develop your ideas.

"In sickness and in health, 'til death do us part." With those familiar words, millions of people each year are married, a public affirmation of a private bond that both society and the newlyweds hope will endure. Yet for nearly four years, Karen Thompson was denied the company of the one person to whom she had pledged lifelong devotion. Her partner is a woman, Sharon Kowalski, and their home state of Minnesota, like every other jurisdiction in the United States, refuses to permit two individuals of the same sex to marry.

Karen Thompson and Sharon Kowalski are spouses in every respect except the legal. They exchanged vows and rings; they lived together until November 13,

1983—when Ms. Kowalski was severely injured when her car was struck by a drunk driver. She lost the capacity to walk or to speak more than several words at a time, and needed constant care.

Ms. Thompson sought a court ruling granting her guardianship over her partner, but Ms. Kowalski's parents opposed the petition and obtained sole guardianship. They moved Ms. Kowalski to a nursing home three hundred miles away from Ms. Thompson and forbade all visits between the two women. Last month, as part of a reevaluation of Ms. Kowalski's mental competency, Ms. Thompson was permitted to visit her partner again. But the prolonged injustice and anguish inflicted on both women hold a moral for everyone.

Marriage, the Supreme Court declared in 1967, is "one of the basic civil rights of man" (and, presumably, of woman as well). The freedom to marry, said the Court, is "essential to the orderly pursuit of happiness."

Marriage is not just a symbolic state. It can be the key to survival, emotional and financial. Marriage triggers a universe of rights, privileges, and presumptions. A married person can share in a spouse's estate even when there is no will. She is typically entitled to the group insurance and pension programs offered by the spouse's employer, and she enjoys tax advantages. She cannot be compelled to testify against her spouse in legal proceedings.

The decision whether or not to marry belongs properly to individuals—not the government. Yet at present, all fifty states deny that choice to millions of gay and lesbian Americans. While marriage has historically required a male partner and a female partner, history alone cannot sanctify injustice. If tradition were the only measure, most states would still limit matrimony to partners of the same race.

As recently as 1967, before the Supreme Court declared miscegenation statutes unconstitutional, sixteen states still prohibited marriages between a white person and a black person. When all the excuses were stripped away, it was clear that the only purpose of those laws was, in the words of the Supreme Court, "to maintain white supremacy."

Those who argue against reforming the marriage statutes because they believe that same sex marriage would be "antifamily" overlook the obvious: Marriage creates families and promotes social stability. In an increasingly loveless world, those who wish to commit themselves to a relationship founded upon devotion should be encouraged, not scorned. Government has no legitimate interest in how that love is expressed.

And it can no longer be argued—if it ever could—that marriage is fundamentally a procreative unit. Otherwise, states would forbid marriage between those who, by reason of age or infertility, cannot have children, as well as those who elect not to.

As the case of Sharon Kowalski and Karen Thompson demonstrates, sanctimonious illusions lead directly to the suffering of others. Denied the right to marry, these two women are left subject to the whims and prejudices of others, and of the law.

Depriving millions of gay American adults the marriages of their choice, and the rights that flow from marriage, denies equal protection of the law. They, their families and friends, together with fair-minded people everywhere, should demand an end to this monstrous injustice.

 ## Writing Assignment 13-5

Imagine that you have just received the following letter from your friend Tami Borden, a high school biology teacher. As she says in the letter, she has written several of her former students for advice on a matter of extreme importance to her: whether she should teach sex education in her classes. After you have read the letter closely, jot down your thoughts. Then go to the library and study the issue. You may want to begin by looking up the topic in the *Encyclopedia Americana,* the *Readers' Guide,* and the *SIRS.*

Next, write Tami a personal letter in which you give your advice. Try to present both sides of the question, but then take a position, using all your skills in making an argument. Remember that Tami Borden is your friend and wants your advice, not a lecture.

Dear _____,

I am writing to a few of my former students to ask their advice on a matter that is very important to me. As you probably know, the state legislature has recently made it possible for biology teachers to offer sex education in our high school classes.

I was delighted when I heard the news because I have long thought that sex education should be a part of the curriculum. In the last few weeks, however, there has been a loud public protest against teaching anything connected with sex in high school. I know a few of the people involved in this protest, and they seem like responsible, loving parents. While I disagree with them, I do respect their position. They are afraid that if we offer sex education in the schools, their teenagers will be tempted to indulge in sexual promiscuity.

Because you did not receive sex education in high school, I thought your advice would be helpful. What I would like from you is your opinion on the importance of sex education to the high school student. If I am convinced that this subject really will help my students in their personal lives, I am going to teach it. If it does not seem to matter that much, however, I am not going to stick my neck out. Why fight a battle that does not have to be fought?

Please write me as soon as possible and tell me, from your reading and your experience, just how important you believe it would be for me to offer sex education in my biology classes. Do you think the arguments against sex education in high school are valid? Thank you in advance for your help.

Sincerely yours,

Tami Borden

The Writing Process

GATHER your ideas and information
ANALYZE your ideas and information
IDENTIFY your theme or main point
PLAN your essay
WRITE your essay
REVISE AND EDIT your essay (STSOE)

14

Writing the Research Paper

- **Applying the Writing Process to Your Research Paper**
- **Quoting Published Material**
- **Sample Research Format**

WRITING A RESEARCH paper provides an opportunity to explore a topic about which you want to know more. Have you ever wanted to find out what scientists think about the possibility of life on another planet? Or wished to investigate whether antigang dress codes can prevent violence in schools? Should children be allowed to divorce their parents? Are curfew laws fair and effective means of reducing crime? What determines whether someone is lesbian or gay? Developed through your own analysis of evidence and argued with documented facts, a research paper can provide a convincing answer to any of these questions.

Applying the Writing Process to Your Research Paper

If you have never written a research paper before, it will be especially helpful for you to understand at the outset what kind of paper you will be creating. Broadly defined, a research paper is a documented essay developed with your own ideas and the information you have gathered from other sources about a topic. A research paper differs from other essays you have written in several ways: (1) it is generally longer; (2) it makes extensive use of information sources beyond the writer's personal experience, including books, magazines, journals, and newspapers; and (3) it acknowledges the writer's use of other sources by citing them in the text and also listing them in a Works Cited section at the end of the paper. This task involves learning the correct way of citing and listing the sources consulted.

A research paper also resembles other essays you have written, in several important ways. The text of a research paper consists of an *introduction,* which gives necessary background information and states the purpose or *thesis;* a *body,* which is composed of paragraphs that develop the thesis in more detail and provide evidence to support it; and a *conclusion,* which sums up the main ideas presented in the paper.

Most importantly, a research paper is similar to other essays you have written because, despite your use of outside sources to support or illustrate ideas, the overall content reflects *your thinking about the topic.* Even when you are writing a ten- or twenty-page research paper, your own ideas, supported by the research you have done, direct the paper's discussion. In writing such a paper, you can still use the same methods you applied to shaping much shorter essays. Here is how to adapt the activities of the Writing Process to your research paper.

Gather Your Ideas and Information

Your instructor may ask you to select the topic for a research paper or assign you a general subject with which to start—dangerous drivers, for example. In either case, part of your job will be to narrow down the topic to a thesis of suitable scope for the length of the assigned paper. For instance, in a ten-page paper, you could not hope to cover every important issue connected with the American education system, but you could examine a more limited question, such as *one* of these: How do students pass through the system without learning to read and write? How does our system compare with that of another country? In what ways can we improve the system without destroying it?

The best way to begin your research is to assess how much you already know about the subject and then make a list of questions about the topic that you would like to find answers to. Brainstorming works well for this step. Given the topic of dangerous drivers, you might come up with questions such as these:

1. How big is the problem of dangerous drivers on the highway?
2. What causes "road rage"?
3. How does road rage differ from other kinds of discourteous or dangerous driving?
4. What can people do to help reduce road rage?

Of course, you are not under any obligation to answer all these questions in the course of your research. However, making the list will help you get a better focus on what interests you. This is the first rule for writing a good research paper: *Choose a part of your topic that you genuinely would like to find out more about.* If you set off with gritted teeth to spend hours in the library researching some topic you don't care about at all, the paper is bound to be a painful experience for you—and for your reader as well.

In addition to your interest in the topic, another very important consideration is the workability of the subject. Is there enough resource material available for you to base a paper on? How much has been written on the subject, and how much of what has been written does your library have? To answer these questions, you will need to head for the library. Your time there will be spent in making a working bibliography, reading and scanning, and taking notes.

Make a Working Bibliography: This is a list of the books, articles, and other resources that might be useful to you in writing your paper. As you begin your research, it is a good idea to keep a record of all the potential sources you locate, including their call numbers, so you can easily go back to them later. The best way to do this is to keep a stack of 3-by-5-inch index cards on which you list the information necessary for locating a source again or for listing it in your paper's Works Cited section. For books, this information includes the author's name, book title, place of publication, publisher name, and date published. For periodicals (magazines, newspapers, and journals), record the author's name, article title, periodical title, date, and the inclusive page numbers. For both types of sources, also list the library call number and perhaps a note concerning the subject of the source. A sample card is shown on page 250. Keeping such a record will help you at several stages of your research—while you are looking up and reading a source, when it is time to quote from the material and cite the source, and when you are preparing the Works Cited section of your paper.

HC   Arnold Nerenberg

2638   Overcoming Road Rage: The 10-Step Compassion Program

C2

N43   Los Angeles: Handsdown, 1995

1995

        Has good data on road rage and means to overcome it.

Investigate a Variety of Sources: While compiling your working bibliography, keep in mind the importance of gathering information from a variety of current and authoritative resources. It is a good idea to begin your research by reading an encyclopedia article for general background on your topic. Your library's card catalog or online catalog can tell you not only what books are available on your topic, but also where useful resources such as the *Readers' Guide to Periodical Literature,* the *Social Sciences Index,* and the *New York Times Index* are located. (Chapter 12 discusses these and other important library resources.) You will find that books provide the most in-depth treatment of a subject, while magazines and newspapers will provide the most current information about popular issues. Scholarly journals may be more difficult to read, but they will supply accounts of the most current research and thinking.

As you check for potential sources to research, remember to keep the working bibliography balanced in terms of the type of sources listed and the point of view they represent. Resist an overreliance on any one or two works, no matter how comprehensive they appear to be, and avoid relying too much on one type of source—all magazine articles, let's say. Search for multiple sources that together will give you a picture of all sides of an issue or of all aspects of the topic. If you are investigating, for example, whether or not SAT scores are legitimate criteria for college admissions, you will need to find out what the makers of the test claim, what its supporters think, and what those who argue against the SAT have to say about it.

Scan and Read: Having located a variety of potential sources and recorded information about them in your working bibliography, you are now ready to begin investigating the books and articles that look most promising. Try scanning the books rather than reading each of them all the way through. First, look at the date the book was published. (If you are writing a paper on recent student dropout rates, you can eliminate a book that was published in 1950.) Then look through the table of contents to see what areas of the topic the writer has examined. By reading a few paragraphs in one of the chapters, you will get a sense of the level of difficulty of the writer's style. Then flip to the index at the back of the book to see how often your area of interest is mentioned. (For example, you might look in the index under the heading "School dropouts." Is the term mentioned once, twice, six times in the book? Do any of the page references represent long segments of the book?) If you do this at the outset, you usually can determine which books or chapters of books warrant a closer reading. Begin by reading the material that is most likely to provide you with an overview of the subject.

Take Notes: If any articles or sections of books are brief enough and are particularly important to you, you may want to photocopy these for your own use. For the most part, though, you will need to make an accurate written record of the ideas and information you may want to use later and to keep track of where they came from. Strive for accuracy when you write down someone else's words. Also write down the author, title, and number of the page on which the quotation was found. Your task will be simplified if you have already made out bibliography cards. If you have, all you need to put in the way of documentation on your notes is the author's last name and the page numbers used. Remember, you will have access to the book only for a limited amount of time, and you may not have it in your hands during the final stage of writing your paper.

Some writers prefer to use loose-leaf paper or notebooks for their note taking, but the most generally accepted technique is to use index cards. If you limit the amount of material on each card to one subject and put a subject heading in the upper right-hand corner, you will be able to shift and rearrange cards as needed, keeping together all the material on a particular subject.

One final note about the information-gathering stage: As you can see, it is much more involved and time consuming than any information gathering you have done in the past. Yet it is crucial that you give yourself the time to do it thoroughly because the information you collect is the foundation on which your research paper will rest. Therefore, be sure to begin well in advance of the date when the paper is due.

Analyze Your Ideas and Information

At this point, you need to take a step away from all your reading and note taking and ask yourself, "What part of this subject am I most interested in pursuing?" You will probably want to expand (or alter) your original list of questions. Then select from the list the question (or group of questions) you want to look at more closely. Do you already have enough information on this limited part of your topic, or do you need to find out more? How can you put together in a meaningful way the information you have? (For example, given the issue of dangerous drivers, do you want to concentrate primarily on the causes of road rage or on what you think can be done to teach drivers to be more courteous toward one another?)

Identify Your Main Point

Your thesis statement will come out of the questions you answered in the preceding activity. The thesis is simply a more explicit statement of the main idea that you want to examine in your paper. Try to say in a sentence or two what you want to prove or show. If you choose to concentrate on how to reduce road rage, you might begin with the following thesis statement:

> Overcoming road rage will require national as well as individual effort from all of America's drivers.

See pages 70–73 for help in writing the thesis statement.

Plan Your Paper

When you are satisfied that your thesis statement is as effective as possible, you are ready to make an outline. While there are many forms of outlines, many writers prefer to use a *topic outline* to organize their thinking and actual writing for a research paper. For a topic outline, you write key phrases that indicate the detailed ideas that will appear in the paper itself. The following example shows how to create a topic outline. Notice how each level of ideas, ranging from broad to particular, is set off by indentation:

Thesis statement: Overcoming road rage will require national as well as individual effort from all of America's drivers.

   I. Introduction: Examples of road rage

  II. Increases in aggressive driving and road rage

 III. Causes of road rage
    A. Traffic incidents
    B. Modern culture
    C. Stress
    D. Traffic congestion

 IV. Cost of road rage
    A. To society
    B. To individuals

  V. Responses to road rage
    A. Public awareness
    B. Increased law enforcement
    C. Internet
    D. Self-control

Write Your Paper

With your thesis statement in front of you, begin to write. Consider this writing effort a rough draft, and don't be concerned if not every detail is perfect. Just concentrate on writing an essay that is coherent (that is, one in which the ideas are closely and logically related) and on using the information you have found to reinforce your main ideas.

Many research papers overdepend on long quotations from outside sources. Even though you do need to borrow the ideas of others from time to time, it is still *your* paper. Let your own voice be heard. Many students find that they can resist the temptation to let other writers' voices "take over" if they put aside their notes and try first to free-write a two- or three-page paper on the subject. Then they can go back and fill out the body paragraphs more fully by using their outside sources. Whatever technique you favor, don't let your paper degenerate into a long string of quotations that are connected loosely by a few words of your own. Four ways to quote other sources are described in detail on the following pages.

All four methods, including paraphrasing, require citing your sources, a way of giving credit to the writers whose ideas you quote. The simplest way to do this is to give the author's name and the page number of the book or article—in parentheses—at the end of the quotation.

When you have finished writing the paper and citing the sources, one final task remains in the writing stage: compiling the bibliography. The *bibliography* is an alphabetized listing of the sources you have consulted. It is placed at the end of the research paper, on a separate page. The bibliography should be titled "Works Cited." See page 278 for sample entries in a Works Cited section.

Revise, Edit, and Submit Your Paper

After you have completed your rough draft, let it rest for a day or two, if at all possible, before you begin the revision process. When you have made all the necessary changes, proofread the final copy carefully for mechanical and grammatical errors. Submit your research paper with a title page, which gives the title of your paper (do not use quotation marks around it), your name, the course title, and the date. (Follow the sample on page 269.)

Quoting Published Material

Use *quotation* when you need to provide the exact written or spoken words of another writer or source. To use quotation effectively in your research paper, observe the following key points:

■ *Quote sparingly and always for a reason.* Few things can dilute the quality of your research paper more than numerous patches of unselected and needless quotations. Quote another author or source when you need to support a claim, present evidence, or clarify an idea. Use paraphrase or ellipsis (see below, page 257) to eliminate any needless parts of a long quotation.

■ *Use quotations to pass on the exact language of a particularly well-written phrase or sentence and whenever paraphrasing would lose an important quality of the original.* You might need to quote someone's exact words to reveal an attitude or feeling, for example, or to record precise language when what was said or intended is disputed by others.

■ *Whenever you quote, always acknowledge the source of the quotation.* Cite the source both in your paper's text and in the Works Cited section of your paper. (See below, pp. 260–266.)

Several methods exist for using quoted material in a research paper. Which ones you use should depend upon your emphasis and the style or tone you adopt for the paper. Following are four of the most basic ways to include quotations in your discussion.

Method 1:   Incorporate the most important parts of the original quotation into the grammar of your own sentence. This method allows you to reduce the amount of quoted material and to emphasize what is important without noticeably interrupting your discussion.

> In his essay "Rising to the Occasion of Our Death," William F. May says that people who know they are going to die soon "have time to engage in acts of reconciliation" (7).

Rules on Form

1. When the quotation is part of the grammar of the sentence, do not capitalize the first word of the quotation, unless it would normally be capitalized anyway (such as a proper noun). Note that the first word in the preceding quotation is not capitalized because it does not begin a whole sentence.
2. Use quotation marks only if you write the *exact* words of the original.
3. If you do not mention the author's name in your sentence, include it with the source page number in parentheses at the end:

> Clearly, too many men mistakenly feel that women in science are "unnecessary, injurious, and out of place" (Cole 21).

Method 2:   Let the quotation stand by itself as at least one full sentence, using your own words to introduce it:

> According to James, "Road rage is a habit acquired in childhood" (2).

Rules on Form

1. If the quotation is itself a full sentence or more, capitalize its first word:

   According to Cole, "The main sorting out of the girls from the boys in science seems to happen in junior high school" (20).

2. Use your own words to introduce or incorporate the quoted sentence into the text, as in the example above. Do not allow the quoted sentence to stand all by itself between quotation marks.

3. When using a verb such as *say, write,* or *state* to introduce the quotation, insert a comma after the verb:

   As May states, "Sometimes the moral life calls us out into a no-man's land where we cannot expect total security and protection under the law" (7).

4. When introducing a full sentence with expressions such as *the following,* use a colon after the introductory phrase:

   May, however, states the following: "On the whole, our social policy should allow terminal patients to die but it should not regularize killing for mercy" (8).

   Note that the quotation is introduced by a statement that is a grammatically complete sentence.

5. Give the page number(s) in parentheses after the closing quotation marks and before the period:

   Boys, Cole points out, learn games that involve "speed, motion, and mass" (20).

Method 3:   Indent any quotation that amounts to more than four lines of *your paper's* text:

> According to James, our society accepts road-raging behavior as part of the norm and something to tolerate because we are taught to admire and imitate it:
>
> > Road rage is a habit acquired in childhood. Children are reared in a car culture that condones irate expressions as part of the normal wear and tear of driving. Once they enter a car, children notice that all of a sudden the rules have changed: It's O.K. to be mad, very upset, out of control, and use bad language that's not ordinarily allowed. By the time they get their driver's license, adolescents have assimilated years of road rage. (2)

Rules on Form

1. Set off a quotation of more than four lines by indentation, not quotation marks. Indent the entire quotation *ten* spaces from the left margin if you are typing, or an inch if you are writing by hand. Do not indent the quotation on the right.

2. Do not skip a line above or below the indented quotation. If you are typing, double-space the quotation throughout.
3. Do not indent the first line of a quotation to show that it is a single paragraph in the original. Begin the first sentence of the quoted paragraph ten spaces from the left margin as you would any other indented quotation. If you quote two or more paragraphs, however, indent the first line of each paragraph three spaces.
4. Introduce indented quotations (such as the example in Method 3) with an introductory sentence and colon.
5. Give the page number(s) in parentheses *two spaces after* the period ending the quotation.

Method 4:   Make the quotation indirect by paraphrasing the source in your own words. The advantage of paraphrasing is that you have much more flexibility in the way you incorporate the original material into your paper. The indirect quotation or paraphrase is often shorter than the original because you are summarizing:

> James argues that we adopt road rage habits as children, learning from adults that it is acceptable to get angry and yell at other drivers when we are in a car. By the time we get our own driver's license, we have absorbed years of road rage culture. (2)

Other Rules on Form

1. Do not use quotation marks for a paraphrase or indirect quotation. However, do remember to use quotation marks for any *exact* language you include.
2. Note that indirect quotations are often introduced by the word *that,* as in the preceding example.

Other Rules for Quoting Published Material

1. Give the full name of the author you are quoting the first time you quote, but thereafter refer to the author by the last name only:

> Author Leon James calls road rage a "habit acquired in childhood." According to James, . . .

2. Put quotation marks around the titles of short pieces, such as articles, essays, poems, songs, and television programs:

> "Why Clinton Got Elected" (article)   "Easter Sunday" (poem)
>
> "America" (song)   "Northern Exposure" (television program)

3. Underline the titles of longer works, such as books, magazines, journals, newspapers, pamphlets, plays, and films:

Woman Warrior (book)   Newsweek (magazine)   Hamlet (play)

New York Times   Avoiding AIDS   Yale Law Journal
(newspaper)   (pamphlet)   (journal)

Men in Black (film)

4. Avoid quotations within quotations, as these can become very awkward. If you must quote in this fashion, use single quotation marks around the inside quotation:

> When a man asked her what the women thought about Carl Sagan, Cole said she "had no idea what 'the women' thought about anything" (21).

5. You may omit unnecessary material from a quotation by using an *ellipsis* to indicate that some part of the original has been left out.

Original quotation   "Most road rage incidents, whether they involve the police or not, are the result of illegal driving and should be regarded that way."

Quotation with ellipsis "Most road rage incidents . . . are the result of illegal driving and should be regarded that way."

The ellipsis is made by three periods (. . .) with a space before and after each period. An ellipsis *plus* a period may be used when a quoted word or phrase comes at the end of a sentence (note that the ellipsis follows the period):

> As Trainer points out, "Most road rage incidents, whether they involve the police or not, are the result of illegal driving. . . ."

The use of ellipsis in cases like this, however, is generally unnecessary. You do not need to use an ellipsis at the beginning or end of a quoted word or phrase because the grammar and punctuation will indicate that you have omitted other parts of the original. The following method of integrating parts of a quotation with your sentence is preferable:

> As Trainer points out, "Most road rage incidents, whether they involve the police or not, are the result of illegal driving" (31).

Use the ellipsis sparingly. You can often avoid it entirely by using paraphrase or indirect quotation. When you must use an ellipsis, make sure the quoted material continues to move smoothly, as though the thought were continuous, as in the preceding examples.

Avoid Plagiarism

Whenever you quote directly or paraphrase ideas or language from another writer, you must give credit to that writer, or source, in your research paper. Because student writers of research papers may be uncertain about when or how to give credit to their sources, they sometimes fall into the trap of *plagiarism,* which is using the words or ideas of another without acknowledgment. Intentional or not, plagiarism is cheating—using another writer's words, ideas, research data, or ways of explaining something as if they were your own. Plagiarism is a serious breach of both personal and academic integrity. Most colleges react to plagiarism with penalties ranging from a failing grade on the research paper or in the course to academic suspension. For these reasons, it is important that you understand both when and how to give your sources credit for any language or ideas you adapt for use in your research paper.

Crediting Your Sources

You will need to *cite,* or give credit to a source, anytime you quote the source directly, paraphrase or summarize ideas from the source, or borrow specific information and ideas not found in most other sources for your topic. You will undoubtedly have no problem remembering to cite an author whom you quote directly in your paper. However, don't forget that you must also cite the source if you paraphrase, for example, another writer's ideas about the ways children learn to read or if you state that "the Library of Congress houses over 20 million books" (who found this out for you?). You will also want to cite a source to give authority to statements such as "most Americans still believe in family values" or "the Beatles are the most famous musical group in the world" (how have you determined this?). In such instances as these, you are drawing upon research others have done for you, and they deserve to be credited for it.

However, keep in mind that the majority of your paper will be composed of your own ideas and general information about the topic, material for which you will not need to assign credit to others. You do not need to credit a source when you mention commonly known facts or concepts in your paper, such as the fact that Franklin D. Roosevelt defeated Herbert Hoover in the 1932 presidential election, or when you define the *solar system* as including the Sun and all the known planets. These ideas are known to most people familiar with the general subjects of American politics or astronomy, and they would most likely appear in several sources on those topics.

The Modern Language Association (MLA) sets the standard followed in most college English courses for crediting or citing sources in research papers. In an MLA-style research paper, you cite sources both in the text of your paper and, additionally, in a final section titled "Works Cited." Study the following sections carefully to understand the correct forms for acknowledging sources in text and in the Works Cited section of your paper.

Citing Sources in the Text

When you quote directly or paraphrase words or ideas from another source in your research paper, cite the source first in the text of your paper. You will acknowledge the source again in the paper's Works Cited pages, but the in-text citation allows you to document immediately and more precisely what you borrowed.

You can cite sources in your text in two ways. The first way is to include the author's name in the sentence introducing the borrowed material, giving the source page number in parentheses right after:

Author named in text   According to Jane Goodall, the people of Gombe can best protect wild chimpanzee habitat by developing what she calls "controlled tourism" (253).

Use this method to cite an author in the text when it is important to emphasize who said or wrote what you have included in your paper.

When *what* you borrow from a source is more important than from *whom,* cite the author's last name and the source page number in parentheses after the borrowed material:

Author cited parenthetically in text   The people of Gombe can protect the habitat of wild chimpanzees best by developing what has been called "controlled tourism" (Goodall 253).

As a general rule, you must always give the page number for any source you cite in text unless the source (1) has no page numbers (such as a film or interview) or (2) when the entire source is a single page, in which case you cite only the author in the text and omit giving a page number:

So successful have lotteries become that one out of every ten Americans has purchased a lottery ticket at least once (Rogers).

The single page number for the source cited here by Rogers would be listed with other information in the Works Cited section of your research paper. For ways to cite various kinds of sources in your text, study the citations in the sample research paper on pages 269–277 and the examples included after each Works Cited entry on page 278.

The Notes Section of Your Paper

You should include all important information and ideas about your topic in the text of the research paper itself. However, if you want to provide further information about a topic but feel that it will take away from the point you are making in the paper's text, you can include a comment in a Notes section that appears just before the Works Cited pages. You signal a reader that you have an additional comment to make in the Notes by placing a note number slightly above the line of text and repeating it again at the start of the comment in the Notes section. Notes are numbered consecutively throughout the paper, starting with 1. Here is an example of a note number as it would appear in the text of a research paper, and then as the note itself would appear in the Notes section:

Note number appearing in the text

Teens often join gangs for self-protection as much as they do out of a desire for a sense of community.[1] The drawback, of course. . . .

Note as it appears in the Notes section

[1]The desire for a sense of belonging to a community, in fact, is greater in older teens than in younger ones (Hansen 34).

The Works Cited Section

Every source cited in your research paper's text or referred to in the Notes must also be listed in the Works Cited section. No other works, not even those you may have examined thoroughly during the research stage but did not cite in the paper or notes, should be included in this section. Remember to list each source alphabetically by the author's last name or, if no author is named in the source, by the work's title. Study the sample research paper's Works Cited page on page 278, and follow the guidelines given below for the sources you list in your own paper's Work Cited section.

Works Cited Forms: MLA Style

Following are general guidelines describing standard Modern Language Association (MLA) practices for the way you should list various kinds of sources in your paper's Works Cited section. Notice that every Works Cited entry includes certain basic information about each source listed. For a book or other whole work, these include the author's name, the work's title, place of publication, the publisher, and the date published:

AUTHOR   TITLE   PLACE PUBLISHED   DATE PUBLISHED

Feynman, Richard P. <u>Six Not-So-Easy Pieces.</u> Reading, MA: Helix, 1997.

For a magazine or newspaper article, or for other sources not published as whole works, the basic information includes these items:

AUTHOR   TITLE   SUBTITLE   SOURCE TITLE   DATE

Adler, Jerry. "Road Rage: We're Driven to Destruction." <u>Newsweek</u> 2 June 1997: 70.

PAGE NUMBER

In all cases, be sure to follow the form exactly as shown in the guidelines and models that follow, especially in regard to such matters as spacing, capitalization, underlining, and punctuation. For more information on citing sources or for a format for listing any source not shown here, consult *MLA Handbook for Writers of Research Papers,* 4th ed., by Joseph Gibaldi (New York: MLA, 1995).

Authors' Names and Order of Appearance

1. List a single or first author by the last name, followed by the first name and initial, if any. List the second or third author's name in usual order, separating the names by a comma or *and.*

   Drucker, Johanna. The Alphabetic Labyrinth: The Letters in History and Imagination. London: Thames and Hudson, 1995.

   Gribbin, John, and Mary Gribbin. Richard Feynman: A Life in Science. New York: Dutton, 1997.

   Boyd, Robert, Carol Haney, and John Thinmer. Hard Going: Hiking the Blue Ridge. New York: Damler, 1997.

2. For a work with more than three authors, list only the first author's name, followed by *et al.* ("and others"):

   Segre, Emilio, et al. National Wealth and Private Rights. Chicago: Hall, 1997.

3. If you cite two or more works by the same author, give the author's name in the first entry and use three unspaced hyphens followed by a period to stand for the name in all following entries. List each work in alphabetical order by title. When citing one of the works parenthetically in your paper's text, name the specific title, in shortened form, followed by the page number.

   Wilson, Edward O. The Diversity of Life. New York: Norton, 1993.

   ———. In Search of Nature. Washington, D.C.: Island, 1996.

   ———. Naturalist. Washington, D.C.: Island, 1994.

   The proper in-text citation form is (Wilson, Diversity 63).

4. If the author of a work is a corporation, committee, or other group, list the work by its corporate or group author, followed by other necessary information:

   Society for Nutrition Education. You're in Charge: Nutrition for Preschool Children. New York: Society for Nutrition Education, 1996.

5. If no author is given in the source, do not use "Anonymous" or "Anon" in place of an author's name. Instead, list the work alphabetically by the first word in the title, but ignore the articles *a, an,* and *the.* For example, the following entry would appear in the Works Cited list as though *Astrologer's* were the first word in the title:

   The Astrologer's Companion. San Francisco: Aquarian, 1997.

Editors' Names

Give an editor's name the same way you would an author's name, but follow it with the abbreviation *ed.* or *eds.* to indicate *editor* or *editors:*

> Springer, Marlene, ed. <u>What Manner of Woman: Essays on English and American Life and Literature</u>. New York: NYU, 1996.

> Whitlock, Donald, and Jason Kerr, eds. <u>The Dinosaur's Endurance</u>. New York: Craig, 1997.

Titles of Books and Other Whole Works

Underline the titles of all complete works, such as books, journals, pamphlets, magazines, newspapers, plays, recordings, and movies. However, do not underline the title of the Bible, the Koran, or other sacred books. Note that you use a colon between the main title and subtitle of a book.

A book	Berenbaum, May R. <u>Bugs in the System: Insects and Their Impact on Human Affairs</u>. Reading, MA: Helix, 1995.
A book including another work	Kyles, Johnathan. "The Only Women He Knew." <u>Century Reader.</u> Eds. Joyce Roth and Dale Newsome. New York: Textualis, 1997. 83–88.
A sacred book	The Bible [Indicates the King James version].
A pamphlet	Kline, Henry. <u>Talk to Your Child About Drugs</u>. Denver: Hatter, 1997.
A magazine	Cook, William J. "Mad Driver's Disease." <u>U.S. News & World Report</u> 11 Nov. 1996: 20.
A journal	Shend, David. "Why Teachers Quit." <u>Educator Quarterly</u> 41 (1997): 261–71.
A newspaper	Puente, Maria. "Students Get Object Lesson in 'Road Rage.'" <u>USA Today</u> 16 Oct. 1997: 3A.
A recording	Washman, Leonard. <u>Orchestralis</u>. Columbia Records, CK73459, 1997.

Articles, Chapters, and Parts of Whole Works

Place double quotation marks around the titles of articles, chapters, songs, or works published as part of another, complete work.

An article:	El-Baz, Farouk. "Space Age Archaeology." <u>Scientific American</u> Aug. 1997: 60–65.
A chapter:	Ambrose, Stephen E. "Jefferson and the West." <u>Undaunted Courage: Meriwether Lewis, Thomas Jefferson, and the Opening of the American West</u>. New York: Simon, 1996. 332–42
A song:	Haggarty, Carol. "Something for You." <u>Sweet Talk.</u> Central, 1997.

Place of Publication

Give the name of the city in which a book was published, followed by a colon and the name of the publisher. When more than one city of publication is given in the source, list only the first city named. If the city has a common name (e.g., "Cambridge, Massachusetts" and "Cambridge, England") or is not well recognized, follow it with a comma and an abbreviation of the state (use standard ZIP code abbreviations) or foreign country where the city is located. (Note the use of *Sp.* for "Spain" in the following example.)

Buendia, J. Rogelio. <u>A Basic Guide to the Prado</u>. Madrid, Sp.: Grefol, 1996.

Sang, Tsu. <u>Simplified Chinese Characters</u>. Union City, CA. Suno, 1997.

Publisher's Name

Use a shortened (usually single) name for the publisher; abbreviate *University* or *Press* with "U" or "P."

Barnwell, William, and Robert Dees. <u>The Resourceful Writer</u>. 4th ed. Boston: Houghton, 1999.

McArthur, Tom. <u>The Oxford Companion to the English Language</u>. Oxford: Oxford UP, 1995.

For other publisher names, use the following examples as guides.

Barnes and Noble Books	Barnes
Cornell University Press	Cornell UP
Government Printing Office	GPO
Houghton Mifflin	Houghton
Alfred A. Knopf, Inc.	Knopf
W.W. Norton and Co., Inc.	Norton
Random House	Random
University of Chicago Press	U of Chicago P

Page Numbers

Give complete pages when citing a particular chapter, part of a book, or periodical article. Separate consecutive page numbers with a hyphen (e.g., 34–41). If a periodical article appears on discontinuous pages (e.g., first on page 40, then on page 73, then on 82), give only the first page number and a plus sign (e.g., 40+), followed by a period.

> Bogert, Carroll. "Oh, to Be Young and Chinese." <u>Newsweek</u> 7 July 1997: 40+.

> Lahr, John. "Fortress Mamet." <u>New Yorker</u> 17 Nov. 1997: 70–82.

Dates of Periodical Entries

List the day before the month, and abbreviate the name of the month, except for the months of May, June, and July. Here are some examples:

> 14 Jan.   6 Apr.   23 Aug.   9 May   11 July

Citing Electronic and Online Sources

Electronic and online sources come in a variety of forms; they also sometimes appear in printed versions, and they may be changed or updated periodically. You will need to indicate such information when it is relevant for the electronic and online sources included in your paper's Works Cited pages. If some information is not relevant to the type of source or if you are unable to locate some required information, give as much as is needed or available (see the entry for "Hypnosis" below).

1. Citing Sources on a CD-ROM
   a. *A CD-ROM source that is updated periodically and has a printed equivalent:*
      List (1) the author's name; (2) the regular publication information for the print equivalent; (3) the database name (if relevant), underlined; (4) CD-ROM; (5) the name of the database provider or vendor; (6) the publication date of the CD-ROM.

> Canno, James. "The Internet Has Holes." <u>New York Times</u> 21 Feb. 1996: B2. <u>New York Times Ondisc</u>. CD-ROM. UMI-Proquest. Nov. 1997.

> "Hypnosis." <u>Encyclopaedia Britannica</u>. CD-ROM. Chicago: Encyclopaedia Britannica, 1997.

   b. *A CD-ROM source that is updated periodically with no printed equivalent:*
      Give (1) the author's name; (2) the title of the accessed source (in quotation marks); (3) the date of the source; (4) the title of the database (underlined); (5) CD-ROM; (6) the name of the vendor (if relevant); (7) the electronic publication date.

> Sheldon, Sandra. "Demographic Profiles for the City of Anderson." 1997. <u>Illinois Population Census</u>. CD-ROM. Oakland. 1997.

c. *A CD-ROM source that is not updated and has no print equivalent:*

Some CD-ROM are issued like books, that is, as whole works not intended to be updated or changed. To cite such sources, give (1) the name of the author; (2) the title of the part of the work you are citing (in quotation marks if appropriate); (3) the title of the work, underlined; (4) the edition, release, or version (if relevant); (5) CD-ROM; (6) the city of publication; (7) the publisher's name; (8) the publication year.

> Stratton, William H. "The Apache Today." Native Americans: Their History and Future. CD-ROM. Chicago: Oakley, 1997.

2. Citing Sources from a Commercial Online Service

For sources you access through a commercial online network such as America Online, Nexis and Lexis, Prodigy, or the Microsoft Network, give the (1) author's name; (2) full information for the printed equivalent of the source, (3) database name (underlined); (4) Online; (5) the name of the computer service; (6) the date you accessed the source material.

> Kern, Walter. "Living the Pharmaceutical Life." Time 29 Sept. 1997: 82. Time Online. Online. AOL. 7 Oct. 1997.

3. Citing Sources from the Internet

Many of the Internet sources you locate will not contain all the information needed for full bibliographic description. In such cases, cite as much information as you can: (1) the author's name; (2) printed form information (if the source is available only electronically, include [a] the underlined title of the major component (e.g., journal, conference, newsletter), [b] any volume or issue numbers, [c] the date of the electronic posting, [d] the number of pages or paragraphs (use "n. pag." if there is no pagination given, "pp." for *pages,* and "par." or "pars." for *paragraph* or *paragraphs*); (3) Online; (4) the database or site title; (5) the computer network; (6) the date of your access; (7) the electronic address, or URL, between angle brackets.

> Altman, Kyoko. " 'Road Rage' Runs Rampant in High-Stress U.S. Society." U.S. News & World Report 18 July 1997. 3 pp. Online. CNN Interactive. 9 Nov. 1997. <http://www.cnn.com.US/9707/18/aggressive-driving/index.html>.

> "Don't Get Mad—Get Even!" Online. D.U.D.s—The Database of Unsafe Driving. Internet. 1 Nov. 1997. <http://www.comnet.ca/~chezken/duds.html>.

Other Types of Sources

For most sources such as those given here, indicate the medium (such as "personal interview" or "videocassette") as shown. For performances (such as films or plays) you may specify the roles of various individuals who may be relevant to your text discussion.

An interview	Miller, Francis. Personal interview. 17 June 1996.
A speech or lecture	Mendoza, Michael. "Disclosure Ethics." Lecture. San Jose State University. San Jose, CA, 19 Mar. 1997.
An advertisement	"You Can't Pick Your Relatives." Advertisement. <u>Wired</u>. Dec. 1997: 135.
E-mail	Nguyen, Kathy. <kath@globe.com>. "Job Openings." E-mail to Barbara Kaelman. 20 Aug. 1997.
News group	Dolson, Greg. "Volunteers." 8 May 1997. Online posting. Community News. Chatlines. 12 May 1997.
A film	Sonnenfeld, Barry, dir. <u>Men in Black</u>. Paramount, 1997.
A videocassette	Griggs, Tara, host. <u>Where Are the Jobs?</u> Videocassette. Dir. Gayle Olney. Seaforth, 1997.

Research Paper Format

Your instructor will probably require that you type your research paper or print it from a computer file. Follow these guidelines as you prepare the final research paper manuscript:

Paper, Type, and Ribbon: Use standard 8½- by-11-inch white paper of a common weight and thickness (16–20 pound bond paper is usual). Type or print the paper in easily readable size type, such as 10-point (elite) or 12-point (pica) throughout, and use a good-quality black ribbon that produces sharp, readable print.

Margins and Spacing: Use a one-inch margin at the top and bottom of your paper, as well as on both sides. Double space throughout the paper, including after the title and for indented quotations, notes, and the Works Cited entries.

Indentations: Indent each paragraph of the text five spaces in from the left margin; indent quotations of more than four lines ten spaces from the left margin. Type the first line of each entry in the Works Cited list flush with the left margin, but indent the second and all following lines five spaces.

Page Numbers: Beginning with the first page of the paper's text, number each page consecutively in arabic numerals (1, 2, 3, and so on). Count and put a page number on every page of the text, including the first page. Use small roman numerals for the page numbers of any pages appearing before the paper's text pages. (Although you would not actually put a number on it, the title page is considered page i.) Type each page number one-half inch down from the top of the paper and one inch in from the right edge. On each page, include your last name, followed by a space, before each page number: Johnson 2.

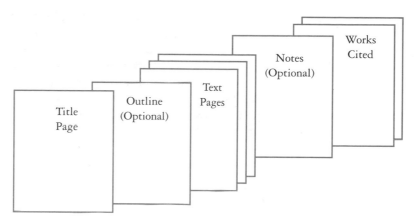

The parts of a research paper

Organizing the Paper: Unless your instructor asks you to put the research paper in a folder, staple all the pages together in the upper left-hand corner so that they appear in this order: title page, outline (optional), text pages, notes (optional), Works Cited pages (see illustration).

A Sample Research Paper

The following sample research paper on road rage demonstrates the practices you should observe as you compose your own paper. Carefully read and study the sample paper several times, paying attention to the way the writer has integrated his own ideas and information from research sources. Note also the way sources are first cited parenthetically in the text and then listed in the Works Cited section at the end of the paper. The comments in the margin of the paper point out writing strategies and technical practices that you may want to adopt for your own research paper.

Writing Your Research Paper on a Computer

Writing a research paper with the aid of a computer offers several advantages for storing, arranging, and editing research material as you work. If you have access to a computer and plan to use one as you do your research and write the paper, here are several uses to keep in mind.

   1. *Use the computer to store your research notes.* You can use the computer first to store research notes and, later, to revise, rearrange, or copy from them as you start to write various parts of the paper. You can begin by first

creating two separate files, one titled "NOTES.TXT" (or some other title of your own) for your research notes, and another called "BIBLIO.TXT," in which you can record the list of sources for your working bibliography. Using your computer software's ability to copy or to move text, you will find it easy to organize your notes under subcategories with distinctive headings, as well as to copy quotations or directly merge other material from the notes into your research paper as you write it. You will find a working bibliography file called "BIBLIO.TXT" (or another name) handy for listing sources alphabetically by author or title as you first enter them, and for later copying them directly into your "Works Cited" list when the paper is finished.

2. *Make an outline for your paper.* Some computer software programs include an outline-making feature that you can use to create an outline for your research paper. If you don't have this option on your computer, you will find the regular margin or tabbing functions of your word-processing program helpful in setting up the correct indentation and spacing required for a formal outline.

3. *Write the drafts of your paper.* Composing on a computer is easier than typing or writing by hand because a computer allows you to add, rearrange, change, or move text as you write. Inserting new text or deleting what you no longer want is fast and easy on a computer, and most word-processing programs let you switch back and forth between pages or even view more than one page at a time as you write. You can use the computer's copy feature to reproduce quotations, technical details, or any other material directly from the notes you have stored in the same or another file, and you may be able to use your computer's graphic functions to create a chart or graph to illustrate your research findings. The computer's word-processing program also makes it easy to set the proper margins and spacing for your paper, to insert raised note numbers, to center the title on the title page and the first page, and to number the paper's pages automatically as you write.

4. *Edit and revise the final draft of your paper.* Your computer's "move" function will allow you to rearrange any portion of the final text that would be more effective in a different part of the paper, and you can use the delete and insert features to eliminate wordiness or to sharpen your word choices as you revise. If you have a spelling-, grammar-, or style-checking function in your word-processing program, check the paper's correctness in these matters. However, do not rely entirely on these features to make your paper error free. Don't forget that the spelling checker cannot distinguish between *its* and *it's,* for instance, or that the style checker may not know when you have omitted citing a source or have used needless or imprecise vocabulary.

5. *Back up your files.* If your computer has a hard disk drive, you can store whatever you write each time you work by saving the particular file to the computer's hard disk. Since any kind of technical error or power shortage may lose what is stored on the hard disk, it is important that you make backup copies of any

If your instructor prefers that you include a separate title page, follow this example.

Center the paper's title, your name, and all other information on the title page.

Road Rage: Violence Takes Over
America's Highways

by

Richard Lerma

English 101
Professor Nora Tansey
December 14, 1997

Place your last name in front of each page number; use lowercase roman numerals for pages coming before the paper's text.

Include the paper's thesis at the start of the outline.

Follow standard outline form.

Thesis statement: Overcoming road rage will require national as well as individual effort from all of America's drivers.

  I. Introduction: Examples of road rage

 II. Increases in aggressive driving and road rage

III. Causes of road rage
    A. Traffic incidents
    B. Modern culture
    C. Stress
    D. Traffic congestion

IV. Cost of road rage
    A. To society
    B. To individuals

 V. Responses to road rage
    A. Public awareness
    B. Increased law enforcement
    C. Internet
    D. Self-control

Road Rage: Violence Takes Over America's Highways

In Durham, Maryland, when another car cut aggressively in front of theirs, high school driving instructor David Cline ordered his student driver to chase after the offender. When they caught up to the other car, Cline got out and punched the other driver in the nose (Puente). In Colorado Springs, Colorado, when Vern Smalley pulled off the road with the 17-year-old driver who had been tailgating him, Smalley, 55, neither lectured nor punched the teenager; he shot and killed him (after the youth had threatened him) (Vest, Cohen, and Tharp 24).

Incidents like these are textbook examples of what popular and scholarly literature have come to term "road rage," an irrational, hostile driving response intentionally aimed at harming another motorist or vehicle. In 1997 road rage accounted for one in every three vehicle crashes and two-thirds of the 41,000 traffic deaths in this country (Rosenfeld 1). So widespread has road rage become that the House of Representatives has held hearings about it, and state and national authorities are instituting dozens of new safe-driving campaigns and special laws to reduce its surging incidence. Its causes and what to do about road rage are complex. However, as the phenomenon one psychologist has labeled a contagious "mental disorder" (Altman 2) continues to spread, it becomes clear that overcoming road rage in this country will require national as well as individual effort from all of America's drivers.

The current surge in road rage comes at a time of increasingly aggressive driving in general. A recent USA Today/CNN/Gallup poll found that a majority of Americans (74 percent) think people are driving more aggressively today than they did five years ago[1] (Puente); another study found that nearly 90 percent of drivers surveyed said they had had an aggressive driving experience within the past year (AAA 2). In Washington, D.C., aggressive driving has reached such proportions that motorists view it as a greater threat to highway safety than drunk driving (Vest, Cohen, and Tharp 24). Such perceptions are corroborated by a 1997 American Automobile Association study showing traffic incidents related to violence and aggressive driving have increased nationwide nearly 7 percent each year since 1990; and that figure does not include hundreds, possibly thousands, of cases that are not reported (AAA 5).

Center the paper's title at the top of the first page.

This paper begins with two brief narrative examples.

Cite sources parenthetically in the text.

Include definitions for key terms in the paper.

The paper's thesis appears at the end of the second paragraph.

Use raised numerals to indicate material in the paper's Notes section.

Include up to three authors' names in the citation, as shown.

Lerma 2

Use single quotation marks to indicate a quotation appearing within a quotation.

Perhaps most surprising is that the majority of road rage cases grow out of relatively minor, everyday traffic incidents. Most of them are hardly worth arguing over, let alone killing for. Yet according to David Willis, president of the American Automobile Association's Foundation for Traffic Safety, "Motorists are being shot, stabbed, run over for totally inane reasons. Like 'She wouldn't let me pass,' or, 'Nobody gives me the finger.' People have been shot because they drove too slowly or played the radio too loud" (Altman 1). In one road rage incident, a driver was attacked because he could not turn off the antitheft alarm on his rented jeep; another case involved a woman being shot because "the bitch hit my new Camaro" (AAA 5–6). In another encounter, a teenager murdered the passenger in another vehicle simply because, as he put it, "We was dissed" (AAA 6).

Once upset, these angry, out-of-control drivers use their vehicles as weapons, dangerously tailgating, ramming, or swerving at other cars; running down other motorists or bystanders, as well as purposely crashing into light posts or buildings, is also common. In some 65 percent of road rage cases studied by the AAA, motorists also used other weapons, including pepper spray, guns, knives, tire irons, hatchets, baseball bats, skis, and even eggs and water pistols (AAA 7). In Massachusetts, a 54-year-old bookkeeper and church deacon used a crossbow and arrow to kill the other driver with whom he was arguing (Willis 3); in California, famed actor Jack Nicholson retaliated against a driver he thought had cut him off by repeatedly striking the windshield and roof of the other car with a golf club (Willis 7).[2]

These examples include details that enhance their effectiveness.

Experts who study such incidents say their causes are multiple, ranging from the personalities involved in a road rage incident to broader cultural influences that celebrate aggressiveness on the road. Some blame drivers' sense of power and combativeness on the size and design of today's vehicles, as well as on the emphasis on "power" used to sell modern cars and trucks; others point to the influences of the "Road Warrior" image popularized in the 1981 film of that name and reinforced by other movies and car advertisements (Willis 4–5).

Cite encyclopedia articles by title, without page numbers.

Road rage also seems prompted by the plain stress of driving today. Authorities agree that just living—and therefore driving—in a modern, technological society imposes a significant amount of "unavoidable" psychological stress ("Stress") on everyone, a con-

Lerma 3

Give only the last two digits of long, continuous page numbers.

dition that has been shown since the 1960s to correlate with violent road incidents among drivers (Selzer, Rogers, and Kern 1022–36). Americans are driving 35 percent more miles now than in 1987—but on only 1 percent more roads and highways. The result is that nearly 70 percent of urban freeways are congested today, as opposed to just 55 percent in 1983 (United States 2). As roads become more clogged with traffic, drivers feel more pressed for time; aggressive drivers react by trying to assert more control. Professor John Palmer of the Health Education and Safety Department at St. Cloud State University, Minnesota, says that when people perceive "someone is impeding their progress or invading their agenda, they respond with what they consider to be 'instructive' behavior, which might be as simple as flashing their lights to something more combative" (Vest, Cohen, and Tharp 28).

State qualifications for cited authorities as needed.

Another cause, says Sandra Ball-Rokeach, codirector of the Media and Injury Prevention Program at the University of Southern California, is that aggressive behavior at the wheel is "now the most common way of driving. It's not just a few crazies—it's a subculture of driving" (Vest, Cohen, and Tharp 27). Professor of psychology Leon James, who maintains an Internet site on aggressive driving and also teaches courses on traffic psychology at the University of Hawaii, agrees, stressing that a good deal of road rage comes from cultural influences. According to James, our society accepts road-raging behavior as part of the norm and something to tolerate because we are taught to admire and imitate it:

Introduce indented quotations with a colon.

Indent quotations longer than four lines ten spaces.

Cite sources or page number parenthetically *after* an indented quotation and any final punctuation mark.

> Road rage is a habit acquired in childhood. Children are reared in a car culture that condones irate expressions as part of the normal wear and tear of driving. Once they enter a car, children notice that all of a sudden the rules have changed: It's O.K. to be mad, very upset, out of control, and use bad language that's not ordinarily allowed. By the time they get their driver's license, adolescents have assimilated years of road rage. (2)

The cost of assimilating road rage behavior into our culture comes at a price, however, to society and to the individuals who are caught up in it. One insurance expert estimates the nationwide dollar cost of discourteous, aggressive driving in the billions, not to mention the thousands of lives lost or indirectly harmed by

Lerma 4

Cite a source with no author by title.

Include quoted material in your own sentences when possible.

These multiple examples help to illustrate the author's ideas.

Give the full name of organizations before using initials.

its fallout ("Coalition" 1). The cost in human suffering is clearly great. The more than 25,000 deaths a year attributed to road rage include children and other innocent bystanders, the indirect victims of crashes, gunfire, or other lethal action that was originally aimed at someone else (AAA 11). Family members are also victims: besides losing a loved one, they are left with what one mother called the "eternal questioning of why somebody else's craziness" killed their child or other relative (Bays 6).

While no single profile describes the overtly aggressive or road-raging driver, the majority are relatively young, poorly educated males from lower socioeconomic backgrounds, although not all—including the roughly 4 percent who are female—fit that profile (AAA 4). A large number are average men and women, many of whom are also educated, respected members of their communities. What sets them apart is their experience of getting suddenly caught up in the fury of a moment's road rage—often with tragic results. Thus, in Hawaii, a 17-year-old high school student faces manslaughter charges because the man he argued and then scuffled with over a traffic dispute fell from the highway and died during the incident (Bays A4). In California, a respected 42-year-old restaurateur was convicted of manslaughter for shooting and killing the unarmed driver he said harassed him for miles over a mountainous road (Gammon A1); and in Cincinnati, Ohio, a 24-year-old mother was sentenced to eighteen months in prison for causing the death of an unborn fetus in a car she purposely cut off and caused to crash after it had entered her lane (Adler 1). According to John Larson, director of the Institute of Stress Medicine, such drivers "are not predators in the usual sense. They don't have a history of assaultive behavior, and, following the incident, are embarrassed, and usually recognize that they over-reacted and had gotten out of hand" (AAA 15).

Recognizing that road rage itself has gotten out of hand, Americans are beginning to take steps to remedy it. In conjunction with House of Representatives hearings, the Coalition for Consumer Health and Safety (CCHS) has recently announced the launching of a nationwide safe-and-courteous driving campaign. Together with the American Driver & Traffic Safety Education Association, the CCHS will publicize guidelines on safe driving and the dangers of road rage ("Coalition" 1).

Lerma 5

States are also reacting to curb road rage and generally aggressive driving. In addition to adding heavier fines for aggressive drivers, Maryland has also instituted a new "#77" program in which motorists dial a special number to alert police about an aggressive or dangerous driver's presence on the road (Willis 6). In addition, new electronic anti–road rage messages now light up Maryland's interstate highways as part of the state's "End of the Road for Aggressive Drivers" campaign (Vest, Cohen, and Tharp 26). In a similar effort, Delaware, Pennsylvania, and New Jersey have set up special highway patrols to target aggressive drivers, and Massachusetts has started a new "3-D" program aimed at arresting "drunk, drugged, and dangerous" drivers (Bays A4). In California, new automated cameras record license plates of vehicles running red lights (Altman 2).

The new rage against road rage has also given rise to a variety of local and individual efforts. In Los Angeles, drivers who have just been victimized by an aggressive driver or who are themselves beginning to fume out of control can use their cellular phones to talk with psychologist Arnold Nerenberg, an expert in traffic psychology who also likes to refer to himself as a "Doctor of Road Rage" (Bays A2). And in Hawaii, Professor Leon James, as mentioned earlier, not only teaches a university course on driving, but as "Dr. Driving" also maintains a well-known Internet site devoted to safe driving advice and psychology.

The Internet, in fact, is proving a popular forum for frustrated drivers to vent their hostilities. One San Francisco Web site, for example, displays "Jerque du Jour" photographs of vehicles whose overly aggressive drivers have been caught on camera by the site's authors; their fans also send in e-mail descriptions of their own photographs of other "Jerques" (Lefevre 1–2). Another site, "The Knoxville Road Rage Action Page," publishes reports of people who drive like "a potato-head" and includes the make and license numbers of offending cars. At the "Database of Unsafe Driving," frustrated motorists can "get even" with "D.U.D." drivers by posting their own descriptions. One entry reads as follows: "Tyrannus Jerkasauras. Cuts off cars at high speeds. Like the Kindergarten kid, can't stay in the lines" ("Don't" 17). The following example is also typical:

> Little black Dodge Shadow which almost ran my wife and I off the road (literally), sped up so that we could not pass, cut in front of us so that we could not proceed, then got off the high-

Use quotation marks around online sources.

Lerma 6

way in Southington, CT laughing his fool head off. If anyone encounters this guy, post it to this page and I'll make sure a couple of guys . . . give him some driving lessons. ("Don't" 10)

While Internet responses may provide frustrated drivers valuable but short-lived relief, motorists will ultimately need to learn to deal with road rage while actually on the road, starting with examining their own driving habits. As psychologist Arnold Neremberg explains, however, self-examination—especially for those who need it—does not come easily. "Road ragers need to admit they have a problem" he says. "And frankly, road ragers don't consider road rage a problem" (Altman 2). Although once-popular driver's education courses have been traditionally considered the way to train drivers, they rarely teach anything about driver personalities and the importance of courtesy on the road (James 17). More promising results have come from a new Massachusetts program that allows motorists convicted of aggressive driving offenses to take an eight-hour video course focused specifically on road rage and driver attitudes. So far the program has reduced by seventy-seven percent the number of accidents the course's drivers had within a year (United States 3).

Such programs have strong endorsement from safety and traffic experts, who agree that leading motorists to examine their own driving habits and to be more patient with other drivers is the best way to improve behavior behind the wheel. Professor James encourages his students, as they make their way through heavy traffic, to tape record their feelings about other drivers. James maintains motorists can consciously modify their driving by "self-witnessing" their attitudes about other drivers and by examining their own behaviors (Cook 3). He also suggests that rather than practice "defensive driving," which presumes confrontation, we should instead exercise "supportive driving" or driving with the "aloha spirit" he practices in Hawaii (Vest, Cohen, and Tharp 28).

In his book Overcoming Road Rage: The 10-Step Compassion Program, Arnold Nerenberg reminds readers that other drivers are human, too. The best response when we feel anger brewing over the mistakes of others on the road, he says, is to "Take a deep breath and just let it go" (16). That may not always be easy, of course. But given the potential for any driver to be involved in a violent incident today, it may be the surest—and the safest—way to begin getting road rage off the road for good.

Underline the titles of books.

The paper ends with a restatement of the thesis ideas.

Center the title <u>Notes</u> at the top of the page.

Begin each note entry with a raised numeral; indent the first line of each entry five spaces.

Use note entries to provide important explanations to or clarifications of your paper's content.

Lerma 7

Notes

[1]See a slightly different figure (64 percent) for those surveyed saying others are driving worse now than five years ago in "Coalition" 2.

[2]Targets of road rage are not always only other drivers or their vehicles. The AAA study also found that angry drivers have intentionally rammed their cars into crowds of pedestrians, utility poles, gasoline pumps, hospitals, banks, schools, hotels, and restaurants—and even purposely driven themselves in spiteful rage off hillsides and piers. See AAA 9.

Works Cited

Center the title <u>Works Cited</u> at the top of the page.

If given, include the page numbers of online sources; include online service provider where applicable, and date of access. "Available" access information may be required by your instructor.

Indent the second and following lines of each entry five spaces.

List sources alphabetically, by the authors' last names.

List a work with no author by its title.

Use <u>n. pag.</u> when there is no pagination for an online source.

AAA Foundation for Traffic Safety. "Aggressive Driving: Three Studies." March 1997. 33 pp. Online. Internet. 10 Nov. 1997. <http://www.aaafts.org/Text/research/agdrtext.htm#Road Rage>.

Adler, Jerry. "Road Rage: We're Driven to Destruction." <u>Newsweek</u> 2 June 1997: 70.

Altman, Kyoko. " 'Road Rage' Runs Rampant in High-Stress U.S. Society." <u>U.S. News & World Report</u> 18 July 1997. 3 pp. Online. <u>CNN Interactive.</u> Internet. 9 Nov. 1997. <http://www. cnn. com.US/9707/18/aggressivedriving/index.html>.

Bays, Corrine. "Road Rage Takes Its Toll—Again." <u>Texas Sun Sentinel</u> 14 Mar. 1997: A1+.

"Coalition Announces Safe, Courteous Driving Campaign." 26 Aug. 1997. Online. Internet. 12 Nov. 1997. <http://www. healthandsafety.org//courteous.html>.

"Don't Get Mad—Get EVEN!" <u>D.U.D.s—The Database of Unsafe Driving</u>. n. pag. Online. Internet. 1 Nov. 1997. <http://www. comnet.ca/~chezken/duds.html>.

Drevik, Steve. "The Knoxville Road Rage Action Page." n. pag. Online. Internet. 6 Nov. 1997. <http://www.geocities.com/ TimesSquare/Castle/3130/complain.html>.

James, Leon. "Aggressive Driving and Road Rage: Dealing with Emotionally Impaired Drivers." Congressional Testimony Before the House Committee on Transportation and Infrastructure. Subcommittee on Surface Transportation. 17 July 1997. 15 pp. Online. 5 Nov. 1997. <http:www.house.gov/ transportation/surface/sthearin/ist717/james.htm>.

Include the place and date of publication for book entries.

Include the volume number for journal entries.

List encyclopedia articles by title; cite CD-ROM source as shown.

List government sources by government, followed by agency or agencies.

List three authors as shown here.

Use the + sign to indicate that source material appears on discontinuous pages.

Lerma 9

Lefevre, Greg. "Web Page 'Shames' Bad Drivers." 20 Dec. 1995. *CNN Interactive*. 2 pp. Online. Internet. 10 Nov. 1997. <http://www.cnn.com/TECH/9512/web_shame/index.html>.

Nerenberg, Arnold. Overcoming Road Rage: The 10-Step Compassion Program. Los Angeles: Handsdown, 1995.

Puente, Maria. "Students Get Lesson in 'Road Rage.'" USA Today 16 Oct. 1997: 3A.

Rosenfeld, Harry. "Where Does 'Road Rage' Come From?" Albany Times Union 30 June 1997: A2.

Selzer, M. L., J. E. Rogers, and S. Kern. "Fatal Accidents: The Role of Psychopathology, Social Stress, and Acute Disturbance." American Journal of Psychiatry 124 (1968): 1028–36.

"Stress." Encyclopaedia Britannica. CD-ROM. Chicago: Encyclopaedia Britannica, 1997.

United States. Cong. House. Subcommittee on Surface Transportation. Hearings on "Road Rage." 17 July 1997. 5 pp. Online. Internet. 7 Nov. 1997. <http://www.house.gov/transportation/surface/sthearin/ist717/ist717.htm#PURPOSE>.

Vest, Jason, Warren Cohen, and Mike Tharp. "Road Rage." *U.S. News & World Report* 2 June 1997: 24+.

Willis, David K. "Research on the Problem of Violent, Aggressive Driving." Congressional Testimony Before the House Committee on Transportation and Infrastructure. Subcommittee on Surface Transportation. 17 July 1997. 7 pp. Online. 5 Nov. 1997. <http:www.house.gov/transportation/surface/sthearin/ist717/willis.htm>.

files you create for your research paper material, including the files containing your notes, working bibliography, and the research paper itself. You can back up such files by periodically copying them onto a separate floppy disk as you add material or make other changes to them, or you can print a paper-copy backup, or hard copy, of each file as you work. Some experienced writers do both—that is, copy each file to a floppy disk and make a hard copy—just to make sure none of their important effort is ever lost. Once your research paper is finished, print an extra copy of it for yourself and others to read and enjoy, also.

Writing Assignment 14-1: Gathering Ideas for a Research Assignment

The two essays on the following pages were selected to give you one or more possible starting points for your own research. In addition to focusing on the socially significant issues of assisted suicide and the role of women in science, the essays touch as well upon a number of related topics that you could profitably investigate for a research paper assignment: the ways other countries cope with dying, our country's treatment of the aged and disabled, female vs. male education, and nontraditional roles for women with careers, to name a few. Next, review the Questions for Discussion and Writing at the end of each selection with your classmates to determine two or three additional topics you might want to examine further. Use your library's resources and those listed after each essay in Sources for Further Reading and Research to find out more about a topic or to begin your research.

Rising to the Occasion of Our Death

William F. May

For many parents, a Volkswagen van is associated with putting children to sleep on a camping trip. Jack Kevorkian, a Detroit pathologist, has now linked the van with the veterinarian's meaning of "putting to sleep." Kevorkian conducted a dinner interview with Janet Elaine Adkins, a 54-year-old Alzheimer's patient, and her husband and then agreed to help her commit suicide in his VW van. Kevorkian pressed beyond the more generally accepted practice of passive euthanasia (allowing a patient to die by withholding or withdrawing treatment) to active euthanasia (killing for mercy).

Kevorkian, moreover, did not comply with the strict regulations that govern active euthanasia in, for example, the Netherlands. Holland requires that death be imminent (Adkins had beaten her son in tennis just a few days earlier); it demands a more professional review of the medical evidence and the patient's resolution than a dinner interview with a physician (who is a stranger and who does not treat patients) permits; and it calls for the final, endorsing signatures of two doctors.

So Kevorkian-bashing is easy. But the question remains: Should we develop a judicious, regulated social policy permitting voluntary euthanasia for the terminally ill? Some moralists argue that the distinction between allowing to die and killing for mercy is petty quibbling over technique. Since the patient in any event dies—whether by acts of omission or commission—the route to death doesn't really matter. The way modern procedures have made dying at the hands of the experts and their machines such a prolonged and painful business has further fueled the euthanasia movement, which asserts not simply the right to die but the right to be killed.

But other moralists believe that there is an important moral distinction between allowing to die and mercy killing. The euthanasia movement, these critics contend, wants to engineer death rather than face dying. Euthanasia would bypass dying to make one dead as quickly as possible. It aims to relieve suffering by knocking out the interval between life and death. It solves the problem of suffering by eliminating the sufferer.

The impulse behind the euthanasia movement is understandable in an age when dying has become such an inhumanly endless business. But the movement may fail to appreciate our human capacity to rise to the occasion of our death. The best death is not always the sudden death. Those forewarned of death and given time to prepare for it have time to engage in acts of reconciliation. Also, advanced grieving by those about to be bereaved may ease some of their pain. Psychiatrists have observed that those who lose a loved one accidentally have a more difficult time recovering from the loss than those who have suffered through an extended period of illness before the death. Those who have lost a close relative by accident are more likely to experience what Geoffrey Gorer has called limitless grief. The community, moreover, may need its aged and dependent, its sick and its dying, and the virtues which they sometimes evince—the virtues of humility, courage, and patience—just as much as the community needs the virtues of justice and love manifest in the agents of care.

On the whole, our social policy should allow terminal patients to die but it should not regularize killing for mercy. Such a policy would recognize and respect that moment in illness when it no longer makes sense to bend every effort to cure or to prolong life and when one must allow patients to do their own dying. This policy seems most consonant with the obligations of the community to care and of the patient to finish his or her course.

Advocates of active euthanasia appeal to the principle of patient autonomy—as the use of the phrase "voluntary euthanasia" indicates. But emphasis on the patient's right to determine his or her destiny often harbors an extremely naïve view of the uncoerced nature of the decision. Patients who plead to be put to death hardly make unforced decisions if the terms and conditions under which they receive care already nudge them in the direction of the exit. If the elderly have stumbled around in their apartments, alone and frightened for years, or if they have spent years warehoused in geriatrics barracks, then the decision to be killed for mercy hardly reflects an uncoerced decision. The alternative may be so wretched as to push patients toward this escape. It is a huge irony and, in some cases, hypocrisy to talk suddenly about a compassionate killing when the aging and dying may have been starved for compassion for many years. To put it bluntly, a country has not earned the moral right to kill for mercy unless it has already sustained and supported life mercifully. Otherwise we kill for compassion only to reduce the demands on our compassion. This statement does not charge a given doctor or family member with impure motives. I am concerned here not with the individual case but with the cumulative impact of a social policy.

I can, to be sure, imagine rare circumstances in which I hope I would have the courage to kill for mercy—when the patient is utterly beyond human care, terminal, and in excruciating pain. A neurosurgeon once showed a group of physicians and an ethicist the picture of a Vietnam casualty who had lost all four limbs in a landmine explosion. The catastrophe had reduced the soldier to a trunk with his face transfixed in horror. On the battlefield I would hope that I would have the courage to kill the sufferer with mercy.

But hard cases do not always make good laws or wise social policies. Regularized mercy killings would too quickly relieve the community of its obligation to provide good care. Further, we should not always expect the law to provide us with full protection and coverage for what, in rare circumstances, we may morally need to do. Sometimes the moral life calls us out into a no-man's-land where we cannot expect total security and protection under the law. But no one said that the moral life is easy.

Questions for Discussion and Writing

1. What reasons does May give for opposing Kevorkian's assistance in Janet Elaine Adkins's death? Do you agree with his reasons? Why or why not?
2. What does May mean when he says we live in an "age when dying has become such an inhumanly endless business"? What has such an "endless business" to do with his argument about euthanasia?
3. May postpones stating his thesis until late in the essay. Where does his thesis statement appear in the essay? Do you find it difficult to recognize? If so, why?
4. Under what circumstances would May consider killing another out of mercy? Does his position in this case contradict what he says elsewhere in the essay?
5. What does May mean when he says, at the end of the essay, "Sometimes the moral life calls us out into a no-man's-land where we cannot expect total security and protection under the law"?
6. Explain the title of May's essay in your own words.

Sources for Further Reading and Research

In addition to readings in this text on the subject of assisted suicide (pages 280–282), consult the following sources, as well as your library's *Readers' Guide to Periodical Literature*, the *SIRS*, or relevant databases and World Wide Web sites available online:

Broadway, Bill. "Faith and Assisted Suicide." Washington Post 15 Nov. 1997: B08.

Cole-Adams, Kenneth. "Kinder, Gentler Death?" Time 12 June 1995: 36.

Oregon Death with Dignity Act, 1997. [Full text of the law available online at http://www.islandnct.com/~deathnet/ergo_orlaw.html]

Stilson, Theodore. Death with Dignity. Chicago: Blason, 1997.

Women in Science

by K. C. Cole

I know few other women who do what I do. What I do is write about science, mainly physics. And to do that, I spend a lot of time reading about science, talking to scientists, and struggling to understand physics. In fact, most of the women (and men) I know think me quite queer for actually liking physics. "How can you write about that stuff?" they ask, always somewhat askance. "I could never understand that in a million years." Or more simply, "I hate science."

I didn't realize what an odd creature a woman interested in physics was until a few years ago when a science magazine sent me to Johns Hopkins University in Baltimore for a conference on an electrical phenomenon known as the Hall effect. We sat in a huge lecture hall and listened as physicists talked about things engineers didn't understand, and engineers talked about things physicists didn't understand. What *I* didn't understand was why, out of several hundred young students of physics and engineering in the room, less than a handful were women.

Sometime later, I found myself at the California Institute of Technology reporting on the search for the origins of the universe. I interviewed physicist after physicist, man after man. I asked one young administrator why none of the physicists were women. And he answered: "I don't know, but I suppose it must be something innate. My seven-year-old daughter doesn't seem to be much interested in science."

It was with that experience fresh in my mind that I attended a conference in Cambridge, Massachusetts, on science literacy, or rather the worrisome lack of it in this country today. We three women—a science teacher, a young chemist, and myself—sat surrounded by a company of august men. The chemist, I think, first tentatively raised the issue of science illiteracy in women. It seemed like an obvious point. After all, everyone had agreed over and over again that scientific knowledge these days was a key factor in economic power. But as soon as she made the point, it became clear that we women had committed a grievous social error. Our genders were suddenly showing; we had interrupted the serious talk with a subject unforgivably silly.

For the first time, I stopped being puzzled about why there weren't any women in science and began to be angry. Because if science is a search for answers to fundamental questions then it hardly seems frivolous to find out why women are excluded. Never mind the economic consequences.

A lot of the reasons women are excluded are spelled out by the Massachusetts Institute of Technology experimental physicist Vera Kistiakowsky in a recent article in *Physics Today* called "Women in Physics: Unnecessary, Injurious, and Out of Place?" The title was taken from a nineteenth-century essay written in opposition to the appointment of a female mathematician to a professorship at the University of Stockholm. "As decidedly as two and two make four," a woman in mathematics is a "monstrosity," concluded the writer of the essay.

Dr. Kistiakowsky went on to discuss the factors that make women in science today, if not monstrosities, at least oddities. Contrary to much popular opinion, one of those is *not* an innate difference in the scientific ability of boys and girls. But early conditioning does play a stubborn and subtle role. A recent *Nova* program, "The Pinks and the Blues," documented how girls and boys are treated differently from birth—the boys always encouraged in more physical kinds of play, more active explorations of their environments. Sheila Tobias, in her book, *Math Anxiety,* showed how the games boys play help them to develop an intuitive understanding of speed, motion, and mass.

The main sorting out of the girls from the boys in science seems to happen in junior high school. As a friend who teaches in a science museum said, "By the time we get to electricity, the boys already have had some experience with it. But it's unfamiliar to the girls." Science books draw on boys' experiences. "The examples are all about throwing a baseball at such and such a speed," said my stepdaughter, who barely escaped being a science drop-out.

The most obvious reason there are not many more women in science is that women are discriminated against as a class, in promotions, salaries, and hirings, a conclusion reached by a recent analysis by the National Academy of Sciences.

Finally, said Dr. Kistiakowsky, women are simply made to feel out of place in science. Her conclusion was supported by a Ford Foundation study by Lynn H. Fox on the problems of women in mathematics. When students were asked to choose among six reasons accounting for girls' lack of interest in math, the girls rated this statement second: "Men do not want girls in the mathematical occupations."

A friend of mine remembers winning a Bronxwide mathematics competition in the second grade. Her friends—both boys and girls—warned her that she shouldn't be good at math: "You'll never find a boy who likes you." My friend continued nevertheless to excel in math and science, won many awards during her years at the Bronx High School of Science, and then earned a full scholarship to Harvard. After one year of Harvard science, she decided to major in English.

When I asked her why, she mentioned what she called the "macho mores" of science. "It would have been O.K. if I'd had someone to talk to," she said. "But the rules of comportment were such that you never admitted you didn't understand. I later realized that even the boys didn't get everything clearly right away. You had to stick with it until it had time to sink in. But for the boys, there was a payoff in suffering through the hard times, and a kind of punishment—a shame—if they didn't. For the girls it was O.K. not to get it, and the only payoff for sticking it out was that you'd be considered a freak."

Science is undeniably hard. Often, it can seem quite boring. It is unfortunately too often presented as laws to be memorized instead of mysteries to be explored. It is too often kept a secret that science, like art, takes a well-developed esthetic sense. Women aren't the only ones who say, "I hate science."

That's why everyone who goes into science needs a little help from friends. For the past ten years, I have been getting more than a little help from a friend who is a physicist. But my stepdaughter—who earned the highest grades ever recorded in her California high school on the math Scholastic Aptitude Test— flunked calculus in her first year at Harvard. When my friend the physicist heard about it, he said, "Harvard should be ashamed of itself."

What he meant was that she needed that little extra encouragement that makes all the difference. Instead, she got that little extra discouragement that makes all the difference.

"In the first place, all the math teachers are men," she explained. "In the second place, when I met a boy I liked and told him I was taking chemistry, he immediately said 'Oh, you're one of those science types.' In the third place, it's just a kind of a social thing. The math clubs are full of boys and you don't feel comfortable joining."

In other words, she was made to feel unnecessary, injurious, and out of place.

A few months ago, I accompanied a male colleague from the science museum where I sometimes work to a lunch of the history of science faculty at the University of California. I was the only woman there, and my presence for the most part was obviously and rudely ignored. I was so surprised and hurt by this that I made an extra effort to speak knowledgeably and well. At the end of the lunch, one of the professors turned to me in all seriousness and said: "Well, K. C., what do the women think of Carl Sagan?" I replied that I had no idea what "the women" thought about anything. But now I know what I should have said: I should have told him that his comment was unnecessary, injurious, and out of place.

Questions for Discussion and Writing

1. Do you agree with Cole that most people—and males in particular—regard women scientists as somewhat different or unusual?
2. Contact a male and female professor of science on your own campus, and discuss Cole's essay with each of them. How do they regard female science majors or the role of women in science generally? Do their views differ? Why?

3. In what ways do you agree with Cole that our society discourages women from developing an interest in science?

4. Cole maintains that women are "discriminated against as a class" in a variety of ways throughout our culture. Do you agree? What evidence is there that would support Cole's assertion?

5. Are men discouraged from entering any particular professions in our society? Which ones? Who or what discourages them from doing so?

Sources for Further Reading and Research

The following sources focus directly on the topic of women in science and the women's movement generally:

Holloway, Margaret. "A Lab of Her Own." <u>Scientific American</u> Nov. 1993: 94–103.

Hubbard, Ruth. The <u>Politics of Women's Biology</u>. New Jersey: Rutgers UP, 1990.

Penry, Deborah, "Puppy Peek-A-Boo." <u>AWIS Magazine</u> Vol. 25, No. 4. Summer: July/Aug/Sept. 1996: 3–4.

Zuckerman, Harriet, John R. Cole, and John T. Bruer, eds. <u>The Outer Circle: Women in the Scientific Community</u>. New York: Norton, 1991.

In addition to consulting your library's catalog, *Readers' Guide to Periodical Literature,* and the resources in *SIRS,* you may find the following reference guides helpful:

Abstracts and Indexes:

<u>The Chicana: A Comprehensive Bibliographic Study</u>

<u>Education Index</u>

<u>Feminist Periodicals: A Current Listing of Contents</u>

<u>Women Studies Abstracts</u>

<u>Women of Color in the United States: A Guide to the Literature</u>

Journals

<u>Journal of Women Studies</u>

<u>Sage: A Scholarly Journal on Black Women</u>

<u>Studies on Women</u>

Suggested Research Topics

If your instructor prefers that you devise your own research paper topic, you may find the following possible topics and research questions worth investigating:

- *The Internet:* How sexist is the Internet? Do we need stronger controls over pornographic, racial, or political material? How is the Internet changing education?

- *Euthanasia:* Do those afflicted with painful or incurable illnesses have the right to choose death through suicide over suffering? Should those who assist such people in committing suicide be charged with murder?

- *Family Divorces:* Should children be allowed to divorce their parents? Do parents have the right to divorce unwanted problem children?

- *Gun Control:* Is it time to ban all handguns or other types of guns? What can we do to control the problem of too many guns causing too many deaths?

- *Women in Careers:* Are women really able to compete equally with men in the same career? How successful has the women's rights movement really been?

- *Rape on Campus:* Are colleges doing enough to protect males and females who might become victims of rape? Are victims' rights being ignored to protect rapists or the colleges' reputations?

- *Bilingual Education:* Are non-native speakers of English being punished by English only education? What should schools do to protect students' cultural heritage and identities?

- *Gene Splicing and Cloning:* Can science take us too far? Should we clone extinct species to bring them back to life? Should we clone human beings?

- *Gangs:* Are we doing all we can to control the gang problem in America? What is working, and what else should we be doing?

- *Generation X:* Is there a "Generation X"? What is it? Who belongs to it? Where is it going?

- *Drugs:* Heroin is popular again, marijuana is stronger than ever, and crack is killing hundreds of people daily. Is it time to give up and legalize drugs?

PART IV

A Writer's Workbook

Many students have wondered aloud why some instructors stress the mechanics of English so heavily. "Isn't it much more important that you write well than it is to know what a conjunctive adverb is?" "Why should we learn all the rules about commas when everyone seems to use them differently anyway?" "Grammar is for grammar school."

It is true that many fine writers would be hard pressed to define a conjunctive adverb or to list ten rules for using commas. It is also quite possible that these same writers have not thought much about the mechanics of writing since their school days. Over time, however, avid readers pick up the mechanics of writing naturally without thinking a lot about it. If these readers also do a lot of writing, they gradually master the skills of standard written English.

If you are such a reader, the mechanics of English will come easily to you as you practice writing the essays assigned in Parts I, II, and III. Still, you will gain better control over your writing if you learn the vocabulary and rules for the mechanics of English presented in Part IV.

If you are just beginning to develop good reading habits, this workbook should give you a shortcut to writing correct English. In no way, however, should it be seen as a substitute for essay writing; you learn to write well only by doing a lot of reading and composition writing. Rather, Part IV should give you the tools for writing strong and varied sentences and for editing your writing.

Many exercises are offered in Part IV: Some are objective; others require that you compose your own sentences or even paragraphs. You can check your answers to the objective exercises in the Appendix. The review exercises at the end of each chapter will help test your knowledge of the material in that chapter. Your instructor will advise you on which exercises you should complete and which you may skip.

15

Parts of Speech

15.0   Introduction

In this chapter you will learn how the eight parts of speech function in a sentence. As you study the rules of grammar and punctuation, you will need to know how to identify the parts of speech, especially subjects and verbs.

Parts of Sentences

A sentence is made up of parts: clauses, phrases, and words. A sentence stands by itself as a complete unit: It has a subject and a verb. A sentence may be a statement or a question:

STATEMENT

subject verb

↓   ↓

<u>They</u> <u>are</u> in a high tax bracket.

QUESTION

verb subject

↓   ↓

<u>Are</u> <u>you</u> hungry?

A clause is one part of a sentence; a clause also has a subject and a verb.

CLAUSES

subject   verb   subject   verb

↓   ↓   ↓   ↓

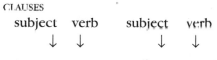

<u>When we were young,</u> <u>stamps cost fifteen cents.</u>
(first clause)   (second clause)

A phrase is another part of a sentence, but it does not have a subject and a verb.

PHRASES

into the house

singing in the rain

never too much

Practice 1

In the following exercises, identify sentences with an *S,* clauses with a *C,* and phrases with a *P.*

1. _____ Over the most dangerous mountain range.

2. _____ While Rome burned.

3. _____ Who is on the phone?

4. _____ It is the lady from the paint company.

5. _____ Because you are ill.

6. _____ Soon it will rain.

7. _____ Climbing higher and higher into the sky.

8. _____ For the sake of humankind.

9. _____ Which is over there.

10. _____ Not in my class.

Parts of Speech

Eight parts of speech make up sentences: nouns, pronouns, verbs, prepositions, adjectives, adverbs, conjunctions, and interjections. As you study the various parts of speech, remember that many words can be used as different parts of speech in different contexts; for example, the word *hate* can be used in three different ways:

I <u>hate</u> pain. (verb)

His expression revealed <u>hate.</u> (noun)

The senator received many <u>hate</u> letters. (noun used as an adjective)

15.1   Nouns

A *noun* is a part of speech that names a person, place, thing, or idea. Nouns are often preceded by the following groups of words:

a, an, the
this, these, that, those
my, your, his, her, its, our, their
in, of, on, by, with, to

Practice 2

Underline each of the nouns in the following sentences. (The number of nouns in each sentence is given in parentheses after the sentence; there are twelve altogether. The words *they* and *you* are not nouns, but pronouns.)

1. An essay on a test need not be a difficult task. (3)

2. First, students should gather their thoughts and, if time permits, write an outline. (4)

3. Next, they should write all their ideas in the most logical order. (2)

4. Be sure your sentences are clear and complete. (1)

5. If you have the time, proofread your essay. (2)

Proper Nouns

Nouns that refer to particular people, places, or things are called *proper nouns* and are capitalized. The underlined words in this sentence are proper nouns:

> Edgar Allan Poe, who lived in both England and the United States, is the author of many short stories, including "The Gold Bug" and "The Tell-Tale Heart."

Practice 3

Underline the proper nouns in the following sentences.

1. In 1937, Richard Wright wrote his great book, *Black Boy.*

2. It is the story of a black American growing up in the Deep South between 1905 and 1925.

3. Most of the story is set in the cities of Memphis and Jackson.

4. The book is about how Wright freed himself from the bondage of his youth.

Practice 4

Underline *all* nouns, including proper nouns, in the following sentences. (The number of nouns in each sentence is given in parentheses after the sentence.)

1. Richard Wright had many obstacles to overcome. (2)

2. It was especially hard for him to obtain a good education because when he was young the schools for blacks were inferior to those for whites. (4)

3. His family was so poor that Wright often went to bed hungry. (3)

4. He had to buy his own clothes, books, and much of his food. (3)

5. But Wright did free himself from his hardships. (2)

6. Many things enabled him to escape: his reading, his defiance, his learning to cope, and his determination. (5)

7. He always found a way to obtain magazines and books to read. (3)

8. After the long, hard struggles of his youth, Wright entered the adult world as a free man. (5)

9. But the struggles of his youth had left him with scars. (3)

10. Most college students enjoy the book *Black Boy.* (3)

Nouns as Subjects

A noun can function as the subject of a sentence. When a noun is a subject, it is responsible for the action of a verb and is what the sentence is about. For example,

The hurricane blew down houses, turned over cars, and destroyed most of the trees in the area.

The noun *hurricane* is the subject; it is responsible for the action of the verbs *blew, turned,* and *destroyed,* and is what the sentence is about. All sentences must have subjects. Here are two more sentences in which the subject is a noun:

My ninety-year-old grandmother is a spunky lady.

The baby cried half the night.

 ### Practice 5

Underline the subjects of the following sentences.

1. The United States Marine Corps officially began in 1798 as part of the navy.
2. The Marine Corps is composed of three divisions, three aircraft wings, and supporting troops.
3. Despite recent cutbacks by Congress, more than 190,000 men and women serve in the Marine Corps today.
4. Known for their courage and tough training, the marines have been active in every U.S. military operation since the War of 1812.
5. Every marine is proud of what the corps has done for this country.

15.2   Verbs

A *verb* is a part of speech that says what a subject is (was, will be) or does (did, will do). Here is an example of a verb that says what a subject is:

subject   verb
↓   ↓

My grandmother is ninety years old.

Below is a verb that says what a subject does:

subject   verb
↓   ↓

The deer leaps over the fence to escape the hunters.

Practice 6

Write sentences (thoughts that will stand on their own), using the following subjects and verbs.

1. (criminals, lead) _____

   _____

2. (president, takes) _____

   _____

3. (looks, tell) _____

   _____

4. (architect, designed) _____

   _____

5. (tests, measure) _____

   _____

6. (smoking, causes) _____

   _____

7. (high school bands, _____) _____
                         (supply verb)

   _____

8. (police officers, _____) _____
                     (supply verb)

   _____

9. (_____, swam) _____
   (supply subject)

   _____

10. (_____, kissed) _____
    (supply subject)

   _____

Simple Verbs and Verb Phrases

A verb that is just one word is called a *simple verb*. A verb that is made up of more than one word is called a *verb phrase*. The words that go along with a main verb to make up a verb phrase are called *helping verbs*.

SIMPLE VERB

love

VERB PHRASES

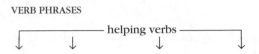

<u>do</u> love, <u>can</u> love, <u>should have</u> loved, <u>will</u> love

Practice 7

In the following sentences, underline the subjects once and the verbs twice. Be sure to underline the helping verbs as well as the main verbs.

1. <u>I</u> <u><u>do believe</u></u> the testimony.
2. The testimony could hurt the defendant.
3. The troop should go on more hikes.
4. The extra five minutes should have made the difference.
5. The Marines want a few good people.
6. David should have been chosen.

Practice 8

Write sentences, using the following verb phrases.

1. (can understand) _____

2. (should know) _____

3. (must wait) _____

4. (can eat) _____

5. (will be seated) _____

Linking Verbs

Linking verbs tell what a subject is, was, or will be. Thus they can be any form of the verb *to be,* such as *am, is, are, was, were, has been,* or *will be.* Other linking verbs are *become, feel, seem, look,* and *appear.* For example,

My ninety-year-old <u>grandmother</u> *<u>is</u>* a spunky <u>lady.</u>

Grandmother is the subject of the sentence, or what it is about. *Lady* is a *predicate nominative:* It renames the subject and is linked to the subject by the verb *is.* Think of the linking verb as an equal sign in an equation:

grandmother = lady

In the following two examples, the subjects and predicate nominatives are underlined once and the linking verbs twice:

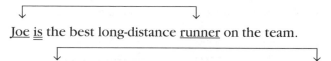

Joe is the best long-distance runner on the team.

The recruits at the police academy will become officers soon.

 ## Practice 9

In the following sentences, underline the subjects and predicate nominatives once and the linking verbs twice.

1. Yesterday was the last day of the concert series.
2. Many popular movies of the early 1970s were disaster films.
3. Mr. Reynolds has been the chair of the department for years.
4. Under the circumstances, that solution seems the best one.
5. This painting is an example of Impressionist work.

Subjects Placed After Verbs

Sometimes the subject comes not at the beginning of the sentence, but after the verb. This may happen in a question:

Did the instructor say that?

The sentence is about the instructor, so you know *instructor* is the subject. You can identify the verb by making the sentence into a statement:

The instructor said that.

 ## Practice 10

Change the following questions to statements in the spaces provided. Then underline the subjects once and the verbs twice in the questions themselves. Be sure to underline the helping verbs as well as the main verbs.

1. Will the teller cash our check?

   The teller will cash our check.
   _____

2. Are Mary and Martha the sisters mentioned in the story?

   _____

3. Should the employees insist on collective bargaining?

   _____

4. Is physics the most difficult freshman course?

_____

5. Should we have listened to Einstein when he warned against atomic power?

_____

Another type of sentence in which subject and verb are reversed is one that begins with an *expletive expression* such as *there is, there are, here is, here are,* and *it is:*

There are three possible answers to that question.

Expletives like *there* point to and introduce subjects, but they are not subjects themselves. The subject in the preceding sentence is *answers;* the verb is *are.*

Practice 11

In the following sentences, underline the subjects once and the verbs twice, and draw an arrow from the expletive expression to the subject.

1. There is a bug in my Coke.
2. There are five volunteers for the job.
3. Here is all my change.
4. Here are four examples of prejudice in our newspaper.
5. There is still one of us left.
6. There are still three of us left.
7. It was a bad day at Black Rock.

Practice 12

In the following sentences, underline the subjects once and the verbs twice. Be sure to underline helping verbs as well as main verbs.

1. Will television ever replace classrooms and teachers?
2. Many children regularly watch *Sesame Street* and other educational programs.
3. Perhaps such programs will occupy more and more of our children's time in the future.
4. What did Neil Armstrong say when he set foot on the moon?
5. There are two main advantages to such a computerized system.
6. Students learn best in a nonthreatening environment.
7. In her class, no one feels embarrassed about making mistakes.

8. Second, students can progress at their own speed.

9. However, one drawback is the isolation of television viewing.

10. Will the space program survive the budget cutbacks?

11. There are no opportunities for a person to relate to others.

12. The team should have chosen her as captain.

13. A young couple often has difficulty establishing credit.

14. Teaching techniques should combine both traditional and innovative approaches.

15.3   Objects and Prepositions

Direct Objects

A *direct object* is a noun that receives the action of a verb. Here are two examples:

John threw the <u>javelin.</u>

Javelin is the direct object of the action verb *threw.* You can check this by asking the question "John threw *what?*"

Mark invited his <u>girlfriend.</u>

Girlfriend is the direct object of the action verb *invited.* You can check by asking "Mark invited *whom?*"

Practice 13

In the sentences that follow, underline the subject once and the verb twice, and circle the direct object. Say whether the direct object tells *what* or *whom.*

1. <u>We</u> <u><u>watched</u></u> (television) on Thursday evening. *tells what*

2. The girls baked peanut-butter cookies.

3. Andy asked Melissa for a date.

4. Andy ate two dozen cookies and drank a quart of apple cider.

5. Andy had a stomachache on Friday.

6. The math instructor returned the tests.

7. Karen defeated Janice in the tennis tournament.

8. She finished the problems in an hour.

9. After studying for at least two hours every night, she easily passed the test.

10. The teacher wrote a helpful comment on the paper.

Objects of Prepositions

A noun also may serve as the *object of a preposition.* A preposition, which is usually a short word, connects a noun to the rest of the sentence. For example:

It is a difficult job even <u>for</u> a hardworking person.

For is the preposition, and it connects *hardworking person* to the rest of the sentence. *Person* is the object of the preposition, and *hardworking* is the modifier of the object.

Below are some of the most common prepositions. The underlined words are examples of objects of the prepositions.

above (above the <u>city</u>)
across (across the <u>river</u>)
after (after his <u>death</u>)
among (among his <u>strengths</u>)
at (at the <u>crossroads</u>)
before (before <u>breakfast</u>)
behind (behind the <u>door</u>)
below (below <u>sea level</u>)
between (between <u>you</u> and <u>me</u>)
by (by <u>train</u>)
down (down the <u>street</u>)
during (during <u>class</u>)
for (for <u>whom</u>)
from (from <u>John</u> and <u>Polly</u>)

in (in those <u>days</u>)
into (into the <u>unknown</u>)
like (like <u>King Kong</u>)
of (of human <u>bondage</u>)
on (on the <u>mountain</u>)
onto (onto the <u>roof</u>)
over (over <u>hill</u> and <u>dale</u>)
through (through the <u>woods</u>)
to (to his <u>house</u>)
under (under the <u>chair</u>)
up (up the <u>stairs</u>)
upon (upon this <u>rock</u>)
with (with your <u>personality</u>)
without (without <u>me</u>)

Practice 14

Write your own prepositional phrases for each of the 28 prepositions listed above. Then use ten of these phrases in sentences, and underline the objects of the prepositions. For example, you might write this prepositional phrase:

above the water

Your sentence could then be something like this:

She had a hard time keeping her head above the water.

Practice 15

In the following sentences, place parentheses around the prepositional phrases, and underline the objects of the prepositions. (The number of prepositional phrases in each sentence appears in parentheses after the sentence.)

1. (During the <u>sixties</u>) many people became interested (in <u>drugs.</u>) (2)

2. You could hear the names of particular drugs, such as LSD and marijuana, on the news every day. (2)

3. Experimentation with drugs increased dramatically at this time. (2)

4. With the increase in drug use came the danger of drug abuse. (3)

5. Unfortunately, drugs led to an early death for some. (2)

6. Others were not harmed by drugs. (1)

7. Most experts believe that the drug problem is getting worse in large cities. (1)

8. For some people, crack is the most addictive drug available on the street. (2)

9. "X," a street name for Ecstasy, is one of the most dangerous drugs to appear on the American scene. (3)

10. A psychologist at our university believes that parents who drink too much alcohol contribute greatly to the drug problem because they demonstrate their own addiction to their children. (3)

Indirect Objects

An *indirect object* is a noun that tells for whom or to whom something is done. It usually comes between an action verb and its direct object.

> Tony gave his younger <u>sister</u> a quarter.

What Tony gave his sister was a quarter; therefore, *quarter* is the direct object. The person *to whom* he gave the quarter was his sister; therefore, *sister* is the indirect object.

You can identify indirect objects by seeing if they can be converted to prepositional phrases, as follows:

> The worried mother sent her <u>son</u> a care package during his first week of college.

This same thought can be expressed with a prepositional phrase:

> The worried mother sent a care package <u>to her son</u> during his first week of college.

Because *son* can be shifted to become the object of the preposition *to,* you can assume that it is an indirect object.

Practice 16

Convert the following sentences with prepositional phrases to sentences with indirect objects. Underline the indirect objects.

1. Tom brought a basket of fruit to his friend.

   Tom brought his <u>friend</u> a basket of fruit.

2. Elizabeth gave some free advice to her instructor.

   _____

3. The news gave a shock to the family.

_____

4. The real estate agent offered a special deal for her clients.

_____

5. That thief sold a stolen car to my husband.

_____

6. She made a beautiful dress for her daughter.

_____

Practice 17

Complete the following sentences, using both indirect and direct objects. Underline the indirect objects and circle the direct objects.

1. The President sent   *his ally a thousand troops*_____

2. The people gave _____

3. The tailor made _____

4. The waiter brought _____

5. She sold _____

6. The woman bought _____

15.4   Pronouns

A *pronoun* is a word that substitutes for a noun:

Dr. Lawson chuckles when <u>he</u> starts to pull a tooth. (The pronoun *he* takes the place of *Dr. Lawson.*)

Representative Taylor was delighted when *she* received the award. (The pronoun *she* replaces *Representative Taylor.*)

Pronoun Case

Some pronouns change their form, or *case,* according to their use in a sentence. A pronoun in the subjective case serves as the subject of a sentence:

<u>He</u> is the one who is guilty.

A pronoun in the possessive case shows ownership:

The birds did not make <u>their</u> nests this year.

A pronoun in the objective case can be a direct object, an indirect object, or the object of a preposition.

DIRECT OBJECT
When he caught the ball, he threw <u>it</u> back.

INDIRECT OBJECT
The pitcher threw <u>him</u> the ball.

OBJECT OF A PREPOSITION
My parents were most excited when the prize was awarded to <u>them</u>.

Study the different cases of personal pronouns listed below. (A personal pronoun usually refers to a person.)

Singular Personal Pronouns

	Subjective	Possessive	Objective
FIRST PERSON	I	my, mine	me
SECOND PERSON	you	your, yours	you
THIRD PERSON	he, she, it	his, her, hers, its	him, her, it

Plural Personal Pronouns

	Subjective	Possessive	Objective
FIRST PERSON	we	our, ours	us
SECOND PERSON	you	your, yours	you
THIRD PERSON	they	their, theirs	them

Two other pronouns change form depending on how they are used in a sentence: *who* and *whoever.* Study these forms as well.

	Subjective	Possessive	Objective
WHO	who	whose	whom
WHOEVER	whoever	—	whomever

Practice 18

Using the preceding lists, supply the specified pronoun for each of the following sentences.

1. (third-person singular, subjective case) Kathleen is much taller than
   _____*he*_____ .

2. (first-person singular, subjective case) John and _____ are studying together.

3. (first-person singular, objective case) Just between you and _____ , I think she is a fine instructor.

4. (first-person singular, subjective case) Clarence and _____ are the best of friends.

5. (first-person singular, objective case) The letter was addressed to your mother and _____.

6. (third-person singular, possessive case) The bird built _____ nest inside the bumper of the car.

7. (first-person plural, possessive case) Their team is no better than _____.

8. (third-person plural, objective case) Please give the information to _____ before it is too late.

9. (*who,* objective case) With _____ do you play tennis?

10. (first-person singular, subjective case) "Who is it?" she asked. "It is _____," he replied.

11. (first-person singular, possessive case) The police staked out Antonio's and _____ house.

The Subjective Case: The subjective case must be used in such situations as the following:

He runs as fast as <u>I.</u>

The pronoun *I* is used instead of *me* because the sense of the sentence is actually "He runs as fast as I run." *I* is thus the subject of the verb *run,* which is understood.

This is <u>she.</u>

She is linked to the subject, *this,* by the verb *is* and is thus in the subjective case.

Compound Constructions: Pronouns used in compound constructions should be treated the same way as single pronouns:

My friend and <u>I</u> ate cereal for breakfast.

Choose *I,* not *me.* You would not say "Me ate cereal for breakfast."

She bought the present for Jim and <u>me.</u>

Choose *me,* not *I.* You would not say "She bought the present for I."

Practice 19

In the following sentences, circle the correct pronoun.

1. Margarita and (I, me) took the test before John took it.

2. Rachel brought Mary and (I, me) the notes to study.

3. John saw (we, us) on the practice field.

4. David cannot type as fast as (she, her).

5. Was it really (she, her) that you saw?

6. The near crash alarmed neither Maria nor (I, me).

7. The answer was apparent to both (he and I, him and me).

8. Dad gave my brother and (I, me) the stereo as a birthday present.

9. Harry and (I, me) have three children.

10. Just between you and (I, me), Mr. Norton has been acting strangely lately.

11. José does not jog as often as (I, me).

12. (Who, Whom) is your advisor?

13. (Whoever, Whomever) wants this day-old sandwich may have it.

14. Give the invitation to (whoever, whomever) you can find.

15. For (who, whom) does the bell toll?

16. This is (he, him).

Seven Kinds of Pronouns

1. Personal Pronouns: *Personal pronouns* distinguish between the person speaking (first person), the person spoken to (second person), and the person spoken about (third person).

FIRST PERSON
I, me, we, us, my, mine, our, ours

SECOND PERSON
you, your, yours

THIRD PERSON
he, she, it, him, his, her, hers, its, they, them, their, theirs

2. Demonstrative Pronouns: *Demonstrative pronouns* point to specific persons or things. The demonstrative pronouns are *this, that, these,* and *those.* They are often the subjects of sentences.

This is my problem.

These are the facts.

That is your belief.

Those should make the difference.

You may do this but not that. (Here, *this* and *that* are objects.)

3. Indefinite Pronouns:
Indefinite pronouns do not identify specific individuals or things:

any	either	many	neither	some
anybody	everybody	more	nobody	somebody
anyone	everyone	most	none	someone
anything	everything	much	no one	something
each				

> <u>Somebody</u> is missing a pen.

> <u>Everyone</u> misses you.

Indefinite pronouns are usually singular, but they can be plural. See Section 16.8 for a discussion of this.

4. Intensive Pronouns:
Intensive pronouns emphasize a particular noun or pronoun.

Singular	Plural
myself	ourselves
yourself	yourselves
herself	themselves
himself	themselves
itself	themselves

Note that the plural of *self* is *selves*. Also, there are no such words as *hisself* and *theirselves*.

> The players <u>themselves</u> refused to cheat.

> I <u>myself</u> will take the blame.

Players is emphasized in the first sentence; *I* is emphasized in the second.

5. Reflexive Pronouns:
Reflexive pronouns show that the subject acts upon itself. They are formed like intensive pronouns.

> I hurt <u>myself</u> in the game.

> You can fool other people, but you cannot fool <u>yourself.</u>

The person *I* hurt was *myself;* the person *you* cannot fool is *yourself.*

6. Interrogative Pronouns:
Interrogative pronouns ask questions:

Who?	Whoever?	What?
Whom?	Whomever?	Whatever?
Whose?	Which?	

Who is the best dressed?

Whose is that?

7. Relative Pronouns: **Relative pronouns** introduce dependent clauses:

who	whoever	whose	that
whom	whomever	what	which

The company makes pens that do not write.

The tree, which is outside my window, was hit by lightning.

The people who live on our block are very friendly.

Use *who* or *that* to refer to people and *that* or *which* to refer to things. See Section 16.8 for a more complete discussion of how relative pronouns function in a sentence.

Practice 20

The pronouns in the following paragraph are underlined. Identify each pronoun by type, using the following abbreviations: *per* (personal), *dem* (demonstrative), *ind* (indefinite), *int* (intensive), *inter* (interrogative), *reflex* (reflexive), and *rel* (relative). Note that the word *that* can be used as a demonstrative or relative pronoun.

My Aunt Birdie is a rare species of aunt that will soon become extinct. She is so considerate of other people that sometimes you can actually see a halo over her head. My aunt is seventy-nine years old, five feet tall, and shaped like a loosely rolled sleeping bag. She talks to herself all the time about her old boyfriends. Her hair is snow-white, which matches her teeth that sit upon her bureau every night. She has a huge hernia that forces her to tilt to the left when she walks. Although Aunt Birdie has a hard time getting around, she will not let anyone help her. She does everything for herself. That is how she likes it.

15.5   Adjectives

An *adjective* modifies, or describes, a noun or pronoun. Here are some examples:

the scorching sun

the blinding glare

unfriendly people

a <u>frozen</u> pond

a <u>terrible</u> day

the <u>worst</u> storm

Special Types of Adjectives

1. *Articles:*　*a, an, the*

   <u>a</u> house

   <u>a</u> batch

   <u>an</u> apple

   <u>an</u> image

   <u>an</u> hour

   <u>the</u> truth

Note that *an* is used before words beginning with a vowel *(a, e, i, o, or u)* or a vowel sound (such as the *o/oh* sound in *hour* or *honest*).

2. Predicate Adjectives

My canary is <u>sick.</u>

The trip seemed <u>dangerous</u> to me.

Predicate adjectives function like predicate nominatives: They follow a linking verb and refer to the subject of the sentence. In the preceding sentences, *sick* modifies *canary,* and *dangerous* modifies *trip.*

3. Demonstrative Adjectives:　*this, that, these, those*

<u>This</u> place is prettier than <u>that</u> place.

<u>These</u> places are prettier than <u>those</u> places.

Demonstrative adjectives have the same form as demonstrative pronouns. However, instead of serving as subjects or objects, they modify nouns.

4. Indefinite Adjectives:　*some, few, any, each,* and the like

<u>some</u> people

a <u>few</u> dollars

any approach

each person

Practice 21

Underline the adjectives in the following sentences, and draw arrows to the nouns or pronouns they modify. The number of adjectives in each sentence is in parentheses after the sentence. (Remember that the articles *a, an,* and *the* are classified as adjectives.)

1. The Kool Jazz Festival is a mixture of soul music and jazz. (3)
2. These concerts attract different types of people. (2)
3. They bring out the rowdy ones, the dreamy lovers, the smokers, the ones who stand against the walls the whole night, and the people who use profane language. (11)
4. The rowdy ones are young. (3)
5. They dance, scream, push, and blow those loud whistles. (2)
6. The dreamy lovers sit through the whole concert watching one another with moony eyes. (5)
7. The smokers fill the air with the disgusting smell of marijuana. (4)
8. The wall-standers are unfriendly to everyone, even to one another. (2)
9. The cursers sit everywhere and do not show any respect for anyone, not even for the older people. (4)
10. Still, the Kool Jazz Festival is terrific; I never miss it. (2)

Practice 22

Use the following adjectives in sentences. (Consult a dictionary for any meanings you do not know.) Draw arrows to the nouns or pronouns the adjectives modify.

1. (gleaming) *His gleaming eyes met mine.* _____

2. (ferocious) _____

3. (malignant) _____

4. (superior) _____

5. (pernicious) _____

6. (magnanimous) _____

7. (caustic) _____

8. (abundant) _____

9. (patronizing) _____

10. (detailed) _____

Comparative and Superlative Adjectives

Many adjectives change in form when the nouns they modify are compared and contrasted with other nouns. You may describe a farm scene as *lovely,* but if you think it is prettier than another farm scene, you say that it is *lovelier* than the other one, and if you think it is the prettiest farm scene anywhere, you say that it is the *loveliest* of them all. In comparing two nouns, use *comparative adjectives;* in comparing three or more nouns, use *superlative adjectives.*

COMPARATIVE ADJECTIVES

The work is <u>harder</u> than it was before. (Here you are comparing present work with previous work.)

The grass is not <u>greener</u> in California. (Here you are comparing grass in California to grass elsewhere.)

The work is <u>more fulfilling</u> than before. (If an adjective has three or more syllables, use *more* before the adjective instead of changing the ending.)

SUPERLATIVE ADJECTIVES

My cat is the <u>smartest</u> in the neighborhood. (Here the cat is compared with all the cats in the neighborhood.)

My cat is the <u>most unpredictable</u> cat in the neighborhood. (Use *most* before superlative adjectives of three or more syllables.)

Irregular Forms: A few adjectives change form completely when used as comparative or superlative adjectives:

Basic Form	Comparative Form	Superlative Form
bad	worse	worst
good	better	best
far	farther	farthest
little	less	least
much	more	most

Practice 23

In the following sentences, supply comparative and superlative forms of appropriate adjectives.

1. Halloween is a pretty cat, but Full Moon is _prettier_. They are the _prettiest_ cats on the block.

2. She is difficult, but her husband is even _____ . As a couple, they are the _____ people I know.

3. Yesterday was cold, but today is _____. This is the _____ winter we have had in some time.

4. She has a bad attitude, but Molly's attitude is _____. And Emily's is the _____ of all.

5. Uncle Ed doesn't eat much at night, but Aunt Buzzy eats _____. And their daughter eats the _____ of all.

6. That essay was pretty good, but you have done _____. I have yet to see your _____ work.

7. The dessert was tasty, but the chicken pie was _____. In fact, it was the _____ chicken pie I have ever eaten.

8. The middle school is not far, but it is _____ than the elementary school. The high school is the _____ from my house.

9. It is a little traveled road. It is _____ traveled than the other road at East Fork. It may, in fact, be the _____ traveled road in the entire national park.

10. My work is already fulfilling, but I would like it to be even _____. I have always wanted to find the _____ work possible.

15.6   Adverbs

An *adverb* modifies a verb, an adjective, or another adverb:

He drove <u>wildly.</u>

The child wept <u>quietly.</u>

The preceding adverbs tell how he *drove* and how the child *wept:* They modify verbs.

The <u>very</u> large man is my father.

She is <u>extremely</u> sick.

These adverbs tell just how *large* the man is and just how *sick* she is: They modify adjectives.

He was running <u>so</u> rapidly that no one could keep up with him.

The car was going <u>quite</u> slowly on the interstate.

These adverbs tell just how *rapidly* he was running and just how *slowly* the car was going: They modify other adverbs.

Adverbs often end in *-ly:*

beautifully	hardly	poorly	triumphantly
cruelly	incompetently	quietly	wholly
daily	nicely	smoothly	wisely

Some adverbs do not have *-ly* endings:

almost	more	quite
always	most	too
even	never	very
fast	not	well

Practice 24

Underline the adverbs in the following sentences, and draw arrows to the verbs, adjectives, or other adverbs they modify. (The number of adverbs in each sentence is given in parentheses after the sentence.)

1. It was <u>so</u> dark that I stumbled and fell <u>noisily</u> over the chair. (2)
2. The flowers were so beautifully arranged that all the children noticed them. (2)
3. Although they conducted the investigation very incompetently, they did catch the thief, who had been quietly stealing from everyone. (3)
4. My neighborhood is just too noisy to enjoy. (2)
5. He generously gave his mother a most lovely home. (2)
6. The lady in the lounge has been waiting for you most impatiently. (2)
7. With his ragtag band, he entered the city triumphantly, riding very slowly on the back of a donkey. (3)
8. It is extremely hard to work forty hours a week, attend school, raise children, and not complain. (2)
9. The Reverend Davis always begins his sermon with an unnecessarily long prayer. (2)
10. Dr. Nguyen never admits a patient who has not been carefully screened. (3)

15.7   Conjunctions

A *conjunction* joins words, phrases, or clauses in a sentence. There are three types of conjunctions: coordinating conjunctions, subordinating conjunctions, and correlative conjunctions.

Coordinating Conjunctions

A *coordinating conjunction* joins elements that are grammatically equal. There are seven coordinating conjunctions:

and	yet
but	or
for	nor
so	

Here is how they are used:

TO JOIN WORDS
the <u>dog</u> <u>and</u> his <u>bone</u>

TO JOIN PHRASES
not <u>into darkness</u> <u>but</u> <u>into light</u>

TO JOIN CLAUSES
<u>He stayed at home,</u> <u>and</u> <u>she went to work.</u>

See Section 21.2 for a discussion of coordinating conjunctions in compound sentences.

Subordinating Conjunctions

A *subordinating conjunction* introduces a subordinate or dependent clause in a sentence. For example,

<u>Although we were tired,</u> we went to work anyway.

Although introduces a dependent clause (underlined) and joins this clause to the rest of the sentence. Here are other examples of dependent clauses introduced by subordinating conjunctions:

He acts that way to his family <u>because he hates himself.</u>

<u>When he went to the psychiatrist,</u> he found out that he was bored with life.

These are some of the most common subordinating conjunctions:

after	before	so that	where
although	even though	though	wherever
as	if	till	whether
as if	in order that	unless	while
as though	since	until	
because	so	when	

See Section 21.4 for a discussion of subordinating conjunctions in complex sentences.

Correlative Conjunctions

Correlative conjunctions are always used in pairs:

either . . . or	both . . . and
neither . . . nor	not only . . . but also

Here are two examples of the use of correlative conjunctions:

<u>Either</u> you fix the car, <u>or</u> I will take it to the shop.

<u>Not only</u> should you listen, <u>but</u> you should <u>also</u> take notes.

See Section 16.7 for a discussion of the use of subjects and verbs with correlative conjunctions.

Practice 25

In the following sentences, underline all conjunctions and then label them with the following abbreviations: *cc* (coordinating conjunction), *sub* (subordinating conjunction), or *cor* (correlative conjunction).

1. It was <u>both</u> my happiest <u>and</u> my saddest summer.
2. When the wind is from the south, it blows the hook into the fish's mouth.
3. Many people are walking the streets of London because, while they were playing blackjack, they drew cards whose points went over twenty-one.
4. One door closes, and another door opens.
5. If you look closely, you will discover that a good man or woman is not hard to find.
6. You will bloom where you are planted.

7. You can fool some of the people some of the time, but you cannot fool all of the people all of the time, or can you?

8. Every creature in the world either eats or is eaten.

9. Because you love, you will live.

10. He reads to his grandchildren when they ask him.

11. And he teaches them old sayings while he has their attention.

15.8   Interjections

An *interjection* is used to express either a mild or a strong emotion. Interjections are used more commonly in speech than in writing. An expression of strong emotion is followed by an exclamation point:

Ouch!   Help!   Stop!   Wait!

An expression of mild emotion is followed by a comma and hooked to the sentence:

My, my, you certainly are clever these days.

15.9   Review Exercise

Make a list from 1 to 100, and identify each of the numbered words in the paragraphs below with one of the following abbreviations: *n* (noun), *p* (pronoun), *v* (verb), *prep* (preposition), *adj* (adjective), *adv* (adverb), *c* (conjunction), *i* (interjection), and *e* (expletive).

Once there was a pilgrim who made it his life's work to discover the highest truth
     1   2   3   4   5 6 7

that this world could teach. He heard that a certain wise man might be able to offer him
 8 9 10   11   12

the most important teaching. To find the wise man, the pilgrim mounted his horse and set
    13   14   15   16   17   18 19

out on a long journey. He forded swift rivers and crossed high mountains. After he had
   20   21 22 23   24   25   26

searched for months, the pilgrim finally found the great teacher sitting outside of a cave.
     27   28   29   30   31 32 33

He was an old man with a long white beard. The pilgrim said to him, "At last! Great
34 35   36   37 38 39   40 41   42

teacher, I have heard <u>that</u> <u>you</u> <u>can</u> <u>tell</u> <u>me</u> the <u>most</u> <u>important</u> <u>truth</u> <u>that</u> <u>this</u> <u>world</u> can
                       43 44   45   46   47   48   49   50   51   52

teach. I have been searching <u>for</u> <u>you</u> for months. <u>Will</u> <u>you</u> <u>share</u> your wisdom with me
                             53 54   55   56 55

now?" The wise man <u>listened</u> <u>attentively</u> to the question <u>but</u> <u>made</u> no response. The
                   57   58   59   60

<u>seeker</u> of the truth <u>waited</u> <u>and</u> <u>waited.</u> <u>Hours</u> <u>passed.</u> <u>Finally,</u> after hours of silence, the
61   62   63   64   65   66   67

wise <u>man</u> <u>looked</u> at the horse the pilgrim was riding <u>and</u> <u>asked</u> him why he was <u>not</u>
     68   69   70   71   72

looking <u>for</u> a horse instead of <u>enlightenment.</u> The pilgrim responded <u>that</u> <u>obviously</u> he
        73   74   75   76

<u>already</u> had a horse. The wise <u>man</u> <u>smiled</u> <u>and</u> <u>retreated</u> <u>to</u> his cave.
77   78   79   80   81   82

The pilgrim thought <u>about</u> <u>this</u> <u>experience</u> <u>for</u> a <u>long</u> <u>time</u> <u>and</u> <u>finally</u> <u>figured</u> <u>out</u>
                    83   84   85   86   87   88   89   90   91

<u>what</u> the wise man <u>was</u> <u>telling</u> <u>him.</u> <u>What</u> <u>do</u> you <u>think</u> the <u>message</u> <u>was?</u> Do <u>you</u> agree
92   93   94   95   96   96   96   97   98   99

<u>with</u> the wise man?
100

16

Subject–Verb Agreement

16.0   Introduction

IN THIS CHAPTER you will study how to make verbs agree with their subjects. When you should add an -*s* to a verb can sometimes be most confusing. When you should choose *is* or *are* or *was* or *were* also can be confusing. This chapter gives the rules for subject-verb agreement and contains many practice exercises.

In standard English, the verb and the subject of a sentence must agree with each other. If the subject is one person, place, or thing, then the verb also must be singular. Here are examples of singular subjects with singular verbs:

The <u>train</u> <u>stops</u> at every station.

<u>Gasoline</u> <u>costs</u> a lot these days.

<u>Roberta</u> <u>cries</u> over the lost children.

Each subject is one: one train, one kind of fuel (gasoline), and one person (Roberta). The -*s* added to the verbs indicates that each verb is also singular. Because the subjects and the verbs are both singular, they are said to *agree* with each other.

Here are examples of plural (more than one) subjects and verbs:

The <u>trains</u> <u>stop</u> at every station.

Every day their <u>colds</u> <u>get</u> worse.

<u>Rudy and Mary</u> <u>plan</u> everything together.

Each of these subjects is more than one: more than one train, more than one cold, and two people named Rudy and Mary. The fact that the verbs do not end with -*s* indicates that they are plural.

The great confusion over subject-verb agreement arises from the fact that you add an -*s* to form the plural of most nouns but omit the -*s* to form the plural of verbs. For example, *one cabin* becomes *two cabins,* but *she lives* becomes *they live. Cabin* is a singular noun. To make the word plural, you add an -*s. Lives* is a singular verb. To make it plural, you omit the -*s.*

Practice 1

Make plural nouns and plural verbs for the following examples.

1. *A boy* becomes *two* ____*boys*____ , but *Mia sews* becomes *they* ____*sew*____ .

2. *A sister* becomes *two* _____ , but *Chris runs* becomes *they* _____ .

3. *One fist* becomes *two* _____ , but *she asks* becomes *they* _____ .

4. *A risk* becomes *two* _____ , but *Tom risks* becomes *they* _____ .

5. *A play* becomes *two* _____ , but *Sue plays* becomes *they* _____ .

Practice 2

Make singular nouns and singular verbs for the following examples.

1. *Two cats* becomes *one* ___*cat*___, but *they hit* becomes *he* ___*hits*___.

2. *Two boxes* becomes *one* _____, but *they cost* becomes *it* _____.

3. *Two buses* becomes *one* _____, but *they love* becomes *she* _____.

4. *Two bills* becomes *one* _____, but *they bill* becomes *he* _____.

5. *Two dances* becomes *one* _____, but *they dance* becomes *she* _____.

16.1   Verb Conjugation

To discuss the different verb forms, it is helpful to illustrate them. Here is an illustration for the verb *decide* in the present tense (showing action going on now):

	Singular	Plural
FIRST PERSON	I decide	we decide
SECOND PERSON	you decide	you decide
THIRD PERSON	he, she, or it decides	they decide
	(Bill, Mary, or the	(the people decide)
	dog decides)	

Such illustrations are called *conjugations*.

As shown above, the first-person plural of the verb *decide* is *we decide;* the third-person singular is *he, she,* or *it decides;* and the third-person plural is *they decide.*

You can see from the preceding conjugation of *decide* that only the third-person singular of a present-tense verb takes an *-s* at the end. If your subject is one of the pronouns *he, she,* or *it,* you know immediately to add the *-s.* If your subject is *they,* you know to omit the *-s.* If your subject is a singular noun, add the *-s* ending; if the noun is plural, omit it.

Look at these sentences:

(he)
John <u>plays</u> the stock market.

(she)
Mary <u>seems</u> to be understanding.

(it)
The <u>ship</u> <u>sails</u> around the world.

Because you can substitute *he* for *John, she* for *Mary,* and *it* for *ship,* each subject is singular and each verb must be singular (with the *-s* ending).

Now look at these examples:

(they)
John and Carlos <u>play</u> the stock market.

(they)
Mary and Martha <u>seem</u> to be understanding.

(they)
The <u>ships</u> <u>sail</u> around the world.

Because you can substitute *they* for each of these subjects, you must use a third-person plural verb for each—that is, a verb that does not end in *-s.*

Practice 3

Write the pronoun that you would substitute for each of the following noun subjects above the subject, and then choose the correct verb. Finally, complete the sentences.

1. The apples (~~costs~~, cost) *(they)* *more this year* _____ .

2. Robin Hood (robs, ~~rob~~) *(he)* *from the rich to give to the poor* _____ .

3. The police (complains, complain) _____ .

4. Mrs. Thatcher (stands, stand) _____ .

5. The space program (consists, consist) _____ .

6. Love (makes, make) _____ .

7. Happiness (seems, seem) _____ .

8. Her daughter (seeks, seek) _____ .

9. Their mother and father (keeps, keep) _____ .

10. Grandfather (becomes, become) _____ .

Practice 4

Compose sentences, using the following verbs in the present tense and in the person indicated.

1. (*hope:* first-person plural) *We hope this year will be a year of peace.*

_____

2. (*involve:* third-person singular) *Our mayor involves the citizens in city government.*

3. (*practice:* second-person singular) _____

_____

4. (*spend:* second-person plural) _____

_____

5. (*sew:* third-person plural) _____

_____

6. (*consist:* third-person singular) _____

_____

7. (*give:* first-person singular) _____

_____

8. (*become:* third-person singular) _____

_____

9. (*say:* third-person plural) _____

_____

10. (*use:* third-person plural) _____

_____

11. (*seem:* third-person singular) _____

_____

12. (*seem:* third-person plural) _____

_____

16.2   Irregular Noun Subjects

When used as third-person subjects, the following types of nouns are irregular and thus deserve special attention:

1. Most collective nouns (such as *family, class, team, union,* and *political party*) take singular verbs (those with the *-s* ending):

Her family meets all her needs. (*One family* meets her needs.)

The class seems to like the new instructor.

Our team plays best under pressure.

The union often threatens to go on strike.

The Democratic Party supports the minimum wage.

But note these exceptions:

The police appreciate law-abiding citizens.

The San Francisco 49ers win many more games than they lose.

2. Some collective nouns, such as *jury,* can take either a singular or plural verb depending on the meaning of the sentence:

The jury seems deadlocked. (Here, *jury* is considered as one unit.)

The jury disagree and cannot reach a verdict. (Here, *jury* is considered as a group of individuals.)

3. If the word *people* is understood—but not written—as part of a subject, the subject takes a plural verb:

The rich get richer, and the poor get poorer. (The writer is saying that the *rich people* get richer and the *poor people* get poorer.)

The courageous die, but the cowards live. (The writer is speaking of *courageous people.*)

4. A noun that is plural in form (with an *-s* ending) but singular in meaning usually takes a singular verb:

The United States gives some of its money to Third World countries. (The *United States* is one nation.)

Some think that politics corrupts. (*Politics* is one activity.)

But note these exceptions:

The scissors turn up each time I lose them.

My son's pants tear each time he goes fishing.

Practice 5

In each sentence below, choose the correct verb.

1. The police (raids, (raid)) a different bar every night.
2. The United States (experiences, experience) hard times as well as prosperous times.
3. The jury (eats, eat) fine meals at the government's expense.
4. The poor (pays, pay) the taxes, and the rich (pays, pay) the tax lawyers.
5. Each graduating class (gives, give) the school a nice present.
6. The family (acts, act) as one unit.
7. Politics (makes, make) the world go round.
8. Even the experienced (makes, make) mistakes when they are not careful.
9. The people of the world (needs, need) to unite against nuclear destruction.
10. His pants (shows, show) a lot of wear.
11. Those with disabilities (demand, demands) equal access to public facilities.
12. The jury (argues, argue) among themselves.
13. The police (supports, support) gun control.
14. The people of Russia no longer (want, wants) Stalin's communism.
15. The New Orleans Saints never (quits, quit).
16. The Republican Party usually (supports, support) business interests.
17. The Olympics (is, are) a once-in-a-lifetime experience to those who participate.
18. The powerful (controls, control) all business in that country.

16.3   Verb Endings

For verbs that end in *-ch, -sh, -ss, -x, -z,* or *-o,* add *-es* in the third-person singular of the present tense:

>   I, you, we, and they reach, but he reaches.
>
>   I, you, we, and they boss, but she bosses.
>
>   I, you, we, and they push, but she pushes.
>
>   I, you, we, and they box, but Ali boxes.

You add *-es* to these verbs simply because they would be hard to pronounce if you added only an *-s.* The *-es* adds an extra syllable to the words and makes pronunciation easier. However, note that *ask* and *cost* take an *-s,* not an *-es,* ending: *she asks, it costs.*

Practice 6

Write sentences, using the designated verbs in the present tense and in the person indicated.

1. (*preach:* third-person singular) *My wife preaches to me all the time about my rumpled shirts.*

2. (*pinch:* third-person singular) _____

   _____

3. (*fuss:* third-person singular) _____

   _____

4. (*cost:* third-person singular) _____

   _____

5. (*cost:* third-person plural) _____

   _____

6. (*rush:* third-person plural) _____

   _____

7. (*crush:* third-person plural) _____

   _____

8. (*ask:* third-person singular) _____

   _____

9. (*bless:* third-person singular) _____

   _____

Do and *Go*

Forms of *do* and *go* are particularly troublesome to some students. Note the following conjugations:

I, you, we, and they do, but it does.

I, you, we, and they go, but he goes.

To make *do* or *does* negative, you add the adverb *not* or, in a contraction, the suffix *-n't*. (A *suffix* is a letter or letters that are added to the end of a word.)

I do not (or I don't)

It does not (or it doesn't)

Note: The more formal the writing, the less you should use contractions.

Practice 7

Use *do, does, don't,* or *doesn't* in the following sentences.

1. Dr. Greenway *doesn't* want to be bothered by his children.

2. Our instructor _____ care about her students.

3. This city _____ not have many dry days.

4. Only on the weekends _____ the noise become unbearable.

5. Why make a young woman keep a man she _____ want?

6. They _____ have a lot of money; in fact, you could call them rich.

7. I had to tell her that Santa and his reindeer _____ come to our neighborhood.

8. It _____ hurt anymore; all my tears have been shed.

9. The English _____ seem to cherish the queen.

10. She, in turn, _____ care about her people.

11. _____ it seem strange when our allies go to war with each other?

Verbs That End in *-y*

If a verb ends in *-y* and is preceded by a consonant, change the *-y* to *-i* and add *-es* to form the third-person singular in the present tense. (A *consonant* is any letter other than one of the five *vowels: a, e, i, o, u.*) *I cry* thus becomes *she cries* because the *-y* is preceded by the consonant *r.*

I, you, we, and they spy, but she spies.

I, you, we, and they carry, but it carries.

I, you, we, and they bury, but he buries.

I, you, we, and they dry, but she dries.

If, however, a verb ends in *-y* and is preceded by a vowel, simply add an *-s* to the verb. *They enjoy* thus becomes *he enjoys* because the *-y* is preceded by the vowel *o.*

I, you, we, and they play, but it plays.

I, you, we, and they say, but she says.

I, you, we, and they enjoy, but he enjoys.

I, you, we, and they journey, but it journeys.

Note that when you add *-ing* to a verb ending in *-y,* you do not change the *-y.* Thus *cry* becomes *crying, enjoy* becomes *enjoying,* and *journey* becomes *journeying.*

Practice 8

Supply the correct verb in the present tense.

1. (carry) Mary _____*carries*_____

2. (defy) Ben _____

3. (try) She _____

4. (travel) Mia _____

5. (fly) A bird _____

6. (journey) The team _____

7. (bury) It _____

8. (do) It _____

9. (do + -n't) It _____

10. (go) The van _____

16.4   *Have* and *Has*

The verb *have* is regular except in the third-person singular, where *has* is used instead of *haves.*

	Singular	Plural
FIRST PERSON	I have	we have
SECOND PERSON	you have	you have
THIRD PERSON	he, she, or it has	they have
	(Bob has, Jill has, the cat has)	(the people have)

Since *have* and *has* are frequently used as helping verbs, make sure that you use each form correctly. Here are examples of *have* and *has* used as helping verbs:

The <u>Dolphins have won</u> many games this year.

<u>Becky has broken</u> her arm again.

<u>She has loved</u> many men in her day.

 ### Practice 9

In the following sentences, supply the correct form of the verb *have*.

1. The city of Detroit ____*has*____ many industries.

2. Everyone just gathers and _____ a good time.

3. You _____ been lying to me all along.

4. China _____ more people than the United States.

5. They _____ done what they can to save her.

6. These days a soldier _____ a pretty nice life.

7. The United States _____ offered them a compromise solution.

8. The scissors _____ not cut him so far.

9. The police _____ a difficult job to do.

10. People in Latin America _____ close ties with us.

11. The class _____ elected its representative.

16.5   The *Be* Verbs

Be verbs are irregular. Here are the conjugations of *be* in the present and past tenses.

	Present Tense	
	Singular	*Plural*
FIRST PERSON	I am	we are
SECOND PERSON	you are	you are
THIRD PERSON	he, she, or it is	they are

Past Tense

	Singular	Plural
FIRST PERSON	I was	we were
SECOND PERSON	you were	you were
THIRD PERSON	he, she, or it was	they were

Thus you would write the following:

PRESENT TENSE

I <u>am</u> sick.

You <u>are</u> my friend.

The police officer <u>is</u> leaving.

We <u>are</u> going.

You <u>are</u> my friends.

The police <u>are</u> leaving.

PAST TENSE

The family <u>was</u> disturbed.

The poor <u>were</u> hungry.

Practice 10

Choose the correct form of each verb, and then complete the following sentences.

1. (is, are) The people *are my friends* _____

   _____ .

2. (was, were) My husband and brother-in-law _____

   _____ .

3. (is, are) The jury _____

   _____ .

4. (wasn't, weren't) Uncle Mac _____

   _____ .

5. (wasn't, weren't) They _____

   _____ .

6. (was, were) Congress _____

   _____ .

7. (isn't, aren't) The Rams _____

_____ .

8. (is, are) The police _____

_____ .

9. (wasn't, weren't) You _____

_____ .

16.6   Subject and Verb Reversed

Questions

You reverse the order of the subject and verb when you ask a question. Note the placement of the subjects and verbs in the following questions:

Does your daughter still believe in Santa Claus?

Hasn't that plane left yet?

The verb *does believe* agrees with the subject *daughter; hasn't left* agrees with the subject *plane.*

Practice 11

First turn the following statements into questions. Then underline the subjects once and the verbs twice.

1. He does need more money for the trip. *Does he need more money for the trip?*

2. She is going to dance with you. _____

_____

3. Those children do need heavier jackets. _____

_____

4. They were the ones we were looking for. _____

_____

5. The leg has healed completely. _____

_____

6. The senator doesn't deliver on his promises. _____

_____

Expletives

You also reverse the order of the subject and verb when you use an *expletive,* which is an expression such as *it is, here is, there is, here are,* and *there are.* Note the placement of the subjects and verbs in the following sentences with expletives.

There <u>is</u> one <u>thing</u> you haven't told me.

There <u>have been</u> several <u>occasions</u> when he seemed crazy.

It <u>is</u> the <u>house</u> of my dreams.

Here <u>are</u> my <u>plans.</u>

The expletives in the preceding sentences (*there is, there have been, it is,* and *here are*) are not the subjects, but they do point to the subjects. The subjects come after the verbs but nevertheless must agree with them. *Thing* agrees with *is; occasions* agrees with *have been; house* agrees with *is; plans* agrees with *are.*

Practice 12

Underline the subject in each of the following sentences, and then supply the correct verb.

1. (was, were) There *were* _____ deer everywhere.

2. (is, are) There _____ something I have been meaning to tell you.

3. (is, are) There _____ often street fighting on the next block.

4. (Was, Were) _____ there many survivors from the airplane crash?

5. (wasn't, weren't) There _____ any use in saying it again; the dean had made up her mind.

6. (wasn't, weren't) There _____ a thing the doctors could do for him.

7. (is, are) There _____ just two alternatives left.

8. (has, have) There _____ been more violent crime this year.

9. (hasn't, haven't) There _____ been any reason for the increase that we know about.

10. (has, have) There _____ been fewer murders, however.

11. (has, have) There _____ been some concern in the community.

16.7   Verbs with Two or More Subjects

Many of your verbs will have two or more subjects (called *compound subjects*). Usually they are joined by the conjunction *and:*

<u>Ron</u> and <u>Don</u> <u>are</u> twin brothers. <u>Sally</u> and <u>Julius</u> <u>study</u> together. (Because *Ron* and *Don* together are the subject of the sentence and represent more than one person, they take the plural verb *are.* The same is true of *Sally* and *Julius.*)

<u>What I say</u> and <u>what I do</u> <u>are</u> not always the same. (*What I say* and *what I do* each function as individual nouns, but together take the plural verb *are.*)

<u>Appointing officials</u> and <u>initiating legislation</u> <u>are</u> the governor's primary responsibilities. (*Appointing officials* and *initiating legislation* each function as individual nouns, but together take the plural verb *are.*)

Practice 13

In each of the following, choose the correct verb and then complete the sentence.

1. (sew, sews) Mother and I often *sew together* .

2. (cost, costs) Gas and oil both _____ .

3. (aren't, isn't) What I want and what she wants _____ .

4. (are, is) But what I want _____ .

5. (give, gives) This man and this woman _____ .

6. (are, is) Getting better grades _____ .

7. (are, is) Getting better grades and playing more tennis _____ .

8. (buy, buys) My aunt and uncle sometimes _____ .

9. (seem, seems) The potatoes, corn, and spinach all _____ .

10. (protect, protects) The Bill of Rights and the Constitution _____

_____

11. (are, is) Making clothes for her children _____ .

Other Ways of Joining Subjects

1. Compound subjects are sometimes connected by the conjunction *or* or the correlative conjunctions *either ... or:*

Either <u>Ron</u> or <u>Don</u> <u>is going</u> to medical school. (A singular verb is used; one of the subjects will go to medical school, not both.)

However, if one of the subjects joined by *or* is plural, use a plural verb *when the subject closer to the verb is plural:*

Either <u>Tina</u> or her <u>parents</u> <u><u>are</u></u> mistaken. (The verb *are* is used to agree with the plural subject *parents.*)

But use the singular verb when the subject closer to the verb is singular:

Either the <u>eggs</u> or the <u>bacon</u> <u><u>is</u></u> burning. (Even though *eggs* is plural, *bacon* is closer to the verb and thus determines that it is singular.)

2. The conjunction *nor* and the correlative conjunctions *neither ... nor* and *not only ... but also* function in the same way as *or* and *either ... or:*

Neither <u>Mother</u> nor <u>Father</u> <u>lets</u> me use the car.

Not only my hotel <u>accommodations</u> but also my airplane <u>ticket</u> <u><u>costs</u></u> more this year.

Not only my airplane <u>ticket</u> but also my hotel <u>accommodations</u> <u><u>cost</u></u> more this year.

Practice 14

In each of the following, choose the correct verb and then complete the sentence.

1. (come, comes) Every day Mrs. Appleby or Mrs. St. John *comes by and brings me my supper* .

2. (are, is) Neither you nor they _____

    _____ .

3. (are, is) Abraham and his son, Isaac, _____

    _____ .

4. (are, is) Either Sara Martinez or her friends _____

    _____ .

5. (appear, appears) But then suddenly a bear or some other kind of animal _____

    _____ .

6. (are, is) Not only adults but also children _____

    _____ .

7. (jog, jogs) Not only the grandfather but also the children _____

    _____ .

8. (jog, jogs) Not only the children but also the grandfather _____

_____ .

9. (have, has) Either Sophia or you _____

_____ .

10. (sleep, sleeps) Both the cat and the dog _____

_____ .

11. (experience, experiences) Neither Russia nor the United States _____

_____ .

16.8   Verbs with Pronoun Subjects

Throughout this chapter you have been writing sentences with personal pronouns as subjects: *I, you, he, she, it, we,* and *they.* In this section you will learn the rules for verb agreement when *indefinite, interrogative,* and *relative pronouns* are used as subjects.

One type of pronoun that can cause difficulty in verb-agreement constructions is the *indefinite pronoun.* Although some are plural in meaning, the following *always* take singular verbs:

anybody	everybody	nobody	somebody
anyone	everyone	no one	someone
anything	everything	nothing	something

Thus you would write the following:

> <u>Anything</u> she wants to do <u>is</u> fine with us.
>
> <u>Everybody</u> <u>says</u> that this is the hottest summer in history.
>
> <u>Somebody</u> <u>has</u> made a mistake.

The indefinite pronoun *some* can take either a singular or a plural verb. For example,

> <u>Some</u> of the apple <u>is</u> rotten. (Some of *one* thing is rotten.)
>
> <u>Some</u> of the apples <u>are</u> rotten. (Some of *several* things are rotten.)

Half, part, all, a lot, more, and *most* also can take either singular or plural verbs. You need to ask yourself if they refer to part of one thing or some of several things. For example,

> <u>A lot</u> of your writing <u>is</u> clever.
>
> <u>A lot</u> of the students in this class <u>are</u> good writers.

Practice 15

In each of the following, choose the correct verb and then complete the sentence.

1. (are, is) Some of you *are still my friends* _____.

2. (cost, costs) Everything _____.

3. (are, is) Anyone _____.

4. (were, was) Some of the work _____.

5. (are, is) All of the families on the block _____.

6. (involve, involves) Everything in this life _____.

7. (tell, tells) Half of my brain _____;

   half _____.

8. (Do, Does) everyone _____?

9. (have, has) Most of the prisoners _____.

10. (are, is) Much of their problem _____.

11. (Do, Does) anyone _____?

Interrogative Pronouns as Subjects

A second kind of pronoun that can cause difficulty in verb-agreement constructions is the *interrogative pronoun*—a pronoun used in questions:

   Who?   What?   Which?

When used as subjects, these pronouns can take either singular or plural verbs, depending on the words they stand for:

   What is that woman's name? (*What* refers to *one* woman's name.)

   What are their names? (*What* refers to *several* people's names.)

Interrogative pronouns that do not refer to particular nouns usually take singular verbs:

   What is happening?

   Who is going with us?

Practice 16

In each of the sentences that follow, draw an arrow from the interrogative pronoun to the noun or pronoun it refers to, and then supply the correct verb.

1. (are, is) What _____*is*_____ the best choice?

2. (were, was) What _____ their names before they got married?

3. (are, is) What _____ your agenda for the meeting?

4. (are, is) Which one of the insurance plans _____ best for your family?

5. (were, was) Who _____ the lucky winner?

6. (were, was) Who _____ the lucky winners?

Relative Pronouns as Subjects

A third kind of pronoun that can cause difficulty in verb-agreement constructions is the *relative pronoun*—a pronoun that connects an adjective clause to a main clause:

who   whose   which   that

Like interrogative pronouns, relative pronouns can take either singular or plural verbs, depending on the words they stand for:

The person who means the most to me is my husband.

The people who mean the most to me are my parents.

In the first example, *who* refers to one person and thus takes the singular verb *means*. In the second, *who* refers to more than one person and takes the plural verb *mean*.

Practice 17

In each of the sentences below, underline the pronoun subject of the adjective clause, draw an arrow to the noun or pronoun it refers to, and then supply the correct verb.

1. (were, was) My friends <u>who</u> _____*were*_____ with me stood up for me when I was arrested.

2. (break, breaks) It is hard to remain allies with nations that _____ our treaties.

3. (mind, minds) The one who _____ his or her own business is the one who stays out of trouble.

4. (care, cares) They are the ones who _____ for you the most.

5. (turn, turns) The coins that _____ green are copper.

6. (need, needs) People who _____ others are my kind of people.

7. (believe, believes) The police who _____ in crime prevention contribute a lot to our community.

8. (talk, talks) If I have another date who _____ to me about football, I am going to scream.

9. (know, knows) Will those of you who _____ something about this please leave your names?

10. (cost, costs) The gifts that _____ the most are not necessarily the best.

11. (are, is) I kept the scissors that _____ the sharpest.

Practice 18

Complete these sentences by using the designated subjects with either *is* or *are.*

1. Everybody *is my friend these days* _____.

2. Anyone _____.

3. Everything _____.

4. Some of the shirts _____.

5. Half of the watermelon _____.

16.9   Present-Tense Essay

Many students have found that writing present-tense, third-person singular essays is the best practice for subject-verb agreement. In such assignments, the writer is forced to use the -*s* endings consistently. For example,

> My <u>horse</u>, Pegasus, <u>stands</u> taller than any other horse. His <u>coat</u> <u>shines</u> brighter than any hand-shined leather. <u>He</u> <u>holds</u> his head high, with great dignity. . . .

If you convert such a narrative to the present-tense, third-person *plural,* you of course drop the -*s* from the third-person verbs. The resulting essay may sound somewhat contrived, but it will nevertheless offer excellent practice in subject-verb agreement. For example,

> My <u>horses</u>, Lucky and Zorro, <u>stand</u> taller than any other horses. Their <u>coats</u> <u>shine</u>. . . .

The advantage of writing such third-person essays is that you naturally use your own words and sentence construction rather than those someone has prepared for you. Consequently, what you learn by writing these essays can be more easily converted into other writing you do.

If you are having persistent difficulty in subject-verb agreement, complete the three following assignments.

Practice 19

Using the free-writing technique to gather ideas and information, write a present-tense, third-person singular narrative that has one of the following beginnings. Underline the subjects once and the verbs twice. (Do not worry about your verbs when you are free writing. When you revise and rewrite, however, make sure that your subjects and verbs agree.)

■   He finds himself at the age of twenty on the outskirts of Chicago with no money in his pockets and no relatives or friends to turn to. It is getting dark, and he is cold in the early fall air. He is hungry and does not know what to do, but he knows he must do something fast, so he . . .

■   She has always believed that somewhere in the world there lives the perfect mate for her. One day she finds herself at a small party feeling bored, but when she happens to look up toward the door, she sees him standing there alone. She knows as she has never known anything so definitely before that this is the right person for her. She gathers her courage, and she . . .

■   It is summer time. She is walking along the beach and happens to see an old bottle covered with barnacles. As she approaches the bottle, she sees that there is a piece of paper, a letter, inside the bottle. She has to break off the end of the bottle to get to the letter, and then she reads these words: . . .

16.10 Review Exercises

Review Exercise 1

In the following sentences, underline the subjects and then supply the correct verbs.

1. (is, are) There ____are____ only a few soldiers determined to hold out.

2. (costs, cost) The Social Security program _____ more than we can afford.

3. (is, are) The most educational programs on television _____ the news and the public broadcasting programs.

4. (wasn't, weren't) The people of your country _____ friendly to the people of our country.

5. (begins, begin) The family _____ each morning with exercises.

6. (lives, live) My friends, who _____ nearby, are always there when I need them.

7. (seems, seem) Eggs, which still _____ cheap, are one of the best foods you can buy.

8. (is, are) For the housewives and househusbands who stay home, there _____ soap operas.

9. (uses, use) A car that _____ a lot of gasoline is often cheap.

10. (has, have) I want representatives in Congress who _____ character.

11. (doesn't, don't) It _____ matter what you do.

12. (becomes, become) The police _____ angry when people are sarcastic to them.

13. (Hasn't, Haven't) _____ those things been said before?

14. (breaks, break) She _____ her own record each time she competes.

15. (is, are) Either she or they _____ lying.

16. (costs, cost) Not only the hotel bills but also the flight _____ more this year.

17. (There is, There are) _____ only a few people who know what caused the nuclear disaster.

18. (helps, help) The rain bothers us but _____ the farmers.

19. (does, do) What _____ that expression mean?

20. (doesn't, don't) It _____ seem to matter what witnesses say.

21. (Doesn't, Don't) _____ your father mean anything to you?

Review Exercise 2

Edit the following essay, correcting all the verb agreement errors by writing the corrections above the line.

Uptown Versus Downtown

I now live in Jefferson City East, which is known as the uptown area. I have been living uptown for six years and has enjoyed every moment. Before that I lived downtown and hated every moment. Mother worked hard, sometimes at two jobs, to make enough money for us to move. (1 error)

Living uptown is very pleasant. Around my neighborhood there isn't any gang fights. People are friendly and helps one another in time of trouble. I can go to the corner drugstore and not have to worry about being mugged. My mother has peace of mind knowing that neither she nor her children is going to be hurt in the streets. Mother sometimes invite people over to see the house and is not embarrassed by dirty surroundings. (4 errors)

My experience living downtown was quite different. There was gang fights every day. Sometimes in the fights people would be badly hurt or even killed. You was always scared that you would be the next to get hurt. The people in my neighborhood was not friendly at all. A nice drugstore was on the corner, but we were scared of the drug addicts who gathered there. My mother was always worried about the danger in the streets; she was afraid her children would get mixed up with the wrong crowd. She was also too embarrassed to invite people to the house because of the crime in the neighborhood. This neighborhood weren't the atmosphere my mother wanted for her children. (4 errors)

These are my reasons for choosing uptown, a better place to live than downtown. I hope I can do for my children what my mother have done for us and keep them away from downtown. (1 error)

17

Verb Tense and Practice with Verbs

17.0 Introduction

In this chapter you will learn the different tenses, or forms, of the more common verbs, and then you will learn about and practice correcting subject-verb agreement and verb-tense errors. Learning the spelling rules, mastering the use of the dictionary, and practicing the irregular constructions will all help you to understand verb use.

A *verb* is a part of speech that says what a subject is, was, or will be or does, did, or will do. These examples show how two verbs can be used:

TO BE

My grandmother <u>is</u> ninety years old.

My grandmother <u>was</u> ninety years old.

My grandmother <u>will be</u> ninety years old.

My grandmother <u>has been</u> ninety years old for two days now.

My grandmother <u>had been</u> ninety years old for two days before she died.

TO LEAP

The deer <u>leaps</u> over the fence.

The deer <u>leaped</u> over the fence.

The deer <u>will leap</u> over the fence.

The deer <u>has leaped</u> over the fence.

The deer <u>had leaped</u> over the fence before anyone could catch him.

Each of these verb forms has a different meaning, referring to a different time. This distinction in time is called *verb tense*.

Each verb has four principal parts that are used to indicate different tenses. Here are the principal parts of five verbs:

Base Form	Simple Past	Past Participle	Progressive Form
love	loved	loved	loving
walk	walked	walked	walking
have	had	had	having
begin	began	begun	beginning
be	was	been	being

Of these five verbs, *love* and *walk* are said to be *regular.* What makes them regular is that you add either *-d* or *-ed* to form both the simple past and the past participle. On the other hand, *have, begin,* and *be* are *irregular* because the simple past and the past participle are formed in other ways.

Practice 1

Write the correct form of the designated verb in each of the following sentences. (*Note: Drown, seem, ask,* and *plead* are all regular verbs and consequently take *-ed* endings for the simple past and past participle forms.)

1. (*begin:* past participle) I had ____*begun*____ my work before she came in.

2. (*love:* simple past) They _____ one another from the first.

3. (*begin:* progressive form) The headaches were _____ all over again.

4. (*walk:* past participle) That woman was _____ over once too often.

5. (*begin:* base form) You may _____ when you are ready.

6. (*be:* simple past) The family _____ together.

7. (*drown:* past participle) The child had _____ before they got to her.

8. (*seem:* simple past) They _____ like such nice people.

9. (*ask:* past participle) You were _____ to do your part.

10. (*plead:* simple past) They _____ with him to stay away from drugs.

11. (*have:* progressive form) I was _____ a wonderful time.

17.1   Irregular Verbs

A list of the principal parts of many irregular verbs (and a few regular verbs sometimes mistaken for irregular verbs) follows. Try to learn all the forms as soon as possible. The underlined words remain the same except in the progressive.

Base Form	Simple Past	Past Participle	Progressive Form
arise(s)	arose	arisen	arising
awake(s)	awoke	awakened	awaking
beat(s)	beat	beaten	beating
become(s)	became	become	becoming
begin(s)	began	begun	beginning
bite(s)	bit	bitten	biting
blow(s)	blew	blown	blowing
break(s)	broke	broken	breaking
bring(s)	brought	brought	bringing
build(s)	built	built	building
buy(s)	bought	bought	buying
catch(es)	caught	caught	catching
choose(s)	chose	chosen	choosing

Base Form	Simple Past	Past Participle	Progressive Form
come(s)	came	come	coming
cost(s)	cost	cost	costing
cut(s)	cut	cut	cutting
dig(s)	dug	dug	digging
do(es)	did	done	doing
draw(s)	drew	drawn	drawing
dream(s)	dreamed	dreamed	dreaming
drink(s)	drank	drunk	drinking
drive(s)	drove	driven	driving
drown(s)	drowned	drowned	drowning
eat(s)	ate	eaten	eating
fail(s)	failed	failed	failing
fall(s)	fell	fallen	falling
feel(s)	felt	felt	feeling
fight(s)	fought	fought	fighting
find(s)	found	found	finding
fly(ies)	flew	flown	flying
forget(s)	forgot	forgotten	forgetting
forgive(s)	forgave	forgiven	forgiving
freeze(s)	froze	frozen	freezing
get(s)	got	gotten	getting
go(es)	went	gone	going
grow(s)	grew	grown	growing
hang(s)	hung	hung	hanging
have (has)	had	had	having
hear(s)	heard	heard	hearing
hide(s)	hid	hidden	hiding
hit(s)	hit	hit	hitting
hurt(s)	hurt	hurt	hurting
keep(s)	kept	kept	keeping
know(s)	knew	known	knowing
lay(s) (to put or place something)	laid	laid	laying
lead(s)	led	led	leading
leave(s)	left	left	leaving
lend(s)	lent	lent	lending
let(s)	let	let	letting
lie(s) (to recline)	lay	lain	lying
lose(s)	lost	lost	losing
make(s)	made	made	making
meet(s)	met	met	meeting

Base Form	Simple Past	Past Participle	Progressive Form
pass(es)	passed	passed	passing
pay(s)	paid	paid	paying
plead(s)	pleaded	pleaded	pleading
prove(s)	proved	proven	proving
put(s)	put	put	putting
quit(s)	quit	quit	quitting
raise(s)	raised	raised	raising
read(s)	read	read	reading
ride(s)	rode	ridden	riding
ring(s)	rang	rung	ringing
rise(s)	rose	risen	rising
run(s)	ran	run	running
say(s)	said	said	saying
see(s)	saw	seen	seeing
seem(s)	seemed	seemed	seeming
sell(s)	sold	sold	selling
send(s)	sent	sent	sending
set(s)	set	set	setting
(to put something down)			
shoot(s)	shot	shot	shooting
sing(s)	sang	sung	singing
sit(s)	sat	sat	sitting
speak(s)	spoke	spoken	speaking
stand(s)	stood	stood	standing
steal(s)	stole	stolen	stealing
stick(s)	stuck	stuck	sticking
swear(s)	swore	sworn	swearing
swim(s)	swam	swum	swimming
take(s)	took	taken	taking
teach(es)	taught	taught	teaching
tear(s)	tore	torn	tearing
tell(s)	told	told	telling
think(s)	thought	thought	thinking
throw(s)	threw	thrown	throwing
wake(s)	woke	wakened	waking
wear(s)	wore	worn	wearing

The Forms of *Be*

The forms of *be* are also irregular and deserve special attention. Here are the principal parts:

BASE FORM
be

SIMPLE PAST
was

PAST PARTICIPLE
been

PROGRESSIVE FORM
being

The present tense is *conjugated,* or related to a subject, as follows:

	Singular	Plural
FIRST PERSON	I am	we are
SECOND PERSON	you are	you are
THIRD PERSON	he, she, or it is	they are

The simple past tense is conjugated as follows:

	Singular	Plural
FIRST PERSON	I was	we were
SECOND PERSON	you were	you were
THIRD PERSON	he, she, or it was	they were

Practice 2

Insert the indicated form of the irregular verbs in the following sentences. Check the verbs against the preceding list.

1. (*break:* past participle) I have ____*broken*____ my hand.

2. (*lay:* simple past) Yesterday I _____ my watch on the desk.

3. (*lie:* simple past) I was so tired that I _____ down.

4. (*set:* simple past) He _____ his watch two hours fast.

5. (*lie:* past participle) They had just _____ down when the alarm sounded.

6. (*lay:* past participle) The soldier has _____ down his sword and shield.

7. (*lie:* base form) She loves to _____ out in the sun.

8. (*drown:* simple past) The little girl almost _____ in the pool.

9. (*cost:* past participle) It has _____ us a lot to live in the city.

10. (*go:* past participle) She has _____ over that with me many times.

11. (*begin:* past participle) We have _____ to see daylight.

12. (*see:* simple past) The instructor _____ to it that we did our work.

13. (*begin:* progressive form) We are _____ a long journey.

14. (*lay:* progressive form) They are _____ their cards on the table.

15. (*hurt:* progressive form) We were always _____ one another.

16. (*break:* present tense) That country _____ its treaties whenever it wishes.

17.2   The Base Form

The base form of a verb is used in the following ways:

1. To serve as the present tense of a verb:

	Singular	*Plural*
FIRST PERSON	I love	we love
SECOND PERSON	you love	you love
THIRD PERSON	he, she, or it loves	they love

Note that you add an *-s* to the third-person singular form.

2. To serve as the main verb with the helping verb *do:*

I do love   she does love   they did love

3. To serve as an *infinitive* when introduced by *to:*

I try to love   she tries to love   they tried to love

Note: You do not add *-d* or any other ending to the base form of a verb when it is used as an infinitive.

4. To serve as the main verb when used with one of the nine helping verbs called *modals: will, would, shall, should, must, can, could, may,* and *might.* Modals show various degrees of possibility or probability. For example,

I will love   I shall love   I can love   I may love

I would love   I should love   I could love   I might love

I must love

Note: You do not add *-d* or any other ending to the base form of a verb when it is used with a modal.

Practice 3

Choose a different modal verb for each of the sentences that follow.

1. Your friends ____can____ come if they want to.

2. Jannie _____ ride a rodeo mule.

3. The jacket _____ dry quickly.

4. I really _____ read this text more closely.

5. We _____ adopt a child.

6. If I did not know Herb so well, I _____ think he was crazy.

7. Antonio _____ have his grades by now.

8. It _____ rain this afternoon.

9. You _____ pass this course!

10. He _____ do it if he _____ .

Modal Verbs and Verb Tense

Ordinarily you should use *will, can,* and *may* with present-tense verbs and *would, could,* and *might* with past-tense verbs, as follows:

> You <u>know</u> you <u>will do</u> well in that class. (present tense)
>
> You <u>knew</u> you <u>would do</u> well in that class. (past tense)
>
> He <u>says</u> that I <u>can</u> go to that school. (present tense)
>
> He <u>said</u> that I <u>could</u> go to that school. (past tense)
>
> You <u>may be</u> making a mistake. (present tense)
>
> I <u>told</u> her that she <u>might be</u> making a mistake. (past tense)

Note: The modal *may* and the main verb *be* are written as two separate words, *may be. Maybe* is an adverb, as in "*Maybe* you are right."

Practice 4

Choose the correct modal verb for each of the following.

1. (can, could) When I was young, you ____could____ buy a cola for a dime.

2. (can, could) When darkness falls out there, you _____ hear strange sounds in the woods.

3. (can, could) He thought he _____ pass the test, but unfortunately he was wrong.

4. (can, could) I hope you _____ come with us.

5. (can, could) You _____ have knocked me over with a straw.

6. (will, would) Leroy knew that he _____ win some day.

7. (will, would) If we arrive on time, we _____ get the best seats.

8. (will, would) If they had known we were coming, they _____ have hired a band.

9. (will, would) Mother said she _____ give the ring to me when I got married.

10. (will, would) The pants _____ fit when I lose weight.

11. (will, would) I thought we _____ win.

12. (may, might) The president _____ be right about inflation, but many disagree.

13. (may, might) The president _____ have been right about inflation.

14. (may, might) Regina told the dean that she _____ be thinking of another career.

15. (may, might) Students with outside jobs and children to raise _____ not find enough hours in the day to do everything.

17.3   The Simple Past Tense

When you want to write about something that happened in the past—whether a moment ago, a year ago, or a million years ago—you will often use the *simple past tense* of the verb. To form the simple past of regular verbs, add *-d* or *-ed* to the base form:

I love becomes I loved

I walk becomes I walked

If you are in doubt about how to form the simple past for irregular verbs, check the list on pages 342–344 or consult a dictionary. Here are two simple past conjugations:

Seem (Regular)		*Begin (Irregular)*	
I seemed	we seemed	I began	we began
you seemed	you seemed	you began	you began
he, she, or it seemed	they seemed	he, she, or it began	they began

 ### Practice 5

In the first sentence of each pair below, supply the appropriate *present-tense* form of the designated verb (remembering to add *-s* or *-es* when necessary); in the second sentence, supply the *simple past form*. Use the list of irregular verbs on pages 342–344 as necessary.

1. (dress) a. Carlos ____*dresses*____ "fit to kill" every day.

   b. When he was a young man, he ____*dressed*____ "fit to kill."

2. (cut) a. Lee _____ his finger when he chops onions.

   b. But yesterday, he nearly _____ his finger off.

3. (begin) a. Each time I _____ to study, someone interrupts me.

   b. The moment I _____ to study, my daughter came in for a chat.

4. (choose) a. _____ me to represent the class, please.

   b. They said that you _____ me.

5. (read) a. My husband _____ to the children every night.

   b. Last night, he _____ *Tom Sawyer*.

6. (cost) a. Gasoline _____ more each year.

   b. Ten years ago, it hardly _____ anything.

7. (drown) a. David _____ her with his love.

   b. When she rejected him, he _____ himself in tears.

8. (wake) a. When she _____ me up, the cat awakes also.

   b. When she _____ me up, the cat awoke also.

9. (have) a. Dr. Sanders _____ good attendance in her class.

   b. Dr. Sanders _____ good attendance in her class until this semester.

10. (feel) a. I _____ you have been unfair to me.

    b. I _____ you were unfair to me.

11. (get) a. Mrs. Joseph _____ up with the birds.

    b. But yesterday, she _____ up before the birds.

Past-Tense Endings

When writing verbs in the simple past, it is often necessary to double the final letter before adding *-ed:*

hum becomes hummed

refer becomes referred

<u>stop</u> becomes <u>stopped</u>

<u>commit</u> becomes <u>committed</u>

Before doubling the final letter, make sure the verb meets the following tests:

1. The final letter is a consonant, not a vowel (*a, e, i, o,* or *u*), and not *y.* For example, the preceding verbs end in *m, r, p,* and *t.*
2. The final letter is preceded by a single vowel (not a double vowel and not a consonant). This is true of all the preceding examples. What are the vowels that precede the final consonants?
3. The word is either one syllable *or* the accent is on the last syllable. *Hum* and *stop* are both one-syllable words; *refer* and *commit* are both accented on the last syllable. We say:

comMIT, not COMmit

reFER, not REfer

Travel, however, is pronounced TRA-vel. Thus the simple past is *traveled.* Likewise, the simple past of *happen* is *happened.*

Practice 6

Applying the three rules above, tell why you do *not* double the final letter of the following words to form the simple past.

1. help_____
2. loom_____
3. enjoy_____
4. differ_____
5. return_____

Practice 7

Form the simple past of the following verbs.

1. (enjoy) Mary _____ my company those many years.
2. (prefer) Clarence said that he _____ meat and potatoes.
3. (gas) We stopped at the pump and _____ up the car.
4. (step) They _____ up their passing attack in the third quarter.
5. (suppose) Chou told me that he _____ he would study medicine.

Verbs That End in -*y*

To form the simple past of verbs that end in *-y preceded by a consonant*, change the *-y* to *-i* and add *-ed:*

> cry becomes cried
>
> apply becomes applied
>
> marry becomes married

For verbs that end in *-y preceded by a vowel*, just add *-ed* without changing the *-y:*

> enjoy becomes enjoyed
>
> journey becomes journeyed
>
> obey becomes obeyed
>
> employ becomes employed

Note: If you add *-ing* to a verb that ends in *-y*, you do not change the *-y: fry* becomes *frying.*

 Practice 8

Form the simple past of the following verbs.

1. (cry) She _____ a river of tears over me.

2. (fry) They _____ it in bacon grease.

3. (obey) Hartford always _____ his mother.

4. (marry) They _____ when they were much too young.

5. (bury) Rover _____ the bone in the yard.

17.4   The Past Participle

The *past participle* is the verb form that is used with the helping verbs *have, has,* and *had* to form the *perfect tenses* and with *am, are, is, was,* and *were* to form the *passive voice.*

The Past Participle with *Have, Has,* and *Had*

If a past-tense verb is written as one word, it is called the *simple past.* Other past-tense constructions are formed with *have, has,* and *had.* The main verb in such constructions is called a *past participle.* To form the past participle of regular verbs, add *-d* or *-ed* to the base form of the verb:

love becomes <u>has loved</u>, <u>have loved</u>, or <u>had loved</u>

walk becomes <u>has walked</u>, <u>have walked</u>, or <u>had walked</u>

Note that the simple past and the past participle of regular verbs are formed in the same way. I *loved* and I *have loved.*

If you are in doubt about how to form a past participle for an irregular verb, check the list on pages 342–344 or consult a dictionary. Here are two sample conjugations:

Join *(Regular)*

PRESENT PERFECT	I have joined	we have joined
	you have joined	you have joined
	he, she, or it has joined	they have joined
PAST PERFECT	I had joined	we had joined
	you had joined	you had joined
	he, she, or it had joined	they had joined

Begin *(Irregular)*

PRESENT PERFECT	I have begun	we have begun
	you have begun	you have begun
	he, she, or it has begun	they have begun
PAST PERFECT	I had begun	we had begun
	you had begun	you had begun
	he, she, or it had begun	they had begun

Practice 9

Supply the past participles of the designated irregular verbs in the sentences below. (If necessary, consult the list on pages 342–344.) Notice how *have* and *has* are used differently from *had.*

1. (teach) Mother had already ___*taught*___ me how to read when I began school.

2. (rise) The sun had _____ before I arose.

3. (begin) I have _____ to develop a taste for sweets.

4. (choose) You have _____ well.

5. (sit) I have _____ in that English class one semester too many.

6. (come) It has _____ to a showdown.

7. (become) He wanted to know what had _____ of them.

8. (run) Richard had _____ completely out of money before he got that job.

9. (quit) He had _____ before he was fired.

10. (put) Tomas has _____ his money where his mouth is.

11. (hit) Hurricane Andrew has _____ with all its force.

12. (lead) Debra had _____ a proper life before she met Lewis Funicella.

13. (lay) He has _____ down his sword and shield.

14. (lie) We have _____ down to rest from our labors.

15. (ring) They have not _____ that church bell for ninety years.

16. (begin) He has _____ to get a little deaf.

When to Use *Have, Has,* and *Had*

Have and *has* are used as helping verbs to form the *present perfect tense,* which shows either of the following:

  1. Action that was begun in the past but continues into the present:

He has begun to get a little deaf. (The deafness came on him in the past and is still with him.)

Georgia has decided to go to college. (She made her decision to go to college in the past, and the decision still stands.)

  2. Action that was completed in the *recent* past:

I have spoken to her about the bill. (The speaker has *just* spoken to her about the bill.)

Had is used as a helping verb to form the *past perfect tense,* which shows action that began in the past and ended in the past:

He had begun to get a little deaf, but he hears perfectly well now. (At some point in the past deafness came on him, but it ended in the past.)

Georgia had decided to go to college, but then she met Philip. (Georgia's decision to go to college was made in the past; however, after Philip came into her life, she changed her mind.)

Note: Many students overuse *had* in their writing. When you do use *had,* be sure it is necessary. The simple past will often work just as well.

Practice 10

In the first sentence of each pair below, supply either *have* or *has* and the correct past participle. In the second sentence, supply *had* and the correct past participle.

1. (love) a. I ___*have*___ ___*loved*___ and lost many times.

   b. I ___*had*___ ___*loved*___ and lost many times, but then I met you.

2. (happen) a. It _____ _____ before and will probably happen again.

   b. It _____ _____ once too often; I called the police.

3. (legalize) a. The legislatures _____ _____ it in some states.

   b. The legislatures _____ _____ it, but then they discovered that the situation became worse.

4. (guess) a. I _____ _____ the correct answer.

   b. I thought I _____ _____ the correct answer, but, as usual, I was wrong.

5. (finish) a. I _____ _____ my work.

   b. I thought I _____ _____ my work, but then I found out I had two more assignments.

6. (build) a. The British _____ _____ a ship that will not sink.

   b. The British said they _____ _____ a ship that would not sink, but when it hit an iceberg it sank quickly.

Have, Has, and *Had* in Stories

When telling a story in the present tense, use *have* or *has.* When telling a story in the past tense, use *had.* For example,

> He <u>says</u> he <u>has</u> lost his way. (present)
>
> He <u>said</u> he <u>had</u> lost his way. (past)

Practice 11

The following sentences are written in the present tense. Rewrite them in the past tense, changing not only *have* and *has* but other verbs as well. Remember, infinitives do not change form when the tense changes.

1. I have been shy most of my life.
2. In college I keep to myself because I have made no friends.

3. However, I soon get to know Dr. Rosen, a drama instructor, who has taken a liking to me.
4. She has been put in charge of a school play and asks me to play an important role.
5. I can soon say that I have made many friends among the cast.
6. I have a lot to thank her for.

The Past Participle with *Am, Is, Are, Was,* and *Were*

So far, you have been studying verbs in the *active voice,* that is, verbs that tell what the subject is or does in the present, past, or future:

The girl pushes the car.

Girl is the subject because she is what the sentence is about, *pushes* is the verb because it tells what the girl does, and *car* is the object because it receives the action. In the *passive voice,* however, the subject and object are reversed:

The car is pushed by the girl.

Now the subject is *car,* but instead of doing something, the car receives the action. *Girl* becomes the object of the preposition *by.*

To form the passive voice:

1. Use some form of the *be* verb as a helper, usually *am, are, is, was,* or *were.*
2. Use the past participle of the main verb. For irregular forms, consult the list on pages 342–344 or a dictionary.

Here are two sample conjugations in the passive voice:

Suppose (Regular)

PRESENT PASSIVE

I am supposed	we are supposed
you are supposed	you are supposed
he, she, or it is supposed	they are supposed

PAST PASSIVE

I was supposed	we were supposed
you were supposed	you were supposed
he, she, or it was supposed	they were supposed

Understand (Irregular)

PRESENT PASSIVE   I am understood   we are understood
                    you are understood   you are understood
                    he, she, or it is understood   they are understood

PAST PASSIVE   I was understood   we were understood
                    you were understood   you were understood
                    he, she, or it was understood   they were understood

Practice 12

Change the following from the active to the passive voice. The object will become the subject. Either make the subject the object of a prepositional phrase beginning with *by* or, if this is awkward, omit it altogether.

1. They built that bridge to withstand hurricanes. *That bridge was built by them to withstand hurricanes.*

2. I ate all of the dessert before the movie started. _____

   _____

3. They tore my shirt while we were playing football. _____

   _____

4. The splinter of glass cut his knee wide open. _____

   _____

5. John and Alicia built their house on a hill. _____

   _____

When to Use the Passive Voice

Avoid overusing the passive voice in your writing. Ordinarily, your sentences are stronger when your subjects act themselves instead of being acted on. If you want to say that Hans read the play Julius Caesar, write

> Hans read *Julius Caesar.*

instead of

> *Julius Caesar* was read by Hans.

If you want to say that the bank cashes your checks, write

> The bank cashes my checks.

instead of

My checks are cashed by the bank.

However, when the receiver of the action is more important than the doer of the action, you may need to use the passive voice. For example,

She was mugged right outside the grocery store. (The writer is calling attention to the person who was mugged, not to the unknown mugger.)

Ali was finally beaten in the ring. (The writer is calling attention to the long-time boxing champion, not to the person who defeated him.)

Practice 13

The passive voice is appropriately used in the following sentences. Supply the correct past participle, using the list on pages 342–344 for irregular forms.

1. (suppose) You are ___*supposed*___ to spend no more than an hour on the test.

2. (write) It is _____ that you should love one another.

3. (use) They were _____ to his being late all the time.

4. (swear) I was then _____ in before the judge.

5. (hurt) My finger was _____ when I fell from the roof.

6. (say) It is _____ that I am a fine cook.

7. (drive) Alvina was _____ crazy by the gossip before she left her job.

8. (know) Nantucket is _____ as the "Gray Lady."

9. (use) I will never get _____ to having five children.

10. (freeze) The lakes were _____ over.

11. (set) My alarm clock is _____ to go off at five.

Practice 14

The passive voice is inappropriately used in the following sentences. Rewrite them in the active voice.

1. What you have done is greatly appreciated by me. *I greatly appreciate what you have done.*

2. The supplies were really needed by us._____

_____

3. The money will be used by them to buy a car. _____

_____

4. The doctor was called by her father. _____

_____

5. His lecture was understood by me. _____

_____

6. The various verb forms have been carefully learned by you. _____

_____

17.5   The Progressive Form

You have studied three parts of the verb: the base form, the simple past, and the past participle. The fourth part of the verb is the *progressive form,* which is used to show continuing action either in the present or in the past. For example,

> I love becomes I am loving or I was loving
>
> I walk becomes I am walking or I was walking

The general rule for constructing the progressive form is to add *-ing* to the base form of the verb or, if the verb ends in *-e,* to drop the *-e* and add *-ing.* Here are two sample conjugations:

Walk

PRESENT PROGRESSIVE	I am walking	we are walking
	you are walking	you are walking
	he, she, or it is walking	they are walking

PAST PROGRESSIVE	I was walking	we were walking
	you were walking	you were walking
	he, she, or it was walking	they were walking

Write

PRESENT PROGRESSIVE	I am writing	we are writing
	you are writing	you are writing
	he, she, or it is writing	they are writing

PAST PROGRESSIVE	I was writing	we were writing
	you were writing	you were writing
	he, she, or it was writing	they were writing

But note the following exceptions to the general rule for constructing the progressive form:

1. Do not drop the *-e* when the verb ends in double *-e:*

see becomes seeing

flee becomes fleeing

2. Do not drop the *-e* in *singe* and *dye:*

singe becomes singeing

dye becomes dyeing

3. For verbs that end in *-ie,* drop the *-i* and the *-e,* and add *-y + -ing:*

lie becomes lying

die becomes dying

vie becomes vying

4. For one-syllable verbs (or verbs that are accented on the last syllable) that end in a consonant preceded by a single vowel, double the final consonant before adding *-ing:*

hum becomes humming

begin becomes beginning

occur becomes occurring

quiz becomes quizzing

5. Do not drop the *-y* when the verb ends in *-y:*

fry becomes frying

say becomes saying

If you are in any doubt as to whether you should drop an *-e* or double a letter before adding *-ing,* consult a dictionary.

Practice 15

Supply the progressive form of the designated verb below. Be sure to use the right tense. Remember, the present progressive is used with present-tense verbs; the past progressive is used with past-tense verbs.

1. (look) You ___*are looking*___ very handsome these days.

2. (begin) We left because we ___*were beginning*___ to wear out our welcome.

3. (help) She _____ me when Mrs. Malloy walked in.

4. (ask) The paper says they _____ five thousand dollars for their car.

5. (quiz) Dr. Ward _____ us on that material tomorrow.

6. (quit) Maureen told me she _____ her job and moving to Texas.

7. (travel) We _____ in Europe when we heard the news.

8. (lie) The old man _____ face down on the sidewalk when they found him.

9. (lay) I _____ down my sword and shield and will practice war no more.

10. (say) Now that we are in the second week of the play, she _____ her lines perfectly.

11. (hit) She became so angry that she _____ everything in sight.

17.6   Using the Dictionary for Verbs

Anytime you are in doubt as to what a particular verb form is, look it up in the dictionary. A dictionary appropriate for college use will give you the parts of irregular and troublesome verbs. For example, suppose you look up the verb *break* (the base form). To find the various parts of the verb, first make sure you have located a verb. Verbs, designated *v* or *vb,* are further classified as *vt* or *tr* (transitive verbs—those which take objects), or *vi* or *intr* (intransitive verbs—those which do not take objects). Nouns are marked *n.*

In a medium-length dictionary, you will probably see the following entry:

break (brāk) *vt.* **broke, broken, breaking**

break is the base form
(brāk) is the pronunciation
broke is the simple past
broken is the past participle
breaking is the progressive form

In a more complete dictionary, you may see an entry like this:

break (brāk) *vt.* **broke** *or Archaic* **brake, broken, breaking, breaks**

brake is an alternative for *broke* but is no longer in use
breaks is the third-person singular, present-tense form

If you are given a choice of using one simple past over another, one past participle over another, or one progressive form over another, always choose the first alternative. For example, choose *broke* over *brake.*

In looking up a regular verb such as *love* or *walk* in a medium-size dictionary, you probably will not see any parts of the verb listed. This means that all constructions are regular. That is, you add -*d* or -*ed* to the base form for both the simple past and the past participle, and you add -*ing* to the base form for the progressive form. (If the verb ends in -*e,* you drop the -*e* and add -*ing* to construct the progressive form.)

If you look up the irregular verb *bring* in a medium-size dictionary, you probably will see the following:

bring (bri̯ng) *vt.* **brought, bringing**

bring is the base form
brought is both the simple past and the past participle
bringing is the progressive form

Here are two other examples of irregular verbs from a medium-size dictionary:

hit (hit) *vt.* **hit, hitting**

hit is the base form
hit is both the simple past and past participle
hitting is the progressive form

counsel (koun's'l) *vt.* **counseled** or **counselled, counseling** or **counselling**

counsel is the base form
counseled and *counselled* are two alternatives for both the simple past and the past participle (if you have a choice, use the first)
counseling and *counselling* are two alternatives for the progressive form (if you have a choice, use the first)

Practice 16

Find the base form of the following verbs in a dictionary, and write the other three parts of the verb in the designated blanks.

Base Form	Simple Past	Past Participle	Progressive Form
1. creep	*crept*	*crept*	*creeping*
2. weave			
3. mow			
4. bend			
5. shine (to give light)			
6. forbid			
7. shoulder			
8. hang (to execute)			
9. harken			
10. happen			
11. spay			

17.7   Avoiding Tense Shifts

Ordinarily, you write in either the present tense or the past tense, but not in both. For example, you write

> She <u>says</u> she <u>pushes</u> the car while her <u>father</u> <u>watches</u>.

or

> She <u>said</u> she <u>pushed</u> the car while her <u>father</u> <u>watched</u>.

but not

> She <u>says</u> she <u>pushed</u> the car while her <u>father</u> <u>watches</u>.

Note: *Will* and *can* are ordinarily used with present-tense verbs, while *could* and *would* are ordinarily used with past-tense verbs. For example,

> The <u>president</u> <u>is going</u> to veto the budget so that <u>he</u> <u>can get</u> more money for defense. (present tense)

> The <u>president</u> <u>vetoed</u> the budget so that <u>he</u> <u>could get</u> more money for defense. (past tense)

> He <u>says</u> he <u>can</u> eventually <u>get</u> the appropriation. (present tense)

> He <u>said</u> he <u>could get</u> the appropriation, but it failed. (past tense)

Practice 17

In the following sentences, some of the verbs are in the present and some are in the simple past. Write them all in the simple past.

1. They ~~surprise~~ *surprised* us when they came to our school.
2. When I was young, I use to tear the heads off my sister's paper dolls.
3. She got so mad that she turns red.
4. They always dress up when they went out to eat.
5. We work, we work, and we work, but we got nowhere.
6. When we return, we freed the prisoners.
7. My wife said you advertise a car in the morning paper.
8. They act as if they had never seen a young lady before.
9. Maria said that she will study harder this semester.
10. The president told the nation that he can balance the budget.
11. We come home after the war, just as we said we will.

Practice 18

Write a three-paragraph paper in the past tense telling what you did in the morning, afternoon, and evening of one particular day. You may choose either a typical day or an unusual day. Proofread carefully to make sure the past tense is used correctly. You might begin your paper something like this:

> One morning during my senior year in high school, I woke up while it was still dark. Hearing the sound of someone walking through the house, I got up . . . .

17.8   Verbals: Infinitives, Participles, and Gerunds

Verbals are words that come from verbs but are used as adjectives, adverbs, and nouns. There are three kinds of verbals: infinitives, participles, and gerunds. Like verbs, verbals sometimes take objects.

Infinitives

The *infinitive,* which is introduced by *to,* is the same as the base form of the verb. It can be used as a noun, an adjective, or an adverb:

> To live is to grow. (These two infinitives are used as nouns, the first as a subject, the other as a predicate nominative.)

> There must be another way to solve that problem. (This infinitive phrase is used as an adjective modifying *way.* Within the infinitive phrase, *problem* is the object of *to solve.*)

> Tezeta came out to say good-bye. (This infinitive phrase is used as an adverb modifying *came out.* Within the infinitive phrase, *good-bye* is the object of *to say.*)

Keep the following in mind when using infinitives:

1. The form of the infinitive does not change when the tenses change. Even when writing in the past tense, you do not add *-d* or *-ed* to the infinitive:

> I did not like to walk those long distances when I was in the army.

2. When an infinitive or an infinitive phrase is the subject in present-tense constructions, use the third-person singular verb:

> To jog the entire distance requires months of training.

If you use two or more infinitives as subjects, you need to use a plural verb:

> To live and to love were the two things he asked.

3. As a general rule, do not split infinitives. Choose

It is not always easy <u>to like</u> the one you love.

instead of

It is not easy <u>to</u> always <u>like</u> the one you love.

 ### Practice 19

Compose sentences using the following infinitives as subjects.

1. (to love) *To love others does not come easily to our friend.*

_____

2. (to succeed) _____

_____

3. (to read and to fish) _____

_____

4. (to spend) _____

_____

5. (to understand the Chinese)_____

_____

6. (to make me happy)_____

_____

7. (to have seen) _____

_____

Participles

The *present participle* is the same as the progressive form of the main verb and is constructed with an *-ing* ending. The *past participle* used as a verbal is the same past participle you have been studying. It often ends in *-ed.*

Present Participle	Past Participle
seeing	seen
beginning	begun
loving	loved
prejudicing	prejudiced
handicapping	handicapped
shocking	shocked

Both the present and past participles can be used as adjectives:

It was a <u>disturbing</u> day at the bank. (The present participle modifies the noun *day.*)

<u>Seeing what happened,</u> the boy pulled out his cap pistol. (The present-participle phrase modifies the subject *boy. What happened* is the object of the participle *seeing.*)

<u>Shocked,</u> the robber handed over the money to the boy. (The past participle modifies the subject, *robber.*)

<u>Satisfied,</u> the boy put his pistol back in his pocket. (The past participle modifies the subject, *boy.*)

Practice 20

Supply the correct participle of the designated verb in each of the following sentences.

1. (see) ___*Seeing*___ Sandra ahead, he walked as fast as he could to catch up with her.

2. (love) Although _____ by her parents, the child still had severe emotional problems.

3. (begin) Having _____ the climb to Long's Peak, we were determined to finish.

4. (shock) _____ at the news, his parents broke down in tears.

5. (begin) _____ again, we picked up our packs and moved on.

Practice 21

Using the sentences in Practice 20 as models, compose sentences with the following participles.

1. (determined to pass) *Determined to pass his physics class, Tom studied for two hours every night.*

2. (prejudiced by their ignorance) _____

_____

3. (finally beaten) _____

_____

4. (having begun) _____

_____

5. (shocked by the news) _____

_____

6. (singing to herself) _____

_____

Gerunds

The *gerund* is formed like a present participle, but it is always used as a noun:

subject   predicate nominative

↓   ↓

<u>Seeing</u> is not always <u>believing.</u> (The first gerund is the subject; the second is a predicate nominative.)

subject

↓

<u>Living the good life</u> was no longer possible for him. (The gerund phrase is the subject of *was. Life* is the object of the gerund *living.*)

object

↓

To my way of <u>thinking,</u> he is a fool! (The gerund is the object of the preposition *of.*)

subject   subject

↓   ↓

Are <u>fishing</u> and <u>hunting</u> what you enjoy most? (Since two gerunds serve as the subject, a plural verb is necessary.)

Practice 22

Supply the correct gerunds of the designated verbs in the following sentences.

1. (shock) Dr. Kahn enjoys _____*shocking*_____ all the students in her biology class.

2. (begin) In the _____, God created the heavens and the earth.

3. (do, be) _____ is _____.

4. (give) We reached an agreement without our _____ in.

5. (wait) They like _____ on us.

Practice 23

First underline the subject or subjects in each sentence below, and then choose the correct verb.

1. (make, makes) Seeing all those dishes ___*makes*___ Enrique wish he was not so liberated.

2. (are, is) Seeing the sun rise over the Cumberland Hills _____ something that has great meaning for me.

3. (are, is) To work hard, to play hard, and to have a cooperative family _____ what I want most in life.

4. (are, is) To be or not to be _____ the question.

5. (prepare, prepares) Working hard in English and math _____ you for college.

6. (discover, discovers) In this chapter the hero _____ the truth about his real father's identity.

17.9 Practice Using Standard and Nonstandard Verbs: Subject-Verb Agreement

If you are still having difficulty with verbs, do not despair. Many students have great trouble mastering standard verbs. The problem usually arises because these students are used to hearing and speaking nonstandard verb forms. When they are asked to write standard forms, they have to use verbs that do not sound right to them. Then they start overcorrecting and making errors they did not make before. If you have this problem, you *can* master standard verb forms, but you will probably need a lot of practice. Sections 17.9–17.15 are designed to give you this practice.

If you are confused about when to add the final *-s* to a verb and when to leave it off, be sure that you first know the easier subject-verb constructions. Review the conjugations of the regular verbs *love* and *carry:*

	Singular	Plural
FIRST PERSON	I love	we love
SECOND PERSON	you love	you love
THIRD PERSON	he, she, or it loves	they love

	Singular	Plural
FIRST PERSON	I carry	we carry
SECOND PERSON	you carry	you carry
THIRD PERSON	he, she, or it carries	they carry

You can see immediately that if your subject is *I, you, we,* or *they,* you form the verb without the *-s.* Of course, you must first be able to identify the verb. To do this, ask what your subject *is* or *does.*

Now review the conjugation of *have:*

	Singular	Plural
FIRST PERSON	I have	we have
SECOND PERSON	you have	you have
THIRD PERSON	he, she, or it has	they have

Notice that the verb *have* is regular, like the other two shown above. The only difference is that the third-person singular of *have* is *has,* not *haves.* But for *I, you, we,* and *they,* the correct form is always *have.*

Finally, review the conjugation of *do:*

	Singular	Plural
FIRST PERSON	I do (don't)	we do (don't)
SECOND PERSON	you do (don't)	you do (don't)
THIRD PERSON	he, she, or it does (doesn't)	they do (don't)

The verb *do* is also regular, except for the third-person singular, which is *does* (or *doesn't*).

Practice 24

In the following sentences, underline the subjects once and the verbs twice. Using the four conjugations above as models, determine whether the subjects and verbs agree. If they do not agree, change the verbs to correct the sentence.

1. We refuse their money, and we ~~keeps~~ *keep* our pride.
2. You say you love your country, but you acts in a different way.
3. I says to myself, "Bingo, you're in trouble again."
4. They like our country, but they just loves our tourists.
5. We in the dancing troupe does our best.
6. I don't care what we do, I don't care what you do, and I don't care what they do, but I do care about what the world do.
7. They, in their own way, loves their children.
8. They seems to know what they believe.
9. We carries a heavy burden, but we don't complain.
10. As for shoes, they costs more each year.
11. Haven't they had enough trouble for a while?

12. You and your family has to pay attention.

13. Hasn't those summer days been beautiful?

14. You have my trust, and I have your trust.

15. We surely has a lot to be thankful for.

16. We asks, and we do receive.

17.10   Third-Person Endings

Making verbs agree with subjects is more complicated when the subjects are in the third person. For example, which of the following forms do you use?

loves *or* love   carries *or* carry   does *or* do (doesn't *or* don't)

has *or* have

If the pronoun subject is *he, she,* or *it,* you always use the form with the *-s* ending:

he loves	he carries	he does (doesn't)	he has
she loves	she carries	she does (doesn't)	she has
it loves	it carries	it does (doesn't)	it has

If the pronoun subject is *they,* you always use the form without the *-s* ending:

they love   they carry   they do (don't)   they have

But what form do you use when the subject is not a pronoun (that is, not *he, she, it,* or *they*), but a noun? Which of the following verb forms is standard?

Robin Hood <u>robs</u>	*or*	Robin Hood <u>rob</u>
the house <u>costs</u>	*or*	the house <u>cost</u>
the cat <u>doesn't</u>	*or*	the cat <u>don't</u>
the people <u>lives</u>	*or*	the people <u>live</u>
Mary and Will <u>sees</u>	*or*	Mary and Will <u>see</u>

To decide which verb form to use, all you need to do is to ask yourself if the subject is one or more than one. If the subject is one, use the verb with the *-s* ending. If the subject is more than one, use the verb without the *-s* ending, as follows:

Robin Hood (one) robs

the house (one) costs

the cat (one) doesn't

the people (more than one) live

Mary and Will (more than one) see

 ### Practice 25

Read each of the following sentences carefully. If the subject is singular, write *S* above it. If the subject is plural, write *P* above it. Change the verbs to agree with the subjects. (One sentence is correct.)

1. The police ~~asks~~ him for his license, and he ~~give~~ it to them.   *P ask   S gives*
2. Mary don't like to discipline her mischievous little boy.
3. Her husband try out the merchandise before he buys it.
4. What interest me most about New York is Central Park.
5. She clean her house while her daughters just sits around.
6. It don't cost as much this year.
7. Mia fix her van just as good as new.
8. Let me tell you about all the things she do for me.
9. The government employs a lot of people at the naval yard.
10. If Stan push me again, he is going to regret it.
11. In the summer Ferdinand sleeps, eats, and watch a lot of television.
12. Each time the class sings, the music teacher ask me to not sing.
13. The people comes running and climb down the bank toward me.
14. Serena is very loving and care a lot for lonely children.
15. If the recipe don't come out the way it should, try, try again.

17.11   The *Be* Verbs

Review these conjugations for the *be* verbs:

Present Tense

	Singular	Plural
FIRST PERSON	I am	we are
SECOND PERSON	you are	you are
THIRD PERSON	he, she, or it is	they are

Past Tense

	Singular	Plural
FIRST PERSON	I was	we were
SECOND PERSON	you were	you were
THIRD PERSON	he, she, or it was	they were

If the subject is *I,* always use *am* in the present tense and *was* in the past tense.

If the subject is *you, we,* or *they,* always use *are* in the present tense and *were* in the past tense.

If the subject is *he, she,* or *it,* always use *is* in the present tense and *was* in the past tense.

If, on the other hand, the subject is a noun, ask if it is one or more than one. If it is one, use *is* or *was.* If it is more than one, use *are* or *were.* For example,

John (one) is going

Gina (one) is my sister

the family (one) was together

the dog (one) was sleeping

the police (more than one) are coming

the sisters (more than one) are together

the families (more than one) were together

Tom and Gina (more than one) were seen

Practice 26

Choose the correct verb for each of the following sentences.

1. They said that we (was, were) not chosen.
2. I am what I (am, are), you are what you (is, are), and we are what we (is, are), so let's live and let live.
3. We (was, were) the last survivors to return.
4. (Weren't, Wasn't) they the winners?
5. (Isn't, Aren't) that the truth!

Practice 27

Underline the noun subjects of the following sentences. If the subject is singular, write *S* above. If the subject is plural, write *P* above. When necessary, change the verbs to agree with the subjects. (Some verbs are correct.)

1. The <u>governments</u> of those countries ~~wasn't~~ *weren't* at all cooperative.
2. Those fish was delicious.
3. The soldiers wasn't so sure of their position.
4. There was some students still in doubt.
5. There isn't a chance of your going.

6. It is surprising that there isn't more of them going.

7. The so-called boat people either died or were brought to this country.

8. The nations who was gathering their armies for battle met one last time.

9. Weren't the police called to the scene of the accident?

10. Isn't the United States trying to mediate that controversy?

11. Neither Red nor his parents was responsible.

 Practice 28

Use *is* or *are* or *was* or *were* to complete the following sentences.

1. Yesterday, the Chicago Bulls _____.

2. Today, the family who _____.

3. Either the House or the Senate _____.

4. There _____ some of the dinner left.

5. Neither you nor we _____.

17.12   Subjects with Two or More Verbs

When you use two or more verbs with one subject, be sure that all verbs agree with the subject. For example,

> <u>Ron and Don</u> <u>are</u> twin brothers and <u>look</u> exactly alike.

> Every night, <u>Juan</u> <u>studies</u> his notes and <u>reads</u> the assigned chapters but <u>seems</u> to get nowhere.

In the first sentence, the plural subject *Ron and Don* takes the plural verbs *are* and *look*. In the second sentence, the singular subject *Juan* takes the singular verbs *studies, reads,* and *seems.*

 Practice 29

Underline the subjects of the following sentences, and supply appropriate present-tense verbs.

1. <u>She</u> gives her check to her parents and ___*does*___ most of the housework as well.

2. I clean the dishes, scrub the floors, and work in the yard; much of the time I

_____ like Cinderella.

3. She is selfish with her possessions and also _____ a bad temper.

4. The radio and television are on all the time and _____ so much noise that I cannot think.

5. The people on my street sometimes yell at their children and

_____ things I do not want to repeat.

6. My husband does not drive himself but _____ everyone else how to drive.

Practice 30

Write a sentence using each pair of verbs below *with the same subject.*

1. (loves, hates) *Our dog loves winter but hates summer.* _____

_____

2. (sings, dances) _____

_____

3. (defends, accuses) _____

_____

4. (lives, dies) _____

_____

5. (is, is not) _____

_____

6. (does, does not) _____

_____

7. (has, hasn't) _____

_____

Practice 31

In the following sentences, rewrite the nonstandard verbs in standard English. (Some sentences are correct.)

were
1. She and I ~~was~~ the smartest students in kindergarten.

2. I hope this paper gives you some ideas about what to do on a rainy weekend and help make your rainy weekends more pleasant.

3. When we arrived, they had stopped serving dinner and was now serving breakfast.

4. A good newspaper reporter goes out and face the world directly to get a story.

5. On weekends, she usually goes to parties or attends school events.

6. Every evening about six o'clock, she sits on the front porch and gossips with the neighbors.

7. Sometimes he catch himself before things become too rough and makes a joke out of what has been happening.

8. I think the way I was brought up and the schools I attended have a lot to do with the problems I am having now.

9. April drives in the car pool five days a week and take the children to swimming class twice a week.

10. When night falls, the young people in the neighborhood come out and play their radios.

11. They love each other and plans to get married soon.

17.13   Subjects and Verbs Separated

Many times in your writing your verbs will not come immediately after your subjects but instead will be separated by words, phrases, and clauses. These constructions sometimes cause verb-agreement difficulty. The following samples are correct:

> I always take the easy way out.
>
> The programs that I have mentioned teach children quite a lot.

Subjects Separated from Verbs by Prepositional Phrases

Prepositional phrases often separate subjects from verbs, as in these examples:

> One of us is crazy.
>
> The people in my neighborhood are nice.

In the first example the prepositional phrase *of us* separates the subject, *one,* from the verb *is.* In the second the prepositional phrase *in my neighborhood* separates the subject, *people,* from the verb *are.* Many prepositional phrases that separate subjects from verbs begin with *of, on,* or *in.*

Practice 32

In the following sentences, underline the subjects once and the verbs twice, and put parentheses around the prepositional phrases. Change the verbs to agree with the subjects where necessary.

1. The <u>sounds</u> (of my neighborhood) <s>changes</s> *change* from hour to hour.
2. All the houses on my block are brick.
3. Everybody in my classes are working very hard.
4. My first few years of school was my most difficult ones.
5. The sounds in my neighborhood is so loud that they disturb the dogs.
6. My great-grandmother, in most people's eyes, seem to be just a mean old woman.
7. Just the thought of her children are quite satisfying to Mother.
8. The construction work on the houses begin next month.
9. One of us is able to do the job alone.
10. Harold Muskie of Metropolitan Bank recommends the *Wall Street Journal.*
11. Their dreams for a better life was fulfilled that day.

Subjects Separated from Verbs by Adjective Clauses

Sometimes subjects and verbs are separated by adjective clauses, as follows:

> My <u>friends,</u> who saw me get up out of that muddy water and then fall back in again, <u>were laughing</u> at me.

> The <u>attempts</u> that she makes to help others sometimes <u>fail</u>.

> The <u>book</u> she was reading <u>was stolen</u> from her desk.

Note that in the last sentence the relative pronoun *that* is omitted but understood.

Practice 33

In the following sentences, underline the subjects once and the verbs twice, and put parentheses around the adjective clauses. Change the verbs to agree with the subjects where necessary.

1. Small <u>children</u> (who are not in school) <u><s>has</s></u> *have* more time to play.
2. Those who don't have the money gets the long sentences.
3. The things she has left behind means so much to her family.
4. The children who live in my neighborhood play baseball every afternoon.
5. The school where my mother taught for the last seven years is closing.
6. The gifts he brings to my son comes from his heart.

Practice 34

Write sentences with the following phrases and clauses. Place them between the subjects and verbs, and keep the verbs in the present tense.

1. (who wears her hair down to her shoulders) *Geraldine, who wears her hair down to her shoulders, washes it every night.*

2. (which is my most difficult course) _____

3. (which are the best cars on the market) _____

4. (of the people I will write about) _____

5. (who is hard to control) _____

6. (who eat too much ice cream) _____

17.14   Refining Your Use of Verb Tense

As you have learned, each verb has four parts:

	Base Form	Simple Past	Past Participle	Progressive Form
REGULAR	I love	I loved	I have loved	I am loving
IRREGULAR	I begin	I began	I have begun	I am beginning

Verbs are regular if you add *-d* or *-ed* at the end to form both the simple past and the past participle. Thus the verb *love* is regular. Verbs are irregular if the simple past or the past participle is formed in any other way. Study the following conjugation of *love* carefully and notice how the principal parts of the verb are used either alone or with helping verbs. If you need to know a particular form of an irregular verb, simply substitute the irregular verb in the *love* construction. For example, you can see that *I had loved* is the past perfect of *love* and that this construction takes a past participle. Therefore, you must use a past participle with *begin* to express the past perfect: *I had begun.*

	Singular	*Plural*

Present Tense

	Singular	Plural
FIRST PERSON	I love	we love
SECOND PERSON	you love	you love
THIRD PERSON	he, she, or it loves	they love

Simple Past Tense

	Singular	Plural
FIRST PERSON	I loved	we loved
SECOND PERSON	you loved	you loved
THIRD PERSON	he, she, or it loved	they loved

Perfect Tense with Have *or* Has

	Singular	Plural
FIRST PERSON	I have loved	we have loved
SECOND PERSON	you have loved	you have loved
THIRD PERSON	he, she, or it has loved	they have loved

Perfect Tense with Had

	Singular	Plural
FIRST PERSON	I had loved	we had loved
SECOND PERSON	you had loved	you had loved
THIRD PERSON	he, she, or it had loved	they had loved

Passive Voice with Am, Is, *or* Are

	Singular	Plural
FIRST PERSON	I am loved	we are loved
SECOND PERSON	you are loved	you are loved
THIRD PERSON	he, she, or it is loved	they are loved

Passive Voice with Was *or* Were

	Singular	Plural
FIRST PERSON	I was loved	we were loved
SECOND PERSON	you were loved	you were loved
THIRD PERSON	he, she, or it was loved	they were loved

Progressive Tense with Am, Is, or Are

FIRST PERSON	I am loving	we are loving
SECOND PERSON	you are loving	you are loving
THIRD PERSON	he, she, or it is loving	they are loving

Progressive Tense with Was or Were

FIRST PERSON	I was loving	we were loving
SECOND PERSON	you were loving	you were loving
THIRD PERSON	he, she, or it was loving	they were loving

Now turn to page 341 and review the principal parts of each verb.

Practice 35

Write sentences using the following regular and irregular verbs. Refer to the preceding conjugation of the verb *love* as necessary, but try to write the irregular forms without looking at the list on pages 342–344.

1. (*find:* progressive form) *I am finding my work more satisfying these days.*

   _____

2. (*love:* passive voice) _____

   _____

3. (*love:* perfect tense with had) _____

   _____

4. (*drown:* passive voice) _____

   _____

5. (*find:* perfect tense with have) _____

   _____

6. (*fly:* present tense, third-person singular) _____

   _____

7. (*freeze:* passive voice) _____

   _____

8. (*go:* perfect tense with had) _____

   _____

9. (*happen:* progressive form) _____

   _____

10. (*lay:* simple past) _____

    _____

11. (*lead:* simple past) _____

    _____

12. (*lie:* progressive form) _____

    _____

13. (*lose:* base form with *do, does,* or *did*) _____

    _____

14. (*pay:* perfect tense with *had*) _____

    _____

15. (*see:* simple past) _____

    _____

16. (*set:* progressive form) _____

    _____

17. (*sing:* simple past) _____

    _____

18. (*steal:* passive voice) _____

    _____

19. (*take:* passive voice) _____

    _____

20. (*teach:* simple past) _____

    _____

21. (*throw:* perfect tense with *has*) _____

    _____

Now check your irregular verbs against the list on pages 342–344.

 Practice 36

Correct the verbs in the following sentences. (Three of the sentences are correct.)

1. The writer Richard Wright's mother almost ~~beated~~ *beat* him to death when he was four years old.

2. In his youth he lied, stolen, and struggled to contain his seething anger.

3. And there was the time that he proved to his family that he was his own boss.
4. He went to all the bars, stayed out late at night, and try to impress his friends.
5. As he stood and watch a man being kicked, he felt pity and disgrace.
6. He wrote what he felt and what he want to express.
7. Richard did not have any money, so he lied and say he was not hungry.
8. He was talking to the woman who hire him for his first job.
9. Richard had struggle and worked to get ahead.
10. He went home when he had finish.
11. When he was young, he use to sell newspapers on Saturday.
12. He had gave the speech that the principal write.
13. There were many things that enable him to break free.
14. His stubbornness did help him in some ways, but it hurt him in other ways.
15. Another obstacle he have to overcome was that he could not earn enough money.
16. As time went on, he manage to free himself from his bondage.
17. He slipped into Nishelle's room and took the book from her shelf.
18. He had hided the books to read, and he learn many things from them.
19. He then took the book and run home to his mother.
20. In the end he went north and escape his bondage.
21. The conditions begun to change after he left.

17.15   More Practice Avoiding Tense Shifts

Ordinarily, you must keep the tenses of your verbs consistent. If a sentence has one verb in the present tense, for example, the other verbs in the sentence should usually be in the present as well. The verb tenses in these two sentences are consistent:

> When the wind <u>is</u> from the south, it <u>blows</u> the hook into the fish's mouth.

> When the wind <u>was</u> from the south, it <u>blew</u> the hook into the fish's mouth.

But the tenses in this sentence shift:

> When the wind <u>was</u> from the south, it <u>blows</u> the hook into the fish's mouth.

The following suggestions should help you avoid tense shifts when you write in the past tense:

1. It is hard to hear the *-d* or *-ed* endings of some verbs. If you cannot hear the endings, follow the rules for forming past-tense or past-participle endings:

INCORRECT
She is <u>suppose</u> to know.

CORRECT
She is <u>supposed</u> to know.

INCORRECT
I <u>use</u> to go fishing.

CORRECT
I <u>used</u> to go fishing.

INCORRECT
He <u>ask</u> me to sing.

CORRECT
He <u>asked</u> me to sing.

INCORRECT
It <u>seem</u> to be raining.

CORRECT
It <u>seemed</u> to be raining.

2. Ordinarily, use *will, can,* and *may* with present-tense verbs and *would, could,* and *might* with past-tense verbs:

I <u>will</u> believe her if she <u>tells</u> me she is innocent.

I <u>would</u> believe her if she <u>told</u> me she was innocent.

Also, as a general rule, use *have* or *has* with present-tense verbs and *had* with past-tense verbs:

The council <u>says</u> we <u>have</u> spent too much money.

The council <u>said</u> we <u>had</u> spent too much money.

3. Sometimes when you are writing in the past tense, you will want to make a comment in the present. In this case, be sure to write that comment in the present tense:

past   present
So those <u>were</u> the good old days. I <u>wish</u> I could be eleven again.

Practice 37

Correct the tense shifts by putting present-tense verbs in the past tense in the following sentences.

began
1. When the birds ~~begin~~ to sing, it meant spring had come.
2. When the passengers got off the plane, they seem terrified.
3. The woman at the bank ask me how much insurance I wanted.
4. When Representative Taylor asks me to support her reelection, I said yes.
5. Uncle Charlie always sang that corny old song about how he love to go "swimmin' with the women."
6. When we were young, we use to help milk the cows.
7. When the tomatoes ripened, we have to stop what we were doing so that we can help harvest them.
8. Neddie come in the barn and started throwing tomatoes at me.
9. My grandfather say he had never seen two boys who could get into so much trouble.
10. We use to help him grind the corn for golden grits.
11. He ask us to see if the chickens were "a sittin' or a settin'."

Practice 38

Correct the tense shifts and other verb errors in the following student narrative.

Test Anxiety

One Saturday morning in 1997, I stood in line with a few hundred other students to enter the Science Hall at Campbell City College to take the dreaded SAT, or Scholastic Aptitude Test, for entrance into college. I know that colleges usually accepted or rejected students on the basis of their SAT score, so I was understandably nervous and very anxious to have the whole thing over as soon as possible. (1 error)

At about ten minutes before 9:00 a.m. a woman wearing a blue vest appear at one side of the line and start giving us instructions. "You may bring no more than your identification and a pen and pencil into the testing room," she was shouting to us. "Once you enter the testing room, go to your assigned aisle and sit where the row monitor tells you," the woman said. Just as she finishes, the line moved forward, and we began to enter the building. (3 errors)

Once inside, I moved quickly to my assigned aisle, where a young man wearing a blue vest like the woman's told me where to sit. No one is talking. Signs around the room says, "No talking during the testing session." (2 errors)

A man at the front of the room next gives us directions for the test. He told us to take the top booklet off the stack of tests being handed down the aisle and then to pass the stack on to the next person. We were to write our code number on the front of our test booklet and wait for further instructions. I do as I was told. (2 errors)

When everyone has a test, the man say we would have one hour for the first part of the test. Then he told us to start the test. I opened my test booklet and began reading the first question. Suddenly, the young man who was our row monitor shouts "Stop!" and ask the girl next to me and me to stand up. He come down the aisle and stopped directly in front of us, grabbing the girl's test booklet and mine in what seemed a single, angry swoop. "Did you switch tests?" he ask, looking accusingly at both of us. "N-no," I stammered, trying to answer; I was too embarrassed to talk. The girl did not say anything. "You both have even-numbered tests," the young man said. "One of you is supposed to have an odd-numbered test." (6 errors)

I had not switch any tests, but I was so scared, I was shaking all over. The girl and I look at one another, both of us suspecting the other of having somehow changed the order of the tests. We stood in embarrassed silence while the testing people talk together and examine each of the test booklets in our aisle. Finally, the woman who had spoken to us outside came over to the girl and me. (4 errors)

"It's all right," she say. "You can sit down. The tests are both different. They was just improperly numbered. I'm sorry about the mistake. Please don't be upset." (2 errors)

But I was very upset, and I could see that the girl is, too. Nonetheless we both mumbled something and sit down. I am still shaking. The man in the front of the room said everyone could open the test booklets and start again. I open mine, but I could not concentrate. I felt like I had just escaped being branded for life as someone who got caught cheating on the SAT! Then, after about five minutes, I felt myself start to get over the incident and to think about the test. I began reading the questions again and writing down my answers. After a few minutes, I was back to normal, and my mind was clearly focused on the test. (4 errors)

I was really scared that day, although I am able to laugh about the whole thing later. I even managed to do well enough on the test to score in the top percentile of my class—better than I ever expected. Maybe all that adrenaline rushing through my veins stimulate my brain, too! (2 errors)

17.16   Review Exercises

Review Exercise 1

The following sentences are written in the present tense. Rewrite them in the simple past. Some sentences will require two or more changes in tense.

1. Lucia ~~minds~~ *minded* the children while John ~~travels~~ *traveled* to Europe.
2. The wise men journey on their way.
3. They fry the fish as soon as they catch them.
4. She tries to do everything her father asks her to do.
5. Deshawn visits me when I am sick.
6. He says that one person can make a difference.
7. After they walk away, they just vanish from my life.
8. What I like best about the play is the scenery.
9. They bus the children to school from the next county.
10. They train for months before the season starts.
11. He lies to me about this and that.
12. Mrs. Sanchez snaps at us when we are misbehaving.
13. For the first time in his life, he breaks down and cries when he hears the news.
14. They prefer to fly rather than to drive.
15. We forget that communist countries might differ a lot from each other.
16. They cherish their children and tend to them gently.
17. The preacher says that God caused Scripture to be written.
18. I apply for that job at least once a year.
19. Joe finishes shaving and combs his hair.
20. It suddenly occurs to the senator that he is mistaken.
21. They never fly if they can avoid it.

Review Exercise 2

Correct the verb errors and the shifts in tense in the following student essay.

Two Children—Two People

I am the mother of two fine children. I have been bless with a child of each sex. My daughter, Corinne, is seventeen years old and thinks she is a woman of the world. Will, my son, is fourteen. He has suddenly discover a light brown mustache, deep voice, and girls! Although I love my children dearly, I sometimes wonder how they can be brother and sister; they are so different. (2 verb errors)

Attitudes about the value of money in our home are most interesting. Will is very concern about cash at all times. He keeps both his hard-earned money and his birthday money locked in the top drawer of his dresser. He is know in our home as one who is "tight with a buck." When you ask him for a loan of perhaps one dollar, he may or may not give it to you. We are wondering when he will start charging us interest on each dollar we borrow. Corinne, on the other hand, still has uncashed checks earned from her job at Walgreen's dating back to July 1997. She does not realize that she has not cash them. When one walks through Corinne's bedroom, one sees nickels, dimes, and quarters that are spreaded all over her dresser, desk, and night table. One thing is true about Corinne, though: She cheerfully lends you money and is anything but a miser. (4 verb errors)

Entering Will's bedroom is a pleasure. Everything has a place. Books are pile neatly on the desk; the bed is rarely unmade. The closet is always very well organize, with clothes hung up and shoes lined up in a neat row. Will is a systematic and methodical young man, and his room speaks for his neatness. Corinne's room, on the other hand, is mass confusion. Shoes are everywhere. Clothes are hung over chairs and laying on the bed, which, by the way, is hardly ever made. It would not surprise me to find an old apple core under the bed. That's Corinne for you; she is disorganized but very relaxed. (3 verb errors)

Will's and Corinne's personalities are like the sun and the moon. Will is extremely quiet and basically a loner, with only one or two close friends. Corinne was just the opposite. She always has had an effervescent personality. She felt immediately at ease with strangers and has had many friends. Despite their differences, however, my two children have one important thing in common: They really care deeply for each other. It is my hope that they will continue to care for one another for the rest of their lives. (2 shifts in tense)

Review Exercise 3

Underline the subjects in the following sentences, and then change the verbs to agree with these subjects. (Some verbs are correct.)

1. A child believe what he or she sees.
2. If a child watch certain television programs, he or she learns many useful things.
3. My Aunt Yoshiko always say she is going to live forever.
4. Best of all, television informs its viewers of the local and national news.
5. As far as snacks is concerned, no one needs them.
6. It seems to me that the president try to do the right thing.
7. When the sauce starts to boil, reduce the heat and simmer it for ten minutes.
8. If Mrs. Frances ask me to stop, I do what she ask.
9. Sal knows better than to call me that name again.
10. Marlene always hurt the man she love.

Review Exercise 4

Underline the subjects in the following sentences, and then change the verbs to agree with the subjects. (Some verbs are correct.)

1. Uncle Sam have a good job waiting for you.
2. Those teenagers are the ones who has been causing the problem.
3. There hasn't been any more problems since you spoke to her.
4. The drunkards on the corner is called "the birds" because they are on the corner before the birds gets up.
5. Junkyard Joe is the kindest man in the entire downtown.
6. The people in Little Rock is the nicest people you will meet anywhere.
7. There weren't anyone left that I could trust.
8. Lourdes don't mean what she says.
9. Was they listening to what I said?
10. Doesn't it make sense to look at all the possibilities?
11. No, it don't.

12. New Orleans have many streets with French and Italian names.
13. The victim who have complained is the one they are watching.
14. Hasn't someone claimed the victory?
15. The people who live in darkness has seen a great light.

Review Exercise 5

Correct the errors in subject-verb agreement in the following student essay. (Do not change any verbs inside quotation marks.)

Sweet Albert Dee

There is only one Sweet Albert Dee, and he's my uncle. Sweet Albert is about 5'2" tall and look like a child, even though he is in his fifties. He have a head shaped like an apple. Albert Dee "smokes" old cigar butts although he never light them because, he say, "Smokin' is not good for you." (4 errors)

Albert is an unusual person and never do anything he don't feel like doing. If he don't feel like talking, he don't. His reasoning is a little strange on subjects such as bathing and working. I remember once I asked, "Uncle, why don't you like to take baths?" He replied, "Mary, just 'cause God made a lot of water, that don't mean he want you to use it all up." When my mother asked him why he didn't get a job, he answered, "As long as I can eat free, I don't need a job." Albert Dee think it is enough to enjoy life. (5 errors)

Unfortunately, my uncle is a very heavy drinker. He drink anything from moonshine to what he call "mad dog." And he say he don't care if the alcohol destroy his liver because he believe he can always get another one. Poor Albert Dee won't live too long. Besides drinking and not taking baths, he love to sing silly songs. When he drink too much, he always sing what he call a "lover's chant." It go something like this: "Ooh-ya-ya-ya-haya-ha-ha." He repeats this over and over until he fall asleep. (12 errors)

Sweet Albert Dee isn't a bad person. He just have his own philosophy about life and how to live it—that's all. Albert is really a nice old man who happen to be a little weird and to have a drinking problem. Sometimes I thinks that maybe everyone should be a little weird, and then maybe the world could be as happy as Sweet Albert Dee. (3 errors)

18

Using Pronouns Correctly

18.0   Introduction

PRONOUNS CAN BE misused in many ways. In this chapter you will learn how to avoid various types of pronoun errors. Before beginning, review the introduction of pronouns in Section 15.4.

18.1   Avoiding Errors in Pronoun Case

The way a pronoun is used in a sentence is called the *case*. The following are typical errors in case:

INCORRECT

Marcus and <u>me</u> were always getting into trouble. (*Marcus and me* is the subject, but the subjective case of *me* is *I*.)

CORRECT

Marcus and <u>I</u> were always getting into trouble.

INCORRECT

To <u>who</u> should I address this letter? (The preposition *to* takes the objective case, which is *whom*, not *who*.)

CORRECT

To <u>whom</u> should I address this letter?

INCORRECT

Are those <u>them</u>? (The personal pronoun is used as a predicative nominative. Thus, the subjective case, which is *they*, is necessary.)

CORRECT

Are those <u>they?</u>

INCORRECT

The apartment is just right for you and <u>I</u>. (The preposition *for* takes the objective case, which is *me*, not *I*.)

CORRECT

The apartment is just right for you and <u>me</u>.

INCORRECT

Carlos is older than <u>her</u>. (The sentence is saying that "Carlos is older than *she is*." Thus, the subjective case, *she*, is needed for the pronoun.)

CORRECT

Carlos is older than <u>she</u>.

Practice 1

Correct the pronoun case errors of the underlined words.

1. Marcus was very hurt and began spreading many lies about Troy and ~~I~~. *me*
2. Because he was older than <u>me</u>, he graduated before me and went away to college.
3. When Michael and <u>me</u> broke up, Mother knew just how hurt I was.
4. Now I realize that the little girl and <u>me</u> are closer than ever.
5. Just between you and <u>I</u>, that man is crazy.
6. It was <u>her</u> who finally spoke up.

Practice 2

Correct the errors in pronoun case in the following student paper, and be prepared to explain why you made the changes.

My Summer at Nantucket

Students who work at resorts in the summer often have unusual experiences. Last summer, my friend Regina and me traveled a thousand miles to work at Nantucket, which is a resort island twenty miles from the Massachusetts shore. We arrived with very little money in our pockets, and it was still quite cold. We didn't bring enough clothes and were nearly freezing. Someone told Regina and I go to to the local thrift shop, where we could buy cheap coats. Regina bought a fine old overcoat for three dollars, but I didn't have as much luck as her, so I had to huddle up in my blanket to keep warm. (3 errors)

Besides being cold, we were also hungry. Our friend Randy from Penn State was working as a dishwasher and brought Regina and I scraps of food every night. Regina and me did not have any regular place to live, so we stayed with various friends in rooms they had rented, sleeping on the floor. We looked and looked for jobs, but no one wanted to give either she or me employment. (3 errors)

At this point I was getting desperate. I did not know to who I could turn for help. I was determined not to ask my parents for money. Just between you and I, they were furious with me for leaving home to go to Nantucket. "Whom do you girls think you are," my dad said, "traveling a thousand miles to work at some funny resort island?"

But us "girls" (I am nineteen and Regina is twenty) went anyway. (4 errors)

Just before starvation set in, I got a job as a janitor at a hotel, and Regina got a job as a "bag boy" in a supermarket. When I wrote my father and told him about our jobs, he thought Regina and me were completely crazy. "You mean you traveled a thousand miles to mop floors?" he wrote back. My summer in Nantucket was an unusual experience, and it was also the most fun Regina and me ever had. Whomever said that parents are always right? (3 errors)

18.2   Avoiding Pronouns with Unclear Antecedents

The noun or pronoun for which a pronoun stands is called its *antecedent* (meaning it goes *before* the pronoun). When you use a pronoun, make sure the antecedent is clear. Examine this sentence:

<u>April</u> is the worst month of the year. <u>It</u> is the time when <u>they</u> make you pay your taxes.

The antecedent of *It* is clearly *April,* so there is no problem. But what is the antecedent of *they?* The writer assumes you will think of the federal government, but such an assumption is not enough. Follow this important rule: *If there is no clear antecedent for a pronoun, replace the pronoun with an appropriate noun.* The two sentences could read:

April is the worst month of the year. It is the time when the federal government makes you pay your taxes.

Practice 3

In the following sentences, the antecedents of the underlined pronouns are unclear. Replace them with appropriate nouns or pronouns. Also, change verbs as necessary.

1. Sex education should be taught in high school because parents are either too scared or too busy to teach the facts of life to <u>them</u>. *their children*

2. In the final game, I was playing defense and tried to make a tackle. When I hit <u>him</u>, he fell on his side and landed on my finger.

3. When I was in the service, <u>they</u> would not let me grow my hair longer than an inch.

4. One thing I don't like about that restaurant is that <u>they</u> are always trying to rush you.

5. No one likes living on the brink of nuclear war. There have been many attempts to change <u>this</u>.

6. I took my automobile to the dealer to be fixed, but <u>they</u> wanted far too much for the repairs.

7. My son would like to major in business, but <u>they</u> are a bit too demanding for him.

8. Congress has passed much new legislation, but our unemployment rate continues to rise. I don't know what the president should do about <u>this</u>, but he should do something.

9. My computer is broken, but <u>he</u> said that he would fix it for almost nothing.

10. I hope to be out of my apartment soon; <u>they</u> are charging too much rent and do not want to make any repairs.

11. When I was in the hospital, <u>they</u> took very good care of me.

18.3   Avoiding Errors in Pronoun Agreement

Personal pronouns (*I, you, she, they,* and the like) must agree with the nouns they replace in both *number* and *person.* (The nouns they replace are their antecedents.)

> Popular music is an art form, and <u>it</u> is the principal art form for many young people.

Instead of repeating the word *music,* you naturally substitute the pronoun *it;* otherwise, the sentence would be awkward:

> Popular music is an art form, and popular music is the principal art form for many young people.

Thus it is appropriate to use a pronoun to replace *music* the second time it is used, but the pronoun must agree with its antecedent in number and person.

The following list of personal pronouns in the subjective case shows why *it* appropriately replaces *music* in the preceding example:

	Singular	Plural
FIRST PERSON	I	we
SECOND PERSON	you	you
THIRD PERSON	he, she, or it	they

Agreement in number means that singular pronouns must be used to replace singular antecedents and plural pronouns must be used to replace plural antecedents. In the preceding sentence, it is therefore appropriate to use *it* instead of *they,* because *music* is singular.

Agreement in person means that first-person pronouns must be used to replace first-person antecedents, second-person pronouns to replace second-person antecedents, and third-person pronouns to replace third-person antecedents. It is therefore appropriate to use the third-person pronoun *it* to replace *music,* because *music,* as a noun, is in the third person.

Pronouns used as objects or to show possession should be written in the objective or possessive case. For example,

> Francine was so nice to me that I will never forget her.

Her is in agreement with *Francine* and is the object of the verb *forget.*

Practice 4

Choose the correct pronoun in each of the following, and draw an arrow to the noun or pronoun (the antecedent) that it replaces. In two sentences, you will have to choose the correct verb as well.

1. Movies rated X are for adults only because (it, <u>they</u>) often (contains, <u>contain</u>) explicit sex and violence.
2. The world would have more crime than (it, they) could handle if everyone saw X-rated movies.
3. Ticket clerks at theaters that show X-rated films often take advantage of my son by selling (him, them) a ticket without asking for proper identification.
4. Hawaii is known for the many beautiful islands (it, they) (has, have).
5. When I go downtown and see an old lady begging with a cup, I feel sorry for (her, them).
6. Most mystery stories do not end the way you expect (it, them) to.
7. The government is the worst offender; (it, they) (wastes, waste) more money than anyone else.
8. When Mexico suffered a great earthquake, (it, they) asked other nations for assistance.

Practice 5

In the first part of each exercise below, use the designated noun in a sentence. In the second part, write another sentence in which an appropriate pronoun replaces the noun.

1. (bird) a. *Each morning a bird sits outside my window.*

   b. *I am going to feed it today.*

2. (computer) a. _____

   b. _____

3. (car) a. _____

   b. _____

4. (person) a. _____

   b. _____

5. (Canada) a. _____

   b. _____

6. (woman) a. _____

   b. _____

 ### Practice 6

In the sentences that follow, change the pronouns to agree with their antecedents. Change other words as necessary. (One sentence is correct.)

them

1. My glasses are very important to me because without it I could not function.
2. Because the United States uses more oil than they can produce, they have to import great quantities from other countries.
3. In conclusion, each state is unique in their own culture, industry, and natural environment.
4. Marge was determined to help her father and brother because she loved him.
5. I have had three jobs since I began working, and each has been rewarding in its own way.
6. My husband gets furious at neighbors who borrow things and never think to return it.
7. When people first met my grandfather, he found him charming.
8. As they got to know my grandfather, however, you found him less charming and more cantankerous.
9. The United Arab Emirates was in an oil crisis; they imported too much of their oil.
10. These working mothers have more responsibility than they can handle. She needs a lot more help from her husband.
11. When one joins a car pool to get to work, they help save oil.

18.4   Avoiding Pronoun Gender Confusion

When a pronoun refers to a male, use *he, him,* or *his:*

Dr. Carl Regaldo asked me to come to see him.

When a pronoun refers to a female, use *she, her,* or *hers:*

> Senator Barbara Newburn asked people to trust <u>her</u> new program.

But what do you do when the antecedent is a person whose gender is unknown, or if it is a word like *lawyer, teacher, parent,* or *someone,* which could refer to both men and women? You could say

> A lawyer has to work hard to build <u>his</u> practice.

But many women, as well as men, are lawyers. Thus you could say

> A lawyer has to work hard to build <u>her</u> practice.

But many men, as well as women, are lawyers. Therefore, you *might* say

> A lawyer has to work hard to build <u>their</u> practice.

However, the pronoun *their* is clearly wrong because its antecedent is the singular word *lawyer.*

Until fairly recently, most English texts instructed students to use the male pronoun if the antecedent was not clearly female. Thus they taught that you should say "A lawyer has to work hard to build <u>his</u> practice." Although this use of the masculine pronoun is still correct, more and more textbooks and teachers are turning away from it and suggesting the following alternatives:

1. To avoid gender confusion, avoid the pronoun altogether whenever possible. Simply say

> A lawyer has to work hard to build a practice.

Or make the *antecedent* plural:

> <u>Lawyers</u> have to work hard to build <u>their</u> practices.

2. If it is not possible to avoid using the pronoun or to make the antecedent plural, use the double pronouns *he or she, him or her,* or *his or her.* If you were announcing to a group of men and women that a car parked outside had its lights on, you could say

> <u>Someone</u> has left <u>his or her</u> car lights on.

If you do use a double-pronoun expression, try not to do so more than once in a paragraph, and never use it more than once in a sentence. Never write

> <u>He or she</u> left <u>his or her</u> umbrella in the auditorium.

Practice 7

In the following sentences, avoid the problem of gender confusion by either omitting the male and female pronouns or making the antecedents and their verbs plural. You will have to change some other words as well.

1. These days a good teacher has a hard time keeping his job.

   These days a good teacher has a hard time keeping a job.

   _____

2. A doctor must be available to his patients all of the time.

   _____

   _____

3. This type of nurse is always ready to help a patient with any problem he may have.

   _____

   _____

4. Then there is the nurse who is concerned about her work only when someone is watching her.

   _____

   _____

5. This person is at the bottom of society; he lives in poverty.

   _____

   _____

6. Each of my parents helps me in his own way, and I am grateful for what each has done.

   _____

   _____

7. It is difficult for a parent to relate to his child these days.

   _____

   _____

8. A person with a problem should make sure that she sees somebody trained to help.

   _____

   _____

9. A teacher should be completely fair to his students.

   _____

   _____

10. In addition, a teacher should plan all her classes carefully.

_____

_____

Indefinite Pronouns and Gender Agreement

A special problem arises in gender agreement when you use a personal pronoun to replace an indefinite pronoun such as *each, anyone, someone, everyone, no one,* and so on. (See page 306 for a more complete list.) Most indefinite pronouns are singular, which means that you probably will need to use *he or she, him or her,* or *his or her* for agreement. For example,

Anyone may submit <u>his or her</u> application now.

No one should go on such a strict diet without <u>his or her</u> doctor's permission.

You can bet that someone will not do <u>his or her</u> share.

As pointed out above, however, try to limit the use of the double pronoun to once in a paragraph.

On occasion, when the indefinite pronoun *clearly* refers to a group of people, it is appropriate to use it with a plural pronoun—*they, them,* or *their.* For example,

Everyone was clapping <u>their</u> hands.

Everybody worked as hard as <u>they</u> could.

Practice 8

Write sentences in which the indefinite pronouns shown below are the subjects. Use the designated possessive pronouns to refer to them.

1. (anyone, his or her) *Anyone who wants his or her paper should see me after class.*

2. (someone, his or her) _____

_____

3. (anybody, he or she) _____

_____

4. (no one, his or her) _____

_____

5. (each one, himself or herself) _____

_____

6. (everybody, their) _____

_____

18.5   Avoiding Pronoun Person Shifts

A fairly common pronoun-agreement problem is a shift in person within the same sentence. For example,

> I came to realize that because <u>you</u> are on earth for only a short time, <u>one</u> should do the things <u>one</u> wants.

The writer began with the second-person *you* and shifted to the third-person *one.* Here are two ways to correct the error:

> I came to realize that because <u>you</u> are on earth for only a short time, <u>you</u> should do the things <u>you</u> want.

> I came to realize that because <u>one</u> is on earth for only a short time, <u>one</u> should do the things <u>one</u> wants.

Practice 9

Correct the shifts in pronoun person in the following sentences. (One sentence is correct.)

1. If you have ever lived as a "navy brat," you know that such a life can be frustrating, especially if ~~one has~~ *you have* moved around as much as I have.

2. When one goes to see her, you should plan on spending the whole day because she always has to bake something for you to eat.

3. Mrs. Lewis passes everyone in her class, whether you have good grades or not.

4. One's social class has more to do with your personality than you think.

5. They were always there when I needed them and would always talk to you in a nice tone of voice.

6. Someone has stolen your bicycle.

7. This statement is very strong because it tells me that you should forgive people who have sinned against me.

8. When one sees the view of that saltwater marsh, you are moved by its beauty.

9. Parents' great fear is that their children will use drugs that are dangerous to you.

10. We should be careful before believing what they tell you.

11. One should not listen to all you hear.

18.6   Avoiding Other Pronoun Errors

Other pronoun errors include the following:

1. Reversing the order of pronouns:

INCORRECT
She took <u>me</u> and Robert for a ride.

CORRECT
She took Robert and <u>me</u> for a ride.

Always put yourself last.

2. Using the wrong personal pronoun with a gerund:

INCORRECT
She was driven crazy by <u>him</u> nagging.

CORRECT
She was driven crazy by <u>his</u> nagging.

Use the possessive form of the personal pronoun with a gerund.

3. Using the incorrect relative pronoun:

INCORRECT
The woman <u>which</u> lived next door was an alcoholic.

CORRECT
The woman <u>who</u> lived next door was an alcoholic.

Use *who* and *whose* with people and *which* and *that* with things.

18.7   Summary of Common Pronoun Errors

The following are typical pronoun errors or awkward constructions:

1. Errors in case:

INCORRECT
<u>Sal and me</u> drove to Minneapolis.

CORRECT
<u>Sal and I</u> drove to Minneapolis.

INCORRECT
Just between <u>you and I</u>, the trip was terrible.

CORRECT

Just between <u>you and me,</u> the trip was terrible.

2. Unclear antecedents:

INCORRECT

When my mother was in the hospital, <u>they</u> treated her well.

CORRECT

When my mother was in the hospital, <u>the staff</u> treated her well.

3. Pronouns that do not agree with their antecedents:

INCORRECT

<u>Anyone</u> who wants to join should see <u>their</u> counselor.

CORRECT

<u>Anyone</u> who wants to join should see <u>his or her</u> counselor.

Note: Do not overuse *his or her* constructions.

CORRECT

If <u>you</u> want to join, see <u>your</u> counselor.

INCORRECT

<u>Washington</u> is known for <u>their</u> outdoor concerts.

CORRECT

<u>Washington</u> is known for <u>its</u> outdoor concerts.

4. Awkward gender use:

AWKWARD

If a <u>person</u> wants to succeed in nursing, <u>she</u> must study hard.

BETTER

If <u>one</u> wants to succeed in nursing, <u>one</u> must study hard.

AWKWARD

Each <u>parent</u> should give <u>his</u> child love.

BETTER

<u>All parents</u> should give <u>their</u> children love.

5. Pronoun-person shifts:

INCORRECT

The way <u>one</u> dresses will have much to do with <u>your</u> success.

CORRECT

The way <u>you</u> dress will have much to do with your success.

6. Pronouns out of order:

INCORRECT

They showed <u>me and Rosa</u> a good time.

CORRECT

They showed <u>Rosa and me</u> a good time.

  7. Incorrect relative pronouns:

INCORRECT

The <u>people which</u> you befriend will not forget you.

CORRECT

The <u>people whom</u> you befriend will not forget you.

INCORRECT

The <u>people which</u> befriend you are the ones you will not forget.

CORRECT

The <u>people who</u> befriend you are the ones you will not forget.

18.8   Review Exercise

Correct all pronoun errors and awkward constructions in the following sentences, rewriting as necessary. (Three sentences are correct.)

  1. You can test the loaves by tapping them with your finger; it should sound hollow.

  _____

  2. When the bread is thoroughly cooled, wrap them securely with foil.

  _____

  3. Mrs. Williams does not mind paying high taxes because she feels you should support your government.

  _____

  4. The people you think are carefree are often the very ones who take life most seriously.

  _____

  5. I think a child's interest in reading depends on the material he or she is given in his or her early years of schooling.

  _____

  6. It was a first for Mary and I.

  _____

  7. The old lady took the drug because the doctors prescribed them for her.

  _____

8. If you drive Manuel and I to work every day, we will pay you well.

    _____

9. Just because you are older than I, that does not give you the right to boss me around.

    _____

10. Our parents gave me and Deborah a good home.

    _____

11. When one takes Spanish from Dr. Fernandez, you should plan on having a lot of work.

    _____

12. To who is the letter addressed?

    _____

13. Anyone turning in their paper late will lose a letter grade.

    _____

14. I came to realize that he and I would never work out our problems unless we got help.

    _____

15. Someone should pick up their phone and call the police.

    _____

19

Spelling Skills

19.0 Introduction

IN THIS CHAPTER you will learn how to write tricky plural nouns and verb endings, how to distinguish sound-alike words, and how to use the hyphen. A list of the words most frequently misspelled in the papers of beginning college students is also included.

Some people are naturally good spellers; others are not. One of the authors of this text is not a naturally good speller. Once he sent a manuscript to a publisher with a reference to the parable of the shepherd who left his flock of ninety-nine sheep to find the one that had strayed. In his most solemn voice, he wrote that to seek the one that was lost, the shepherd had left the "*nighty and the nine.*" He still cannot spell *accommodate*—or is it *acommodate* or *acomodate?* Nor is he ever quite sure when to insert a hyphen and when not to. Frankly, he doesn't like hyphens. For example, he always resists using a hyphen with *first class* when it is used as an adjective, as in *first-class restaurant.* And he has just about given up trying to remember when to write *awhile* and when to write *a while.* But there is hope for the likes of him—the dictionary! Ask your instructor to recommend a dictionary that you can easily carry with you to check your spelling.

In addition to constant use of the dictionary, extensive reading also will help your spelling. Without even thinking about it, you will remember how various words are formed. The following suggestions can also help:

1. As you write, concentrate on each syllable of each word. You can usually avoid the following types of mistakes by carefully pronouncing each word, syllable by syllable, as you write it:

necessry for necessary (ne-ces-sa-ry)

practicly for practically (prac-ti-cal-ly)

goverment or govment for government (gov-ern-ment)

craddle for cradle (cra-dle)

2. Begin your own dictionary, keeping a list of every word you ever misspell in any course in college. Anyone can misspell a word like *kindergarten* or *sacrilegious* or *shillelagh,* but you do not have to keep misspelling the same words. Before writing each of your essays, review your list.

3. Learn the rules of noun plurals and verb endings, which are given in Sections 19.1 and 19.2.

4. Learn the rules for contractions and how to distinguish them from the personal pronouns, such as *its,* that sound like contractions (see Section 19.3).

5. Learn to distinguish homonyms, or sound-alike words, such as *there* and *their* (see Section 19.4).

6. Learn the rules or the uses of the hyphen that are given in Section 19.5.

7. Study the list in Section 19.6 of the most commonly misspelled words in college writing. Even if you later forget how to spell some of these words, you will probably remember to look them up in your dictionary.

8. Proofread your papers carefully.

If you are still having problems, ask your instructor to suggest a spelling workbook. One that has helped many students is *College Spelling Skills* by James F. Shepherd (Boston: Houghton Mifflin, 1986).

19.1 Plurals of Nouns

Most noun plurals are made simply by adding an *-s* to the singular form: *experience* becomes *experiences, American* becomes *Americans*. Plurals formed in other ways can be tricky. Learn the rules below. As you read them, fill in the blanks.

1. Add *-es* to nouns that end in *x, ss, z, sh,* and *ch:*

box becomes _____*boxes*_____   church becomes_____

sex becomes _____   business becomes_____

bus becomes___ _____   rash becomes _____

2. Add *-es* to a few nouns that end in *-o.* For example,

tomato becomes_____*tomatoes*_____   veto becomes_____

hero becomes_____   echo becomes _____

potato becomes _____

Add *-s* to most other nouns that end in *-o:*

ego becomes_____*egos*_____   radio becomes_____

zero becomes_____   two becomes_____

zoo becomes _____   tattoo becomes _____

3. Follow these rules for nouns that end in *y:*

If the *-y* is preceded by a consonant (a letter other than *a, e, i, o, u*), change the *-y* to *-i* and add *-es:*

cry becomes_____*cries*_____   library becomes_____

navy becomes_____   berry becomes_____

If the *-y* is preceded by a vowel (*a, e, i, o, u*), add only *-s:*

play becomes _____   journey becomes _____

    If a proper name ends in *-y,* add only *-s;* otherwise, the name would be changed:

Kennedy becomes_____   January becomes_____

    4. Change *-f* or *-fe* endings of most nouns to *-ves:*

self becomes_____*selves*_____   knife becomes _____

life becomes_____   leaf becomes_____

elf becomes_____   loaf becomes_____

    Note: Roof becomes *roofs* and *belief* becomes *beliefs.*

    5. The singular and plural for some nouns, especially animals that are hunted and certain fish, are the same:

deer remains_____*deer*_____   elk remains_____

trout remains_____   bass remains _____

    6. Change the noun itself to form yet other plurals:

man becomes_____*men*_____   ox becomes _____

woman becomes_____   mouse becomes_____

    7. You may use *-'s* to form the plural of letters, numerals, and symbols. (**However, many publishers omit the apostrophe.**)

       the t becomes the t's

       1980 becomes the 1980's

       & becomes &'s

Do *not* use *-'s* to form any other plurals.

    If you are in doubt about a plural, look up the noun, designated *n,* in a dictionary, and you will find the plural, designated *pl.* If you look up *alumnus,* for example, you will see something like this:

    a-lum-nus (ə-lŭm'nə) *n., pl.* **-ni** (-nī).

You thus know that the plural is *alumni.* (The suffix *-ni* replaces *-nus.*) If two plural suffixes are given, always use the first alternative.

Practice 1

Give the plurals for the following.

1. watch _watches_ ax _____ first _____

2. candy _____ sash _____ two _____

3. potato _____ Lindsay _____ woman _____

4. leaf _____ hero _____ lady _____

5. life _____ echo _____ honey _____

6. 1990 _____ deer _____ m _____

7. roof _____ policeman _____ bath _____

8. self _____ stereo _____ Monday _____

9. hippopotamus _____ (Use your dictionary.)

10. analysis _____ (Use your dictionary.)

 Practice 2

Correct the noun plurals in the following paragraph. (Six plural endings have been omitted; two have been misspelled.)

The area where I live is called Graveyard because of the two graveyard located nearby. I have lived in Graveyard for twelve year now and know all the thing that go on there. I get tired of seeing the same people standing on the corner talking to each other all day long. They try to start conversation with the ladys who pass by, and they try to bum money from you so that they can buy beer, soft drink, and various kind of candys from the store down the street.

19.2   Verb Endings

The rules governing verb endings are given in Chapters 16 and 17. Here is a summary:

1. Add *-s* to most verbs to form third-person singular constructions in the present tense:

He, she, or it <u>loves</u>

He, she, or it <u>walks</u>

2. Add *-es* to verbs to form third-person singular constructions in the present tense if the verbs end in *-o, -x, -ss, -z, -sh,* or *-ch:*

He, she, or it <u>does</u>

He, she, or it <u>reaches</u>

3. If the verb ends in a *-y* that is preceded by a consonant, change the *-y* to *-i* before adding *-es* or *-ed:*

<u>spy</u> becomes <u>spies</u> or <u>spied</u>

<u>bury</u> becomes <u>buries</u> or <u>buried</u>

but

<u>journey</u> becomes <u>journeys</u> or <u>journeyed</u> (The *-y* is preceded by a vowel, *e.*)

4. When adding *-ed* or *-ing* to one-syllable verbs or verbs accented on the last syllable, double the final consonant if it is preceded by a single vowel. (See pages 348–350 and 358–359 for more explanation.)

<u>drum</u> becomes <u>drummed</u> or <u>drumming</u>

<u>occur</u> becomes <u>occurred</u> or <u>occurring</u>

but

<u>happen</u> becomes <u>happened</u> or <u>happening</u>. (The accent is on the first syllable.)

5. When adding *-ing* to verbs that end in *-y*, do not change the *-y:*

<u>fly</u> becomes <u>flying</u>

<u>satisfy</u> becomes <u>satisfying</u>

Practice 3

Supply the correct verb forms.

Base Form	Third-Person Singular, Present	Simple Past and Past Participle	Progressive Form
1. try	*tries*	*tried*	*trying*
2. comply			
3. hum			
4. bus			
5. bevel			
6. defer			

7. satisfy   _____   _____   _____

8. open   _____   _____   _____

9. counsel   _____   _____   _____

10. study   _____   _____   _____

11. occupy   _____   _____   _____

12. journey   _____   _____   _____

13. jog   _____   _____   _____

14. travel   _____   _____   _____

15. refer   _____   _____   _____

19.3   Contractions and Possessive Pronouns

Using Contractions

One meaning of *contract* is "to reduce in size." For example, ice contracts when it melts. To make a *contraction* in grammar, you join two words by reducing their number of letters:

> it is becomes it's
>
> there is becomes there's
>
> cannot becomes can't
>
> I would becomes I'd
>
> let us becomes let's
>
> Linda is going becomes Linda's going

Notice that in each of the preceding, an *apostrophe* (') replaces the missing letter or letters:

> it is becomes it's
> ↑
> cannot becomes can't
> ↑
> I would becomes I'd
> ↑
> Linda is becomes Linda's
> ↑

Except for *will not,* which becomes *won't,* all contractions are formed by using the apostrophe to *replace* the missing letter or letters.

Some people tend to overuse contractions in their writing. It is fine to use some contractions, but give your papers variety by writing out *it is, will not, I would,* and the like most of the time. In formal writing—such as a research paper—use contractions seldom, if at all. Avoid the following contractions:

<u>there's</u> for <u>there is</u> (It is too easy to make a verb-agreement error, as in *There's two of us left.* Write out *There are two of us left.*)

<u>it's</u> for <u>it has</u> (Save *it's* for *it is.* Write out *it has.*)

<u>Linda's going</u> for <u>Linda is going</u> (The contraction is unnecessarily informal.)

Do not try to make a contraction of *there are.* Also, note that if you spell out the contraction *can't,* you write *cannot,* not *can not.*

Practice 4

Make contractions of the following words.

1. who is _____ *who's* _____   6. would not _____

2. they are _____   7. they would _____

3. cannot _____   8. should not _____

4. let us _____   9. do not _____

5. will not _____   10. you are _____

Contractions and Possessive Pronouns

Because some contractions sound like the possessive forms of certain pronouns, they are often confused with the pronouns in writing:

Contractions	*Possessive Pronouns*
It's (it is) raining.	The dog went to <u>its</u> house.
<u>They're</u> (they are) ready.	<u>Their</u> knowledge is great.
<u>There's</u> (there is) the knife.	The knife is <u>theirs</u>.
<u>Who's</u> (who is) going to pass?	The ones <u>whose</u> papers are turned in on time are going to pass.
<u>You're</u> (you are) a pleasant person.	<u>Your</u> manner is pleasant.

To determine whether you need a contraction or the possessive pronoun, apply a simple rule: Try to convert the word in question into two words. If you can, the contraction is the correct form:

You can say, "It is raining."   You cannot say, "The dog went to it
 (Thus *it's* is correct.)   is house." (Thus *its* is correct.)
You can say, "They are ready."   You cannot say, "They are knowledge
 (Thus *they're* is correct.)   is great." (Thus *their* is correct.)
You can say, "Who is going to pass?" You cannot say, "The ones who is papers
 (Thus *who's* is correct.)   are turned in on time are going
                                       to pass." (Thus *whose* is correct.)

Practice 5

Choose either the contraction or the possessive pronoun for each of the following.

1. I began to work there in 1987. (It's, Its) location was on Tanis Drive in Lexington.

2. If (you're, your) lucky, you might find peace.

3. When (you're, your) living at home, you cannot leave when you want to, as you can when you are staying in the dorm.

4. You can count on Linda's cooking because you know (it's, its) going to be good.

5. Sometimes you can't even tell what (they're, their) talking about.

6. (There's, Theirs) is the least costly way.

7. (There's, Theirs) only one of us left.

8. (It's, Its) not a question of whom you are serving: You must always be polite. (You're, Your) reputation is at stake.

9. There are so many people in the program that (it's, its) impossible to know them all.

10. (Who's, Whose) going to be the first to jump in?

11. Most of the classes are large, although (there's, theirs) at least one small one.

19.4   Other Sound-Alike Words

Besides pronouns and contractions that sound alike, there are a number of other words that sound similar. Read the definition of the following sound-alike words and the tricks provided to help you remember them:

1. accept—a verb that means "receive." (I accept your offer.)
   except—a preposition that means "not including." (She likes everything except meatloaf.)

2. affect—a verb that means "influence." (The storm affected the crop.)
   effect—a noun that means "result." (The effect of the storm was great.)

3. <u>choose</u>—a verb that means "decide for." (I <u>choose</u> to go this way.)
<u>chose</u>—past tense of choose. Yesterday, I <u>chose</u> to go that way in-stead.)

4. <u>hear</u> —a verb that means "listen." (I <u>hear</u> with my ear.)
<u>here</u>—an adverb that means "place." (Bring the luggage <u>here</u>.)

5. <u>whole</u>—entire. (The <u>whole</u> class sent her a get-well card.)
<u>hole</u>—a noun that means "a round opening." (He dug a <u>hole</u> in the ground.)
<u>hold</u>—a verb that means "to grasp." (I <u>hold</u> on tightly.)

6. <u>new</u>—an adjective that means the opposite of <u>old</u>. (She welcomed the <u>new</u> day.)
<u>knew</u>—the past tense of <u>know</u>. (I <u>knew</u> better than that.)

7. <u>loose</u>—an adjective that means "not tight." (The knot is <u>loose</u>.)
<u>lose</u>—a verb that means "to misplace." (I might <u>lose</u> my hat.)

8. <u>may be</u>—a verb that shows possibility. (You <u>may be</u> president someday.)
<u>maybe</u>—an adverb that shows possibility. (<u>Maybe</u> you will go with him.)

9. <u>of</u>—a preposition that means "belonging to." (She is a member <u>of</u> the club.)
<u>off</u>—an adverb that means "from" or "away." (It fell <u>off</u> the shelf.)

10. <u>pass</u>—a present-tense verb that means "to successfully complete." (I hope to <u>pass</u> the test.)
<u>passed</u>—the past tense of <u>pass</u>. (You <u>passed</u> the test!)
<u>past</u>—a noun or adjective that means "at an earlier time." (In the <u>past</u> week, you have taken three tests.)

11. <u>quiet</u>—an adjective that means "free of noise." (I like a <u>quiet</u> park.)
<u>quit</u>—a verb that means "to stop doing something." (He <u>quit</u> his job.)
<u>quite</u>—an adverb that means "completely." (He was <u>quite</u> alone.)

12. <u>read</u>—a verb that means "to understand printed words" (rhymes with <u>bead</u> in the present tense and <u>bed</u> in the past tense). (I <u>read</u> to my chil-dren every day when they come home from school. My parents <u>read</u> to me every day when I was a child.)
<u>red</u>—an adjective that refers to a color. (She photographed the <u>red</u> evening sky.)

13. <u>sense</u>—a noun that means "understanding." (He has good <u>sense</u>.)
<u>since</u>—a preposition that means "after a certain time." (She has been waiting for him <u>since</u> daybreak.)

14. <u>then</u>—an adverb that means "afterward." (We ate dinner, and <u>then</u> we left.)
<u>than</u>—a conjunction that is used to compare two things. (This car is big-ger <u>than</u> the other.)

15. there—an expletive or adverb that means "a place not so close by." (He flew out there for vacation.)
    their—a possessive pronoun that shows ownership. (Their house is on fire.)

16. though—a conjunction that means "in spite of." (He was able to walk, though it was painful for him.)
    thought—the past tense of think. (I thought I saw her.)

17. threw—the past tense of throw. (I threw the javelin in high school.)
    through—a preposition that means "into and out of." (We rode through the forest.)

18. too—an adverb that means "more than enough" or "to an excessive degree." (I am going too. The dog was too sick and too small.)
    to—a preposition with several uses. (They went to the store in order to buy a camera.)
    two—a noun or adjective that is the written form of the numeral 2. (I have two sisters.)

19. weather—a noun that means "temperature" or "climate." (How is the weather in the mountains?)
    whether—an adverb that means "condition." (Whether or not you should go, I don't know.)

20. were—the third-person plural, past tense, of the verb to be. (The skiers were cold at the end of the day.)
    where—an adverb that means "at the place of." (Those fish live where the water is cold.)

19.5 Using the Hyphen

One of the most difficult elements in spelling is the use of the hyphen (-). The following rules will help, but if you are in any doubt as to whether a hyphen is necessary, look up the word in your dictionary. Use the hyphen

1. To carry a word from one line to the next:

                                                    . . . an unnec-

essary remark.

Avoid breaking a word between lines, but if you must, divide it with a hyphen between syllables. Do not divide short words like *also* or *into*. A dictionary will show the breakdown of a word by syllables.

2. To write compound numbers from *twenty-one* to *ninety-nine*.

3. To write fractions such as *three-fifths, two-thirds, one and one-half.*

4. After a prefix that is joined to a proper name, such as *non-European, un-American.*

5. After certain other prefixes, such as *ex-wife, semi-invalid.*

6. To write certain compound nouns, such as *secretary-treasurer,* a *two-year-old, mother-in-law, president-elect.* Consult a dictionary. *If the compound noun is not listed, write it as two separate words.*

7. To join two words used as a single adjective, such as *first-place team, horn-rimmed glasses, big-league coach.* Some compound adjectives, such as *high school* (as in *high school team*), are so familiar that many professional writers omit the hyphen.

19.6   Words Often Misspelled

In addition to the words you have already studied, the following are among those most often misspelled by beginning college students. If you are unsure o what any of the words mean, look them up in the dictionary. Try to learn to spell them all.

Single and Compound Words

almost	everything	something	a lot
already	forever	somewhere	all right
altogether	itself	themselves	each one
always	meantime	throughout	each other
anyway	meanwhile	weekday	even though
anywhere	nevertheless	weekend	every time
apart	nowadays	whenever	high school
awhile	nowhere	whereas	in order that
cannot	postcard	wherever	no one
everyone	someday	whoever	one day
		without	

Numbers, Days, and Months

one-half	eighth	nineteenth	ninety-one	Wednesday
fourth	ninth	twentieth	ninetieth	Saturday
sixth	twelfth	forty		January
eight	thirteenth	ninety		February

Other Frequently Misspelled Words

(See the rule on page 417 on when to use *ie* and *ei.*)

A

absence
academic
accidentally
accommodate
accumulate
achieve
across
advice (*n*)
advise (*v*)
agreeable
amateur
analysis
analyze
apologize
apology
apparent
appearance
argument
ascend
athlete
attendance
average
awful

B

bath (*n*)
bathe (*v*)
beautiful
beginning
belief (*n*)
believe (*v*)
bookkeeping
boundaries
breath (*n*)
breathe (*v*)
Britain
buried
bury
business
businesslike

C

calendar
category
ceiling
certain
college
coming
commission
commitment
committed
committee
competent
conceivable
conscience
conscious
council (*n*)
councilor
counsel (*v*)
counselor
criticize

D

deceased
decision
develop
dictionary
difference
dilemma
discussed
disgust
dormitory

E

earliest
echoes
either
embarrass
emphasis (*n*)
emphasize (*v*)
employee
envelope
equip
equipment

equipped
especially
existence
expense
explanation
extraordinary

F

familiar
fascinate
fiery
foreign
freight
fulfill

G

gauge
generalize
government
grammar
grateful
guess (*n, v*)
guest (*n*)

H

handicapped
handkerchief
handsome
height
hoping

I

identical
illegible
immediately
incident
incompetent
inconceivable
independence
independent
intelligence
interest

J, K

jewelry
judgment
know
knowledge

L

later
latter
leisure
library
license
literature
loneliness
lounge

M

machinery
maintain
maintenance
marriage
mathematics
miniature
mischief
mischievous
misspell
moderate

N

necessary
neither
niece
northeast
noticeable
nowadays

O

occasion
occur
occurred
occurrence
o'clock

okay (OK)
omitted
organization

P

paid
parallel
participant
pastime
peace (not war)
perceive
percent
permanent
permitted
personal
personnel
physical
piece (part of)
possession
potatoes
practical
precede
prejudiced
pressure
principal (one in charge)
principle (a rule)
privilege
proceed

R

realize
receive
recognize
recommend
referred
relieve
rhyme
rhythm
ridiculous

S

salary
secretary

seize
sense
sensible
separate
sergeant
similar
sophomore
succeed
successful
suppose
supposed to
surprise

T

taxable
technical
thorough
till (or *until*)
tragedy
traveled

U, V

used to
useful
valuable
vein
vice versa

W

wage
weird
while
women
writing
written

Y, Z

yearbook
yield
zealous

The *ie, ei* Rule

Use *i* before *e,* except after *c,* or when sounded as *a,* as in *neighbor* and *weigh* (*nay-bor* and *way*):

   1. Use *i* before *e:*

achieve	conscientious	niece	thief
believe	earliest	piece	twentieth
conscience	mischief	relieve	yield

   2. Except after *c:*

ceiling	conceivable	perceive	receive

   3. Or when sounded as *a:*

freight	neighbor	sleigh	vein	weigh

   4. Memorize these exceptions:

either	height	neither	their
foreign	leisure	seize	weird

Practice 6

Correct the one misspelled word in each of the following groups.

                  all right

1. almost, always, ~~alright~~, altogether, already
2. apart, awhile, alot, nowhere, no one
3. everything, someday, throughout, weekend, highschool
4. anywhere, mean time, whereas, without, meanwhile
5. when ever, whoever, cannot, postcard, somehow
6. one-half, fourth, twelth, ninetieth, ninety
7. January, Febuary, Wednesday, thirteenth, nineteenth
8. appearance, accidentally, accommodate, agreeable, absense
9. achieve, arguement, apology, apologize, analysis
10. attendence, agreeable, accumulate, across, athlete
11. businesslike, buried, Britain, bookeeping, breathe

12. begining, boundaries, beautiful,business,believe
13. committed, commitment,commitee,conceivable, counselor
14. ceiling, commission,counsel,coming,competant
15. develope, dilemma,disgust,dictionary, dormitory
16. existence, equipped,especially, emphasize,earlyest
17. envelope, emphasis,embarrass, explanation, existance
18. fiery, familiar, freight, fulfill, foriegn
19. guest, grammer, grateful, gauge, generalize
20. hoping, height,handsome,handkercheif
21. incompetent, independant,intelligence, illegible, inconceivable
22. judgment, jewelry, know, knowlege
23. leisure, loneliness,license,libary, literature
24. miniature, misspell,mathmatics,mischievous, maintenance
25. northeast, necessary, neither, neice,noticeable
26. o'clock, occurrence, okay, occured, occasion
27. percent, personnel, percieve, parallel, principle
28. potato, physical, possession,pastime,privilige
29. participent, permitted, precede, proceed, piece
30. rhyme, rhythm, relieve, rediculous, realize
31. seize, separate, sergeant, sensable, sophomore
32. suppose, supprise, similar, succeed,successful
33. traveled, tragedy, til,taxable, technical
34. used to, vice versa, usefull,vein, valuable
35. yield, weird, writing, writen, wage

19.7   Review Exercise

Choose the correctly spelled words in each sentence below:

1. After they had (<u>carried</u>, carryed) the (radioes, <u>radios</u>) upstairs, they began bringing in the other furniture.

2. The travelers (journied, journeyed) to the remote wilderness of (their, there) dreams.

3. The people gave the space travelers a welcome reserved for (heros, heroes), and then one of the (ladys, ladies) made a speech.

4. I (studyed, studied) a book on the (lives, lifes) of the saints.

5. It (occurred, occured) to Henry Ford that he could make cars more cheaply on an assembly line. He thus (opened, openned) a new factory.

6. You (cannot, can not) have both of your (wishs, wishes).

7. (Let's, Lets) not (deccive, decieve) ourselves.

8. (Its, It's) a shame (your, you're) paper was late.

9. (Who's, Whose) children were they? Did they (appologize, apologize) for what they did?

10. I'd rather have (to, too) much (then, than) too little.

11. (Their, There) was no reason for (their, there) misbehavior.

12. They (threw, through) her into the (hole, hold) in the ground.

13. When my father turned (forty-five, forty five), he said that his life was (one-half, one half) over.

14. We (almost, allmost) forgot to include the (secretary, secretery).

15. You (all ways, always) (achieve, acheive) what you set out to accomplish.

16. His (appearence, appearance) before the (counseler, counselor) left much to be desired.

17. Our nation faces a (dilema, dilemma) in dealing with workers from (forcign, foriegn) countries.

18. The (mischievous, mischeivous) child did (permenent, permanent) damage to the house.

19. Our (handicapt, handicapped) students have not lost (interest, intrest) in trying to make the campus barrier free.

20. (Now a days, Nowadays) there is no (occasion, ocassion) to rebel.

20

Capitalization, Punctuation, and Numbers

20.0   Introduction

IN THIS CHAPTER you will learn the basic rules of capitalization and punctuation. A special section on writing numbers and numerals is also included.

Punctuation refers to all the marks and symbols used in writing: the period, the apostrophe, the comma, the hyphen, and so on. Punctuation is used to clarify the meaning of writing. In the words of the popular novelist Kurt Vonnegut, "If I broke all the rules of punctuation, had words mean whatever I wanted them to mean, and strung them together higgledy-piggledy, I would simply not be understood." This chapter should help you to be understood better in your writing.

It is difficult to learn all the rules of punctuation in a short time. But you can improve your use of punctuation if you consult this chapter while you are editing your writing. The more often you check your punctuation, the more quickly you will master the rules.

20.1   Capitalization

Since many people tend to overuse capital letters, the first rule of capitalization is *do not use a capital letter unless you have a particular reason to do so.* Here are twelve reasons for using capital letters:

1. Capitalize the pronoun *I.*

2. Capitalize the beginning of every sentence.

3. Capitalize the first word of a quoted sentence or part of a sentence:

She said, "You are not too young for Geritol."

Hamlet said, "To be or not to be."

4. Capitalize proper nouns (names of particular people, places, and things) but not general nouns:

Capitalize	Do Not Capitalize
Kennedy High School	my high school
Minneapolis, Minnesota	my home city and state
Labor Day	a holiday
Edward Manly Royall	my grandfather
the United States Constitution	a treaty
Mississippi River	the river
The Institute of Growth	the institute

(Capitalize *t* only if *The* is part of the official name.)

5. Capitalize titles when they are used with proper names:

Capitalize	*Do Not Capitalize*
Dr. Anita Zervigon	our family doctor
Senator Marion Smith	one of the senators
Mr. and Mrs. Johnson	the family next door
Peter B. Morial, Ph.D.	a professor of math

6. Capitalize the days of the week and the months, but not the seasons and general measures of time:

Capitalize	*Do Not Capitalize*
Sunday	summer
Monday	autumn
February	weekend
January	month

7. Capitalize the names of specific courses, language courses, and languages:

Capitalize	*Do Not Capitalize*
Mathematics 102	math
English	physics
Spanish	political science

8. Capitalize the names of relatives when used as proper nouns:

Shall we give Mom her present now?

9. In all titles, capitalize the first and last word and all other words except articles (*a, an,* and *the*), short prepositions (*of, in, on,* and the like), and short conjunctions (*and, or, but,* and so on):

Professor Kahn assigned *The Protestant Ethic and the Spirit of Capitalism.*

10. You may (but do not have to) capitalize the titles of heads of nations:

You May Capitalize	*Do Not Capitalize*
the President of the United States	the president of the college
	the chairman of the board
	the senators in the United States Congress

11. Capitalize *north, east, northwest,* and the like when these words are used to designate recognized geographic areas, but not when used to show direction. *Deep South* is also capitalized.

You must travel east from Hawaii to reach the West.

12. Capitalize words referring to a particular deity, belief, or religious object.

Capitalize	*Do Not Capitalize*
God	the gods are angry
Trinity	divine
Ten Commandments	deity
Hinduism	holy
Bible	a church
Torah	religion
Jehovah	
Koran	

Pronouns referring to deity are often capitalized:

Jehovah, as presented in the Bible, sometimes shows His anger.

 Practice 1

Capitalize as necessary in the sentences that follow.

1. The rules that govern our electoral politics need to be changed.
2. President ~~jimmy carter~~ *Jimmy Carter* lost his attempt for a second term after wasting time, money, and energy working for his reelection.
3. In an article in *newsweek* titled "the six-year presidency," Jack Valenti wrote, "a president's noblest stirring is toward his place in history."
4. willie morris, who wrote *north toward home,* moved to the north but now lives in oxford, mississippi, the deep south.
5. The torah is the jewish name for the first five books of the bible.
6. One wednesday last fall, i began sitting in on a world history class and found it so interesting that i signed up for history 102.
7. My five-year-old son, ted, asked me, "what makes a car run, dad?"
8. I told him, "gasoline, sonny boy."
9. My favorite teacher at carver high school was mr. harry berger, but he is teaching at some junior high school now.
10. As homework, she asked us to write an essay titled "a time I would like to forget."

20.2 End Punctuation

Use either a period (.), a question mark (?), or an exclamation point (!) to end all sentences.

1. Use a period to end a sentence that makes a statement or expresses a command:

Capital punishment is a controversial issue.

Turn in your papers by Friday.

Instead of saying "I do," the bride said, "I don't."

Note that the period is placed inside the quotation marks. A period is also used to indicate most abbreviations:

Mr. (mister)

M.D. (medical doctor)

M.A. (Master of Arts)

P.M. (post meridiem)

Jan. (January)

Note that certain abbreviations—A.M., P.M., B.C., A.D., B.C.E., and C.E.—often appear in typeset materials in "small caps" (capital letters the size of lowercase letters). Consult your dictionary as to the meaning of these terms.

2. Use a question mark to end a sentence that asks a question:

Will you come with me?

"Will you come with me?" he asked.

Note that the question mark is placed inside quotation marks when the quotation is a question. Place the question mark outside the quotation marks when the quoted material is not a question:

Did he say, "I'm ready"?

3. Use an exclamation point to end a sentence that expresses strong emotion:

Stop that fighting!

An exclamation point is also used to indicate an interjection, which may not be a sentence:

Ouch!

Nonsense!

Practice 2

Insert periods, question marks, and exclamation points in the following sentences as necessary.

1. Dr. Sosnoski didn't say, "Will you stop smoking"
2. He said, in a quiet voice, "Stop smoking right now"
3. "Ouch" I said. "That hurts"
4. Can you say, "I will stop smoking right now"
5. "May I wait until after Christmas" I asked
6. "No" he almost shouted "now"
7. Are the surgeon general and Dr. Sosnoski right about smoking

20.3   The Apostrophe

The apostrophe (') has varied uses: to mark the omission of one or more letters or numbers; to form plurals of letters, numerals, and symbols; and to show possession or ownership.

1. Use the apostrophe to mark the omission of one or more letters in contractions:

cannot becomes can't

let us becomes let's

that is becomes that's

it is becomes it's

See pages 409–411 for more examples and for practice in forming contractions.

2. Use the apostrophe to mark the omission of letters and numbers in the following:

of the clock becomes o'clock

the class of 1984 becomes the class of '84

3. Use the apostrophe to mark the omission of letters in quoted dialogue:

He said, "I've just been sittin' and waitin' for my dinner."

4. Use the apostrophe to form the plurals of letters, numerals, and symbols:

one t becomes two t's

one 5 becomes two 5's

one $ becomes two $'s

(Many publishers have dropped the apostrophe in such uses and print the preceding plurals as *two* **ts,** *two 5s, two $s.*) *Note:* **Do** *not* **use the apostrophe to form any other plurals.**

 Practice 3

Supply the necessary apostrophes in the following sentences.

1. Its a long way to his house, but well go there anyway before it is too late.
2. The feminist movement began in about 63 or 64 and is still strong in the 90s.
3. Havent you ever eaten her chicken? Im tellin you, its better than finger lickin good.
4. Its theirs; you cant have it.
5. My children are sick and tired of my telling them to dot their *i*s and cross their *t*s.

Using the Apostrophe to Show Ownership

Use the apostrophe to show ownership.

1. Add *'s* to a singular noun or an indefinite pronoun (*anyone, everyone,* and the like):

the house of Barry becomes Barry's house

the house of Bess becomes Bess's house

the opinion of everyone becomes everyone's opinion

the trials of today becomes today's trials

Do *not* use the apostrophe for the possessive case of personal pronouns:

The new car is ours.

The choice is theirs.

The computer can't make up its mind.

2. Add *'s* to a plural noun that does not end in -*s:*

the play of the children becomes the children's play

the will of the people becomes the people's will

3. Add just the apostrophe to a plural noun that ends in -*s:*

the home of the boys becomes the boys' home

the blades of the propellers becomes the propellers' blades

4. If there is joint ownership between two or more nouns, the final noun takes the apostrophe:

the house of my mother and father becomes my mother and father's house

But notice how the apostrophe is used in the following cases:

Rico's and Donna's watches were stolen. (Here the ownership is not joint because Rico and Donna own their watches separately.)

Gladys's and my house is up for sale. (When the pronoun *my* or *our* is used in such compounds, the apostrophe is added to the noun even though the noun comes first. Note also that *mines* and *my's* are not words.)

5. Add *'s* or just the apostrophe to the last element in a compound word:

the demands of a mother-in-law becomes a mother-in-law's demands

Practice 4

Form the possessive of each of the following.

1. the room of the teachers *the teachers' room* _____

2. the address of the Smiths _____

3. the address of Chen _____

4. the events of today _____

5. the activities of the ladies _____

6. the husband of a woman _____

7. the relationship of a man and a woman _____

8. the good fortune of a son-in-law _____

9. the attitude of the boy _____

10. the attitude of the boys _____

11. the attitude of the people _____

Practice 5

Correct the errors in apostrophe use in the following sentences. Some of the apostrophes have been misused; others have been omitted, along with the *-s*. (One sentence is correct.) *Remember:* Do not use an apostrophe when you are simply adding an *-s* to make a plural.

1. President Carter recognized the ~~Peoples~~ *People's* Republic of China.

2. Her ~~sons~~ *sons'* wives all call her Mother, and she calls them her daughters.

3. His victory was everyones victory.

4. Sandra many boyfriends got together for a reunion.

5. The childrens constant crying is driving me insane.

6. The peoples' fear of crime is increasing.

7. My daughter Marys name for ballet is *baleg*.

8. Her two boys' call a window a *windoor.*

9. I like to shop at Natures Way.

10. The Joneses rent is due.

11. Pierre's and Violette's car is in the shop.

12. Uziel's and Boaz's names come from the Bible.

13. There is so much smoke from the factories that the air smells as though someone house is on fire.

14. My neighbors lawns have almost been ruined by that garbage truck.

15. In our neighborhood we have different committee's to keep things running smoothly.

16. About seven o'clock you can hear the children mother screaming, "Tommy, Angela, come in! It's time to eat."

17. Next to Saint Raymonds Catholic Church is the priests home, where eight of these padres live.

20.4   The Comma

Conventional use of the comma (,) is perhaps the most difficult punctuation skill to master. Professional writers themselves often disagree about certain uses of the comma. Students tend to overuse commas, perhaps because they were taught to use a comma anytime they wanted to indicate a pause in a sentence. To avoid comma errors, it is best to learn the general rules for comma use and to follow the advice of the old saying: *When in doubt, leave it out.* As you learn the ten rules given in this text, you can begin to insert commas. Refer frequently to these rules when you are editing your papers.

Rule 1:   Use a comma before a coordinating conjunction when it joins two independent clauses. The coordinating conjunctions are *and, but, for, yet, so, or,* and *nor:*

> The weather was stormy, and it was very late.

> The weather was stormy, but I was not cold.

Do *not* use a comma before a coordinating conjunction when it joins two words, two phrases, or two dependent clauses:

> <u>Carlos</u> and <u>Lucia</u> are going swimming. (two nouns)

> At lunchtime we <u>were throwing</u> our food away and <u>were creating</u> quite a disturbance. (two verb phrases)

> When you see those things happen, you will know <u>that the time</u> has <u>come for action</u> and <u>that everyone should help.</u> (two dependent clauses)

 ### Practice 6

Supply the necessary commas.

> The fire that raged through our town last year started at a grassy intersection and quickly spread until it reached the village. Firemen were on the scene almost at once but the huge numbers of cars parked downtown blocked them from keeping up with the fire. People soon began to move their cars and the fire fighters were finally able to get the blaze under control. Luckily, no one was injured nor was there any serious damage to people's property.

Rule 2:   Use a comma after a subordinate clause when it begins a sentence. Subordinate clauses begin with such conjunctions as *when, if, because, after, although, as, while, since, even though, before,* and *whenever:*

> While the girl pushed the car, her father watched.

However, when the dependent clause comes at the end of the sentence, you do not ordinarily need a comma. (See Rule 10 below for exceptions.)

> Her father watched while the girl pushed the car.

 ### Practice 7

Supply the necessary commas.

> We were greatly surprised when we found out that Mr. Morales had cancer. But we are not depressed. While there is life there is hope. We know he will get well be-

cause he is such a fighter. If Mr. Morales will just do what the doctor says he will live many more years.

Rule 3:   Use commas to set off an adjective clause if the clause is not *essential* to the meaning of the sentence. Adjective clauses usually begin with *who, which,* or *that:*

> My mother, who likes sardine sandwiches, is an unusual person.

You can omit the clause *who likes sardine sandwiches,* and the sentence will still make sense. Therefore, you need the commas. But if the adjective clause is *essential* to the meaning of the sentence, do not use commas:

> My mother is the only one in our family who likes sardine sandwiches.

This time, if you omit the clause *who likes sardine sandwiches,* the sentence does not make sense.
   Hint: Which clauses usually take commas; *that* clauses seldom do.

Practice 8

Supply the necessary commas.

> Great Britain who was our ally went to war with Argentina who was also our ally. Americans who sided with either Argentina or Britain were criticized. This war which caused many deaths was a tragedy and should never have happened.

Rule 4:   Use a comma or commas to set off most conjunctive adverbs (words and phrases like *however, for example, on the other hand, nevertheless, moreover, particularly, especially, therefore,* and *consequently*):

> I know I said I would go; however, I have since changed my mind. (Here, *however* follows a semicolon.)

> I agree that is what I should do. However, I just cannot bring myself to do it. (Here, *however* begins a new sentence.)

> Children learn to read, however, in spite of poor teaching. (Here, *however* comes in the middle of a simple sentence.)

You usually do not use a comma to set off *then* and *also,* although if you want to indicate a significant pause, you may.

Practice 9

Supply the necessary commas.

Joseph's brothers had sold him into slavery; however he not only forgave them but also extended to them the hand of friendship. When his father Jacob heard the news, he decided to travel to Egypt. Jacob was an old man; nevertheless he was determined to see his son. When his father arrived, Joseph fell at his knees; then he wept. Joseph had many fine qualities for example his courage, his determination, and his love.

Rule 5:   Use a comma or commas to set off an *appositive,* a word, phrase, or clause used as a noun that identifies or explains another noun or pronoun.

Those were the happiest days of my life, the days when I was young and foolish. (The noun *days* is repeated and then explained.)

One of their neighbors, Boo Radley, was a very mysterious person. (The pronoun *one* is identified as Boo Radley.)

We like starches, especially grits, rice, and barley.

Practice 10

Supply the necessary commas.

She lived her entire life in that house a house that had once been admired by all. When I knew her, the building was dilapidated. The porch a beautifully constructed work of art was now rotting. The front door, which had been brought over from England, was nailed shut. Curtains now nothing but rags hung wearily behind cloudy windows. Aunt Kathleen, however, a woman in her eighties did not change. She was poor but still proud.

Rule 6:   Use commas between items in a series (three or more words, phrases, or clauses). Unless your teacher instructs otherwise, use the comma before the conjunction that connects the last item to the others:

She bought <u>apples</u>, <u>oranges</u>, and <u>bananas</u>. (nouns)

Chitty Chat likes <u>to eat tuna</u>, <u>climb Christmas trees</u>, and <u>chase Hubert</u>. (infinitive phrases)

<u>We went home</u>, <u>we took a dip in the pool</u>, and <u>then we ate breakfast</u>. (independent clauses)

When adjectives occur in a series, use a comma between the adjectives *only* if you could replace the comma with the word *and.* For example,

He was a tall, lean man.

The comma is correct because you could write *He was a tall and lean man.* But look at the next sentence:

He was a nice old man.

A comma is not correct because you would not be apt to write *He was a nice and old man.*

Practice 11

Supply the necessary commas.

You are so civilized so intelligent and so self-possessed that you ought to be *Time's* "Man of the Year." But *Time* named that determined courageous man from Poland instead.

Rule 7:   Use a comma or commas with direct quotations:

The ranger said, "Watch out for bears."

"Watch out for bears," said the ranger.

"Watch out for bears," said the ranger, "and don't leave any food for them."

The ranger said, "Watch out for bears," and then he left them.

Note: The comma is always placed inside the quotation marks.
Do not use commas with indirect quotations:

The ranger said to watch out for bears.

The ranger said that we should watch out for bears.

Practice 12

Supply the necessary commas.

"If I were you" my dad said "I wouldn't go out in the rain." "Well" I answered "be glad you aren't me." "I am" he said.

"This will be the first time I have voted in a national election" replied Martin.

Rule 8:   Use a comma or commas to set off items in dates and addresses, but not ZIP codes:

I was born Friday, October 12, 1968, in Charleston, South Carolina.

His address is Apt. A, 1426 M Street, Washington, DC 20012.

Practice 13

Supply the necessary commas.

> Abraham Lincoln was born in Hardin County Kentucky on February 12 1809.
>
> He died on April 15 1865 in Washington DC.
>
> The family living at 225 Goddard Avenue moved in on July 22 1997.

Rule 9:   Use a comma after an introductory phrase if the comma makes the meaning of the sentence clearer:

> After eating, my horse and I set out on our lonesome trip.
>
> In the still of the night, groans can sometimes be heard from the chest in the attic.

Avoid using commas after short introductory phrases if the meaning of the sentence is clear without the comma:

> Later that day they came to our rescue.

 Practice 14

Supply the necessary commas.

> While visiting Anna suddenly became ill. After trying for hours to locate her husband my sister and I took her to the hospital. At about ten o'clock her husband finally arrived.

Rule 10:   Use a comma or commas to set off words, phrases, or clauses if they *clearly* break the flow of the sentence. Sometimes the word or words will be at the beginning of the sentence:

> Darren, please drop what you are doing and give me a hand.

Sometimes the word or words will be in the middle of the sentence:

> My grandmother, known for her habit of chewing tobacco, is nearly ninety. (This break in the middle of a sentence is often a nonessential adjective clause or an appositive. See Rule 3 and Rule 5.)

Sometimes the word or words will be at the end of the sentence, almost as an afterthought:

> Anthony was completely honest about what he had done, not that I would have expected him to act any differently. (You are safe using a comma before all such constructions with *not.*)

You do agree with me, don't you?

I think we should do everything possible to find a peaceful solution, although I must say that I am not optimistic. (Even though the dependent clause comes at the end of a sentence, the comma is necessary because the clause is clearly an afterthought.)

They ended the day in complete silence, knowing that any sound would give them away.

Practice 15

Supply the necessary commas.

Bob said to me, "Carlos that game was the greatest wasn't it?" I turned to my friend who was grinning at me devilishly and said, "Great for you my friend not for me." One of these days I am going to beat Bob in Scrabble although lately I haven't even come close.

Practice 16

Using Rules 1 and 2, supply commas as needed in the following sentences, citing the rule that applies in each case. (Not all sentences need commas.)

1. My name is Bobby Carter, and I'm looking forward to writing this paper. _Rule 1_

2. As I have already said job opportunities in my field are not good. _____

3. I will know how to handle my clients and will be able to represent them well. _____

4. If you can survive this course you will do well in your chosen career. _____

5. I may never become rich but I will be able to acquire the things I want. _____

6. If I were to study nursing I know I would like it. _____

7. She wants to complete college but does not know for sure what the future holds for her. _____

8. My aunt wants to help open the daycare center but she does not want to work there. _____

9. I wanted to be a bank robber when I was young. _____

10. Although a degree is not needed to open a nursery school it would help. _____

11. Because you work hard you will succeed. _____

12. You will succeed because you work hard. _____

Practice 17

Using Rules 3 to 5, supply commas as needed in the following sentences, citing the rule or rules that apply in each case.

1. Sybil, who is a member of the Symphony Club, gave us two tickets for the performance.   *Rule 3*

2. Joe registered late; consequently, he will have to pay a five-dollar fine

    _____

3. Edgar Allan Poe the master writer of horror stories did not enjoy great popularity during his lifetime. _____

4. Only one person a carpenter was injured.

5. My English textbook which had been lost all semester turned up the day classes ended. _____

6. Our family likes living near the coast because we all love fresh seafood especially shrimp, redfish, and crab. _____

7. Many plants are killed by owners who pay too much attention to them; for example overwatering has killed many a plant. _____

8. André who had been cramming the whole night slept through the test. _____

9. We rushed to the theater to see the movie from the beginning; however it had already started when we arrived. _____

10. Chico our eccentric next-door neighbor is the only person I know who mows his lawn in a bathing suit. _____

11. Immunizations are now available for diphtheria, one of the most dangerous childhood ailments. _____

12. My aunt spends most of her free time involved in outdoor activities particularly fishing, hunting, and camping. _____

Practice 18

Using Rules 6 to 10, supply commas as needed in the following sentences, citing the rule or rules that apply in each case:

1. I told her not to worry but to stay cool,

   calm, and collected.   *Rule 6*

2. It was a dark rainy spring day when we first met wasn't it? _____

3. Before riding in the automobile with my father my sister always takes a tranquilizer. _____

4. The city council voted yesterday to increase the sales tax although they know the citizens will rise up in protest. _____

5. As director you will be responsible for the management of the center the hiring and training of the personnel and the development of new

   programs. _____

6. "Ask not what your country can do for you" President Kennedy said "ask what you can do for your country." _____

7. In the middle of the night time stands still, and you can hear the lonely sound of a hoot owl. _____

8. Make love not war. _____

9. "War is not what I want" he said "but peace." _____

10. I left home suitcase in hand not knowing what I would do next. _____

11. Malcolm X, the controversial leader of a movement to unite black people throughout the world, was assassinated in New York City on February 21 1965. _____

Practice 19

Using Rules 1 to 10, supply commas as needed in the following sentences, citing the rule or rules that apply in each case. (Some sentences are correct.)

1. *Dictionary* spelled backwards is *yranoitcid,* but *madam* spelled backwards is *madam.*   *Rule 1*

2. We ended up walking in circles and bumping into the same security officer.

   _____

3. As the three of us walked outside we argued about where we had parked the car. _____

4. He said that he wanted the choir to sing at his wake and that he wanted to be buried in his choir robes. _____

5. That afternoon we divided into groups and searched the library for the items on the list. _____

6. All the girls wanted the leading part because it was that of a glamorous woman. _____

7. After we unloaded the bus our next task was to pitch the tent. _____

8. I tried to light the stove but I was unsuccessful because the matches were wet. _____

9. I tried to light the stove but was unsuccessful because the matches were wet. _____

10. Finally when we arrived at the Rivergate the people applauded us and the whole effort seemed worthwhile. _____

11. I love seafood especially crab shrimp and oysters. _____

12. I was guarding Tim Owens a 6'6" guard and I am only 6'. _____

13. If you look back you will turn into a pillar of salt. _____

14. You will turn into a pillar of salt if you look back. _____

15. Dwight Eisenhower the thirty-fourth president of the United States was born in Denison Texas on October 14 1890. _____

16. As I continued to walk down the road I noticed a small inviting brown cabin with smoke coming from the chimney. _____

17. We shared some very hard times but through it all we stuck together and became like sisters. _____

18. "Life is like walking in the snow" Granny used to say "because every step shows." _____

19. In 1985 the navy sent our family to Los Angeles California where I attended Grossmand High School and met Kim Steve and Colleen. _____

20. Honestly I am about ready to scream; these commas are just too much! _____

20.5   The Semicolon

The semicolon (;) can be used to join independent clauses in compound sentences. Sentences take semicolons when the following occur:

   1. The pronoun subject of the second independent clause refers to a noun in the first independent clause:

The <u>prisoners</u> at the penitentiary are rioting; <u>they</u> claim that the new warden has been unfair.

After just three days Gina quit her <u>job;</u> <u>it</u> didn't hold her interest.

   2. One independent clause is related to another by a conjunctive adverb, such as *then* or *however:*

We first tried giving money to that country; <u>then</u> we sent soldiers.

The governor refused to grant the pardon; <u>however,</u> he did say he might consider the case again next year.

Use the semicolon to make a compound sentence *only* if the two independent clauses are closely related in content and *only* if a period could be substituted for the semicolon. The following sentence is incorrect because the semicolon makes the last part of the sentence into a fragment:

In those days he tried various drugs; for example, marijuana, LSD, and cocaine.

If you substituted a period for the semicolon, the last part of the sentence would also be a fragment:

For example, marijuana, LSD, and cocaine.

The semicolon can be used to set off items in a series if any one of the items has internal punctuation:

For the climb up Long's Peak, we took a tent, which weighed only five pounds; two very light goose-down sleeping bags; and enough food for a large, hungry army.

   Practice 20

Correct the misused semicolons in the following sentences. (Five sentences are correct.)

   1. Chief Donald Sartisky completed twenty years in the Coast Guard ⁄ and then decided to go back to college to finish his degree.

2. He found college quite different from the way he remembered it; however, he adjusted quickly to the new atmosphere.

3. He likes to say, "It is even more difficult; than I remember, but I like the challenge."

4. To his surprise, he found that he had much in common with quite a few of the students; many of them were as old as he.

5. The chief was a hospital corpsman in the Coast Guard; and he wants to pursue a career in nursing when he finishes college.

6. Bridge is more than a game of cards; it is a science.

7. Vacations are not a luxury these days; they are a necessity.

8. Marlene is pleased with the pay at Hibernia National Bank, moreover; she likes the people.

9. The president is correct about inflation being an immense problem, however; he doesn't know what to do about it.

10. I wish everyone would hike in the Smoky Mountains; they are spectacular.

20.6   The Colon

The colon (:) can be used in various situations:

1. After the salutation in a business letter:

Dear Dr. Rittenberg:

Note: A comma is used after the salutation in a personal letter.

2. To separate numbers in the time of day and in biblical passages:

1:15 A.M.

Exodus 3:15 (chapter 3, verse 15)

3. Before items in a series that follow what could be written as a grammatically complete sentence:

Be sure to buy the following: dates, pecans, raisins, and honey.

But do not use a colon when the items in the series are necessary for the sentence to be complete:

INCORRECT
As for me, I like: sugar, canned foods, and lots of meat.

CORRECT

As for me, I like sugar, canned foods, and lots of red meat.

4. To introduce indented quotations and quotations that are preceded by grammatically complete sentences:

Dr. Hume wrote the following in his book *Doctors East, Doctors West:* "Only those can enter into her life who approach China's citadel by way of friendship."

When you introduce a written quotation with verbs like *write, say,* and *state,* it is usually appropriate to use only a comma:

In his book Dr. Hume writes, "Only those can enter into her life who approach China's citadel by way of friendship."

20.7   Quotation Marks and Underlining

Quotation marks (" ") are always used in pairs. (Do not allow end quotation marks to carry over to the beginning of a new line, and do not end a line with beginning quotation marks.) Quotation marks have several functions.

Direct Quotations

Quotation marks are used to set off direct quotations, which are the exact words someone says or writes. The quoted words are often a sentence within a sentence:

The coach said to his team, "Go out there and win!"

Note the following about this sentence:

1. The words the coach said, *Go out there and win!,* can function as a complete sentence. (The subject *you* is understood.)

2. The comma comes before the direct quotation.

3. The second set of quotation marks comes after the exclamation point.

Here are two variations of the preceding quotation. Notice the position of the quotation marks, commas, exclamation points, and question marks and the use of capitalization.

"Go out there and win!" the coach said to the team.

"Go out there," the coach said to the team, "and win!"

The following sentences also demonstrate how quotations can be presented:

"Will you help with the work?" Alan asked. "We'll need your strength!"

"Will you help with the work? We'll need your strength," said Alan.

Alan said, "Will you help with the work? We'll need your strength."

Notice that in the last two sentences, quotation marks are used only at the beginning and end of what Alan said, not at the end of each sentence.

If you must use a quotation mark within another quotation, use single quotation marks (' ') to indicate the inside quotation:

The speaker stated his position as follows: "I firmly believe that fantasy is an important part of life. I always think of the newspaper editor who answered the letter of a young girl by writing, 'Yes, Virginia, there *is* a Santa Claus.'"

Practice 21

Supply quotation marks, other punctuation, and capitalization as needed in the following sentences.

1. What's the matter Richard's mother asked. *"What's the matter?"*
   Richard's mother asked.

2. It's those same boys he said. They'll beat me. _____

   _____

3. You've got to get over that. Now go on she said. _____ _____

   _____

4. Richard replied but I'm scared. _____

   _____

5. She said how can I let you back down now. _____

   _____

6. Please Momma he said don't make me fight. _____

   _____

Indirect Quotations

Do not use quotation marks to set off indirect quotations, which are *not* the exact words that someone says or writes. For example,

She said she would try harder next time.

The words she actually used were these: "I will try harder next time." She did *not* say "She would try harder next time." The writer used these words to tell what she said. Here are two more examples of indirect quotations:

> Dr. Hume wrote that to enter into the life of China one must approach that nation by way of friendship.

> The union members carried signs saying that they would not compromise.

Practice 22

Rewrite the following direct quotations as indirect quotations. Change verbs to the past tense as necessary.

1. The school board said to the union, "You are demanding far too much money."

   The school board said to the union that it was demanding far too much money.

2. The union replied, "We want only a fair wage." _____

   _____

3. The school board said, "Take your case to the taxpayers." _____

   _____

4. The union then said, "The school board is responsible for the wages of teachers." _____

   _____

Practice 23

Rewrite the following indirect quotations as direct quotations. Change verbs to the present tense as necessary.

1. The police chief said that he needed more cooperation from the judges. *The police chief said, "I need more cooperation from the judges."*

2. The judges said that they were already giving out much stiffer sentences.

   _____

   _____

3. The police chief responded that dangerous criminals were still being allowed to roam the streets. _____

   _____

4. The judges said that they could not be blamed for the amount of crime in the streets. _____

_____

5. The police chief said that the judges could help. _____

_____

Other Uses of Quotation Marks and Underlining

Quotation marks have other uses as well:

1. To set off words used as words:

Students often confuse "their" with "there."

However, it is just as correct to underline such words:

Students often confuse their with there.

Use underlining, not quotation marks, for foreign words:

coup de grâce

femme fatale

Note: In print, italics replace underlining.

2. To set off the titles of short published works:

a magazine article—"The Power of Islam"

a book chapter—"A Time to Laugh"

a poem—"Freedom"

an essay—"The Time I Learned Humility"

Longer works are underlined (italicized in print):

a book—To Kill a Mockingbird

a play—Macbeth

a magazine—Newsweek

Longer works (which are underlined) often contain shorter works (which take quotation marks). For example, a book contains chapters, and a magazine contains articles.

3. To set off the titles of television programs and songs:

"60 Minutes"

"Hey Jude"

However, the titles of movies are underlined:

<u>The Lion King</u>

20.8   Other Punctuation: The Hyphen, the Dash, and Parentheses

Since the hyphen is an important part of spelling, it is discussed in Section 19.5. Use the dash (—) and parentheses [( )] as follows:

1. Use the dash to emphasize certain words, usually at the end of the sentence:

One punctuation mark is misused more than any other—the comma.

There is just one course that I can never seem to pass—Math 110.

2. Use the dash to indicate an aside to the reader:

She said the "girls"—they are all over sixty—would play bridge tonight.

The game between Alabama and Michigan—it is sure to be close—will be played in the Superdome.

Note: When typing, use two hyphens for a dash, and do not leave a space on either side of it.

3. You may substitute parentheses for the dash when you make an aside to the reader:

She said the "girls" (they are all over sixty) would play bridge tonight.

The game between Alabama and Michigan (it is sure to be close) will be played in the Superdome.

4. Use parentheses to indicate a span of dates:

Booker T. Washington (1856–1915) was a black American educator.

In her article in the *Atlantic Monthly* (May 1986), Barbara Wallraff wrote about the various kinds of pens.

20.9 Numbers and Numerals

Numbers can be either spelled out or written as numerals. As a general rule, spell out numbers that can be written as one or two words: *forty, sixty-three, five hundred, two million, three-fourths.* Use numerals for all other numbers (110,401; 325; 6,179).

Exceptions

1. Spell out all numbers that begin sentences:

Two hundred forty-one people are still missing.

2. Use numerals for the following:

   a. Most dates:
       October 12, 1938

But spell out *the twelfth of October.*

   b. Most dollar amounts:
       $10.51 $3.01 $17.00

But spell out numbers used to indicate general amounts (*a hundred dollars, five million dollars*).

   c. Street numbers:
       42 Legare Street

   d. Percentage amounts:
       20 percent of your earnings

   e. Times used with A.M. and P.M.:
       8:00 A.M.

But spell out *five o'clock* and *six-thirty* when used without A.M. and P.M.

   f. Page and line numbers:
       page 42, line 15

   g. Numbers in a list, such as the following:
       5 lbs. chicken   3 onions
       2 cups cream   1 lb. bacon
       1 1/2 cups flour   1/2 lb. mushrooms

3. If you write one number in a sentence as a numeral, write all the other numbers as numerals:

I caught 416 pounds of fish, 50 pounds of shrimp, and 91 dozen crabs last summer.

Hyphens

Use a hyphen (-) with all two-word numbers from twenty-one to ninety-nine and with all fractions (three-fourths, nine-tenths, and so forth).

Practice 24

Correct the use of numerals and words in the following. (Five are correct.)

1. ~~Nineteen hundred and one~~ (a date)   *1901*
2. Six o'clock
3. 5:30 P.M.
4. Five dollars and fourteen cents
5. Page sixteen
6. 51 Canal Street
7. 8 o'clock
8. 56 percent
9. $10,550.00
10. Two-thirty P.M.

20.10   Review Exercise

Choose the correct alternative in the following sentences. (*NP* means no punctuation is needed.)

1. Stop that fighting (! *or* .)
2. She said, "Will you help me with my car ("? *or* ?")
3. (Let's *or* Lets) be on our way.
4. Our (children's *or* childrens') friends fill our house with excitement.
5. We now have diplomatic relations with the (Peoples' *or* People's) Republic of China.
6. It was the hottest day of the year (, *or* ;) but we were comfortable inside with our air conditioning turned on.
7. We became stuck on the mud bank (, *or* NP) because the tide fell several feet.
8. When I knew her (, *or* NP) she was already eighty years old.
9. "Give me cold weather anytime (", *or* ,") she said.
10. Be sure to include the following (: *or* ;) a purpose statement, good transition sentences, effective details, and a conclusion.
11. They said that (" *or* NP) they would try harder next time (." *or* .)
12. My favorite movie of all time is ("The African Queen." *or The African Queen.*)
13. "If you come to work with me," he said, ("You *or* "you) will be rich."
14. (Everyones' *or* Everyone's) opinion has changed since the last election.
15. Mona was (president *or* President) of her high school class.
16. Kyle said that he was angry about the sale (, *or* NP) and that he would protest.

17. "People (, *or* NP) who need people (, *or* NP) are the luckiest people in the world."

18. We first tried to make peace (, *or* ;) then we sent in soldiers.

19. He looked up the article in ("Newsweek." *or* *Newsweek*.)

20. At the last count, (46 *or* forty-six) people were still missing.

21

Writing Effective Sentences

21.0   Introduction

IN THIS CHAPTER you will learn different ways of expressing yourself in sentences. As you study simple, compound, and complex sentences, you will learn how to give variety to your writing. You also will review several ways to use commas.

A *sentence* is a group of words expressing a thought that can stand on its own. Most everything that you write in a freshman English course should be in sentence form. Exceptions are titles of essays and sometimes quotations from conversations. Here are two tests that will help you determine whether a statement is a sentence:

1. If you made the statement to someone, would it make sense by itself? If someone wrote only the statement on a note to you, would it make sense?
2. Does the statement have a subject (at least understood) and a verb?

Writing in complete sentences is a natural process because we usually talk in sentence form. To write consistently in complete sentences, the most important thing to remember is to *listen* to what you are writing. Read your writing aloud, sentence by sentence, and ask if each sentence can stand alone.

Practice 1

Identify which statements on the list below are sentences (mark these *S*) and which are not sentences (mark these *N*). Apply this test: If you made the statement to someone, would it make sense? Would it make sense if you received it by itself in a note? Remember that whole sentences can begin with pronoun subjects.

1. __S__ Shut the door.

2. _____ Will you help me with my homework?

3. _____ Because they live on Park Place.

4. _____ When I leave home at seven to catch the 7:15 bus.

5. _____ The novel about the best of times and the worst of times.

6. _____ The time I went to see Aunt Nancy in Philadelphia.

7. _____ Which is a most controversial law.

8. _____ You should know what to do.

9. _____ To dress up my walls with brightly colored paintings.

10. _____ First, how my pet and I are alike.

Practice 2

Choose ten people whom you know, and write one complete sentence about each person. You may want to write about their work, their personality, or what they were doing the last time you saw them. Apply the sentence test: Does your statement make sense by itself? Underline the subject once and the verb twice. For example:

Wendy Johnson has studied karate for seven years.

21.1   The Simple Sentence

A *simple sentence* consists of only one independent clause. Clauses can be dependent (those which cannot stand alone) or independent (those which can stand alone). The following are dependent clauses:

because they are our neighbors

when the test is administered

which she gave us

as the president says

Each clause has a subject (underlined once) and verb (underlined twice), but none can stand alone; thus they are called *dependent.* (If written by themselves, they would be fragments.)

However, the following clauses are independent:

they are our neighbors

the test is administered each Friday

she gave us a dictionary

the president said it

Each could be written as a simple sentence, as follows:

They are our neighbors.

The test is administered each Friday.

She gave us a dictionary.

The president said it.

These are sentences because each has a subject and verb and can stand alone; they are simple sentences because each consists of one independent clause. Notice that, as sentences, each begins with a capital letter and ends with a period.

A simple sentence often has two or more subjects (called *compound subjects*) or two or more verbs (called *compound verbs*):

Ahmad and Alice made A's. (compound subjects)

They walked and jogged for three hours. (compound verbs)

Practice 3

Write simple sentences, using the designated words as subjects. Underline the subjects once and the verbs twice.

1. (Charlie Brown) *Charlie Brown has a very common name.*

_____

2. (the catcher) _____

_____

3. (Bill Clinton) _____

_____

4. (tennis and swimming) _____

_____

5. (Jackie and Susan) _____

_____

Practice 4

Write simple sentences, using the designated words as verbs. Underline the subjects once and the verbs twice.

1. (strutted) *She strutted down the aisle.*

_____

2. (teased and flirted) _____

_____

3. (loves) _____

_____

4. (comes and goes) _____

_____

5. (devoured) _____

_____

Practice 5

Underline the four simple sentences in the following paragraph.

This story began in 1948, when my mother was a girl. One day she was running and playing in a cornfield. A crow flew around the field and suddenly lit on my mother's shoulder, and she gave him an ear of corn. Every day from then on the crow and my mother would meet in the cornfield. Mother fed the crow, and the crow perched on her shoulder. They walked together that way all over the field. One day, Mother went to the field to play, and the crow was lying in the dirt, dead. She told her mother, who said, "Baby, the dead crow means that someone close to you is going to die." That night her uncle Al died of a heart attack.

21.2   The Compound Sentence

A *compound sentence* consists of two or more independent clauses, each of which has its own subject and verb and is able to stand alone. For example,

> The slender girl pushed the big car, and her father gave her encouragement.

Both underlined clauses are independent: They could each be written separately as simple sentences. The joining word *and* is called a *coordinating conjunction* because it joins two clauses. There are seven coordinating conjunctions. Memorize them.

> and   but   for   or   nor   yet   so

Here are three more compound sentences with coordinating conjunctions:

> He really did not mean to do it, but he could not help himself.
>
> The jurors' faces were tense, for they were about to sentence a man to die.
>
> He could rush into battle and be killed, or he could desert and be executed.

Notice that a comma is used before each coordinating conjunction. A comma is *not* used before the conjunction *so,* however, if you could write or say the word *that* after it.

> We left the party so that we could get to bed early.

Practice 6

In the following paragraph, underline the compound sentences and insert the necessary commas before the coordinating conjunctions.

This past Tuesday night, my husband and I were shopping at Maison Blanche and we were about to call it a night. Just before we left, we met Ed, an old friend from high school days. I asked the usual question about how his family was. To our shock, we discovered that Ed and his wife had been divorced. I have come across this unhappy situation many times but each time it shocks and saddens me. The rising divorce rate is especially distressing for many of the marriages could have been saved. Since Tuesday night I have been depressed and have been wondering how secure my own marriage is.

Using Coordinating Conjunctions

As pointed out above, compound sentences consist of two or more independent clauses. If you leave out the coordinating conjunction and substitute a period for the comma, each clause can function as a simple sentence. For example,

Our club sponsored a car wash on Saturday. ~~and~~ we were quite successful.

I like strawberry ice cream. ~~but~~ Sal prefers chocolate chip.

Notice that if you leave out *and* in the first sentence, you would have two separate sentences. However, by using *and* you show a close relationship between two ideas. In the second sentence, *but* shows a contrast between two ideas. Each of the seven coordinating conjunctions has a special function:

1. *And* means addition:

The Bernados sisters are having a big party Saturday night, <u>and</u> everyone is invited.

2. *But* means contrast:

The Bernados sisters are having a big party Saturday night, <u>but</u> their parents do not know it.

3. *For* shows reason and thus means roughly the same as *because:*

The Bernados sisters are having a big party Saturday night, <u>for</u> it is the only time everyone can come.

4. *Or* shows choice:

The Bernados sisters may have a party Saturday night, *or* they may choose to have it Friday night instead.

5. *Nor* (like *or*) shows choice, but *nor* shows negative choice:

Tony does not plan to come, <u>nor</u> will he encourage his friends to come.

Notice that when *nor* joins clauses, the order of the second clause is inverted, as in a question, and the first clause contains a negative word such as *not*.

6. *Yet* (like *but*) shows contrast:

Tony does not plan to attend the party, <u>yet</u> he admits it will probably be fun.

7. *So* shows results and thus means roughly the same as *therefore:*

Tony does not plan to attend the party, <u>so</u> he will be free on Saturday night.

 ## Practice 7

Combine the following pairs of sentences, using *and, but, for,* and *or* at least once.

1. It is best not to thrash around in shark-infested waters. The movement and the sound might attract the sharks.
2. My family is planning to leave town on the tenth. We will be gone about two weeks.
3. Our house is small and dark. I like it.
4. You need to make a decision quickly. Time is running out.
5. We may go to a movie tonight. We may stay home and watch TV.
6. I am usually in bed by 10:00 P.M. My roommate is a night owl.
7. Our tennis match is scheduled for late afternoon. We plan to have dinner afterward.
8. I may decide to continue my subscription to *Time* for another year. I may cancel it now.

Did you insert commas before the coordinating conjunctions?

 ## Practice 8

Combine the pairs of sentences below, using *nor, yet,* and *so* at least once. (*Remember:* You must change the order of the wording of the sentence when you use *nor.*)

1. My sister is not fond of raw oysters. She does not like any other shellfish.
2. This movie is rated PG. We probably should not take your four-year-old niece.
3. Julio is rather an odd-looking character. Many women find him attractive.

4. Amy will enter an ice-skating competition next month. She practices several hours a day.

5. In buying his clothes, George does not listen to his friends' advice. He does not pay attention to current fashion either.

6. Marcus Duffy is in his sixties. He still jogs several miles a day.

Did you insert commas before the coordinating conjunctions?

21.3   The Compound Sentence with a Conjunctive Adverb

One way to join two independent clauses is with a *conjunctive adverb*. Conjunctive adverbs include *then, moreover, consequently, however,* and *for example*. Sometimes the conjunctive adverbs are preceded by the conjunction *and*, as follows:

First, they held up the store, <u>and</u> <u>then</u> they shot the owner.

More often, conjunctive adverbs are preceded by a semicolon (;):

It is a good day for catching pompano; <u>however</u>, with my luck we will probably catch toadfish instead.

Here are some of the most common conjunctive adverbs, organized by function:

1. Time—*then, next:*

First, we visited the Washington Monument, and <u>then</u> we toured the White House.

2. Addition—*also, moreover, furthermore:*

We saw Saint John's Church, and <u>also</u> we toured some of the exhibits in the Smithsonian.

We saw Saint John's Church; <u>moreover</u>, we toured some of the exhibits in the Smithsonian.

3. Results—*consequently, thus, therefore:*

Summer vacation begins on the first of June; <u>consequently</u>, I cannot begin to work until then.

4. Contrast—*however, nevertheless, on the other hand:*

Rudolfo originally planned to join us; <u>however</u>, he later changed his mind.

5. Illustration—*for example, for instance:*

We have many privileges in this country that we take for granted; <u>for example,</u> almost everyone has easy access to a public library.

Note that a comma follows most conjunctive adverbs, as shown in four of the examples above. However, a comma does not usually follow *then* or *also.* (See the first two examples above.)

Practice 9

Using the preceding examples as models, write five of your own compound sentences, using a conjunctive adverb from each group. Be sure to use commas and semicolons correctly. You might write something like this:

First, I will finish college, and then I will go to law school.

Practice 10

Combine the following pairs of sentences with *and* and a conjunctive adverb or with a semicolon and a conjunctive adverb. Use at least one conjunctive adverb from each of the five groups above. Supply commas as needed.

1. I must study first, ~~After that~~ *, and then* I may go to the movies with you.
2. I was not sick after eating the pizza and marshmallows, *; however,* Helen and Tom missed two days of school because of their indulgence.
3. We had many things to talk about. The time passed quickly.
4. The poet Keats died in his mid-twenties. His poetry is more valued than that of many a writer who lived to a ripe old age.
5. The barbeque restaurant will probably be more successful now that it is in a better location. Its new management is first rate.
6. Paula knows how to fix anything. She even fixed her grandfather's cuckoo clock.
7. It was only a small, inexpensive gift. It was a well-chosen one.
8. I enjoy working in the early morning because I feel rested then. It is the only time the house is quiet.
9. Every day Mrs. Carr picks whatever is ripe. After that she feeds the chickens.
10. Christy Brown was an Irish writer who was severely physically disabled from birth. He published several extraordinary books in his lifetime.
11. The day was clear and sunny. We decided to move the party out-of-doors.
12. Thousands of people greet each other every day in the Los Angeles airport. It is not the place to form a lasting relationship.

21.4   The Complex Sentence with a Subordinating Conjunction

A *complex sentence* consists of an independent clause and one or more dependent clauses. Here are two ways to write the same sentence:

dependent clause   independent clause
        ↓   ↓

Because I was sick, I stayed home.

independent clause   dependent clause
        ↓   ↓

I stayed home because I was sick.

Notice that a comma is used after the dependent clause when it begins a sentence, but that a comma is not used when the dependent clause comes after the independent clause. You can usually recognize dependent clauses in complex sentences by the words that introduce them. There are two classes of these words: *subordinating conjunctions* (such as *when, while, because, if, before*, and *unless*) and *relative pronouns* (such as *who, whom, which*, and *that*).

Here are some of the most common subordinating conjunctions, arranged by function:

1. To show time: *as* (at the same time), *after, before, when, while*

<u>As</u> I ate (was eating) my supper, the disk jockey called.

2. To show cause or reason: *as, because, since, in order that, so that*

He will do anything for you <u>because</u> you are his best friend.

She married a man she hardly knew <u>so that</u> she would not be alone.

3. To show condition: *if, in the event that, till, until, unless*

<u>If</u> the two countries go to war, we will have to take sides.

I cannot tell you how you are doing <u>until</u> you turn in your essays.

4. To show a contrasting thought: *although, even though, even if, though, whether, while*

I am still going fishing, <u>even though</u> it is raining.

I am still going fishing, <u>whether</u> it is raining or not.

Shopping with money is fun, <u>while</u> shopping without it is simply challenging.

Note that commas are usually inserted before contrasting-thought clauses.

5. To show place: *where, wherever*

<u>Wherever</u> Naomi goes, Ruth will go.

6. To show how or the manner in which: *as if, as though*

We felt <u>as if</u> we would never make the last mile.

 Practice 11

Write complex sentences, using the following dependent clauses. Circle the subordinating conjunction, and at the end of the sentence indicate which of the six functions it serves.

1. (When) the moon comes over the mountain, *the witches come out to dance.*
   #1--time

2. Although candy is dandy _____

   _____

3. While Mrs. Toodle was looking out of the window _____

   _____

4. If you mail in one Fritzie box top and two dollars _____

   _____

5. Because Mary talks to her plants _____

   _____

6. Unless I pass this math test _____

   _____

If you did not put a comma after each introductory dependent clause, do so now.

 Practice 12

Write complex sentences, using the following dependent clauses. Circle the subordinating conjunction, and indicate which of the six functions it serves.

1. _____ after you went home.

2. _____ because it was stormy.

3. _____ while we were watching the news.

4. _____ before I get really angry.

5. _____ unless you really want me to.

If you put in commas, go back and take them out.

Practice 13

Write complex sentences, using the following subordinating conjunctions to introduce dependent clauses.

1. *You should always check your oil* _____ before
   you leave on a long trip. _____

2. _____ because
   _____

3. _____ since
   _____

4. _____ unless
   _____

5. _____ while
   _____

6. _____ if
   _____

Practice 14

Now reverse the independent and dependent clauses you wrote for Practice 13, and supply commas where needed. You might write something like this:

1. *Before you leave on a long trip, you should always check your oil.*
   _____

2. _____
   _____

3. _____
   _____

4. _____
   _____

5. _____
   _____

6. _____
   _____

Combining Sentences

If you are going to say what you want to say in your writing, you will write many complex sentences. There is nothing wrong with using simple sentences—they can be strong and will give your writing variety—but if you write only simple sentences, your writing will sound flat and unnatural. The following choppy simple sentences can be combined as indicated. (The dependent clauses are underlined.)

CHOPPY

The show was over. The last person had left. We finally went home.

COMBINED

<u>When the show was over and the last person had left,</u> we finally went home. (Note that a comma follows the dependent clause.)

CHOPPY

I was sweeping the rug. I saw a little mouse staring at me.

COMBINED

<u>While I was sweeping the rug,</u> I saw a little mouse staring at me. (Note that a comma follows the dependent clause.)

CHOPPY

I know you will not change your mind. You have shown courage in the past.

COMBINED

I know you will not change your mind <u>because you have shown courage in the past.</u> (Note that there is no comma before a dependent clause that follows an independent clause.)

 ## Practice 15

Combine the following sentences by using the subordinating conjunctions *although, because,* or *when.* If the dependent clause comes at the beginning of the sentence, put a comma after it.

1. The president stood by what he said/ ~~He~~ *because he* was a man of great conviction.
2. I am leaving. I am afraid I will get caught in the rain.
3. It is easy to see a glass as half-empty. It is better to see it as half-full.
4. The terrorists attacked the embassy. Two people were killed.
5. Eighteen-year-olds should be able to buy alcohol. They are old enough to fight and old enough to vote.
6. Eighteen-year-olds are old enough to fight and vote. They still should not be able to buy alcohol.

Practice 16

Combine the following sentences by using each of the following subordinating conjunctions at least once: *when, while, since, because,* and *although.* (You will need to change some of the wording.)

1. We moved to a new town. At that time I was five years old.

   We moved to a new town when I was five years old.

   _____

2. Josh does not have enough money to live comfortably. For that reason he is looking for a new job.

   _____

   _____

3. I moved to Jefferson City about five years ago. At that time I was puzzled by certain words I heard people use.

   _____

   _____

4. Some words were very hard to understand. The reason was that people pronounced them in a funny way.

   _____

   _____

5. I frequently had to ask people to repeat themselves. I could not understand what they were saying.

   _____

   _____

6. Some words, like *yat,* were clearly pronounced. All the same, they were so odd that they sounded foreign.

   _____

   _____

7. I finally asked someone what *yat* meant. I was told that *yat* came from the greeting *whereya at.*

   _____

   _____

8. Some people in the city use *yat* all the time. For that reason they are called *yats*.

    _____

    _____

9. Many *yat* mothers call their children by such names as Precious, Sweetheart, and Darlin'. Angry *yat* mothers call their children Noodlebrain.

    _____

    _____

21.5   The Complex Sentence with an Adjective Clause

Dependent clauses within complex sentences often function as adjectives; that is, they describe nouns or pronouns. *Adjective clauses* usually begin with one of the following relative pronouns:

who, whose, whom
whoever, whomever
that, which, what
whichever, whatever

For example,

Marcia, <u>who is quite talented as a musician</u>, is coming for a visit.

The dependent clause *who is quite talented as a musician* describes the proper noun *Marcia*.

Sometimes the relative pronoun in an adjective clause is omitted but nevertheless understood:

Kurt Vonnegut is a writer <u>I admire.</u>

The relative pronoun *whom* has been omitted.

Kurt Vonnegut is a writer <u>whom</u> I admire.

The dependent adjective clause may begin with *where* or *when*. For example,

I am planning to make a trip to Israel, <u>where three of the world's great religions are centered.</u>

Practice 17

Underline the adjective clauses in the following sentences. Draw arrows to the nouns or pronouns they describe.

1. Everybody wants a life <u>that is filled with good friends and good times.</u>
2. Joe, who is usually the last to leave a party, did not tire until almost dawn.
3. My car, which has not been washed in two years, looks like a piece of junk.
4. The town where I grew up has changed dramatically in the last few years.
5. Anita, who was very tall for her age, took a lot of teasing from her friends.
6. I gave my bike to Karen, who did not have a way to get to school.
7. He is the one I would like to see run for office.
8. The year 1986, when the space shuttle *Challenger* tragedy occurred, was a turning point in my life.

Using Commas with Adjective Clauses

You probably noticed that some adjective clauses in the preceding sentences were set off by commas, whereas others were not. If the adjective clause is essential to the meaning of the sentence, do *not* use commas. For example,

> People who need people are the luckiest people in the world. (If you omitted *who need people,* the sentence would not make sense. Therefore, you do not use a comma.)

If, however, the adjective clause is not essential to the meaning of the sentence, you set it off with a comma or commas. For example,

> Mother, who is nearly eighty, is still in excellent health. (If you omitted *who is nearly eighty,* the sentence would still make sense. Therefore, you need commas.)

Practice 18

Underline the adjective clauses in the following sentences. Then decide whether commas are needed to set off the clauses. (*Hint:* Clauses beginning with *which* are usually set off by commas; clauses beginning with *that* are usually not set off by commas.)

1. Jennifer, <u>who is a very neurotic person,</u> still sleeps with a teddy bear.
2. Rafting down the Colorado River is one experience that he will never forget.
3. The plan that we finally decided upon was our best alternative.
4. My typewriter which has not been cleaned in eight years is in poor condition.
5. Everybody rushed to meet the celebrity who was doing his best to avoid the crowd.
6. The film that Altman directed was the best.

7. Friends who talk behind your back are not friends.

8. I moved to California where the grass was definitely not greener.

Using *Who, Whose, Whom, That,* and *Which* with Adjective Clauses

Use *who, whose,* and *whom* to refer to people. For example,

The person <u>who does the work will be the one to succeed.</u>

He is the player <u>whom we talked about earlier.</u>

Use *that* or *which* to refer to things. For example,

The car, <u>which I bought with my own money,</u> is a beauty.

The things <u>that we enjoy most</u> are free.

Ordinarily, *which* clauses are set off by commas; *that* clauses are not.

Practice 19

Write complex sentences with adjective clauses modifying the following subjects.

1. The space program, *which suffered a great tragedy in 1986, lost some support.* _____

2. My mother, who _____

   _____

3. Cigarettes, which _____

   _____

4. Laws that _____

   _____

5. Friends who _____

   _____

6. The house where _____

   _____

7. Parents whose _____

_____

Check to see if you used commas correctly.

Combining Sentences

By using adjective clauses, you can avoid writing too many simple sentences and thus give variety to your compositions. Notice how these simple sentences can be combined by making one of them an adjective clause.

SIMPLE

The car trip was an unforgettable experience. I took the trip with my brother Tom.

COMBINED

The car trip that I took with my brother Tom was an unforgettable experience.

SIMPLE

Tom and I had been looking forward to the trip for a long time. We both like the outdoors.

COMBINED

Tom and I, who both like the outdoors, had been looking forward to the trip for a long time.

Practice 20

Combine the following pairs of sentences by using *who*, *which*, or *that* to make one of the sentences an adjective clause.

1. The hillsides were covered with trees of fiery red and orange. They extended as far as the eye could see.

    The hillsides, which were covered with trees of fiery red and or-
    ange, extended as far as the eye could see.

2. My parents would love to see a mountainside with trees turning red and gold. They have never been to New England.

    _____

    _____

3. Our decrepit Volkswagen did its best on the mountain roads. It was loaded down with luggage.

    _____

    _____

4. We finally arrived at the ski lodge. It was to be our home for the next few weeks.

    _____

    _____

5. The owner of the lodge helped us unload. He looked like a character out of a Western film.

    _____

    _____

6. I remember watching the first snowfall. It was a sight worth traveling four days to see.

    _____

    _____

7. The local people probably would not share my enthusiasm over snow. They have experienced icy roads and snow shoveling all their lives.

    _____

    _____

21.6   The Sentence with an Appositive

An *appositive* is a word, phrase, or clause that gives more information about a noun, a noun phrase, or a pronoun. Here are several examples of appositives:

> This is Tom, <u>my brother.</u> (The word *brother* further identifies the proper noun *Tom.*)

> She is going to Texas, <u>the second largest state,</u> and then to California. (The phrase *the second largest state* further identifies the proper noun *Texas.*)

> Al found a cushion, <u>the only thing left to sit on.</u> (The phrase *the only thing left to sit on* further identifies the noun *cushion.*)

Notice that the preceding appositives are set off by commas.

Use appositives frequently in your writing. They will help your writing sound smooth and give it variety. These two sentences are choppy:

> John watches television twelve hours a day. He is a nearsighted person.

To combine them, take the "meat" or substance of the second sentence and place it next to *John:*

> John, a nearsighted person, watches television twelve hours a day.

Here is another example:

He will sell you almost anything. For example, he will sell you jewelry, an old bicycle, a new pocketbook, and yesterday's newspaper.

There is no need to repeat *he will sell you.* Simply write this:

He will sell you almost anything, for example, jewelry, an old bicycle, a new pocketbook, and yesterday's newspaper.

Practice 21

Complete the appositives in the following sentences.

1. She plays two sports, _basketball_ and _golf_ .

2. The United States, a nation of _____ , is the home of 225 million people.

3. *Jurassic Park* (or supply your own title _____), a movie about _____ , was a huge success.

4. The Bears are happy about their new quarterback, a man who _____

_____ .

5. Sabrina, a _____ , gives me a ride to school every day.

Practice 22

Using the preceding sentences as models, combine the following pairs of sentences so that one becomes an appositive. Insert commas as necessary.

1. The puppy chewed up everything in sight. He chewed up shoes, newspapers, and even the corner of the couch.

   The puppy chewed up everything in sight, for example, shoes, newspapers, and even the corner of the couch.

2. Greece is a popular vacation spot for Europeans. It is a land of blue skies and whitewashed houses.

_____

_____

3. Barbara Lee's latest novel is supposedly one of her best. It is a book about growing up in China.

_____

_____

4. The defensive-driving coach was a little nervous about his new pupil. His pupil was a man convicted three times of driving while intoxicated.

_____

_____

5. Anton decided not to join the neighborhood softball team. It is a team well-known for its fierce competitive spirit.

_____

_____

21.7   Review Exercises

Your writing will be more effective if you use different kinds of sentences. In this chapter the following kinds of sentences have been discussed:

1. The simple sentence:

She pushed the car.

2. The compound sentence:

The skinny girl pushed the car, and her father watched.

3. The compound sentence with a conjunctive adverb:

She pushed the car; however, her father just watched.

4. The complex sentence with a subordinating conjunction:

She pushed the car while her father watched.

Or:

While her father watched, she pushed the car.

5. The complex sentence with an adjective clause:

The skinny girl, who was not yet sixteen, pushed the car.

6. The sentence with an appositive:

The skinny girl, a close friend of mine, pushed the car.

As you write, try to use different kinds of sentences. You do not speak in sentences that are only simple or compound in structure. You do not need to write that way either. This does not mean that you should avoid all simple or compound sentences, but merely that you should try to make your sentences sound natural and to give them variety.

Review Exercise 1

Complete the following by constructing the designated type of sentence.

1. (a simple sentence) Soap operas *offer entertainment to many* _____ .

2. (a compound sentence) Soap operas are _____ _____ , but _____ .

3. (a compound sentence with a conjunctive adverb) Soap operas _____

_____ ; _____ ,

_____ .

4. (a complex sentence with a subordinating conjunction) Soap operas _____

_____ while _____ .

5. (a complex sentence with an adjective clause) Soap operas, which _____ ,

_____ .

6. (a sentence with an appositive) Soap operas, _____ ,

_____ .

Review Exercise 2

The following essay has been written in mostly simple sentences. Now rewrite it, this time using as many of the six types of sentences listed above as seem appropriate. Remember that it is usually good to use some simple sentences. Be sure to use commas and semicolons correctly.

Mad About Tennis

I have played tennis with my buddy Mike Callanan for over ten years. Very little about either of our games has changed over the years. Mike works very hard at playing tennis. I play just to get the exercise and enjoy what has become a kind of standard routine when we play together.

We always start out by warming up with some old tennis balls. They are usually the ones we used the last time we played. We hit the old balls back and forth for about twenty or thirty minutes. Then Mike will say, "Are you going to get any better?" I try to say something clever. Usually I answer something like, "Not in this lifetime!"

We get out some new tennis balls. Mike spins his racket and asks, "Up or down?" I try to guess in what direction the letter on the end of his racket will come up. If I guess correctly, I get my choice whether to receive or serve first. I usually like to receive. This is because I like to let Mike serve so he can go through his regular routine. His routine consists of first saying, "Let me take three." He means three practice serves, of course. After three practice serves, he finally says, "These go!" This means the next serves count for points. The game will begin.

Mike's tennis is always interesting. He is a noisy player. He grunts, groans, and shouts a lot as we play. Some days he plays exceptionally well. That is when he likes to tell jokes and compliment my backhand or my serve. Some days he misses a number of very easy shots. Then he gets angry at himself. He even talks to himself when his playing is not good. Once he threw his racket at the court fence. Then he looked at me and said, "What's happened to my game?"

My game is always the same. It's neither very weak nor very good. I don't say much as we play. I try to concentrate and watch and listen to Mike. He loves and hates tennis more than anyone I know.

22

Preventing Sentence Errors

22.0   Introduction

IN THIS CHAPTER you will learn how to avoid the following sentence errors:

fragments
run-on sentences
adjective and adverb confusion
dangling modifiers
misplaced modifiers
faulty parallelism

22.1   Preventing Fragments

Be sure that you write consistently, in whole sentences. As pointed out in the last chapter, you can tell that a statement is a sentence if it meets these two tests:

1. If you made the statement to someone, would it make sense by itself? If someone wrote the statement on a note to you with nothing else in the note, would it make sense?
2. Does the statement have a subject (at least understood) and a verb?

A group of words that is not a complete thought (and thus not a sentence) is called a *fragment*.

Practice 1

Applying the two tests given above, mark the following either *S* for whole sentences or *F* for fragments.

1. __*F*__ Which is what I have been thinking.

2. _____ Which one of you is going?

3. _____ Because of the great danger of nuclear fallout.

4. _____ He made the decision because he had to.

5. _____ First, the dangers of the space program.

6. _____ One that anybody who has had basic math should be able to do.

7. _____ Knowing that she would never be alone again.

8. _____ Just knowing her makes me feel good.

9. _____ Although it was against the law.

10. _____ Not the best choice she could have made.

11. _____ It was not I who did it.

Types of Fragments

If you read each sentence you write separately, you will avoid most of these common types of fragments:

   1. The dependent clause fragment:

ERROR

Which is what we should have done in the first place. (You should rarely start a sentence with *which* unless you are asking a question.)

CORRECTION

We finally drove to Oregon, which is what we should have done in the first place.

ERROR

Because it is too late. (A clause that begins with *because* must be accompanied by an independent clause.)

CORRECTION

We will have to live with the consequences because it is too late.

   2. The fragment in which either subject or verb is omitted:

ERROR

First, sex education, a way to prevent early pregnancies. (When you introduce a new topic in a paper, you must write a complete sentence. Here the verb is missing.)

CORRECTION

First, sex education is a way to prevent early pregnancies.

ERROR

There many points of view on the subject. (The verb has been omitted.)

CORRECTION

There are many points of view on the subject.

   3. The appositive fragment:

ERROR

One that the men on board ship are still complaining about. (Use a comma to join an appositive fragment to the preceding sentence.)

CORRECTION

The chief made an unpopular decision, one that the men on board ship are still complaining about.

ERROR

Particularly, Ensign Tomlinson and Lieutenant Dombroski.

CORRECTION

The enlisted personnel were less seasick than the officers, particularly Ensign Tomlinson and Lieutenant Dombroski.

4. The participle fragment:

ERROR

Knowing that the end was near. (Participle phrases written without independent clauses are fragments. You can identify the participles because they are verb forms ending in *-ing:* here, for example, *know* + *-ing.*)

CORRECTION

She called her children to her bedside, knowing that the end was near.

5. Fragments beginning with *not:*

ERROR

Not "Hooligans," as they are called by the navy. (Rarely is it correct to begin a sentence with *not.* Use a comma to join fragments beginning with *not* to the preceding sentence.)

CORRECTION

Coast Guard officers and enlisted personnel are the best, not "Hooligans," as they are called by the navy.

6. Fragments beginning with a contrasting word:

ERROR

Although we did not get out to sea very much. (Statements beginning with words like *although, even though,* and *unless* are sometimes afterthoughts that are written as fragments. Correct them by joining them to the previous sentence with a comma.)

CORRECTION

The *Chilula* was a fine ship to serve on, although we did not get out to sea very much.

Practice 2

Using the preceding corrected sentences as models, make whole sentences out of the following fragments.

1. (which was our policy) *Allowing customers to return merchandise, which was our policy, helped improve our business.*

2. (because they supported terrorists) _____

_____

3. (second, the high cost of the space program)_____

_____

4. (one that you will never forget) _____

_____

5. (helping us whenever she could) _____

_____

6. (not what you think I am) _____

_____

7. (although we did have to break the law to do it) _____

_____

Practice 3

Correct the three fragments in this paragraph.

A salesman must have the ability to handle customers in the right manner. Even if they are hard to handle. I work as a salesman at Danny's Men's Store. Some of the wildest people in the world shop at Danny's. Men do not know what they want to buy, and women do not know what size their husbands wear. A salesman has to try to fit a certain type of garment to a certain type of person. Whether that person is a sportsman, a swinger, or a conservative. I have been working at Danny's for three years and still have not learned how to deal with all the customers. Because some of them are crazy. It is especially hard to serve the ones who come in barefoot.

Practice 4

Correct the four fragments in this paragraph.

Video games are becoming one of the most popular forms of entertainment in this country. Sales last year topped the five-billion-dollar mark. More than Americans spent on movies, in fact. Most of the video games are produced for children; however, adult-oriented interactive video games are also becoming popular. Many of the games or the machines required to run them can be expensive. A problem for parents and one children cannot always understand. Some video games seem to offer too much violence. Kick-boxing, vampires, decapitations, and lots of blood and torn body parts. Makes you wonder what happened to games like chess or rummy.

Practice 5

Correct the five fragments in this paragraph.

Like seaweed? Most people don't know that ice cream contains seaweed. It keeps the ice cream from turning "grainy" in the freezer. You may have seen that happen when you have allowed ice cream to melt. Then frozen it again. The grains are little crystals of water that form the first time the ice cream melts a little. Ice cream manufacturers use a stabilizing material extracted from ordinary red seaweed found along the rocky shores of Europe and North America. Then dried and ground into a powder and mixed with other stabilizing ingredients. Most ice cream has less than a gram of the seaweed extract in it. Actually less than a gram in a whole quart of ice cream. Not much, maybe, but probably more seaweed than you thought you were eating!

Practice 6

Correct the three fragments in this paragraph.

Americans take pride in the wide variety of goods that are available to the public. Thousands of companies, factories, and stores supply us with millions of different products very neatly packaged in colorful, "easy to open" boxes. All tagged with labels saying "new and improved." Many show glossy photos of happy folk enjoying the product. They suggest the image of an ideal, simple way of life. While in reality our lives are growing more complicated all the time. An overabundance of material goods creates many problems. Such as how to operate self-propelled lawn mowers, sensor-touch ovens, and ribbonless typewriters. I ask you, is this progress?

22.2   Preventing Run-on Sentences

Run-on sentences consist of two sentences run together with either no punctuation or only a comma. A run-on sentence with no punctuation is called a *fused sentence;* a run-on sentence with a comma is called a *comma splice.* Here are two examples of run-on sentences:

Capital punishment is ethically unacceptable it is against the morals of civilized societies. (This is a fused sentence. One sentence should end and the other begin after *unacceptable.*)

Capital punishment is ethically unacceptable, it is against the morals of civilized societies. (This is a comma splice, in which two sentences are incorrectly joined, or spliced, with a comma.)

When you edit your papers, read your sentences one at a time to determine if you have run any sentences together. Here are two more examples of run-on sentences:

The work was harder than I thought it was going to be, it almost killed me. (The first independent clause can function alone as a complete sentence because it has a subject, *work,* and a verb, *was going.* The second independent clause can also function by itself as a complete sentence: It has a subject, *it,* and a verb, *killed.*)

The Rangers lost game after game, however, they did not give up. (The first independent clause ends with *game.* It can function alone as a complete sentence because it has a subject, *Rangers,* and a verb, *lost.* The second independent clause begins with *however.* It can also function by itself. It has a subject, *they,* and a verb, *did give.* Note that you can begin sentences with *however.*)

Once you have identified a run on sentence, you can correct it by several methods. Four ways to correct the run-on sentence *I came to the open field, it was not like the one I remember* are listed below:

1. Make two sentences:

I came to the open field. It was not like the one I remember.

2. Insert one of the seven coordinating conjunctions (*and, but, for, yet, so, or,* and *nor*) with a comma:

I came to the open field, but it was not like the one I remember.

3. Insert a semicolon and a conjunctive adverb such as *then, for example, on the other hand, also, however, moreover, consequently,* and *therefore:*

I came to the open field; however, it was not like the one I remember.

4. Make one of the independent clauses into a dependent clause, changing the wording as necessary. (Some dependent clauses begin with subordinating conjunctions such as *while, when, as, because,* and *although;* others begin with relative pronouns such as *which, who,* and *that.*)

When I came to the open field, I realized that it was not like the one I remember.

I came to the open field, although it was not like the one I remember.

I came to the open field, which was not like the one I remember.

Practice 7

Correct the following run-on sentences by making them into two sentences.

1. Today many people are completely dependent on their watches/ ~~they~~ .They would be nervous wrecks without them.
2. Go ahead and check the water it looks good to me.
3. Shut the door it is cold in here.
4. It does not make a lot of difference which one you take both roads will get you there.
5. You are a changed woman your past does not matter to me now.
6. It was not my imagination, it was a little girl.
7. Look at all of those people someone will surely help us.
8. Where I live is only about five blocks from the university, the blocks are not long, and each has only four or five houses.
9. Take me, for instance, I am not your average success story.

Practice 8

Using each of the seven coordinating conjunctions at least once, correct the following run-on sentences. Insert commas as necessary.

1. The cabin was cold ∧ , and there was no more firewood.
2. He was a strange young man, I liked him.
3. She gave me a big shove I fell in the fish pond.
4. Dorm life is unpleasant sometimes, it has been all right on the whole.
5. Cynthia said, "Marry me, I will not see you again."
6. My cat is fed well she is still skinny.
7. Let me go I have to be in class in two minutes.
8. Pedro brought his date home she had not met his parents.
9. I finished high school at Saint Joseph's Academy, now here I am at the university.
10. He will not sleep, he will not eat.

Practice 9

Correct the following run-on sentences by inserting a semicolon before the conjunctive adverbs.

1. He ruined his health/ ; then he ruined his marriage.
2. She is not the most considerate person, however, she is the most intelligent.

3. A few things are still inexpensive, for example, you can still buy water for almost nothing.

4. High school was strict, however, college is not strict enough.

5. You first make a cream sauce, then you brown the shrimp in another pan.

6. The whale turned over on its back as though it were dead, then it started breathing again.

7. If sex education were taught in high school, the number of teenage pregnancies would decline, moreover, young people would protect themselves more effectively against AIDS.

8. Invasion was not our goal, however, it did seem necessary.

9. The surgeon general issued a stern warning against cigarette smoking, consequently, 30 percent of the nation's smokers have quit the habit.

10. He was obviously hiding something, however, we had no way of knowing what it was.

Practice 10

Correct the following run-on sentences by using one of the following subordinating conjunctions—*if, when, since, although, while,* or *because*—to introduce the first or second clause. Insert commas as necessary.

1. I hate to go shopping with Joyce,/she takes so long. *because*

2. He graduates this May, I am going to miss him.

3. You study in our room, I will study in the library.

4. The states of our nation are different in most ways, they do have one thing in common.

5. The Equal Rights Amendment will be proposed again and will eventually pass, it will take many years.

6. Kids are playful, joyful, and bright I decided to write about my little sister.

Practice 11

Correct the following run-on sentences by using any of the four methods described on page 477. (Two sentences are correct.) Remember to use a semicolon or a coordinating conjunction before a conjunctive adverb.

1. I could not believ my eyes /the car was just what I needed.

2. Shut the door, let's keep as warm as possible.

3. The rock hit him beneath his eye it taught him a lesson.

4. Our youth are not the problem, however, they do have a lot to learn.

5. I need those notes, please give them to me.

6. Give me your tired and your poor I will make them into a great nation.

7. The students at this university are not very friendly, in fact they are sometimes hostile.

8. I started college in the fall of 1988 in so doing, I jumped from the frying pan into the fire.

9. Russel is 6'5" he weighs 175 pounds.

10. Usually, I work eight to five, but sometimes I must work many overtime hours.

11. I really enjoy going out with college men, I know they will not be jerks.

12. She had a demanding style of teaching, moreover, she expected perfection.

13. "Try harder," you say to yourself there is one more ball left to play.

14. The noise has stopped, and the lights are out, all except the one that says "tilt."

15. That is how the machine really wins it eats your money.

16. Young drug abusers are responsible for their own actions, however, adults do contribute to the problem by their own addictive behavior.

17. Run-on sentences are often hard to detect, sometimes they flow together very smoothly.

18. We have lost our sense of purpose as a nation, moreover, we seem not to care.

19. The space program will never be what it once was, it has lost much popular support.

20. That country's leader may be our enemy, however, its people are probably very much like ourselves.

Common Types of Run-On Sentences

The following types of run-on sentences are common:

1. Run-on sentences with pronoun subjects in the second clause:

ERROR

Boot camp was just what I had expected, it was terrible. (It is very easy to run these two independent clauses together when writing them because when you say them, you say them in one breath. However, the comma before the pronoun *it* does not correct the run-on.)

CORRECTION

Boot camp was just what I had expected. It was terrible.

ERROR

My drill instructor at Parris Island surprised me, he was actually quite nice. (The comma before *he* does not correct the run-on.)

CORRECTION

My drill instructor at Parris Island surprised me because he was actually quite nice.

2. Run-on sentences with *then:*

ERROR

First you knead the dough, then you smooth it out with a rolling pin. (You cannot join two independent clauses with *then* unless you place a semicolon between them, or use *and* or *but* preceded by a comma.

CORRECTION

First you knead the dough; then you smooth it out with a rolling pin.

Or,

First you knead the dough, and then you smooth it out with a rolling pin.

3. Run-on sentences with other conjunctive adverbs, such as *however, moreover, therefore,* and *consequently:*

ERROR

Bake the cookies for about half an hour, however, if you have a slow oven, bake them a little longer. (When a conjunctive adverb introduces an independent clause, either use a semicolon before it or make two sentences.)

CORRECTION

Bake the cookies for about half an hour; however, if you have a slow oven, bake them a little longer.

Or,

Bake the cookies for about half an hour. However, if you have a slow oven, bake them a little longer.

4. Run-on sentences in narratives:

ERROR

I looked across the field and saw a little boy, the child reminded me of someone I knew. (In telling stories aloud, you probably run sentences together, but in writing you must write them separately or join them correctly.)

CORRECTION

I looked across the field and saw a little boy. The child reminded me of someone I knew.

5. Run-on sentences in quoted speech:

ERROR

The drill sergeant made me say, "This is my rifle, you do not call this weapon a gun." (Make run-on sentences in quotations into sentences.)

CORRECTION

The drill sergeant made me say, "This is my rifle. You do not call this weapon a gun."

Practice 12

Using the preceding corrected sentences as models, correct the following run-on sentences.

1. Heart disease is an extremely dangerous illness/ ~~it~~ ⊙*It* is the number-one killer disease in this country.

2. The president was on the defensive, he could not explain why he had made such a statement.

3. Both houses of Congress must agree on the bill, then it must go to the president for his signature.

4. First you gather the information, then you analyze it.

5. Our dog Lucifer looks ferocious, however, he is as gentle as any dog I know.

6. Eighteen-year-olds can vote and fight for our country, therefore, they should not be able to buy alcohol.

7. We began climbing to the top, the wind was so strong that we could not stand up straight.

8. It was too dark to go any farther, we turned around and went home.

9. She turned to me and said, "Will you just listen to me, I have something to say that will surprise you."

10. I answered, "What do you want from me, I can no longer help you."

Practice 13

Correct the following run-on sentences by using one of the four methods described on page 477.

1. My sister Marie enlisted in the Air Force two years ago, ∧*and* she is stationed in England now.

2. She took a special liking to one elderly couple they accepted her as a member of the family.

3. They gave Marie a standing invitation to stop by on holidays she had only to give them a phone call.

4. Marie was also invited to several dart tournaments darts is a game the British especially love.

5. The beautiful English countryside impressed her as much as the warmth of the people it is a land whose rolling hills remain green all year.

6. Many of these hills are dotted with small farms, one can often see small herds of sheep grazing leisurely on them.

7. Marie also visited France and Italy, she loved the beautiful beaches in the south.

8. She found the French people very friendly, too, they are especially hospitable to those who make an effort to speak their language.

9. However, her favorite European county is Switzerland, it has breathtaking scenery and a brisk, cool climate.

10. The city of Geneva is especially lovely, it is located on a clear, blue lake.

11. Once she went mountain climbing in the Alps, however, snow forced her to turn back before she reached the top of the Matterhorn.

12. She and some friends rode the lift to the lodge, then they set out on foot across a sky-high glacier.

13. The snow was fresh on the glacier, the sun was blinding.

14. She and her party were tied together by ropes, however, no one slipped.

15. They managed to get back down the mountain before dark, everyone had been worried about them.

Practice 14

Correct the run-on sentences in the following student essay by using one of the four methods described on page 477.

The Weekend Camper

If anyone had told me three years ago that I would be spending most of my weekends camping, I would have laughed heartily. Campers, in my eyes, were nothing but masochists who enjoyed insect bites, ill-cooked meals, and damp sleeping bags, they had nothing in common with me. I was to learn a lot about camping since then, however. (1 run-on sentence)

The friends who introduced me to camping thought that it meant being a pioneer. The first trip they took me on, we roughed it, we slept in a tent, cooked over an open fire, and hiked to the shower and bathroom facilities. This brief visit with Mother Nature cost me two days off from work, recovering from a bad case of sunburn. There was no shade, the tallest tree at our campsite was three feet tall. Another memento from the trip was the doctor's bill for my son's poison ivy. (2 run-on sentences)

I was, nevertheless, talked into going on another fun-filled holiday in the wilderness, this time we camped with friends who believed that Daniel Boone would have been proud to use the light bulb if he had known about it. There was no tent, we had a pop-up camper with comfortable beds and an air conditioner. These nature lovers had remembered to bring all the necessities of life they brought lounge chairs, a screened porch, the TV, and even a blender. I can still taste those piña coladas. (3 run-on sentences)

After that trip, my husband and I became quite interested in camping, we have done a lot of it since. Recently, we purchased a twenty-eight-foot travel trailer complete with a bathroom and built-in TV antenna. There is a separate bedroom, a modern kitchen with a refrigerator and roll-out pantry, the trailer even has matching carpet and draperies. (2 run-on sentences)

I must say that I have certainly come to enjoy camping. It must be true that, sooner or later, everyone finds his or her way back to nature, I recommend that you find your way in style. (1 run-on sentence)

22.3   Preventing Adjective and Adverb Confusion

It is easy to confuse adjectives and adverbs. Remember that adjectives must modify nouns or pronouns; adverbs must modify verbs, adjectives, or other adverbs. The following sentence is incorrect:

I did good at that high school.

If you look up *good* in a dictionary, you will see that it cannot be used as it is here: as an adverb modifying the verb *did*. The adverb *well* should be substituted instead:

I did <u>well</u> at that high school.

Likewise, this sentence is incorrect:

He arrived as quick as he could.

Quick is an adjective; the adverb *quickly* must be used to modify the verb *arrived:*

She arrived as <u>quickly</u> as she could.

Adjectives sometimes follow linking verbs such as *is, are, seem,* and *appear.* However, they do not modify these verbs, but rather the subjects of the verbs. For example,

He seems <u>lazy</u> to me.

Lazy, the adjective, modifies the subject *he; lazily,* the adverb, would be incorrect.

Practice 15

Two of the following sentences require adjectives that follow linking verbs. The rest require adverbs. Choose the correct word and draw an arrow to the word(s) it modifies.

1. Carry those dishes just as (careful, <u>carefully</u>) as you can.
2. The librarian looked at me very (curious, curiously).
3. He has fixed up the room very (nice, nicely) for the children.
4. Her fingers were moving across the keys (rapid, rapidly).
5. She looks (beautiful, beautifully) in her wedding gown.
6. These dogs bark so (loud, loudly) that they wake the whole neighborhood.
7. You did (good, well).
8. The WILD jazz band plays (good, well).
9. With her new hairstyle, she certainly looks (good, well).
10. The waiter frowns at me (frequent, frequently).
11. They have been acting (crazy, crazily) lately.

Practice 16

Using the sentences in Practice 15 as models, complete the following exercises by writing whole sentences.

1. Use *well* to describe something that you are not good at doing.

   I do not type well.
   _____   _____

2. Use *quietly* to describe something a cat does that hardly anyone notices.

   _____

3. Use *nicely* to describe how someone always greets you.

   _____

4. Use *well* to describe the skill with which a good quarterback throws the ball.

   _____

5. Use *good* after the verb *looks.*

   _____

22.4   Preventing Dangling Modifiers

What is wrong with the following sentences?

> While sailing, a shark swam close to our boat.

> Having eaten a large meal, it was time to go home.

> To do well, determination is necessary.

Each sentence has the same problem. The subject is not clear. In the first sentence, the shark seems to be the subject, but sharks are not known for sailing. In the second, the reader is not told who ate the large meal; it certainly was not *it*. In the third example, it is not clear who is trying to do well.

In the preceding sentences, *while sailing, having eaten a large meal,* and *to do well* are called *dangling modifiers.* They are supposed to describe subjects in these sentences, but since these subjects are not clear, the modifiers do not connect—they dangle.

The preceding sentences can be corrected as follows:

> <u>While sailing,</u> we saw a shark that swam close to our boat.

> <u>Having eaten a large meal,</u> we realized that it was time to go home.

> <u>To do well,</u> one must have determination.

To correct dangling modifiers, first place the subject that you want your modifier to describe immediately after the modifier; then complete the sentence. In the first sentence, *we* were sailing, so the subject is *we*. In the second, *we* ate the meal, so again the subject is *we*. The goal of doing well applies to anyone, so the subject in the last example is the indefinite pronoun *one;* it could also be *you*.

Practice 17

Complete the following sentences by supplying appropriate subjects for the modifiers.

1. Having breathed her last, *she rolled over and died* .

2. Running from the police, _____.

3. To stop crime, _____.

4. Having witnessed the great event of the century, _____.

5. Watching the deliberations in Congress, _____.

6. Determined to succeed, _____.

7. To love your neighbor, _____.

8. Having been discovered, _____.

9. To succeed in the business world, _____.

10. Spending his money carelessly, _____.

11. Intending to do a good thing, _____.

 Practice 18

Correct these sentences by writing an appropriate subject after the dangling modifier. Change the wording as necessary to convey the intended meaning of the sentence.

1. Having spent all their money, ~~it was time to go home~~. *they headed home.*
2. Built on a rock foundation, there is no problem with a house falling down.
3. To be a good father, it is necessary to spend a lot of time with your children.
4. While swimming in the river, a bad thunderstorm scared us.
5. To do your best, it is important to stay in good shape.
6. While eating his supper, the squirrel ran across the hunter's plate.
7. Convicted of a third felony, the judge sent the man to prison for life.
8. Having awoken early, no one could find them.
9. To bloom where one is planted, it is necessary to make the best of the situation.

22.5   Preventing Misplaced Modifiers

What is wrong with the following sentences?

He left his car to be sold with the dealer.

The president spoke to the terrorists who survived with tough language.

The farmers in our country almost earned ten million dollars.

In each sentence a modifier is out of place. In the first example, it sounds as though the car and the dealer are to be sold together. In the second sentence, it sounds as though the tough language of the terrorists had enabled them to survive. Finally, in the last sentence, it seems as though the farmers, instead of earning an amount close to ten million dollars, did not earn a cent.

In the preceding sentences, *with the dealer, with tough language,* and *almost* are misplaced modifiers. They are intended to describe certain words in the sentences, but because they are misplaced, they modify the wrong words.

The preceding sentences can be corrected as follows:

He left his car <u>with the dealer</u> to be sold.

The president spoke <u>with tough language</u> to the terrorists who survived.

The farmers in our country earned <u>almost</u> ten million dollars.

To correct misplaced modifiers, identify the words that you want your modifiers to describe, and place the modifiers as close to those words as you can. Sometimes you will need to rewrite the sentences. In the first sentence above, *with the dealer* tells where he left the car, so you should move this phrase as close as possible to the verb *left*. In the second, *with tough language* tells how the president spoke, so you should move this phrase next to the verb *spoke*. In the last example, *almost* describes an amount of money that is not quite ten million dollars, so you should move *almost* next to *ten million dollars*.

Practice 19

Rewrite the following sentences, moving the modifiers to their intended places. Then draw an arrow from the modifiers to the words they are intended to modify. Change the wording as necessary.

1. My aunt was rushed to the emergency room at the hospital with a failing heart.

   My aunt, with a failing-heart, was rushed to the emergency room at the hospital.

   _____

2. The interns on duty were able to save her life in the emergency room.

   _____

   _____

3. Her stay in the hospital almost cost her three hundred dollars a day.

   _____

   _____

4. Dr. Regina Watts testified before the House Welfare Committee on behalf of neglected children.

   _____

   _____

5. The committee members listened to her appeal on behalf of the children with great interest.

   _____

   _____

6. Later the legislature passed the bill almost to appropriate one hundred thousand dollars. I believe the exact amount they approved was ninety-seven thousand dollars.

   _____

   _____

7. The children will now be helped by the state representatives who have been neglected.

_____

_____

8. Dr. Watts and the other members of Agenda for Children have made an important contribution to the children of this state with their determined leadership.

_____

_____

9. Dr. Watts has nearly recruited three hundred members for Agenda for Children.

_____

_____

10. The members argue for various priorities they have established convincingly.

_____

_____

11. The legislative victory shows what one person can do to change things with a dream.

_____

_____

22.6   Preventing Faulty Parallelism

What is wrong with these sentences?

I like swimming, hiking, and to collect things.

Capital punishment deters crime, eliminates dangerous criminals, and finally society has a right to demand retribution.

You will need to gather ahead of time the eggs, the flour, baking powder, honey, and the shortening.

Each sentence has the same problem: *faulty parallelism.* When you write words as items in a series, they should have a parallel grammatical structure. In the first sentence, *swimming* and *hiking* are gerunds (verbs made into nouns by adding *-ing*), but *to collect things* is not similar in structure. In the second example, the first two arguments for capital punishment are written as verbs with objects, but the third argument includes a subject (*society*) as well. Thus it is not parallel to the first two arguments. In the third sentence, *the* is included before three items in the series but not before the other two. You can make these items parallel by using *the* only once, before *eggs,* or by using *the* before all five items.

The preceding sentences can be corrected as follows:

I like swimming, hiking, and collecting things.

Capital punishment deters crime, eliminates dangerous criminals, and satisfies society's need for retribution.

You will need to gather ahead of time the eggs, flour, baking powder, honey, and shortening.

 Practice 20

One item in each sentence below is not parallel to the others. Rewrite that item so that it is parallel.

1. The various neighbors on my block could be classified as friendly, indifferent, and ~~some are just plain mean.~~ *just plain mean.*

2. In my view capital punishment does not deter crime, is used only against the poor, and people should not be subject to such cruel and unusual punishment.

3. He enjoys his nap in the afternoon, his bike ride in the early evening, and to read novels at night.

4. Manning watches the soap operas in the morning, the news programs in the late afternoon, and television movies at night.

5. Her responsibilities are to make the customers feel welcome, to show them to a table, and finding them a waiter.

6. When I graduate from this university, I am going to save some money, then open my own business, and finally sitting back and getting rich.

22.7   Review Exercises

Review Exercise 1

Correct the following fragments and run-on sentences, changing the wording as necessary.

1. And finally, ~~the~~ *my neighborhood is filled with* unique sounds ~~in my neighborhood.~~

2. The Reverend Winn did not want to talk about her illness/ ~~instead~~ *. Instead,* she wanted to talk about what we were doing.

3. There very few young people in this neighborhood who go to high school.

4. Because she wanted the room to be just the way it was when her parents died.

5. First you make a roux of white flour and fat, then you add chopped vegetables.

6. She never answers a question with a short answer. While Melvin never answers a question with anything but a grunt or a groan.

7. My instructor gave me a little speech, she said that the time was now or never.

8. This university is not what I had expected, it is not very friendly.

9. Send me the bill, however, I cannot pay everything right now.

10. A person for whom I have the highest respect.

11. My grandmother said, "You have your boyfriend, why can't I have mine?"

12. We have not raised the necessary revenue to fund Social Security, consequently, the money will soon be gone.

Review Exercise 2

Edit the following paragraphs to correct fragments and comma-splice errors. Change the wording of the sentences as necessary.

A Brief History of Coca-Cola

Coca-Cola is one of the most popular and well-known soft drinks in the world. It's surprising to think that it has been so for over a century. Ever since it was invented in 1885 by John S. Pemberton, a pharmacist in Atlanta, Georgia. At first Pemberton made the drink with a mixture of coca leaves and red wine. He later omitted the wine. Used flavor from the cola nut, some sugar, and other ingredients until his new beverage tasted just right. The new mixture proved a great success, people started drinking it as a refreshment and as a "brain tonic." Pemberton's partner, Frank M. Robinson, designed the famous logo for Coca-Cola, the flowing white lettering you still see today on Coca-Cola bottles and cans.

After Pemberton sold his formula for Coca-Cola, ownership changed hands several times. Until Asa G. Candler bought it and added carbonated water to the mixture. Thus making Coca-Cola into a soft drink as we know it today. The formula for Coca-Cola has always been kept very secret, only Pemberton and others to whom he sold the formula ever knew how the drink was made. Although many people have tried to analyze Coca-Cola to discover its combination of ingredients, they have had no success. Coca-Cola is apparently a mixture of several common flavorings, how much of each one is impossible to determine.

At one time the U.S. government took the owners of Coca-Cola to court. Because it was thought that the coca leaf in the formula meant the drink contained cocaine. Thus making the beverage illegal. The court trial was very famous, everyone wanted to know if the coca leaf ingredient made Coca-Cola a drug. Hundreds of tests then and since, however, have shown that there is no cocaine in the drink.

Today Coca-Cola is known and drunk all over the world. From Africa to the Antarctic. Most people refer to drinking Coca-Cola as having a "Coke," maybe they feel the shorter name better represents the drink's refreshing qualities. Coca-Cola has a lot of competition nowadays from other soft drinks, like Pepsi-Cola. And from several new drinks which are mixtures of fruit juice and water. But having a Coke is still part of the American tradition. Whether you like "Classic Coke" or "New Coke," regular or diet.

Anthology

How to Make It in College, Now That You're Here

Brian O'Keeney

Today is your first day on campus. You were a high school senior three months ago. Or maybe you've been at home with your children for the last ten years. Or maybe you work full time and you're coming to school to start the process that leads to a better job. Whatever your background is, you're probably not too concerned today with staying in college. After all, you just got over the hurdle (and the paperwork) of applying to this place and organizing your life so that you could attend. And today, you're confused and tired. Everything is a hassle, from finding the classrooms to standing in line at the bookstore. But read my advice anyway. And if you don't read it today, clip and save this article. You might want to look at it a little further down the road.

By the way, if this isn't your very first day, don't skip this article. Maybe you haven't been doing as well in your studies as you'd hoped. Or perhaps you've had problems juggling your work schedule, your class schedule, and your social life. If so, read on. You're about to get the inside story on making it in college. On the basis of my own experience as a final-year student, and on dozens of interviews with successful students, I've worked out a no-fail system for coping with college. These are the inside tips every student needs to do well in school. I've put myself in your place, and I'm going to answer the questions that will cross (or have already crossed) your mind during your stay here.

What's the Secret of Getting Good Grades?

It all comes down to getting those grades, doesn't it? After all, you came here for some reason, and you're going to need passing grades to get the credits or degree you want. Many of us never did much studying in high school; most of the learning we did took place in the classroom. College, however, is a lot different. You're really on your own when it comes to passing courses. In fact, sometimes you'll feel as if nobody cares if you make it or not. Therefore, you've got to figure out a study system that gets results. Sooner or later, you'll be alone with those books. After that, you'll be sitting in a classroom with an exam sheet on your desk. Whether you stare at that exam with a queasy stomach or whip through it fairly confidently depends on your study techniques. Most of the successful students I talked to agreed that the following eight study tips deliver solid results.

1. Set Up a Study Place.   Those students you see "studying" in the cafeteria or game room aren't learning much. You just can't learn when you're distracted by people and noise. Even the library can be a bad place to study if you constantly find yourself watching the clouds outside or the students walking through the stacks. It takes guts to sit, alone, in a quiet place in order to study. But you have to do it. Find

a room at home or a spot in the library that's relatively quiet—and boring. When you sit there, you won't have much to do except study.

2. Get into a Study Frame of Mind.   When you sit down, do it with the attitude that you're going to get this studying done. You're not going to doodle in your notebook or make a list for the supermarket. Decide that you're going to study and learn *now,* so that you can move on to more interesting things as soon as possible.

3. Give Yourself Rewards.   If you sweat out a block of study time, and do a good job on it, treat yourself. You deserve it. You can "psych" yourself up for studying by promising to reward yourself afterwards. A present for yourself can be anything from a favorite TV show to a relaxing bath to a dish of double chocolate ice cream.

4. Skim the Textbook First.   Lots of students sit down with an assignment like "read chapter five, pages 125–150" and do just that. They turn to page 125 and start to read. After a while, they find that they have no idea what they just read. For the last ten minutes, they've been thinking about their five-year-old or what they're going to eat for dinner. Eventually, they plod through all the pages but don't remember much afterwards.

   In order to prevent this problem, skim the textbook chapter first. This means: look at the title, the subtitles, the headings, the pictures, the first and last paragraphs. Try to find out what the person who wrote the book had in mind when he or she organized the chapter. What was important enough to set off as a title or in bold type? After skimming, you should be able to explain to yourself what the main points of the chapter are. Unless you're the kind of person who would step into an empty elevator shaft without looking first, you'll soon discover the value of skimming.

5. Take Notes on What You're Studying.   This sounds like a hassle, but it works. Go back over the material after you've read it, and jot down key words and phrases in the margins. When you review the chapter for a test, you'll have handy little things like "definition of rationalization" or "example of assimilation" in the margins. If the material is especially tough, organize a separate sheet of notes. Write down definitions, examples, lists, and main ideas. The idea is to have a single sheet that boils the entire chapter down to a digestible lump.

6. Review After You've Read and Taken Notes.   Some people swear that talking to yourself works. Tell yourself about the most important points in the chapter. Once you've said them out loud, they seem to stick better in your mind. If you can't talk to yourself about the material after reading it, that's a sure sign you don't really know it.

7. Give Up.   This may sound contradictory, but give up when you've had enough. You should try to make it through at least an hour, though. Ten minutes here and there are useless. When your head starts to pound and your eyes develop spidery red lines, quit. You won't do much learning when you're exhausted.

8. Take a College Skills Course If You Need It.   Don't hesitate or feel embarrassed about enrolling in a study skills course. Many students say they wouldn't have made it without one.

How Can I Keep Up with All My Responsibilities Without Going Crazy?

You've got a class schedule. You're supposed to study. You've got a family. You've got a husband, wife, boyfriend, girlfriend, child. You've got a job. How are you possibly going to cover all the bases in your life and maintain your sanity? This is one of the toughest problems students face. Even if they start the semester with the best of intentions, they eventually find themselves tearing their hair out trying to do everything they're supposed to do. Believe it or not, though, it is possible to meet all your responsibilities. And you don't have to turn into a hermit or give up your loved ones to do it.

The secret here is to organize your time. But don't just sit around half the semester planning to get everything together soon. Before you know it, you'll be confronted with midterms, papers, family, and work all at once. Don't let yourself reach that breaking point. Instead, try these three tactics.

1. Monthly Calendar.   Get one of those calendars with big blocks around the dates. Give yourself an overview of the whole term by marking down the due dates for papers and projects. Circle test and exam days. This way those days don't sneak up on you unexpectedly.

2. Study Schedule.   Sit down during the first few days of this semester and make up a sheet listing the days and hours of the week. Fill in your work and class hours first. Then try to block out some study hours. It's better to study a little every day than to create a huge once-or-twice-a-week marathon session. Schedule study hours for your hardest classes for the times when you feel most energetic. For example, I battled my tax law textbook in the mornings; when I looked at it after 7:00 P.M., I might as well have been reading Chinese. The usual proportion, by the way, is one hour of study time for every class hour.

In case you're one of those people who get carried away, remember to leave blocks of free time, too. You won't be any good to yourself or anyone else if you don't relax and pack in the studying once in a while.

3. "To-Do" List.   This is the secret that single-handedly got me through college. Once a week (or every day if you want to), write a list of what you have to do. Write down everything from "write English paper" to "buy cold cuts for lunches." The best thing about a "to do" list is that it seems to tame all those stray "I have to" thoughts that nag at your mind. Just making the list seems to make the tasks "doable." After you finish something on the list, cross it off. Don't be compulsive about finishing everything; you're not Superman or Wonder Woman. Get the important things done first. The secondary things you don't finish can simply be moved to your next "to do" list.

What Can I Do If Personal Problems Get in the Way of My Studies?

One student, Roger, told me this story:

> Everything was going OK for me until the middle of the spring semester. I went through a terrible time when I broke up with my girlfriend and started seeing her best friend. I was trying to deal with my ex-girlfriend's hurt and anger, my new girlfriend's guilt, and my own worries and anxieties at the same time. In addition to this, my mother was sick and on a medication that made her really irritable. I hated to go home because the atmosphere was so uncomfortable. Soon, I started missing classes because I couldn't deal with the academic pressures as well as my own personal problems. It seemed easier to hang around my girlfriend's apartment than to face all my problems at home and at school.

Another student, Marian, told me:

> I'd been married for eight years and the relationship wasn't going too well. I saw the handwriting on the wall, and I decided to prepare for the future. I enrolled in college, because I knew I'd need a decent job to support myself. Well, my husband had a fit because I was going to school. We were arguing a lot anyway, and he made it almost impossible for me to study at home. I think he was angry and almost jealous because I was drawing away from him. It got so bad that I thought about quitting college for a while. I wasn't getting any support at home and it was just too hard to go on.

Personal troubles like these are overwhelming when you're going through them. School seems like the least important thing in your life. The two students above are perfect examples of this. But if you think about it, quitting or failing school would be the worst thing for these two students. Roger's problems, at least with his girlfriends, would simmer down eventually, and then he'd regret having left school. Marian had to finish college if she wanted to be able to live independently. Sometimes you've just got to hang tough.

But what do you do while you're trying to live through a lousy time? First of all, do something difficult. Ask yourself, honestly, if you're exaggerating small problems as an excuse to avoid classes and studying. It takes strength to admit this, but there's no sense in kidding yourself. If your problems are serious, and real, try to make some human contacts at school. Lots of students hide inside a miserable shell made of their own troubles and feel isolated and lonely. Believe me, there are plenty of students with problems. Not everyone is getting A's and having a fabulous social and home life at the same time. As you go through the term, you'll pick up some vibrations about the students in your classes. Perhaps someone strikes you as a compatible person. Why not speak to that person after class? Share a cup of coffee in the cafeteria or walk to the parking lot together. You're not looking for a best friend or the love of your life. You just want to build a little network of support for yourself. Sharing your difficulties, questions, and complaints with a friendly person on campus can make a world of difference in how you feel.

Finally, if your problems are overwhelming, get some professional help. Why do you think colleges spend countless dollars on counseling departments and campus psychiatric services? More than ever, students all over the country are taking advantage of the help offered by support groups and therapy sessions. There's no shame attached to asking for help, either; in fact, almost 40 percent of college students (according to one survey) will use counseling services during their time in school. Just walk into a student center or counseling office and ask for an appointment. You wouldn't think twice about asking a dentist to help you get rid of your toothache. Counselors are paid—and want—to help you with your problems.

Why Do Some People Make It and Some Drop Out?

Anyone who spends at least one semester in college notices that some students give up on their classes. The person who sits behind you in accounting, for example, begins to miss a lot of class meetings and eventually vanishes. Or another student comes to class without the assignment, doodles in a notebook during the lecture, and leaves during the break. What's the difference between students like this and the ones who succeed in school? My survey may be nonscientific, but everyone I asked said the same thing: attitude. A positive attitude is the key to everything else—good study habits, smart time scheduling, and coping with personal difficulties.

What does "a positive attitude" mean? Well, for one thing, it means avoiding the zombie syndrome. It means not only showing up for your classes, but also doing something while you're there. Really listen. Take notes. Ask a question if you want to. Don't just walk into a class, put your mind in neutral, and drift away to never-never land.

Having a positive attitude goes deeper than this, though. It means being mature about college as an institution. Too many students approach college classes like six-year-olds who expect first grade to be as much fun as *Sesame Street.* First grade, as we all know, isn't as much fun as *Sesame Street.* And college classes can sometimes be downright dull and boring. If you let a boring class discourage you so much that you want to leave school, you'll lose in the long run. Look at your priorities. You want a degree, or a certificate, or a career. If you have to, you can make it through a less-than-interesting class in order to achieve what you want. Get whatever you can out of every class. But if you simply can't stand a certain class, be determined to fulfill its requirements and be done with it once and for all.

After the initial high of starting school, you have to settle in for the long haul. If you follow the advice here, you'll be prepared to face the academic crunch. You'll also live through the semester without giving up your family, your job, or *Monday Night Football.* Finally, going to college can be an exciting time. You do learn. And when you learn things, the world becomes a more interesting place.

Questions for Discussion and Writing

1. Which suggestions of O'Keeney's would you judge the most valuable for some-one either entering college or returning after a long absence? Which of his suggestions do you follow already? Are there any you plan to adopt as a result of reading this essay? Which ones?

2. Are there any important techniques for succeeding in college that O'Keeney omits? What suggestions would you add to his essay if you were giving advice to new or returning college students?

3. The dropout and failure rate in American colleges nationwide is unfortunately very high. What is it at your college? What obstacles can you think of that often prevent students who drop out of college from finishing?

■ The Answer Is 45 Cents

John Leo

The latest in a long line of depressing reports on the condition of our colleges is "Declining Standards at Michigan Public Universities," put out by the Mackinac Center for Public Policy.

The report finds that Michigan's state universities are "suffering from a general erosion of academic standards and a radical politicization of the undergraduate curriculum." Nothing new there. A 1996 report on New York's state universities said much the same thing, and the National Association of Scholars put out a devastating national analysis of the dumbing down of the modern curriculum, which now bulges with things like "queer theory," the works of Pee-wee Herman, and watching Oprah or Montel Williams for credit.

No wonder a Department of Education study three years ago showed that more than half of American college graduates can't read a bus schedule. Exactly 56.3 percent were unable to figure out how much change they should get back after putting down $3 to pay for a 60-cent bowl of soup and a $1.95 sandwich.

What caught my eye about the Michigan report is how the new stupidity shows up in college writing classes. The report finds that the "process" school of composition dominates freshman writing classes at state institutions According to this school of thought, writing is a continuous process with much rewriting, growth, and self-discovery. So far so good. But embedded in the theory is the notion that standards, grammar, grades, and judgment are bad. Self-expression, self-esteem, and personal rules are good. Students sometimes talk about their "personal languages" and "personal spellings."

Syntax? Don't bother.   Writing in the *Public Interest,* Heather Mac Donald reports that "students who have been told in their writing class to let their deepest selves loose on the page and not worry about syntax, logic, or form have trouble adjusting to their other classes"—the ones in which evidence and analysis are more important than personal revelation or feelings.

In "process" teaching, the gush of feelings about the self often gets tangled up with radical politics and the multicultural makeover of the colleges. Rules, good writing, and simple coherence are sometimes depicted as habits of the powerful and privileged, sometimes as coercion of the poor and powerless. A collection of papers prepared for a course at Central Michigan University takes this politicized stance: "Traditional grammar books were unapologetically designed to instill linguistic habits which were intended to separate those who had made it from those who had not."

So the Michigan report complains about the "politically motivated dismissal of correct, formal prose as oppressive or intimidating to students." Those winds are certainly blowing through colleges. James Sledd, professor emeritus of English at the University of Texas, writes in *College English* that standard English is "essentially an instrument of domination." Arguing against knowledge of grammar and logic, Jay Robinson of the University of Michigan says that "the myth of basic skills" helps sustain a rigid and evil class structure. What college students really need, he says, is reaffirmation as "members of racial, social, and linguistic minorities."

A better example of this school of thought is an article in the *English Leadership Quarterly* urging teachers to encourage intentional errors in English as "the only way to end its oppression of linguistic minorities and learning writers." The pro-error article, written in disappointingly good English by two professors at Indiana University of Pennsylvania, actually won an award from the quarterly, a publication of the National Council of Teachers of English. The NCTE, a group that sometimes seems to be moving away from any contaminating association with actual English, was coauthor of last year's goofy national English standards, attacked on all sides as empty and unreadable, even by the *New York Times.*

In some ways, this anything-goes movement is an attempt to patronize a new wave of unprepared college students, largely members of minority groups, by saying that standards aren't really all that important after all. Mac Donald writes: "Confronted with a barrage of students who had no experience in formal grammar or written language, it was highly convenient for professors to learn that students' natural way of speaking and writing should be preserved, not corrected."

But the good-hearted professors who disparage "the myth of basic skills" are doing students no favors. At some point they have to leave the university and find a job, usually one offered by a company that cares less about oppression and feelings than about those basic skills. "Recruiting Trends 1994–95," by Michigan State Prof. L. Patrick Scheetz, is one of umpteen studies showing how disappointed employers are by many college grads. Scheetz finds that not enough graduates have the ability to write, speak, reason, and relate to others in a satisfactory manner to hold down a job. Should we correct this, or just order up more feel-good, anti-English theory in colleges?

Questions for Discussion and Writing

1. To what extent do you agree with the National Association of Scholars' claim that colleges are "dumbing down" the curriculum to meet student skills and interests? What evidence for and against that view can you find on your own campus?

2. What are some of the examples that Leo cites of what he calls "politicized" views of the curriculum? Can a curriculum be politicized? How? Can you cite any examples at your own or other schools?

3. What skills do employers want in new employees? To what extent and in what ways are colleges ensuring that their students have such skills when they graduate? Could colleges do more? How?

■ The Strange Burden of a Name

Lance Morrow

A name is sometimes a ridiculous fate. For example, a man afflicted with the name of Kill Sin Pimple lived in Sussex, in 1609. In the spring of that year, the record shows, Kill Sin served on a jury with his Puritan neighbors, including Fly Debate Roberts, More Fruit Fowler, God Reward Smart, Be Faithful Joiner and Fight the Good Fight of Faith White. Poor men. At birth, their parents had turned them into religious bumper stickers.

Names may carry strange freights—perverse jokes, weird energies of inflicted embarrassment. Another 17th century Puritan child was condemned to bear the name of Flie Fornication Andrewes. Of course, it is also possible that Andrewes sailed along, calling himself by a jaunty, executive "F.F. Andrewes." Even the most humiliating name can sometimes be painted over or escaped altogether. Initials are invaluable: H.R. (Bob) Haldeman, of the Nixon White House, deftly suppressed Harry Robbins: "Harry Haldeman" might not have worked for him.

Names have an intricate life of their own. Where married women and power are concerned, the issue becomes poignant. The official elongation of the name of Hillary Rodham Clinton suggests some of the effects achieved when customs of naming drift into the dangerous atmospheres of politics and feminism.

The history of "Hillary Rodham Clinton" goes back in time, like a novel: at birth, Bill Clinton was William Jefferson Blythe, his father being a young salesman named William Jefferson Blythe 3rd, who died in a car accident before Bill was born. In a story now familiar, the 15-year-old future President legally changed his name to Bill Clinton in order to affirm family solidarity with his mother and stepfather, Roger Clinton. In 1975, when Bill Clinton got married, his new wife chose to keep the name Hillary Rodham. But five years later, Clinton was defeated in a run for reelection as Arkansas Governor, at which point, to assert a more conventional family image, Hillary Rodham started calling herself Hillary Clinton. But she was not exactly taking Bill's name either, since "Clinton" had not originally been Bill's. Bill was once removed from his own birth name, so now Hillary was, in a sense, twice removed.

A name may announce something—or conceal something. In some societies, the Arab or Chinese, for example, a beautiful child may be called by a depreciating name—"Dog," "Stupid," "Ugly," say—in order to ward off the evil eye. Hillary Rodham knew that in some parts of the political wilds, she attracted the evil eye to the 1992 Democratic ticket. So during her demure, cookie-baker phase, she was emphatically "Hillary Clinton," mute, nodding adorer and helpmate of Bill. She half-concealed herself in "Hillary Clinton" until the coast was clear. With the Inauguration, the formal, formidable triple name has lumbered into place like a convoy of armored cars: Hillary Rodham Clinton.

The name problem for married women is a clumsy mess. Married women have four or more choices. 1) Keep the last name they were given at birth. 2) Take the husband's last name. 3) Use three names, as in Hillary Rodham Clinton; or, as women did in the '70s, join the wife's birth name and the husband's birth name with a hyphen—

a practice that in the third generation down the road would produce geometrically expanded multiple-hyphenated nightmares. 4) Use the unmarried name in most matters professional, and use the husband's name in at least some matters personal and domestic. Most men, if they were to wake up one morning and find themselves transformed into married women, would (rather huffily) choose Option No. 1.

Variations: one woman who has been married three times and divorced three times uses all four available last names, changing them as if she were changing outfits, according to mood or season. More commonly it happens that a woman has made her professional reputation, in her 20s and 30s, while using the name of her first husband, then gets divorced and possibly remarried, but remains stuck with the first husband's name in the middle of her three-name procession.

Names possess a peculiar indelible power—subversive, evocative, satirical, by turns. The name is an aura, a costume. Dickens knew how names proclaim character—although anyone named Lance is bound to hope that that is not always true. Democrats used to have fun with "George Herbert Walker Bush." The full inventory of the pedigree, formally decanted, produced a piled-on, Connecticut preppie–Little Lord Fauntleroy effect that went nicely with the populist crack that Bush "was born on third base and thought he had hit a triple."

How many names does a decent person need? For ordinary getting around, two, as a bird requires two wings. More than two, as a rule, is overweight. Only God should use fewer than two.

The words with which people and things are named have a changeful magic. Some cultures invent different names for people in different stages of life. In Chinese tradition a boy of school age would be given a "book name," to be used in arranging marriages and other official matters. A boy's book name might be "Worthy Prince" or "Spring Dragon" or "Celestial Emolument." (Does a father say, "Hello, have you met my boy, Celestial Emolument?")

Hillary Rodham Clinton may find her name changing still further as her White House power evolves. Perhaps by next year, she will be known as "H.R. Clinton." Maybe the year after that, she will be "H.R. (Bob) Clinton."

Questions for Discussion and Writing

1. How much attention is paid to a person's name in our culture? What evidence can you cite that demonstrates people's concern about their own or others' names?
2. Morrow says that names have "an intricate life of their own." What interesting trends or characteristics are apparent in the way people use and regard names today? Name some of these trends and, if you can, explain their causes and the effects they have upon people.
3. In what ways can a name be a "burden"? How can a name be something positive in a person's life? If you can, describe someone you know and explain how that person's name has been either a burden or a positive influence in his or her life.

How to Write a Personal Letter

Garrison Keillor

We shy persons need to write a letter now and then, or else we'll dry up and blow away. It's true. And I speak as one who loves to reach for the phone, dial the number, and talk. I say, "Big Bopper here—what's shakin', babes?" The telephone is to shyness what Hawaii is to February, it's a way out of the woods, *and yet:* a letter is better.

Such a sweet gift—a piece of handmade writing, in an envelope that is not a bill, sitting in our friend's path when she trudges home from a long day spent among wahoos and savages, a day our words will help repair. They don't need to be immortal, just sincere. She can read them twice and again tomorrow: *You're someone I care about, Corinne, and think of often and every time I do you make me smile.*

We need to write, otherwise nobody will know who we are. They will have only a vague impression of us as A Nice Person, because frankly, we don't shine at conversation, we lack the confidence to thrust our faces forward and say, "Hi, I'm Heather Hooten, let me tell you about my week." Mostly we say "Uh-huh" and "Oh really." People smile and look over our shoulder, looking for someone else to talk to.

So a shy person sits down and writes a letter. To be known by another person—to meet and talk freely on the page—to be close despite distance. To escape from anonymity and be our own sweet selves and express the music of our souls.

Same thing that moves a giant rock star to sing his heart out in front of 123,000 people moves us to take ballpoint in hand and write a few lines to our dear Aunt Eleanor. *We want to be known.* We want her to know that we have fallen in love, that we quit our job, and we're moving to New York, and we want to say a few things that might not get said in casual conversation: *thank you for what you've meant to me, I am very happy right now.*

The first step in writing letters is to get over the guilt of *not* writing. You don't "owe" anybody a letter. Letters are a gift. The burning shame you feel when you see unanswered mail makes it harder to pick up a pen and makes for a cheerless letter when you finally do. *I feel bad about not writing, but I've been so busy,* etc. Skip this. Few letters are obligatory, and they are *Thanks for the wonderful gift* and *I am terribly sorry to hear about George's death* and *Yes, you're welcome to stay with us next month,* and not many more than that. Write those promptly if you want to keep your friends. Don't worry about the others, except love letters, of course. When your true love writes *Dear Light of My Life, Joy of My Heart, O Lovely Pulsating Core of My Sensate Life,* some response is called for.

Some of the best letters are tossed off in a burst of inspiration, so keep your writing stuff in one place where you can sit down for a few minutes and *Dear Roy, I am in the middle of an essay for International Paper but thought I'd drop you a line. Hi to your sweetie too* dash off a note to a pal. Envelopes, stamps, address book, everything in a drawer so you can write fast when the pen is hot.

A blank white 8″ × 11″ sheet can look as big as Montana if the pen's not so hot—try a smaller page and write boldly. Or use a note card with a piece of fine art on the front; if your letter ain't good, at least they get the Matisse. Get a pen that makes a sensuous line, get a comfortable typewriter, a friendly word processor—whichever feels easy to the hand.

Sit for a few minutes with the blank sheet in front of you, and meditate on the person you will write to, let your friend come to mind until you can almost see her or him in the room with you. Remember the last time you saw each other and how your friend looked and what you said and what perhaps was unsaid between you, and when your friend becomes real to you, start to write.

Write the salutation—*Dear You*—and take a deep breath and plunge in. A simple declarative sentence will do, followed by another and another and another. Tell us what you're doing and tell it like you were talking to us. Don't think about grammar, don't think about lit'ry style, don't try to write dramatically, just give us your news. Where did you go, who did you see, what did they say, what do you think?

If you don't know where to begin, start with the present moment: *I'm sitting at the kitchen table on a rainy Saturday morning. Everyone is gone and the house is quiet.* Let your simple description of the present moment lead to something else, let the letter drift gently along.

The toughest letter to crank out is one that is meant to impress, as we all know from writing job applications; if it's hard work to slip off a letter to a friend, maybe you're trying too hard to be terrific. A letter is only a report to someone who already likes you for reasons other than your brilliance. Take it easy.

Don't worry about form. It's not a term paper. When you come to the end of one episode, just start a new paragraph. You can go from a few lines about the sad state of rock 'n roll to the fight with your mother to your fond memories of Mexico to your cat's urinary tract infection to a few thoughts on personal indebtedness to the kitchen sink and what's in it. The more you write, the easier it gets, and when you have a True True Friend to write to, a *compadre,* a soul sibling, then it's like driving a car down a country road, you just get behind the keyboard and press on the gas.

Don't tear up the page and start over when you write a bad line—try to write your way out of it. Make mistakes and plunge on. Let the letter cook along and let yourself be bold. Outrage, confusion, love—whatever is in your mind, let it find a way to the page. Writing is a means of discovery, always, and when you come to the end and write *Yours ever* or *Hugs and Kisses,* you'll know something you didn't when you wrote *Dear Pal.*

Probably your friend will put your letter away, and it'll be read again a few years from now—and it will improve with age. And forty years from now, your friend's grandkids will dig it out of the attic and read it, a sweet and precious relic of the ancient Eighties that gives them a sudden clear glimpse of you and her and the world we old-timers knew. You will then have created an object of art. Your simple lines about where you went, who you saw, what they said, will speak to those children and they will feel in their hearts the humanity of our times.

You can't pick up a phone and call the future and tell them about our times. You have to pick up a piece of paper.

Questions for Discussion and Writing

1. What does Keillor mean when he says we have to write so people know who we are? Do people know who you are from the kinds of writing you do? Why or why not?

2. Why does Keillor feel personal letters are valuable? List at least four of the reasons he gives in his essay. Is he correct? Name two or three reasons of your own why a personal letter may be important today.

3. How would you compare what is communicated by telephone, memo, business letter, or e-mail with what Keillor says is conveyed by a personal letter? Could any of these accomplish the same things as a personal letter? Explain your answer.

■ The New Prohibitionism

Charles Krauthammer

The oddest thing about the current national crusade against tobacco is not its frenzy—our culture lives from one frenzy to the next—but its selectivity. Of course tobacco is a great national killer. It deserves all the pummeling it gets. But alcohol is a great national killer too, and it has enjoyed an amazingly free ride amid the fury of the New Prohibitionism.

Joe Camel has been banished forever, but those beloved Budweiser frogs— succeeded by even cuter Budweiser lizards—keep marching along, right into the consciousness of every TV-watching kid in the country.

For 26 years television has been free of cigarette ads. Why? Because TV persuades as nothing else, and we don't want young people—inveterate TV watchers— persuaded. Yet television is bursting with exhortations to drink. TV sports in particular, a staple of adolescents, is one long hymn to the glories of beer.

And the sports-worshipping years are precisely the time that kids learn to drink. The median age at which they start drinking is just over 13. A 1990 survey found that 56% of students in Grades 5 through 12 say alcohol advertising encourages them to drink. Surprise!

Am I for Prohibition? No. But I am for a little perspective. We tend to think of the turn-of-the-century temperance movement as little blue-haired ladies trying to prevent people from having a good time on Saturday night. In fact, the temperance movement was part of a much larger progressive movement seeking to improve the appalling conditions of the urban working class. These were greatly exacerbated by rampant alcoholism that contributed to extraordinary levels of spousal and child abuse, abandonment and destitution.

Alcohol is still a cause of staggering devastation. It kills 100,000 Americans a year—not only from disease but also from accidents. In 1996, 41% of all U.S. traffic fatalities were alcohol related. It causes huge economic losses and untold suffering. Why, then, do the Bud frogs get to play the Super Bowl while Joe Camel goes the way of the Marlboro Man?

The most plausible answer is that tobacco is worse because it kills more people. Indeed it does. But 100,000 people a year is still a fair carnage. Moreover, the really compelling comparison is this: alcohol is far more deadly than tobacco *to innocent bystanders.* In a free society, should we not consider behavior that injures others more worthy of regulation than behavior that merely injures oneself? The primary motive for gun control, after all, is concern about homicide, not suicide.

The antitobacco folk, aware of this bedrock belief, try to play up the harm smokers cause others. Thus the attorneys general seeking billions of dollars in damages from the tobacco companies are claiming that taxpayers have been unfairly made to pay for the treatment of smoking-related illnesses.

A clever ploy. But the hardheaded truth is that premature death from smoking, which generally affects people in their late-middle and early retirement years, is an economic boon to society. The money saved on pensions and on the truly expensive health care that comes with old age—something these smokers never achieve—surely balances, if it does not exceed, the cost of treating tobacco-related diseases.

The alternative and more dramatic antitobacco tactic is to portray smoking as an assault on nonsmokers via secondhand smoke. Now, secondhand smoke is certainly a nuisance. But the claim that it is a killer is highly dubious. "The statistical evidence," reported the nonpartisan Congressional Research Service in 1994, "does not appear to support a conclusion that there are substantive health effects of passive smoking."

Unlike secondhand smoke, secondhand booze is a world-class killer. Drunk driving alone kills 17,000 people a year. And alcohol's influence extends far beyond driving: it contributes to everything from bar fights to domestic violence. One study found that 44% of assailants in cases of marital abuse had been drinking. Another study found that 60% of wife batterers had been under the influence. Whatever claims you make against tobacco, you'd have quite a time looking for cases of the nicotine-crazed turning on their wives with a butcher knife.

Moreover, look at the *kinds* of people alcohol kills. Drunk drivers kill toddlers. They kill teens. They kill whole families. Tobacco does not kill toddlers and teens. Tobacco strikes late. It kills, but at a very long remove in time. Its victims generally have already had their chance at life. Tobacco merely shortens life; alcohol can deprive people of it.

Still undecided which of the two poisons is more deserving of social disapprobation? Here's the ultimate test. Ask yourself this. If you knew your child was going to become addicted to either alcohol or tobacco, which would you choose?

Questions for Discussion and Writing

1. Summarize the reasons Krauthammer gives for Americans' apparent willingness to tolerate alcohol advertisements more than tobacco ads. What other reasons can you give for this apparent tolerance?

2. What efforts are you aware of in your state or community to reduce the use of tobacco or alcohol, especially among young people? Are these efforts comparable for both substances? How or how not? What else should be done?

3. Read again the question with which Krauthammer ends his essay. If you were to advise your own child about using tobacco or alcohol, what would you say? What ideas would you especially want to emphasize? Why?

Here's to Your Health

Joan Dunayer

As the only freshman on his high school's varsity wrestling team, Tod was anxious to fit in with his older teammates. One night after a match, he was offered a tequila bottle on the ride home. Tod felt he had to accept, or he would seem like a sissy. He took a swallow, and every time the bottle was passed back to him, he took another swallow. After seven swallows, he passed out. His terrified teammates carried him into his home, and his mother then rushed him to the hospital. After his stomach was pumped, Tod learned that his blood alcohol level had been so high that he was lucky not to be in a coma or dead.

Although alcohol sometimes causes rapid poisoning, frequently leads to long-term addiction, and always threatens self-control, our society encourages drinking. Many parents, by their example, give children the impression that alcohol is an essential ingredient of social gatherings. Peer pressure turns bachelor parties, fraternity initiations, and spring-semester beach vacations into competitions in "getting trashed." In soap operas, glamorous characters pour Scotch whiskey from crystal decanters as readily as most people turn on the faucet for tap water. In films and rock videos, trend-setters party in nightclubs and bars. And who can recall a televised baseball or basketball game without a beer commercial? By the age of 21, the average American has seen drinking on TV about 75,000 times. Alcohol ads appear with pounding frequency—in magazines, on billboards, in college newspapers—contributing to a harmful myth about drinking.

Part of the myth is that liquor signals professional success. In a slick men's magazine, one full-page ad for Scotch whiskey shows two men seated in an elegant restaurant. Both are in their thirties, perfectly groomed, and wearing expensive-looking gray suits. The windows are draped with velvet, the table with spotless white linen. Each place-setting consists of a long-stemmed water goblet, silver utensils, and thick silver plates. On each plate is a half-empty cocktail glass. The two men are grinning and shaking hands, as if they've just concluded a business deal. The caption reads, "The taste of success."

Contrary to what the liquor company would have us believe, drinking is more closely related to lack of success than to achievement. Among students, the heaviest drinkers have the lowest grades. In the work force, alcoholics are frequently late or absent, tend to perform poorly, and often get fired. Although alcohol abuse occurs in all economic classes, it remains most severe among the poor.

Another part of the alcohol myth is that drinking makes you more attractive to the opposite sex. "Hot, hot, hot," one commercial's soundtrack begins, as the camera scans a crowd of college-age beachgoers. Next it follows the curve of a woman's leg up to her bare hip and lingers there. She is young, beautiful, wearing a bikini. A young guy, carrying an ice chest, positions himself near to where she sits. He is tan, muscular. She doesn't show much interest—until he opens the chest and takes out a beer. Now she smiles over at him. He raises his eyebrows and, invitingly, holds up another can. She joins him. This beer, the song concludes, "attracts like no other."

Beer doesn't make anyone sexier. Like all alcohol, it lowers the levels of male hormones in men and of female hormones in women—even when taken in small amounts. In substantial amounts, alcohol can cause infertility in women and impotence in men. Some alcoholic men even develop enlarged breasts, from their increased female hormones.

The alcohol myth also creates the illusion that beer and athletics are a perfect combination. One billboard features three high-action images: a baseball player running at top speed, a surfer riding a wave, and a basketball player leaping to make a dunk shot. A particular light beer, the billboard promises, "won't slow you down."

"Slow you down" is exactly what alcohol does. Drinking plays a role in over six million injuries each year—not counting automobile accidents. Even in small amounts, alcohol dulls the brain, reducing muscle coordination and slowing reaction time. It also interferes with the ability to focus the eyes and adjust to a sudden change in brightness—such as the flash of a car's headlights. Drinking and driving, responsible for over half of all automobile deaths, is the leading cause of death among teenagers. Continued alcohol abuse can physically alter the brain, permanently impairing learning and memory. Long-term drinking is related to malnutrition, weakening of the bones, and ulcers. It increases the risk of liver failure, heart disease, and stomach cancer.

Finally, according to the myth fostered by the media in our culture, alcohol generates a warm glow of happiness that unifies the family. In one popular film, the only food visible at a wedding reception is an untouched wedding cake, but beer, whiskey, and vodka flow freely. Most of the guests are drunk. After shouting into the microphone to get everyone's attention, the band leader asks the bride and groom to come forward. They are presented with two wine-filled silver drinking cups branching out from a single stem. "If you can drink your cups without spilling any wine," the band leader tells them, "you will have good luck for the rest of your lives." The couple drain their cups without taking a breath, and the crowd cheers.

A marriage, however, is unlikely to be "lucky" if alcohol plays a major role in it. Nearly two-thirds of domestic violence involves drinking. Alcohol abuse by parents is strongly tied to child neglect and juvenile delinquency. Drinking during pregnancy can lead to miscarriage and is a major cause of such birth defects as deformed limbs and mental retardation. Those who depend on alcohol are far from happy: over a fourth of the patients in state and county mental institutions have alcohol problems; more than half of all violent crimes are alcohol-related; the rate of suicide among alcoholics is fifteen times higher than among the general population.

Alcohol, some would have us believe, is part of being successful, sexy, healthy, and happy. But those who have suffered from it—directly or indirectly—know otherwise. For alcohol's victims, "Here's to your health" rings with a terrible irony when it is accompanied by the clink of liquor glasses.

Questions for Discussion and Writing

1. Basing your answer on your own experience with television and other advertising media, how accurate is Dunayer's portrayal of the way such media promote alcohol? Cite examples of the ways advertisements contribute to the myths about alcohol that Dunayer describes in her essay.
2. Do you feel alcohol consumption is a problem in our society today? Why or why not? What examples could you cite to support, qualify, or refute Dunayer's ideas?
3. In addition to those Dunayer describes, what other myths does our society promote about alcohol consumption? Are the media the only sources that promote such myths? What other influences help to popularize false ideas about alcohol?

■ It's Time to Ban Handguns

Lance Morrow

By a curiosity of evolution, every human skull harbors a prehistoric vestige: a reptilian brain. This atavism, like a hand grenade cushioned in the more civilized surrounding cortex, is the dark hive where many of mankind's primitive impulses originate. To go partners with that throwback, Americans have carried out of their own history another curiosity that evolution forgot to discard as the country changed from a sparsely populated, underpoliced agrarian society to a modern industrial civilization. That vestige is the gun—most notoriously the handgun, an anachronistic tool still much in use. Since 1963 guns have finished off more Americans (400,000) than World War II did.

After one more handgun made it into American history last week (another nastily poignant little "Saturday night" .22 that lay like an orphan in a Dallas pawnshop until another of those clammy losers took it back to his rented room to dream on), a lot of Americans said to themselves, "Well, maybe *this* will finally persuade them to do something about those damned guns." Nobody would lay a dime on it. The National Rifle Association battened down its hatches for a siege of rough editorial weather, but calculated that the antigun indignation would presently subside, just as it always does. After Kennedy. After King. After Kennedy. After Wallace. After Lennon. After Reagan. After . . . the nation will be left twitching and flinching as before to the pops of its 55 million pistols and the highest rate of murder by guns in the world.

The rest of the planet is both appalled and puzzled by the spectacle of a superpower so politically stable and internally violent. Countries like Britain and Japan, which have low murder rates and virtual prohibitions on handguns, are astonished by the over-the-counter ease with which Americans can buy firearms.

Americans themselves are profoundly discouraged by the handguns that seem to breed uncontrollably among them like roaches. For years the majority of them have favored restrictions on handguns. In 1938 a Gallup poll discovered that 84% wanted gun controls. The latest Gallup finds that 62% want stricter laws governing handgun sales. Yet Americans go on buying handguns at the rate of one every 13 seconds. The murder rate keeps rising. It is both a cause and an effect of gun sales. And every few years—or months—some charismatic public character takes a slug from an itinerant mental case caressing a bizarre fantasy in his brain and the sick, secret weight of a pistol in his pocket.

Why do the bloody years keep rolling by without guns becoming subject to the kind of regulation we calmly apply to drugs, cars, boat trailers, CB radios and dogs? The answer is only partly that the National Rifle Association is, by some Senators' estimate, the most effective lobbying organization in Washington and the deadliest at targeting its congressional enemies at election time. The nation now has laws, all right—a patchwork of some 25,000 gun regulations, federal, state and local, that are so scattered and inconsistent as to be preposterously ineffectual.

Firearms have achieved in the U.S. a strange sort of inevitability—the nation's gun-ridden frontier heritage getting smokily mingled now with a terror of accelerating criminal violence and a sense that as the social contract tatters, the good guys must have their guns to defend themselves against the rising tribes of bad guys. It is very hard to persuade the good guys that all those guns in their hands wind up doing more lethal harm to their own kind than to the animals they fear; that good guys sometimes get drunk and shoot other good guys in a rage, or blow their own heads off (by design or accident) or hit their own children by mistake. Most murders are done on impulse, and handguns are perfectly responsive to the purpose: a blind red rage flashes in the brain and fires a signal through the nerves to the trigger finger—**BLAM!** Guns do not require much work. You do not have to get your hands bloody, as you would with a knife, or make the strenuous and intimately dangerous effort required to kill with bare hands. The space between gun and victim somehow purifies the relationship—at least for the person at the trigger—and makes it so much easier to perform the deed. The bullet goes invisibly across space to flesh. An essential disconnection, almost an abstraction, is maintained. That's why it is so easy—convenient, really—to kill with one of the things.

The post-assassination sermon, an earnest lamentation about the "sickness of American society," has become a notably fatuous genre that blames everyone and then, after 15 minutes of earnestly empty regret, absolves everyone. It is true that there is a good deal of evil in the American air; television and the sheer repetitiousness of violence have made a lot of the country morally weary and dull and difficult to shock. Much of the violence, however, results not from the sickness of the society but the stupidity and inadequacy of its laws. The nation needs new laws to put at least some guns out of business.

Questions for Discussion and Writing

1. Morrow uses rich and precise vocabulary to convey many of his central ideas in this selection. Use a dictionary to check the meaning of any words or phrases with which you are unfamiliar. After doing so, explain how the following words reinforce the essay's main point and Morrow's effort to persuade his readers about the need to ban handguns: *vestige, cortex, agrarian, anachronistic, charismatic, itinerant mental case.*
2. What arguments are you aware of that favor or oppose banning handguns? What is your response to such arguments?
3. Would you own a handgun? Explain why or why not.

Hispanic, USA: The Conveyor-Belt Ladies

Rose del Castillo Guilbault

The conveyor-belt ladies were the migrant women, mostly from Texas, I worked with during the summers of my teenage years. I call them conveyor-belt ladies because our entire relationship took place while sorting tomatoes on a conveyor belt.

We were like a cast in a play where all the action occurs on one set. We'd return day after day to perform the same roles, only this stage was a vegetable-packing shed, and at the end of the season there was no applause. The players could look forward only to the same uninspiring parts on a string of grim real-life stages.

The women and their families arrived in May for the carrot season, spent the summer in the tomato sheds and stayed through October for the bean harvest. After that, they emptied the town, some returning to their homes in Texas (cities like McAllen, Douglas, Brownsville), while others continued on the migrant trail, picking cotton in the San Joaquin Valley or grapefruits and oranges in the Imperial Valley.

Most of these women had started in the fields. The vegetable packing sheds were a step up, easier than the back-breaking, grueling work the field demanded. The work was more tedious than strenuous, paid better, provided fairly steady hours and clean bathrooms. Best of all, you weren't subjected to the elements.

The summer I was 16, my mother got jobs for both of us as tomato sorters. That's how I came to be included in the seasonal sorority of the conveyor belt.

The work consisted of standing and picking flawed tomatoes off the conveyor belt before they rolled off into the shipping boxes at the end of the line. These boxes were immediately loaded onto waiting delivery trucks, so it was crucial not to let imperfect tomatoes through.

The work could be slow or intense, depending on the quality of the tomatoes and how many there were. Work increased when the company's deliveries got backlogged or after rainy weather had delayed picking.

During those times, it was not unusual to work from 7 A.M. to midnight, playing catch-up. I never heard anyone complain about the overtime. Overtime meant desperately needed extra money.

I was not happy to be part of the agricultural work force. I would have preferred working in a dress shop or baby-sitting, like my friends. But I had a dream that would cost a lot of money—college. And the fact was, this was the highest-paying work I could do.

But it wasn't so much the work that bothered me. I was embarrassed because only Mexicans worked at packing sheds. I had heard my schoolmates joke about the "ugly, fat Mexican women" at the sheds. They ridiculed the way they dressed and laughed at the "funny way" they talked. I feared working with them would irrevocably stigmatize me, setting me further apart from my Anglo classmates.

At 16 I was more American than Mexican and, with adolescent arrogance, felt superior to these "uneducated" women. I might be one of them, I reasoned, but I was not like them.

But it was difficult not to like the women. They were a gregarious, entertaining group, easing the long, monotonous hours with bawdy humor, spicy gossip and inventive laments. They poked fun at all the male workers and did hysterical impersonations of a dyspeptic Anglo supervisor. Although he didn't speak Spanish (other than "*Mujeres, trabajo, trabajo!*" Women, work, work!), he seemed to sense he was being laughed at. That would account for the sudden rages when he would stamp his foot and forbid us to talk until break time.

"I bet he understands Spanish and just pretends so he can hear what we say," I whispered to Rosa.

"*Ay, no, hija,* it's all the buzzing in his ears that alerts him that these *viejas* (old women) are bad-mouthing him!" Rosa giggled.

But it would have been easier to tie the women's tongues in a knot than to keep them quiet. Eventually the ladies had their way and their fun, and the men learned to ignore them.

We were often shifted around, another strategy to keep us quiet. This gave me ample opportunity to get to know everyone, listen to their life stories and absorb the gossip.

Pretty Rosa described her romances and her impending wedding to a handsome field worker. Bertha, a heavy-set, dark-skinned woman, told me that Rosa's marriage would cause nothing but headaches because the man was younger and too handsome. Maria, large, moon-faced and placid, described the births of each of her nine children, warning me about the horrors of childbirth. Pragmatic Minnie, a tiny woman who always wore printed cotton dresses, scoffed at Maria's stupidity, telling me she wouldn't have so many kids if she had ignored that good-for-nothing priest and gotten her tubes tied!

In unexpected moments, they could turn melancholic: recounting the babies who died because their mothers couldn't afford medical care; the alcoholic, abusive husbands who were their "cross to bear"; the racism they experienced in Texas, where they were branded "dirty Mexicans" or "Mexican dogs" and not allowed in certain restaurants.

They spoke with the detached fatalism of people with limited choices and alternatives. Their lives were as raw and brutal as ghetto streets—something they accepted with an odd grace and resignation.

I was appalled and deeply affected by these confidences. The injustices they endured enraged me; their personal struggles overwhelmed me. I knew I could do little but sympathize.

My mother, no stranger to suffering, suggested I was too impressionable when I emotionally told her the women's stories. "That's nothing," she'd say lightly. "If they were in Mexico, life would be even harder. At least there's opportunities here, you can work."

My icy arrogance quickly thawed, that first summer, as my respect for the conveyor-belt ladies grew.

I worked in the packing sheds for several summers. The last season also turned out to be the last time I lived at home. It was the end of a chapter in my life, but I didn't know it then. I had just finished junior college and was transferring to the university. I was already over-educated for seasonal work, but if you counted the overtime, no other jobs came close to paying so well, so I went back one last time.

The ladies treated me with warmth and respect. I was a college student, deserving of special treatment.

Aguedita, the crew chief, moved me to softer and better-paying jobs within the plant. I went from the conveyor belt to shoving boxes down a chute and finally to weighing boxes of tomatoes on a scale—the highest-paying position for a woman.

When the union's dues collector showed up, the women hid me in the bathroom. They had decided it was unfair for me to have to join the union and pay dues, since I worked only during the summer.

"Where's the student?" the union rep would ask, opening the door to a barrage of complaints about the union's unfairness.

Maria (of the nine children) tried to feed me all summer, bringing extra tortillas, which were delicious. I accepted them guiltily, always wondering if I was taking food away from her children. Others would bring rental contracts or other documents for me to explain and translate.

The last day of work was splendidly beautiful, warm and sunny. If this had been a movie, these last scenes would have been shot in soft focus, with a crescendo of music in the background.

But real life is anti-climactic. As it was, nothing unusual happened. The conveyor belt's loud humming was turned off, silenced for the season. The women sighed as they removed their aprons. Some of them just walked off, calling "*Hasta la próxima!*" Until next time!

But most of the conveyor-belt ladies shook my hand, gave me a blessing or a big hug.

"Make us proud!" they said.

I hope I have.

Questions for Discussion and Writing

1. Explain the author's relationship with the "conveyor-belt ladies." How does she regard them, and how is that shown in the essay? How do they feel about her? How do we know?
2. Citing details from the essay, explain how the experiences Del Castillo Guilbault describes are particularly Hispanic American and unique to that culture. How is her overall experience at the same time universal, that is, also representative of individuals from other cultures as well?
3. Why does the author's role as a college student give her unique status among her coworkers? Have you experienced that same feeling of uniqueness or sensed a similar separateness from others because you are a college student? If so, describe this feeling and the situation in which it occurred. Did you feel good about your uniqueness in this situation? Why or why not?

■ Night Walker

Brent Staples

My first victim was a woman—white, well dressed, probably in her early 20s. I came upon her late one evening on a deserted street in Hyde Park, a relatively affluent neighborhood in an otherwise mean, impoverished section of Chicago. As I swung onto the avenue behind her, there seemed to be a discreet, uninflammatory distance between us. Not so. She cast back a worried glance. To her, the youngish black man—a broad six feet two inches with a beard and billowing hair, both hands shoved into the pockets of a bulky military jacket—seemed menacingly close. She picked up her pace and was soon running in earnest. Within seconds she disappeared into a cross street.

That was more than a decade ago. I was 22 years old, a graduate student newly arrived at the University of Chicago. It was in the echo of that terrified woman's footfalls that I first began to know the unwieldy inheritance I'd come into—the ability to alter public space in ugly ways. It was clear that she thought herself the quarry of a mugger, a rapist, or worse. Suffering a bout of insomnia, however, I was stalking sleep, not defenseless wayfarers. As a softy who is scarcely able to take a knife to a raw chicken—let alone hold one to a person's throat—I was surprised, embarrassed, and dismayed all at once. Her flight made me feel like an accomplice in tyranny. It also made it clear that I was indistinguishable from the muggers who occasionally seeped into the area from the surrounding ghetto. I soon gathered that being perceived as dangerous is a hazard in itself: Where fear and weapons meet—and they often do in urban America—there is always the possibility of death.

In that first year, my first away from my hometown, I was to become thoroughly familiar with the language of fear. At dark, shadowy intersections, I could cross in front of a car stopped at a traffic light and elicit the *thunk, thunk, thunk, thunk* of the driver—black, white, male, female—hammering down the door locks. On less traveled streets after dark, I grew accustomed to but never comfortable with people crossing to the other side of the street rather than pass me. Then there were the standard unpleasantries with policemen, doormen, bouncers, cabdrivers, and others whose business it is to screen out troublesome individuals *before* there is any nastiness.

I moved to New York nearly two years ago and I have remained an avid night walker. In central Manhattan, the near-constant crowd covers the tense one-on-one street encounters. Elsewhere, things can get very taut indeed.

After dark, on the warrenlike streets of Brooklyn where I live, I often see women who fear the worst from me. They seem to have set their faces on neutral, and with their purse straps strung across their chests bandolier-style, they forge ahead as though bracing themselves against being tackled. I understand, of course, that the danger they perceive is not a hallucination. Women are particularly vulnerable to street violence, and young black males are drastically overrepresented among the perpetrators of that violence. Yet these truths are no solace against the alienation that comes of being ever the suspect, an entity with whom pedestrians avoid making eye contact.

It is not altogether clear to me how I reached the ripe old age of 22 without being conscious of the lethality nighttime pedestrians attributed to me. Perhaps it was because in Chester, Pa., the small, angry industrial town where I came of age in the 1960s, I was scarcely noticeable against a backdrop of gang warfare, street knifings, and murders. I grew up one of the good boys, had perhaps a half-dozen fistfights. In retrospect, my shyness of combat has clear sources. As a boy, I saw countless tough guys locked away; I have since buried several, too. They were babies, really—a teen-age cousin, a brother of 22, a childhood friend in his mid-20s—all gone down in episodes of bravado played out in the streets. I chose, perhaps unconsciously, to remain a shadow—timid, but a survivor.

The fearsomeness mistakenly attributed to me in public places often has a perilous flavor. The most frightening of these confusions occurred in the late 1970s and early 1980s, when I worked as a journalist in Chicago. One day, rushing into the office of a magazine I was writing for with a deadline story in hand, I was mistaken for a burglar. The office manager called security and, with an ad hoc posse, pursued me through the labyrinthine halls, nearly to my editor's door. I had no way of proving who I was. I could only move briskly toward the company of someone who knew me.

Relatively speaking, however, I never fared as badly as another black male journalist. He went to nearby Waukegan, Ill., a couple of summers ago to work on a story about a murderer who was born there. Mistaking the reporter for the killer, police officers hauled him from his car at gunpoint and but for his press credentials would probably have tried to book him. Such episodes are not uncommon. Black men trade tales like this all the time.

Over the years, I learned to smother the rage I felt at so often being mistaken for a criminal. Not to do so would surely have led to madness. I now take precautions to make myself less threatening. I move about with care, particularly late in the evening. I give a wide berth to nervous people on subway platforms during the wee hours. If I happen to be entering a building behind some people who appear skittish, I may walk by, letting them clear the lobby before I return, so as not to seem to be following them. I have been calm and extremely congenial on those rare occasions when I've been pulled over by the police.

And on late-evening constitutionals I employ what has proved to be an excellent tension-reducing measure: I whistle melodies from Beethoven and Vivaldi and the more popular classical composers. Even steely New Yorkers hunching toward nighttime destinations seem to relax, and occasionally they even join in the tune. Virtually everybody seems to sense that a mugger wouldn't be warbling bright, sunny selections from Vivaldi's "Four Seasons." It is my equivalent of the cowbell that hikers wear when they are in bear country.

Questions for Discussion and Writing

1. In the third paragraph, Staples gives several examples of what he calls "the language of fear." Discuss these examples and define what Staples means by the term. What examples of the language of fear exist in your own community? For example, how do homeowners where you live demonstrate fear of others by what they do to ensure their own safety or the safety of their property?

2. Discuss a time when, like Staples, you were mistakenly prejudged by others. How did the event make you feel when it happened? How do you feel about it now?

3. How safe are the streets of your community late at night? Write a brief description identifying one or more unsafe elements, and recommend ways to make them safer.

■ The Struggle to Be an All-American Girl

Elizabeth Wong

It's still there, the Chinese school on Yale Street where my brother and I used to go. Despite the new coat of paint and the high wire fence, the school I knew 10 years ago remains remarkably, stoically the same.

Every day at 5 P.M., instead of playing with our fourth- and fifth-grade friends or sneaking out to the empty lot to hunt ghosts and animal bones, my brother and I had to go to Chinese school. No amount of kicking, screaming, or pleading could dissuade my mother, who was solidly determined to have us learn the language of our heritage.

Forcibly, she walked us the seven long, hilly blocks from our home to school, depositing our defiant tearful faces before the stern principal. My only memory of him is that he swayed on his heels like a palm tree, and he always clasped his impatient twitching hands behind his back. I recognized him as a repressed maniacal child killer, and knew that if we ever saw his hands we'd be in big trouble.

We all sat in little chairs in an empty auditorium. The room smelled like Chinese medicine, an imported faraway mustiness. Like ancient mothballs or dirty closets. I hated that smell. I favored crisp new scents. Like the soft French perfume that my American teacher wore in public school.

There was a stage far to the right, flanked by an American flag and the flag of the Nationalist Republic of China, which was also red, white and blue but not as pretty.

Although the emphasis at the school was mainly language—speaking, reading, writing—the lessons always began with an exercise in politeness. With the entrance of the teacher, the best student would tap a bell and everyone would get up, kowtow, and chant, "Sing san ho," the phonetic for "How are you, teacher?"

Being ten years old, I had better things to learn than ideographs copied painstakingly in lines that ran right to left from the tip of a *moc but,* a real ink pen that had to be held in an awkward way if blotches were to be avoided. After all, I could do the multiplication tables, name the satellites of Mars, and write reports on *Little Women* and *Black Beauty.* Nancy Drew, my favorite book heroine, never spoke Chinese.

The language was a source of embarrassment. More times than not, I had tried to disassociate myself from the nagging loud voice that followed me wherever I wandered in the nearby American supermarket outside Chinatown. The voice belonged to my grandmother, a fragile woman in her seventies who could outshout the best of the street vendors. Her humor was raunchy, her Chinese rhythmless, patternless. It was quick, it was loud, it was unbeautiful. It was not like the quiet, lilting romance of French or the gentle refinement of the American South. Chinese sounded pedestrian. Public.

In Chinatown, the comings and goings of hundreds of Chinese on their daily tasks sounded chaotic and frenzied. I did not want to be thought of as mad, as talking gibberish. When I spoke English, people nodded at me, smiled sweetly, said encouraging words. Even the people in my culture would cluck and say that I'd do well in life. "My, doesn't she move her lips fast," they would say, meaning that I'd be able to keep up with the world outside Chinatown.

My brother was even more fanatical than I about speaking English. He was especially hard on my mother, criticizing her, often cruelly, for her pidgin speech—smatterings of Chinese scattered like chop suey in her conversation. "It's not, 'What it is,' Mom," he'd say in exasperation. "It's 'What *is* it, what *is* it, what *is* it!'" Sometimes Mom might leave out an occasional "the" or "a," or perhaps a verb of being. He would stop her in mid-sentence: "Say it again, Mom. Say it right." When he tripped over his own tongue, he'd blame it on her: "See, Mom, it's all your fault. You set a bad example."

What infuriated my mother most was when my brother cornered her on her consonants, especially "r." My father had played a cruel joke on Mom by assigning her an American name that her tongue wouldn't allow her to say. No matter how hard she tried, "Ruth" always ended up "Luth" or "Roof."

After two years of writing with a *moc but* and reciting words with multiples of meanings, I finally was granted a cultural divorce. I was permitted to stop Chinese school.

I thought of myself as multicultural. I preferred tacos to egg rolls; I enjoyed Cinco de Mayo more than Chinese New Year.

At last, I was one of you; I wasn't one of them.

Sadly, I still am.

Questions for Discussion and Writing

1. Explain the meaning of the essay's title. Is there more than one kind of struggle revealed in the essay? What struggles do other young women and men endure as they grow up?
2. Explain the meaning and significance of the last three sentences in the essay. How much truth is in what the sentences state individually as well as together? How do you feel about Wong's final statement?
3. What advice would you give to Elizabeth Wong about her struggle to be an all-American girl? Try putting your ideas in the form of a letter to Wong, or write a brief essay. If you have endured the same or a similar kind of struggle, use your own experiences to illustrate your ideas.

Note: In December of 1996, the Oakland Unified School District Board of Education in California approved a policy recognizing "Ebonics," the language spoken by many of the 53% of African-American students attending that district's schools. The policy endorsed acceptance of Ebonics in the classroom as an enhancement to students' learning standard American English and other subjects. The policy set off a fury of discussion across the nation about educational standards and the role of language diversity in elementary and high school education. The two articles presented here are among the many responses the Ebonics debate has evoked.

■ Ebonics? No Thonics!

John Leo

The nationwide roar of laughter over Ebonics is a very good sign. Talk shows, cartoonists, Internet surfers and famous comedians have all chimed in. A Jewish friend sent along a primer on "Hebonics," the Jewish-American language in which "W" is pronounced as "V," an extra "T" is placed at the end of many words ("hand" becomes "handt") and questions are always answered with other questions (Q: How do you feel? A: How should I feel?). Bill Cosby weighed in with a lighthearted piece in the *Wall Street Journal* calling for English subtitles on Ebonics movies.

Compare this upbeat, satirical commotion with the reaction to the last Ebonic outbreak—the somber silence in 1979 when an imaginative federal judge in Michigan concluded that lack of respect for black English is a form of educational bias. Elementary school teachers in Ann Arbor were forced to attend black English workshops for a while. Then common sense made an unexpected comeback and it all stopped.

Why was the reaction so different this time around? Well, for one thing, we now have a large black middle class that knows very well that institutionalizing Ebonics (maintain the legitimacy and richness of the language, the Oakland, Calif., school board said) is a sure-fire way to help black children avoid success. That many black, middle-class professionals saw this as a scam and an insult allowed others to chime in with ridicule.

As the Hebonics parody suggests, most Americans of all races have a home language or dialect from grandparents or parents that doesn't qualify as a school language and shouldn't. My Italian grandparents never got much beyond broken English set to Italian rhythms, but it never occurred to them that their children should attend pidgin-Italian workshops or ponder the richness of their own homegrown version of English. As Diane Ravitch says, "School is the place to learn how to behave and speak in the public sphere, not how to do a better job with your grandparents' or gang's dialect/slang."

Decreasing Tolerance.   The other big reason for all the chuckling over Ebonics is the decreasing public tolerance for the politically correct notions lurking in the shadows of this debate—identity politics, victimization and self-esteem theory. Identity politics means a constant attempt to stress cultural separateness, so a claim to a separate language, rooted dubiously in "Niger-Congo idioms," fits right in. To the PC-minded, what most of us call the mainstream is known as "the dominant culture," and the same overtones of oppression and bias are turning up in the Ebonics lobby: Standard English is "establishment" language or "standard" English (in quotes to show contempt). So any attempt to educate black children in ordinary English is a psychic assault and a sort of linguistic colonialism.

A familiar trick is being played here: An educational issue (what can we do about the poor school performance of inner-city children) turns into an issue of identity, self-esteem and group power. Some black intellectuals have been quick to point this out. In the *New York Times,* Shelby Steele wrote that identity enhancement won't help black students. "Now we no longer have students with academic deficits; we have racial victims, identity victims." In *Newsweek,* Ellis Cose, author of *Color-Blind: Seeing Beyond Race in a Race-Obsessed World,* made a similar point: "The key to teaching black children . . . is not in convincing them that they speak a foreign language, but that they are capable of mastering any material put in front of them."

Unlike real education, feel-good and identity-enhancing instruction has a way of depending heavily on myths and fake history to achieve the desired effects. Those unproven "Niger-Congo idioms" seem to have a lot in common with certain entrenched teachings in some public schools—the claim, for instance, that Africa staged the world's first industrial revolution and founded math and science.

Ebonics manages to plug in to so much that is declining or discredited in public education. Self-esteem theory—that children won't learn until they feel good about themselves—has been riding high for 10 years, but there is still no credible evidence that the theory is correct. By positioning Ebonics as a plausible extension of bilingualism, the Ebonics lobby mimics another loser. After more than 25 years, at a cost now of $5.5 billion a year, mostly to help Hispanic children, Hispanics have the highest dropout rate of any ethnic group. There is a good amount of evidence, particularly in New York, that those outside the bilingual system do better and learn English faster than those inside it. Many Hispanic parents are now demanding, and getting, all-English programs for their children.

If Hispanic parents are right to fight so their children can escape the language cocoon, it makes no sense for blacks to demand entry into a cocoon of their own. It's true that the muddled Oakland report spoke of teaching standard English, but that seems to have been a matter of building plausible deniability into a report that wanted to put Ebonics on the map and into the school bureaucracy. That mustn't happen. There are many things that inner-city youngsters need to succeed in the real world. Ebonics isn't one of them.

Questions for Discussion and Writing

1. Characterize the tone of John Leo's essay; that is, describe his attitude toward Ebonics and the debate surrounding it. How does his content and use of language establish this tone in the essay? His use of the pun "No thonics" in his title is one example. What others can you identify?

2. What political issues does Leo see involved in the Ebonics issues? Do you agree with him that a "familiar trick is being played" by efforts to incorporate Ebonics into classroom instruction? Why or why not?

3. After reading Leo's essay and the accompanying piece by Joan Walsh (pages 526–527), do you think non-standard varieties of English or bilingual instruction have a place in the classroom? If so, in what ways? If not, why not?

Four Truths About the Ebonics Debate

Joan Walsh

The national debate over ebonics is far more coded and hard to translate than black English, its purported topic. Here are four truths behind the controversy that nobody wants to talk about in plain English.

- Black parents and educators envy—and increasingly resent—the millions of dollars going to Asian and Latino bilingual programs. As immigrant populations grow, these programs are eating up a growing share of bare-bones urban school budgets. While the media framed the issue as Black English v. White America, the ebonics controversy was more a symptom of rising interminority tensions, a product of our zero-sum approach to race relations. Oakland educators insist their ebonics resolution wasn't a ploy to snare bilingual dollars—since they knew from the outset it wouldn't work—but it clearly was an expression of growing black frustration that Latino and Asian kids get programs that help them both succeed in American classrooms and bolster their native language and culture, while African American children get no such help. The ebonics resolution was a rhetorical salvo in a war about resources and respect, and it won't be the last. The questions it raises are profound.

- Programs that help inner city black children "translate" their home speech into standard English seem to work. Without weighing in on the "Is it a language?" debate, many urban districts, including Oakland, are quietly training their teachers to help students translate the language they hear at home into standard English, much the way Spanish speakers think in their native tongue and translate to English as a first step to true bilingualism. Urban isolation means inner city black children aren't around as many people who are fluent in both tongues as in prior generations, and standard English is an idiosyncratic, illogical language that's hard to master without reinforcement. It's too soon to say whether such language programs merit expansion to the funding levels of bilingual education—let alone whether bilingual education's record merits emulation. But the Oakland School Board would easily have been able to defend expanding its successful black language program throughout the district—if that's what its ebonics resolution had done.

- There was an unmistakable tinge of white racism in the ebonics media frenzy. Jesse Jackson and Maya Angelou notwithstanding, the hand-wringing over the Oakland School Board's measure reflected continuing white mistrust of how black people handle their business. There was a clear subtext of "Tsk, tsk, what will those people do next," a familiar objectifying and exoticizing of black culture. You could see the furrowed Caucasian brows as editors cranked out condescending "glossaries" of black English in the daily papers. I can just imagine cautious New York Times researchers—or was it William Safire?—agonizing over how to punctuate the crossover exclamation, "You, go girl!" (I would have written, "You go, girl," but then I'm white.) Only belatedly did some pundits remind us that black English has been a gift to American culture, like jazz and rock and roll, a wellspring of new words and imagery that has replenished the language, not diminished it.

- The Oakland School Board's refusal to amend its ebonics resolution is crazy, but predictable. In the public realm, white disdain yields black intransigence, more reliably than "I" comes before "e." So while black leaders were among the first to attack the nationalistic, pseudo-scientific Oakland measure, the ensuing media firestorm triggered the same circle-the-wagons reaction that made the deracinated O.J. Simpson an unlikely hero to many African Americans. Jesse Jackson recanted, and the school board "clarified" but refused to retract its sorry resolution calling "African Language Systems" the "primary language" of black people and "genetically based" and committing to "instruct African American students in their primary language and in English."

Why not amend the resolution to say what the Board insists it meant—that it wants to expand the successful language programs, without teaching ebonics? "We don't want to appear that we are confused or changing our mind," says Board member Carole Lee Tolvert. This is the traditional wary dance of white and black America, our dysfunctional call and response, depressing but familiar.

Yet there were flickers of new political and cultural life in the ebonics mess. The vital black public debate over ebonics was unique, and marked a growing capacity for black America to have its arguments out in the open, in front of the white folk. Equally important was the acknowledgment by white commentators that black English is our most vivid vernacular—a welcome if belated acknowledgment that our mulatto American culture is ever changing, and belongs to all of us.

Questions for Discussion and Writing

1. Which of the four "truths" that Walsh presents about the ebonics debate do you agree with the most? Which do you agree with the least? Explain why.

2. In what ways does Walsh criticize both African Americans and whites in her essay? What is her purpose in doing so?

3. How do Walsh's ideas compare with those expressed by John Leo in "Ebonics? No Thonics!" (pages 523–524)? To what extent might Walsh and Leo agree about the ebonics controversy?

■ Millennial Woman: Make Her GI Jane, Not June Cleaver

Caryl Rivers

Audience approval of Demi Moore's tough Navy SEAL in "GI Jane" may reflect not just a hit movie but a major shift in gender patterns in the industrialized world. A new reproductive paradigm is developing, and as it does, past constraints on female behavior are easing.

For centuries, Homo sapiens was a fragile, embattled species, beset by predators and struggling for survival. Having large numbers of offspring was an important survival strategy; woman's most important quality often was her fecundity. Women couldn't be spared for combat, even though some women were taller, stronger and more aggressive than some men. A few males, after all, could repopulate a tribe if many men were killed, but one woman could bear and raise only a few children.

Today, the situation is very different. Homo sapiens is not a fragile species but the undisputed master of the planet. Modern medicine has reduced infant mortality to the point where parents can expect most of their children to survive. Today, in fact, the survival of the species and the planet itself depends on curbing population growth.

If there were, indeed, a new reproductive paradigm, we would expect to see women having fewer children and the easing of taboos on risky work behavior for women. That's exactly what is happening. Not only are women moving increasingly into military roles, including combat, but they are also engaging in other kinds of risky behavior. They are driving more aggressively and getting into more accidents, taking part in risky sports such as mountain climbing and boxing. And around the world, female involvement in violent crime is rising rapidly.

Women are rejecting ages-old arguments about their physical frailty. Swimmer Janet Evans' time in the 400 in 1992 was two seconds better than Mark Spitz's time when he won the gold medal in 1968. Olympic speed skater Bonnie Blair's time in the 500 meter in 1992 would have beaten all the male winners through 1976. Today, women hold most of the world records in ultra long distance competition. Women hold the records in open water swimming. UCLA physicians Brian J. Whipp and Susan Ward predict that women soon will match men in all the Olympic running competitions.

Media images are reflecting these facts with more images of strong, active and even aggressive women. "Xena: Warrior Princess" is a TV hit, Rene Russo matched Clint Eastwood scar for scar in the movie "In the Line of Fire," Sigourney Weaver went woman to woman with an alien in the movie of the same name and now Demi Moore guts it out in basic training. Ironically, audiences hated her as the classic sex object, a stripper, but love her as a SEAL.

These media images are emerging because the new reproductive paradigm will not be reversed. Women will continue to move into nontraditional roles.

We'll see more women cops, professional basketball players, world class athletes and combat soldiers. Despite the complaints of some on the right, it's not a few feminists who have changed things, but a new reproductive scenario that is permanently altering old gender roles. GI Jane doing her push-ups may tell us more about the situation of women today than the icon of 1950s womanhood, June Cleaver, vacuuming in her pearls. The old gender roles are no more, and like Humpty Dumpty, all the king's horses and all the king's men can't put them back together again.

Questions for Discussion and Writing

1. Explain what Rivers means when she claims that "a new reproductive paradigm is developing" today regarding women's roles. Summarize the evidence she offers to illustrate and support her claim. Do you agree with her? Can you think of examples in our culture that would contradict what she claims? What are they?

2. How would you categorize the examples of changing women's roles that Rivers offers? Do you agree with her that these changes are good? For example, why is "GI Jane doing her push-ups" a better role model for women than "June Cleaver, vacuuming in her pearls"?

3. In what ways and to what extent do you agree or disagree with Rivers' final statement that "the old gender roles are no more"? Does the statement apply to the roles of men in our culture as well? If so, how?

■ In Defense of Talk Shows

Barbara Ehrenreich

Up until now, the targets of Bill (*The Book of Virtues*) Bennett's[1] crusades have at least been plausible sources of evil. But the latest victim of his wrath—TV talk shows of the *Sally Jessy Raphael* variety—are in a whole different category from drugs and gangsta rap. As anyone who actually watches them knows, the talk shows are one of the most excruciatingly moralistic forums the culture has to offer. Disturbing and sometimes disgusting, yes, but their very business is to preach the middle-class virtues of responsibility, reason and self-control.

Take the case of Susan, recently featured on *Montel Williams* as an example of a woman being stalked by her ex-boyfriend. Turns out Susan is also stalking the boyfriend and—here's the sexual frisson—has slept with him only days ago. In fact Susan is neck deep in trouble without any help from the boyfriend: She's serving a yearlong stretch of home incarceration for assaulting another woman, and home is the tiny trailer she shares with her nine-year-old daughter.

But no one is applauding this life spun out of control. Montel scolds Susan roundly for neglecting her daughter and failing to confront her role in the mutual stalking. A therapist lectures her about this unhealthy "obsessive kind of love." The studio audience jeers at her every evasion. By the end Susan has lost her cocky charm and dissolved into tears of shame.

The plot is always the same. People with problems—"husband says she looks like a cow," "pressured to lose her virginity or else," "mate wants more sex than I do"—are introduced to rational methods of problem solving. People with moral failings—"boy crazy," "dresses like a tramp," "a hundred sex partners"—are introduced to external standards of morality. The preaching—delivered alternately by the studio audience, the host and the ever present guest therapist—is relentless. "This is wrong to do this," Sally Jessy tells a cheating husband. "Feel bad?" Geraldo asks the girl who stole her best friend's boyfriend. "Any sense of remorse?" The expectation is that the sinner, so hectored, will see her way to reform. And indeed, a Sally Jessy update found "boy crazy," who'd been a guest only weeks ago, now dressed in schoolgirlish plaid and claiming her "attitude [had] changed"—thanks to the rough-and-ready therapy dispensed on the show.

All right, the subjects are often lurid and even bizarre. But there's no part of the entertainment spectacle, from *Hard Copy* to *Jade,* that doesn't trade in the lurid and bizarre. At least in the talk shows, the moral is always loud and clear: Respect yourself, listen to others, stop beating on your wife. In fact it's hard to see how *The Bill Bennett Show,* if there were to be such a thing, could

---

[1]William Bennett has held important positions in several Republican administrations and has been a national advocate for traditional morals and culture. His best-selling *The Book of Virtues* (1993) offers a collection of stories and folklore representing what Bennett views as core American values.—Eds.

deliver a more pointed sermon. Or would he prefer to see the feckless Susan, for example, tarred and feathered by the studio audience instead of being merely booed and shamed?

There *is* something morally repulsive about the talks, but it's not anything Bennett or his co-crusader Senator Joseph Lieberman has seen fit to mention. Watch for a few hours, and you get the claustrophobic sense of lives that have never seen the light of some external judgment, of people who have never before been listened to, and certainly never been taken seriously if they were. "What kind of people would let themselves be humiliated like this?" is often asked, sniffily, by the shows' detractors. And the answer, for the most part, is people who are so needy—of social support, of education, of material resources and self-esteem—that they mistake being the center of attention for being actually loved and respected.

What the talks are about, in large part, is poverty and the distortions it visits on the human spirit. You'll never find investment bankers bickering on *Rolonda*, or the host of *Gabrielle* recommending therapy to sobbing professors. With few exceptions the guests are drawn from trailer parks and tenements, from bleak streets and narrow, crowded rooms. Listen long enough, and you hear references to unpaid bills, to welfare, to twelve-hour workdays and double shifts. And this is the real shame of the talks: that they take lives bent out of shape by poverty and hold them up as entertaining exhibits. An announcement appearing between segments of *Montel* says it all: The show is looking for "pregnant women who sell their bodies to make ends meet."

This is class exploitation, pure and simple. What next—"homeless people so hungry they eat their own scabs"? Or would the next step be to pay people outright to submit to public humiliation? For $50 would you confess to adultery in your wife's presence? For $500 would you reveal your thirteen-year-old's girlish secrets on *Ricki Lake?* If you were poor enough, you might.

It is easy enough for those who can afford spacious homes and private therapy to sneer at their financial inferiors and label their pathetic moments of stardom vulgar. But if I had a talk show, it would feature a whole different cast of characters and category of crimes than you'll ever find on the talks: "CEOs who rake in millions while their employees get downsized" would be an obvious theme, along with "Senators who voted for welfare and Medicaid cuts"—and, if he'll agree to appear, "well-fed Republicans who dithered about talk shows while trailer-park residents slipped into madness and despair."

Questions for Discussion and Writing

1. To what extent do you agree with Ehrenreich that the business of talk shows is to "preach the middle-class virtues of responsibility, reason and self-control"? Do the talk shows you have seen fulfill this role? Explain why or why not.

2. Ehrenreich points out that the talk shows sometimes approach "class exploitation." What does she mean by this term? Do you agree that certain classes of people are exploited by the talk shows? Do you agree with Ehrenreich that such exploitation may be helping poor people? Why?

3. Do such television talk shows as Ehrenreich describes serve a positive social purpose? In what ways? Do you think it would be possible to change the shows and still maintain their popular appeal? If so, how?

■ TV Addiction

Marie Winn

The word "addiction" is often used loosely and wryly in conversation. People will refer to themselves as "mystery book addicts" or "cookie addicts." E. B. White writes of his annual surge of interest in gardening: "We are hooked and are making an attempt to kick the habit." Yet nobody really believes that reading mysteries or ordering seeds by catalogue is serious enough to be compared with addictions to heroin or alcohol. The word "addiction" is here used jokingly to denote a tendency to overindulge in some pleasurable activity.

People often refer to being "hooked on TV." Does this, too, fall into the light-hearted category of cookie eating and other pleasures that people pursue with unusual intensity, or is there a kind of television viewing that falls into the more serious category of destructive addiction?

When we think about addiction to drugs or alcohol, we frequently focus on negative aspects, ignoring the pleasures that accompany drinking or drug-taking. And yet the essence of any serious addiction is a pursuit of pleasure, a search for a "high" that normal life does not supply. It is only the inability to function without the addictive substance that is dismaying, the dependence of the organism upon a certain experience and an increasing inability to function normally without it. Thus a person will take two or three drinks at the end of the day not merely for the pleasure drinking provides, but also because he "doesn't feel normal" without them.

An addict does not merely pursue a pleasurable experience and need to experience it in order to function normally. He needs to *repeat* it again and again. Something about that particular experience makes life without it less than complete. Other potentially pleasurable experiences are no longer possible, for under the spell of the addictive experience, his life is peculiarly distorted. The addict craves an experience and yet he is never really satisfied. The organism may be temporarily sated, but soon it begins to crave again.

Finally, a serious addiction is distinguished from a harmless pursuit of pleasure by its distinctly destructive elements. A heroin addict, for instance, leads a damaged life: His increasing need for heroin in increasing doses prevents him from working, from maintaining relationships, from developing in human ways. Similarly an alcoholic's life is narrowed and dehumanized by his dependence on alcohol.

Let us consider television viewing in the light of the conditions that define serious addictions.

Not unlike drugs or alcohol, the television experience allows the participant to blot out the real world and enter into a pleasurable and passive mental state. The worries and anxieties of reality are as effectively deferred by becoming absorbed in a television program as by going on a "trip" induced by drugs or alcohol. And just as alcoholics are only inchoately aware of their addiction, feeling that they control their drinking more than they really do ("I can cut it out any time I want—I just like to have three or four drinks before dinner"), people similarly overestimate their control over television watching. Even as they put off other activities to spend hour after hour watching television, they feel they could easily resume living in a different, less passive style. But somehow or other while the television set is present in their homes, the click doesn't sound. With television pleasures available, those other experiences seem less attractive, more difficult somehow.

A heavy viewer (a college English instructor) observes: "I find television almost irresistible. When the set is on, I cannot ignore it. I can't turn it off. I feel sapped, will-less, enervated. As I reach out to turn off the set, the strength goes out of my arms. So I sit there for hours and hours."

The self-confessed television addict often feels he "ought" to do other things—but the fact that he doesn't read and doesn't plant his garden or sew or crochet or play games or have conversations means that those activities are no longer as desirable as television viewing. In a way a heavy viewer's life is as imbalanced by his television "habit" as a drug addict's or an alcoholic's. He is living in a holding pattern, as it were, passing up the activities that lead to growth or development or a sense of accomplishment. This is one reason people talk about their television viewing so ruefully, so apologetically. They are aware that it is an unproductive experience, that almost any other endeavor is more worthwhile by any human measure.

Finally, it is the adverse effect of television viewing on the lives of so many people that defines it as a serious addiction. The television habit distorts the sense of time. It renders other experiences vague and curiously unreal while taking on a greater reality for itself. It weakens relationships by reducing and sometimes eliminating normal opportunities for talking, for communicating.

And yet television does not satisfy, else why would the viewer continue to watch hour after hour, day after day? "The measure of health," writes Lawrence Kubie, "is flexibility . . . and especially the freedom to cease when sated." But the television viewer can never be sated with his television experiences—they do not provide the true nourishment that satiation requires—and thus he finds that he cannot stop watching.

Questions for Discussion and Writing

1. List some of the adverse effects of television that Winn describes. Do you agree with her about these effects? Discuss any others that you would include in such a list.

2. Consider your own television-viewing habits or those of people you know. Do you think people can become "addicted" to watching television in the ways that Winn describes? Why or why not?

3. What arguments can you make in favor of television viewing? How would you reconcile them with the adverse effects Winn describes?

Appendix

Answers to Practice Exercises in Part IV

Chapter 15   **Practice 1**

1. P   6. S
2. C   7. P
3. S   8. P
4. S   9. C
5. C   10. P

Practice 2

1. essay, test, task   4. sentences
2. students, thoughts, time, outline   5. time, essay
3. ideas, order

Practice 3

1. Richard Wright, *Black Boy*   3. Memphis, Jackson
2. American, Deep South   4. Wright

Practice 4

1. Richard Wright, obstacles
2. education, schools, blacks, whites
3. family, Wright, bed
4. clothes, books, food
5. Wright, hardships
6. things, reading, defiance, learning, determination
7. way, magazines, books
8. struggles, youth, Wright, world, man
9. struggles, youth, scars
10. students, book, *Black Boy*

Practice 5

1. United States Marine Corps   4. marines
2. Marine Corps   5. marine
3. men and women

Practice 7

1. I do believe   4. minutes should have made
2. testimony could hurt   5. marines want
3. troop should go   6. David should have been chosen

Practice 9

1. Yesterday was, day   4. solution seems, one
2. movies were, films   5. painting is, example
3. Mr. Reynolds has been, chair

Practice 10

1. The teller will cash our check. (teller will cash)
2. Mary and Martha are the sisters mentioned in the story. (Mary and Martha are)

3. The employees should insist on collective bargaining. (employees should insist)
4. Physics is the most difficult freshman course. (Physics is)
5. We should have listened to Einstein when he warned against atomic power. (We should have listened)

Practice 11

1. bug is
2. volunteers are
3. change is
4. examples are

5. one is
6. three are
7. day was

Practice 12

1. television will replace
2. children watch
3. programs will occupy
4. Neil Armstrong did say
5. advantages are
6. Students learn
7. no one feels

8. students can progress
9. drawback is
10. program will survive
11. opportunities are
12. team should have chosen
13. couple has
14. techniques should combine

Practice 13

1. We watched television (tells what)
2. girls baked cookies (tells what)
3. Andy asked Melissa (tells whom)
4. Andy ate cookies, drank quart (tells what)
5. Andy had stomachache (tells what)
6. instructor returned tests (tells what)
7. Karen defeated Janice (tells whom)
8. She finished problems (tells what)
9. she passed test (tells what)
10. teacher wrote comment (tells what)

Practice 15

1. (During the sixties), (in drugs)
2. (of particular drugs), (Such as LSD and marijuana), (on the news)
3. (with drugs), (at this time)
4. (With the increase), (in drug use), (of drug abuse)
5. (to an early death), (for some)
6. (by drugs)
7. (in large cities)
8. (For some people), (on the street)
9. (for Ecstasy), (of the most dangerous drugs), (on the American scene)
10. (at our university), (to the drug problem), (to their children)

Practice 16

1. Tom brought his friend a basket of fruit.
2. Elizabeth gave her instructor some free advice.
3. The news gave the family a shock.

4. The real estate agent offered her <u>clients</u> a special deal.
5. The thief sold my husband a stolen <u>car</u>.
6. She made her <u>daughter</u> a beautiful dress.

Practice 18

1. he	7. we
2. I	8. them
3. me	9. whom
4. I	10. they
5. me	11. my
6. its	

Practice 19

1. I	9. I
2. me	10. me
3. us	11. I
4. she	12. Who
5. she	13. Whoever
6. me	14. whomever
7. him and me	15. whom
8. me	16. he

Practice 20

1. that (rel)	13. She (per)
2. She (per)	14. that (rel)
3. you (per)	15. her (per)
4. her (per)	16. she (per)
5. She (per)	17. she (per)
6. herself (reflex)	18. anyone (ind)
7. her (per)	19. her (per)
8. Her (per)	20. She (per)
9. which (rel)	21. everything (ind)
10. her (per)	22. herself (reflex)
11. that (rel)	23. That (dem)
12. her (per)	24. she (per)

Practice 21

1. <u>The</u> (Kool Jazz Festival), <u>a</u> (mixture), <u>soul</u> (music)
2. <u>These</u> (concerts), <u>different</u> (types)
3. <u>the</u>, <u>rowdy</u> (ones), <u>the</u>, <u>dreamy</u> (lovers), <u>the</u> (smokers), <u>the</u> (ones), <u>the</u> (walls), <u>the</u>, <u>whole</u> (night), <u>the</u> (people), <u>profane</u> (language)
4. <u>the</u>, <u>rowdy</u> (ones), <u>young</u> (ones)
5. <u>those</u>, <u>loud</u> (whistles)
6. <u>the</u>, <u>dreamy</u> (lovers), <u>the</u>, <u>whole</u> (concert), <u>moony</u> (eyes)
7. <u>The</u> (smokers), <u>the</u> (air), <u>the</u>, <u>disgusting</u> (smell)
8. <u>The</u>, <u>unfriendly</u> (wall-standers)
9. <u>The</u> (cursers), <u>any</u> (respect), <u>the</u>, <u>older</u> (people)
10. <u>the</u>, <u>terrific</u> (Kool Jazz Festival)

Practice 23

1. prettier, prettiest
2. more difficult, most difficult
3. colder, coldest
4. worse, worst
5. less, least
6. better, best
7. tastier, tastiest
8. far, farther, farthest
9. less, least
10. more fulfilling, most fulfilling

Practice 24

1. <u>so</u> (dark), <u>noisily</u> (fell)
2. <u>so</u> (beautifully), <u>beautifully</u> (arranged)
3. <u>very</u> (incompetently), <u>incompetently</u> (conducted), <u>quietly</u> (had been stealing)
4. <u>just</u> (too), <u>too</u> (noisy)
5. <u>generously</u> (gave), <u>most</u> (lovely)
6. <u>most</u> (impatiently), <u>impatiently</u> (has been waiting)
7. <u>triumphantly</u> (entered), <u>very</u> (slowly), <u>slowly</u> (riding)
8. <u>extremely</u> (hard), <u>not</u> (complain)
9. <u>always</u> (begins), <u>unnecessarily</u> (long)
10. <u>never</u> (admits), <u>not</u> (has been screened), <u>carefully</u> (has been screened)

Practice 25

1. both/and also (cor)
2. When (sub)
3. because (sub), while (sub)
4. and (cc)
5. If (sub)
6. where (sub)
7. but (cc), or (cc)
8. either/or (cor)
9. Because (sub)
10. when (sub)
11. And (cc), while (sub)

Chapter 16   **Practice 1**

1. boys, sew
2. sisters, run
3. fists, ask
4. risks, risk
5. plays, play

Practice 2

1. cat, hits
2. box, costs
3. bus, loves
4. bill, bills
5. dance, dances

Practice 3

1. apples (they) cost
2. Robin Hood (he) robs
3. police (they) complain
4. Mrs. Thatcher (she) stands

5. program (its) consists
6. Love (it) makes
7. Happiness (it) seems

8. daughter (she) seeks
9. mother and father (they) keep
10. Grandfather (he) becomes

Practice 4 (Examples)

1. We hope
2. Our mayor involves
3. You practice
4. You spend
5. Anton and Molly sew
6. It consists

7. I give
8. The dream becomes
9. The people say
10. They use
11. She seems
12. The nations seem

Practice 5

1. police raid
2. United States experiences
3. jury eats
4. poor pay, rich pay
5. class gives
6. family acts
7. Politics makes
8. experienced (people) make
9. people need

10. pants show
11. Those (with disabilities) demand
12. jury argue
13. police support
14. The people want
15. Saints quit
16. Republican Party supports
17. Olympics are
18. powerful (people) control

Practice 6 (Examples)

1. My wife preaches
2. The child pinches
3. My father fusses
4. It costs
5. Apples cost

6. Fools rush
7. The Bears crush
8. The police officer asks
9. The priest blesses

Practice 7

1. Dr. Greenway doesn't
2. instructor does (or doesn't)
3. city does
4. noise does
5. woman doesn't
6. They do

7. Santa and his reindeer don't
8. It doesn't
9. English do (*or* don't)
10. She does (*or* doesn't)
11. Does (*or* Doesn't)

Practice 8

1. Mary carries
2. Ben defies
3. She tries
4. Mia travels
5. A bird flies

6. The team journeys
7. It buries
8. It does
9. It doesn't
10. The van goes

Practice 9

1. city of Detroit has
2. Everyone has

3. You have
4. China has

5. They have
6. soldier has
7. United States has
8. scissors have

9. police have
10. People have
11. class has

Practice 10

1. The people are
2. My husband and brother-in-law were
3. The jury is (or *are* if used for individual jury members)
4. Uncle Mac wasn't
5. They weren't
6. Congress was
7. The Rams aren't
8. The police are
9. You weren't

Practice 11

1. Does he need more money for the trip? (he does need)
2. Is she going to dance with you? (she is going)
3. Do those children need heavier jackets? (children need)
4. Were they the ones we were looking for? (they were)
5. Has the leg healed completely? (leg has healed)
6. Doesn't the senator deliver on his promises? (senator doesn't deliver)

Practice 12

1. deer were
2. something is
3. fighting is
4. survivors were
5. use wasn't
6. thing wasn't

7. there are alternatives
8. crime has been
9. reason hasn't been
10. murders have been
11. there has been concern

Practice 13

1. Mother and I sew
2. Gas and oil both cost
3. What I want and what she wants aren't
4. what is
5. This man and this woman give
6. Getting better grades is
7. Getting better grades and playing more tennis are
8. My aunt and uncle buy
9. potatoes, corn, and spinach seem
10. The Bill of Rights and the Constitution protect
11. Making clothes for her children is

Practice 14

1. Mrs. Appleby or Mrs. St. John comes
2. Neither you nor they are

3. Abraham and his son, Isaac, are
4. Either Sara Martinez or her friends are
5. A bear or some other kind of animal appears
6. Not only adults but also children are
7. Not only the grandfather but also the children jog
8. Not only the children but also the grandfather jogs
9. Either Sophia or you has
10. Both the cat and the dog sleep
11. Neither Russia nor the United States experiences

Practice 15

1. Some are
2. Everything costs
3. Anyone is
4. Some was
5. All are
6. Everything involves
7. Half tells
8. Does everyone
9. Most have
10. Much is
11. Does anyone

Practice 16

1. (choice) is
2. (names) were
3. (agenda) is
4. (one) is
5. (winner) was
6. (winners) were

Practice 17

1. friends who were
2. nations that break
3. one who minds
4. ones who care
5. coins that turn
6. People who need
7. police who believe
8. date who talks
9. those who know
10. gifts that cost
11. scissors that are

Practice 18

1. is
2. is
3. is
4. are
5. is

Chapter 17 **Practice 1**

1. begun
2. loved
3. beginning
4. walked
5. begin
6. was
7. drowned
8. seemed
9. asked
10. pleaded
11. having

Practice 2

1. broken
2. laid
3. lay
4. set

5. lain
6. laid
7. lie
8. drowned
9. cost
10. gone

11. begun
12. saw
13. beginning
14. laying
15. hurting
16. breaks

Practice 3 (Examples)

1. can
2. might
3. will
4. should
5. shall

6. would
7. may
8. could
9. must
10. would, could

Practice 4

1. could
2. can
3. could
4. can
5. could
6. would
7. will
8. would

9. would
10. will
11. would
12. may
13. might *or* may
14. might
15. may

Practice 5

1. a. dresses
2. a. cuts
3. a. begin
4. a. Choose
5. a. reads
6. a. costs
7. a. drowns
8. a. wakes
9. a. has
10. a. feel
11. a. gets

b. dressed
b. cut
b. began
b. chose
b. read
b. cost
b. drowned
b. woke
h. had
b. felt
b. got

Practice 6

1. *help:* it ends in a double consonant
2. *loom:* the final consonant is preceded by a double vowel
3. *enjoy:* it ends in -*y*
4. *differ:* the accent is on the first syllable
5. *return:* it ends with a double consonant

Practice 7

1. enjoyed
2. preferred

3. gassed
4. stepped
5. supposed

Practice 8

1. cried
2. fried
3. obeyed
4. married
5. buried

Practice 9

1. taught
2. risen
3. begun
4. chosen
5. sat
6. come
7. become
8. run
9. quit
10. put
11. hit
12. led
13. laid
14. lain
15. rung
16. begun

Practice 10

1. a. have loved
2. a. has happened
3. a. have legalized
4. a. have guessed
5. a. have finished
6. a. have built

   b. had loved
   b. had happened
   b. had legalized
   b. had guessed
   b. had finished
   b. had built

Practice 11

1. I had been
2. I kept to myself because I made
3. I soon got; who had taken
4. She had; and asked
5. I could soon say that I had made
6. I had

Practice 12 (Examples)

1. The bridge was built by them to withstand hurricanes.
2. All of my dessert was eaten by me before the movie started.
3. My shirt was torn by them while we were playing football.
4. His knee was cut wide open by the splinter of glass.
5. John and Alicia's house was built on a hill.

Practice 13

1. You are supposed
2. It is written
3. They were used
4. I was then sworn

5. My finger was hurt
6. It is said
7. Alvina was driven
8. Nantucket is known

9. I will never get used
10. The lakes were frozen
11. My alarm clock is set

Practice 14

1. I greatly appreciate what you have done.
2. We really needed the supplies.
3. They will use the money to buy a car.
4. Her father called the doctor.
5. I understood his lecture.
6. You have carefully learned the various verb forms.

Practice 15

1. You are looking
2. We were beginning
3. She was helping
4. they are asking
5. Dr. Ward is quizzing
6. I accidentally was dyeing

7. We were traveling
8. The old man was lying
9. I am laying
10. she is saying
11. she was hitting

Practice 16

1. crept, crept, creeping
2. wove, woven, weaving
3. mowed, mowed (or mown), mowing
4. bent, bent, bending
5. shone, shone, shining
6. forbade, forbidden, forbidding
7. shouldered, shouldered, shouldering
8. hanged, hanged, hanging
9. harkened, harkened, harkening
10. happened, happened, happening
11. spayed, spayed, spaying

Practice 17

1. They surprised us when they came to our school.
2. When I was young, I used to tear
3. She got so mad that she turned red.
4. They always dressed up when they went out to eat.
5. We worked, we worked, and we worked, but we got nowhere.
6. When we returned, we freed the prisoners.
7. My wife said you advertised
8. They acted as if they had never seen
9. Maria said that she would study
10. The president told the nation that he could balance the budget.
11. We came home after the war, just as we said we would.

VERBS

Practice 20

1. Seeing
2. loved
3. begun
4. Shocked
5. Beginning

Practice 22

1. shocking
2. beginning
3. Doing, being
4. giving
5. waiting

Practice 23

1. Seeing all those dishes makes
2. Seeing the sun rise is
3. To work, to play hard, and to have a cooperative family are
4. To be or not to be is
5. Working hard prepares
6. the hero discovers

Practice 24

1. We refuse, we keep
2. You say, you love, you act
3. I say, you (are)
4. They like, they love
5. We do
6. I don't care, we do, I don't care, you do, I don't care, they do, I do care, what the world does
7. They love
8. They seem, they believe
9. We carry, we don't
10. they cost
11. they haven't had
12. You and your family have
13. days haven't been
14. You have, I have
15. We have
16. We ask, we do receive

Practice 25

1. police (P) ask, he (S) gives
2. Mary (S) doesn't
3. husband (S) tries, he (S) buys
4. What (S) interests, is
5. She (S) cleans, daughters (P) sit
6. It (S) doesn't
7. Mia (S) fixes
8. she (S) does
9. government (S) employs (correct)
10. Stan (S) pushes, he (S) is going
11. Ferdinand (S) sleeps, eats, and watches
12. class (S) sings, teacher (S) asks
13. people (P) come and climb
14. Linda (S) is, cares
15. recipe (S) doesn't

Practice 26

1. we were
2. I am, you are, we are
3. we were
4. they weren't
5. isn't that

Practice 27

1. governments (P) weren't
2. fish (P) were
3. soldiers (P) weren't
4. students (P) were
5. chance (S) isn't
6. more (P) aren't going
7. people (P) died or were brought
8. nations (P) met, who (nations) (P) were gathering
9. police (P) weren't
10. United States (S) isn't trying
11. Red nor his parents (P) were

Practice 28

1. were
2. is
3. is *or* was
4. is *or* was
5. are *or* were

Practice 29 (Examples)

1. She, does
2. I, feel
3. She, has
4. radio and television, make
5. people, say
6. husband, tells

Practice 31

1. She and I were
2. paper helps
3. they were serving
4. reporter faces
5. (Correct)
6. (Correct)
7. he catches
8. (Correct)
9. April takes
10. (Correct)
11. They plan

Practice 32

1. sounds (of my neighborhood) change
2. houses (on my block) are
3. Everybody (in my classes) is working
4. years (of school) were
5. sounds (in my neighborhood) are
6. great-grandmother (in most people's eyes) seems
7. thought (of her children) is satisfying
8. work (on the houses) begins
9. One (of us) is
10. Harold Muskie (of Chase Metropolitan Bank) recommends
11. dreams (for a better life) were fulfilled

Practice 33

1. children (who are not in school) have
2. Those (who don't have the money) get
3. things (she has left behind) mean

4. children (who live in my neighborhood) play
5. school (where my mother taught for the last seven years) is closing
6. gifts (he brings to my son) come

Practice 35 (Examples)

1. I am finding
2. They are loved
3. The captain had loved
4. The child was drowned
5. We have found
6. She flies
7. The pond is frozen
8. They had gone
9. It was happening
10. I laid down my watch
11. We led
12. You are lying out in the sun
13. I did lose my watch
14. We had paid for the ticket
15. They saw
16. The sun is setting
17. The choir sang
18. The car was stolen
19. It was taken
20. The instructor taught
21. The pitcher has thrown

Practice 36

1. mother beat
2. he lied, stole, and struggled
3. (Correct)
4. He went, stayed, and tried to impress
5. he stood and watched
6. He wrote what he felt and wanted
7. he lied and said
8. (woman) who hired
9. Richard had struggled and worked
10. he had finished
11. he used
12. he had given, principal wrote
13. (things) that enabled
14. (Correct)
15. he had
16. he managed
17. (Correct)
18. He had hidden, he learned
19. He took and ran
20. he went and escaped
21. conditions began

Practice 37

1. birds began
2. they seemed
3. woman asked
4. asked me to support
5. he loved
6. we used
7. we had, we could
8. Neddie came
9. grandfather said
10. We used
11. He asked

Practice 38

1. I knew
2. woman appeared
3. woman started
4. she finished
5. No one was talking.
6. signs said
7. man gave
8. I did
9. everyone had
10. man said
11. man shouted
12. man asked
13. He came
14. he asked

15. I had not switched
16. girl and I looked
17. people talked
18. people examined
19. she said
20. They were

21. girl was
22. we sat down
23. I was
24. I opened
25. I was
26. adrenaline stimulated

Chapter 18   Practice 1

1. about Troy and me
2. older than I
3. Michael and I

4. the little girl and I
5. between you and me
6. It was she

Practice 2

1. my friend Regina and I traveled
2. Someone told Regina and me
3. as much luck as she
4. brought Regina and me
5. Regina and I did not have
6. to give either her or me
7. know to whom

8. Just between you and me
9. "Who do you girls think you are?"
10. But we "girls"
11. Regina and I were completely crazy
12. Regina and I ever had
13. Whoever said

Practice 3 (Examples)

1. their children
2. the ball carrier
3. the authorities
4. the waiters
5. this situation
6. the mechanics

7. the classes
8. this problem
9. the technician
10. the owners
11. the staff

Practice 4

1. they (movies) contain
2. it (world)
3. him (son)
4. it (Hawaii) has

5. her (lady)
6. them (stories)
7. it (government) wastes
8. it (Mexico)

Practice 6

1. without them
2. it can, it has
3. in its own culture
4. she loved them
5. (Correct)
6. return them

7. they found
8. they found
9. it imported, its oil
10. They need, their husbands
11. one helps

Practice 7 (Examples)

1. keeping a job
2. available to their patients
3. to help patients with any problems they may have
4. Then there are nurses who are concerned about their work only when someone is watching them.
5. These people are at the bottom; they live
6. Both of my parents have helped me in their own ways, and I am grateful for what both have done.
7. for parents to relate to their children
8. People with problems should make sure that they see somebody trained to help.
9. fair to students
10. plan all classes

Practice 9 (Examples)

1. if you have moved
2. When you go to see her
3. whether one has good grades or not
4. Your social class
5. always talk to me
6. (Correct)
7. that I should forgive
8. one is moved
9. dangerous to them
10. what they tell us
11. to all one hears

Chapter 19   Practice 1

1. watches, axes, firsts
2. candies, sashes, twos
3. potatoes, Lindsays, women
4. leaves, heroes, ladies
5. lives, echoes, honeys
6. 1990's, deer, m's
7. roofs, policemen, baths
8. selves, stereos, Mondays
9. hippopotamuses
10. analyses

Practice 2

1. two graveyards
2. twelve years
3. all the things
4. conversations
5. ladies
6. soft drinks
7. various kinds
8. candies

Practice 3

1. tries, tried, trying
2. complies, complied, complying
3. hums, hummed, humming
4. buses, bussed, bussing
5. bevels, beveled, beveling
6. defers, deferred, deferring
7. satisfies, satisfied, satisfying
8. opens, opened, opening
9. counsels, counseled, counseling
10. studies, studied, studying

11. occupies, occupied, occupying
12. journeys, journeyed, journeying
13. jogs, jogged, jogging
14. travels, traveled, traveling
15. refers, referred, referring

Practice 4

1. who's
2. they're
3. can't
4. let's
5. won't
6. wouldn't
7. they'd
8. shouldn't
9. don't
10. you're

Practice 5

1. Its
2. you're
3. you're
4. it's
5. they're
6. Theirs
7. There's
8. It's, Your
9. it's
10. Who's
11. there's

Practice 6

1. all right
2. a lot
3. high school
4. meantime
5. whenever
6. twelfth
7. February
8. absence
9. argument
10. attendance
11. bookkeeping
12. beginning
13. committee
14. competent
15. develop
16. earliest
17. existence
18. foreign
19. government
20. handkerchief
21. independent
22. knowledge
23. library
24. mathematics
25. niece
26. occurred
27. perceive
28. privilege
29. participant
30. ridiculous
31. sensible
32. surprise
33. till
34. useful
35. written

Chapter 20   **Practice 1**

1. (Correct)
2. Jimmy Carter
3. *Newsweek,* "The Six Year Presidency,"
4. Willie Morris, *North Toward Home,* North, Oxford, Mississippi, Deep South
5. Torah, Bible

6. Wednesday, I, I, History 102
7. Ted, "What . . . , Dad?"
8. "Gasoline, Sonny boy."
9. Carver High School, Mr. Harry Berger
10. "A Time I Would Like to Forget"

Practice 2

1. Dr. Sosnoski didn't say, "Will you stop smoking?"
2. He said, in a quiet voice, "Stop smoking right now."
3. "Ouch!" I said. "That hurts!"
4. Can you say, "I will stop smoking right now"?
5. "May I wait until after Christmas?" I asked.
6. "No!" he almost shouted. "Now!"
7. Are the surgeon general and Dr. Sosnoski right about smoking?

Practice 3

1. It's, we'll
2. '63 or '64, '90's
3. Haven't, I'm tellin', it's, lickin'

4. It's, can't
5. *i*'s, *t*'s

Practice 4

1. teachers' room
2. Smiths' address
3. Charles's address
4. today's events
5. ladies' activities
6. woman's husband

7. a man and a woman's relationship
8. son-in-law's good fortune
9. boy's attitude
10. boys' attitude
11. people's attitude

Practice 5

1. People's
2. sons'
3. everyone's
4. Sandra's
5. children's
6. people's
7. Mary's
8. boys
9. Nature's Way

10. Joneses'
11. Pierre and Violette's
12. (Correct)
13. someone's
14. neighbors'
15. committees
16. children's
17. Raymond's, priests'

Practice 6

1. once, but
2. cars, and the firefighters
3. injured, nor was

Practice 7

1. While there is life, there
2. doctor says, he

Practice 8

1. Great Britain, who was our ally, went
2. Argentina, who
3. This war, which caused many deaths, was

Practice 9

1. however, he
2. nevertheless, he
3. qualities, for example, his courage

Practice 10

1. that house, a house that had once been
2. porch, a beautifully constructed work of art, was now
3. Curtains, now nothing but rags, hung
4. a woman in her eighties, did not

Practice 11

1. so civilized, so intelligent, and so self-possessed
2. determined, courageous

Practice 12

1. "If I were you," my dad said, "I wouldn't . . . " "Well," I answered, "be glad you aren't me." "I am," he said.
2. election," replied

Practice 13

1. Hardin County, Kentucky, February 12, 1809; April 15, 1865, in Washington, DC.
2. July 22, 1997.

Practice 14

1. While visiting, Mary
2. husband, my sister

Practice 15

1. "Carlos, that game was the greatest, wasn't it?"
2. friend, who was grinning at me devilishly, and
3. "Great for you, my friend, not for me."
4. in Scrabble, although lately

Practice 16

1. Carter, and I'm (Rule 1)
2. said, job (Rule 2)
3. (Correct)
4. course, you (Rule 2)
5. rich, but I (Rule 1)
6. nursing, I (Rule 2)
7. (Correct)

   8. center, but she (Rule 1)
   9. (Correct)
  10. school, it (Rule 2)
  11. hard, you (Rule 2)
  12. (Correct)

Practice 17

   1. Sybil, who is a member of the Symphony Club, gave (Rule 3)
   2. consequently, he (Rule 4)
   3. Poe, the master writer of horror stories, did (Rule 5)
   4. person, a carpenter, was (Rule 5)
   5. textbook, which had been lost all semester, turned (Rule 3)
   6. seafood, especially shrimp (Rule 5)
   7. for example, overwatering (Rule 4)
   8. André, who had been cramming the whole night, slept (Rule 3)
   9. however, it (Rule 4)
  10. Chico, our eccentric next-door neighbor, is (Rule 5)
  11. ailments, diphtheria (Rule 5)
  12. activities, particularly fishing (Rule 5)

Practice 18

   1. cool, calm, and collected (Rule 6)
   2. dark, rainy (Rule 6); first met, wasn't it? (Rule 10)
   3. my father, my sister (Rule 9)
   4. tax, although (Rule 10)
   5. management of the center, the hiring and training of the personnel, and the develop-ment (Rule 6)
   6. for you," President Kennedy said, "ask (Rule 7)
   7. night, time (Rule 9)
   8. Make love, not war (Rule 10)
   9. "War is not what I want," he said, "but peace." (Rule 7)
  10. in hand, not knowing (Rule 10)
  11. February 21, 1965 (Rule 8)

Practice 19

   1. *yranoitcid,* but *madam* (Rule 1)
   2. (Correct)
   3. outside, we (Rule 2)
   4. (Correct)
   5. (Correct)
   6. (Correct)
   7. bus, our next (Rule 2)
   8. stove, but I (Rule 1)
   9. (Correct)
  10. Finally, when (Rule 10); Rivergate, the people (Rule 2); applauded us, and the (Rule 1)
  11. seafood, especially (Rule 5); crab, shrimp, and oysters (Rule 6)
  12. Tim Owens, a 6′6″ guard, and (Rule 5)
  13. look back, you will (Rule 2)

14. (Correct)
15. Eisenhower, the thirty-fourth president of the United States, was (Rule 5); Denison, Texas, on October 14, 1890 (Rule 8)
16. the road, I noticed (Rule 2); small, inviting brown cabin (Rule 6)
17. times, but through (Rule 1)
18. in the snow," Granny used to say, "because (Rule 7)
19. the navy sent our family to Los Angeles, California, where (Rule 8); and met Kim, Steve, and Colleen (Rule 6)
20. Honestly, I am (Rule 10)

Practice 20

1. in the Coast Guard and then decided
2. (Correct)
3. difficult than I
4. (Correct)
5. Coast Guard, and he
6. (Correct)
7. (Correct)
8. Bank, moreover, she
9. problem; however, he
10. (Correct)

Practice 21

1. "What's the matter?" Richard's mother asked.
2. "It's those same boys," he said. "They'll beat me."
3. "You've got to get over that. Now go on," she said.
4. Richard replied, "But I'm scared."
5. She said, "How can I let you back down now?"
6. "Please, Momma," he said, "don't make me fight."

Practice 22 (Examples)

1. The school board said to the union that it was demanding far too much money.
2. The union replied that they wanted only a fair wage.
3. The school board said that the union should take its case to the taxpayers.
4. The union then said that the school board was responsible for the wages of teachers.

Practice 23

1. The police chief said, "I need more cooperation from the judges."
2. The judges said, "We are already giving out much stiffer sentences."
3. The police chief responded, "Dangerous criminals are still being allowed to roam the streets."
4. The judges said, "We cannot be blamed for the amount of crime in the streets."
5. The police chief said, "The judges can help."

Practice 24

1. 1901
2. (Correct)

3. (Correct)
4. $5.14

5. Page 16	8. (Correct)
6. (Correct)	9. (Correct)
7. eight o'clock	10. 2:30 P.M.

Chapter 21   Practice 1

1. S	6. N
2. S	7. N
3. N	8. S
4. N	9. N
5. N	10. N

Practice 5

1. One day she was running and playing in a cornfield.
2. Every day from then on the crow and my mother would meet in the cornfield.
3. They walked together that way all over the field.
4. That night her uncle Al Reynolds died of a heart attack.

Practice 6

1. This past Tuesday night, my husband and I were shopping at Maison Blanche, and we were about to call it a night.
2. I have come across this unhappy situation many times, but each time it shocks and saddens me.
3. The rising divorce rate is especially distressing, for many of the marriages could have been saved.

Practice 7 (Examples)

1. shark-infested waters, for the movement
2. on the tenth, and we will be gone
3. and dark, but I like it.
4. decision quickly, for time is running out.
5. movie tonight, or we may
6. by 10:00 P.M., but my roommate
7. late afternoon, and we plan
8. another year, or I may cancel it now.

Practice 8 (Examples)

1. raw oyster, nor does she like any other shellfish.
2. is rated PG, so we probably
3. odd-looking character, yet many women
4. next month, so she
5. friends' advice, nor does he pay attention
6. his sixties, yet he still

Practice 10 (Examples)

1. I must study first, and then I may go to the movies with you.
2. I was not sick after eating the pizza and marshmallows; however, Helen and Tom

3. We had many things to talk about; therefore, the time passed quickly.
4. The poet Keats died in his mid-twenties; nevertheless, his poetry
5. The barbeque restaurant will probably be more successful now that it is in a better location; moreover, its new management is first rate.
6. Paula knows how to fix anything; for example, she even fixed her grandfather's cuckoo clock.
7. It was only a small, inexpensive gift; however, it was a well-chosen one.
8. I enjoy working in the early morning because I feel rested then; moreover, it is the only time the house is quiet.
9. Every day Mrs. Carr picks whatever is ripe, and then she feeds the chickens.
10. Christy Brown was an Irish writer who was severely brain damaged from birth; nevertheless, he published
11. The day was clear and sunny; therefore, we decided
12. Thousands of people greet each other every day at the Los Angeles airport; however, it is not

Practice 11

1. When—time
2. Although—contrast
3. While—time

4. If—condition
5. Because—reason
6. Unless—condition

Practice 12

1. after—time
2. because—reason
3. while—time

4. before—time
5. unless—condition

Practice 15 (Examples)

1. The president stood by what he said because he was a man of great conviction.
2. I am leaving because I am afraid I will get caught in the rain.
3. It is easy to see a glass as half-empty although it is better to see it as half-full.
4. When the terrorists attacked the embassy, two people were killed.
5. Eighteen-year-olds should be able to buy alcohol because they are old enough to fight and vote.
6. Although eighteen-year-olds are old enough to fight and vote, they should still not be able to buy alcohol.

Practice 16 (Examples)

1. We moved to a new town when I was five years old.
2. Because Josh does not have enough money to live comfortably, he is looking for a new job.
3. When I moved to Jefferson City about five years ago, I was puzzled by certain words I heard people use.
4. Some of the words were very hard to understand because people pronounced them in a funny way.
5. I frequently had to ask people to repeat themselves since (*or* because) I could not understand.
6. Although some words, like *yat,* were clearly pronounced, they were so odd

7. When I finally asked someone what *yat* meant, I was told
8. Because some people in the city use *yat* all the time, they are called *yats.*
9. While many *yat* mothers call their children by such names as Precious, Sweetheart, and Darlin', angry *yat* mothers call

Practice 17

1. that is filled with good friends and good times (life)
2. who is usually the last to leave a party (Joe)
3. which has not been washed in two years (car)
4. where I grew up (town)
5. who was very tall for her age (Anita)
6. who did not have a way to get to school (Karen)
7. [that] I would like to see run for office (one)
8. when the space shuttle *Challenger* tragedy occurred (1986)

Practice 18

1. Jennifer, who is a very neurotic person, still
2. experience that he will never forget.
3. The plan that we finally decided upon was
4. My typewriter, which has not been cleaned in eight years, is in poor condition.
5. the celebrity, who was doing his best to avoid the crowd.
6. The film that Altman directed was the best.
7. Friends who talk behind your back are not friends.
8. I moved to California, where the grass

Practice 20

1. The hillsides, which were covered with trees of fiery red and orange, extended as far as the eye could see.
2. My parents, who have never been to New England, would love to see
3. Our decrepit Volkswagen, which was loaded down with luggage, did its best
4. We finally arrived at the ski lodge, which was to be our home
5. The owner of the lodge, who looked like a character out of a Western film, helped us unload.
6. I remember watching the first snowfall, which was a sight
7. The local people, who have experienced icy roads and snow shoveling all their lives, probably would not

Practice 22 (Examples)

1. The puppy chewed up everything in sight, for example, shoes, newspapers, and even the corner of the couch.
2. Greece, a land of blue skies and whitewashed houses, is a popular vacation spot for Europeans.
3. Barbara Lee's latest novel, a book about growing up in China, is supposedly one of her best.
4. The defensive-driving coach was a little nervous about his new pupil, a man convicted
5. Anton decided not to join the neighborhood softball team, a team well known for its fierce competitive spirit.

Chapter 22   **Practice 1**

1. F
2. S
3. F
4. S
5. F
6. F

7. F
8. S
9. F
10. F
11. S

Practice 3

1. in the right manner, even if they are hard to handle.
2. a certain type of person, whether that person is a sportsman, a swinger, or a conservative.
3. all the customers because some of them are crazy.

Practice 4 (Examples)

1. mark, more than Americans spent on movies, in fact.
2. expensive, a problem for parents
3. violence: kick-boxing, vampires
4. It makes you wonder

Practice 5 (Examples)

1. Do you like seaweed?
2. melt, then frozen it again.
3. North America and then dried
4. extract in it, actually less than
5. That's not much, maybe

Practice 6

1. "easy to open" boxes, all tagged with labels
2. simple way of life, while in reality our lives
3. many problems, such as how to operate

Practice 7

1. on their watches. They would be
2. check the water. It looks good to me.
3. Shut the door. It is cold in here.
4. which one you take. Both roads will
5. woman. Your past
6. my imagination. It was a little girl.
7. people. Someone will surely help us.
8. the university. The blocks
9. for instance. I am not

Practice 8 (Examples)

1. was cold, and there was
2. man, but I liked him.
3. shove, and I fell
4. sometimes, but it has been
5. "Marry me, or I will not see you again."
6. well fed, yet she is still skinny.
7. Let me go, for I have
8. home, for she had
9. Academy, so now I am here
10. He will not sleep, nor will he eat.

Practice 9

1. his health; then he
2. person; however, she is
3. inexpensive; for example, you
4. strict; however, college
5. cream sauce; then you
6. was dead; then it
7. would decline; moreover, young people
8. our goal; however, it did
9. against cigarette smoking; consequently, 30 percent
10. something; however, we

Practice 10 (Examples)

1. with Joyce because she
2. When he graduates this May, I am going to miss him.
3. If you study in our room, I will study in the library.
4. While the states of our nation are different in most ways, they do
5. will eventually pass, although it will
6. Since kids are playful, joyful, and bright, I decided

Practice 11 (Examples)

1. my eyes. The car was
2. the door. Let's keep
3. When the rock hit him beneath his eye, it taught him a lesson.
4. the problem; however, they do
5. I need those notes, so please give them to me.
6. your poor, and I will make
7. very friendly; in fact, they
8. of 1988. In so doing, I
9. Russell is 6'5", and he weighs 175 pounds.
10. (Correct)
11. college men because I know
12. of teaching; moreover, she
13. to yourself because there is one more ball left to play.
14. (Correct)

15. really wins. It eats your money.
16. their own actions; however, adults
17. hard to detect because sometimes they
18. as a nation; moreover, we seem
19. once was because it has lost
20. our enemy; however, its people

Practice 12 (Examples)

1. dangerous illness. It is
2. defensive because he could not.
3. on the bill, and then it
4. the information, and then
5. ferocious, however, he is
6. for our country; therefore, they
7. When we began climbing to the top, the wind
8. any farther, so we
9. "Will you just listen to me? I have something to say. . . ."
10. "What do you want from me? I can no longer help you."

Practice 13 (Examples)

1. two years ago, and she is
2. one elderly couple, who accepted her
3. on holidays. She had only
4. dart tournaments. Darts is a game
5. of the people, for it is a land
6. small farms, and one can see
7. and Italy. She loved
8. friendly, too. They are
9. Switzerland. It has breathtaking
10. especially lovely. It is located
11. the Alps; however, snow
12. the lodge, and then they
13. on the glacier, and the sun
14. by ropes; however, no one slipped.
15. before dark. Everyone had been

Practice 14 (Examples)

1. sleeping bags. They had nothing
2. we roughed it. We slept in a tent
3. no shade because the tallest tree
4. in the wilderness. This time we
5. There was no tent, but we had
6. of life. They brought
7. in camping, and we have
8. pantry. The trailer even has
9. back to nature. I recommend

ERRORS

Practice 15

1. carefully (Carry)
2. curiously (looked)
3. nicely (has fixed up)
4. rapidly (were moving)
5. beautiful (She)
6. loudly (bark)
7. well (did)
8. well (plays)
9. good (she)
10. frequently (frowns)
11. crazily (have been acting)

Practice 18 (Examples)

1. all their money, they headed home.
2. foundation, a house will not fall down.
3. father, you (*or* one) must spend a lot of time with your (*or* one's) children.
4. in the river, we were scared by a bad thunderstorm.
5. your best, you must stay in good shape.
6. The squirrel ran across the hunter's plate while he was eating his supper.
7. Convicted of a third felony, the man was sent to prison for life.
8. Having awoken early, they could not be found.
9. is planted, one must make the best

Practice 19 (Examples)

1. My aunt, with a failing heart, was rushed
2. The interns on duty in the emergency room were
3. cost her almost three hundred
4. testified on behalf of neglected children before the
5. listened with great interest to her appeal
6. passed the bill to appropriate almost one hundred thousand
7. The children who have been neglected will now be helped
8. With their determined leadership, Dr. Watts and
9. has recruited nearly three hundred
10. The members argue convincingly for various
11. what one person with a dream can do to change things.

Practice 20

1. could be classified as friendly, indifferent, and just plain mean.
2. does not deter crime, it is used only against the poor, and it is cruel and unusual punishment.
3. his nap in the afternoon, his bike ride in the early morning, and his novels at night.
4. Manning watches soap operas in the morning, news programs in the late afternoon, and television movies at night.
5. to make the customers feel welcome, to show them to a table, and to find them a waiter.
6. I am going to save some money, then open my own business, and finally sit back and get rich.

Credit Lines

Definition of "desert." Copyright © 1996 by Houghton Mifflin Company. Reproduced by permission from THE AMERICAN HERITAGE DICTIONARY OF THE ENGLISH LANGUAGE, Third Edition.

Howey, Richard, "How to Write a Rotten Poem with Almost No Effort." Reprinted with permission.

Poundstone, Paula, "Be Like Gandhi," MOTHER JONES. May/June 1994: 72. Reprinted with permission from MOTHER JONES Magazine, © 1994, Foundation for National Progress.

"Columbus and the Moon" by Tom Wolfe. Copyright © 1979 by Tom Wolfe. Originally published in THE NEW YORK TIMES. Reprinted by permission of the author.

Noyes, Nicole, "Why Human Cloning Should *Not* Be Banned," COSMOPOLITAN, October 1997: 60. Reprinted by permission.

"Is Sex All That Matters?" by Joyce Garity. Copyright © 1996 by Townsend Press. Reprinted by permission.

Tucker, Carll, "Fear of Dearth," SATURDAY REVIEW MAGAZINE, 1979. Reprinted by permission of the author.

Hamilton, Kendall, and Patricia King, "Playgrounds of the Future: They Ain't Got Swing." From NEWSWEEK, May 12, 1997, © 1997, Newsweek, Inc. All rights reserved. Reprinted by permission.

Kleiman, Mark, "Grant Bachelor's Degrees by Examination," WALL STREET JOURNAL, September 6, 1985. Reprinted with permission of WALL STREET JOURNAL, © 1985 Dow Jones & Company, Inc. All rights reserved.

Humphry, Derek and Daniel Callahan, "Should Doctors Be Allowed to Help Terminally Ill Patients Commit Suicide?" from HEALTH Magazine, May/June 1993, p. 22. Reprinted with permission from HEALTH © 1993.

Stoddard, Thomas B., "Gay Marriages: Make Them Legal," NEW YORK TIMES, March 4, 1989. Copyright © 1989 by The New York Times Company. Reprinted by permission.

May, William F., "Rising to the Occasion of Our Death." Copyright 1990 Christian Century Foundation. Reprinted by permission from the July 11, 1990 issue of CHRISTIAN CENTURY.

Cole, K.C., "Women in Science," NEW YORK TIMES, December 3, 1981. Copyright © 1981 by The New York Times Company. Reprinted by permission.

O'Keeney, Brian, "How to Make It in College Now That You're Here," from J. Langhan's COLLEGE WRITING SKILLS WITH READINGS, 4/e. New York: McGraw-Hill, 1997, pp. 632–43. Used by permission of Ann McClintock and Townsend Press.

Leo, John, "The Answer is 45 Cents." Copyright April 21, 1997, U.S. NEWS & WORLD REPORT. Reprinted by permission.

Morrow, Lance, "The Strange Burden of a Name," TIME, March 8, 1983, p. 76. © 1983 Time Inc. Reprinted by permission.

Krauthammer, Charles, "The New Prohibitionism," TIME, October 6, 1997. © 1997 Time Inc. Reprinted by permission.

"Here's to Your Health" by Joan Dunayer. Copyright © 1990 by Townsend Press. Reprinted by permission.

Rose del Castillo Guilbault, "Hispanic USA: The Conveyor-Belt Ladies," SAN FRANCISCO CHRONICLE, March 5, 1989. Reprinted by permission of the author.

Staples, Brent, Brent Staples is the author of the memoir PARALLEL TIME: GROWING UP IN BLACK AND WHITE and writes editorial for THE NEW YORK TIMES.

Joan Walsh, "Four Truths About the Ebonics Debate." Pacific News Service. Reprinted by permission.

Wong, Elizabeth, "The Struggle to be an All-American Girl." Reprinted with permission.

Rivers, Caryl, "Millenial Woman: Make Her GI Jane, Not June Cleaver," LOS ANGELES TIMES, October 1, 1997, B7. Reprinted by permission of the author.

Ehrenreich, Barbara, "In Defense of Talk Shows," TIME, December 4, 1995. © 1995 Time Inc. Reprinted by permission.

Index